Imagining the Pacific

Imagining

Yale University Press · New Haven and London · 1992

the Pacific

In the Wake of the Cook Voyages

Bernard Smith

Frontispiece: Detail from William Hodges, *View of the part of the Island of Ulieta* (Raiatea) (pl. 128).

Set in Linotron Baskerville by
Best-set Typesetter Ltd, Hong Kong
Printed in Hong Kong by
Kwong Fat Offset Printing Co. Ltd.

Library of Congress Cataloging-in-Publication Data

Smith, Bernard, 1916–
    Imagining the Pacific: In the Wake of the Cook Voyages / Bernard
Smith.
        p.   cm.
    Includes bibliographical references and index.
    ISBN 0-300-05053-4
    1. Cook, James, 1728-1779—Journeys.   2. Voyages around the world.
3. Pacific Area in art.   I. Title.
G420.C73S65   1992
910—dc20   91-38045
                                                                                CIP

A catalogue record for this book is available from the British Library

To my teachers

CHARLES MITCHELL

ARTHUR DALE TRENDALL

CONTENTS

Detail of pl. 116.

imagination, which in truth
is but another name for absolute power
and clearest insight.

Wordsworth, *The Prelude*, xiv, 190–2.

PREFACE

IN THIS BOOK THE IMAGINATION is understood as consisting of two primary components. First there is imaging, in which a person constructs an image in the presence of an object from which the image is fashioned; and then there is imagining, in which a person constructs an image while not in direct sensory contact with the object or objects from which the imagery of the imagining is constructed. Between imaging and imagining there are discontinuities. But for the issues and themes addressed in this book their continuity will be our central concern. Imaging and imagining constitute a spectrum of mental activity not a polarity. Imaging involves not only sensation and perception but also constructive skills and memory. Memory itself involves elements of imaginative recall. As for imagination, even its highest and most complex flights are built upon irreducible perceptual components. To stress these continuities the term imagining is used here to cover all aspects of the image-to-imagination process.

If we are to understand the Pacific world we must also accept the reality of the objects out of which the concept of the Pacific was constructed, together with the reality both of those European minds that sought to understand it and of those Pacific minds that found themselves at once the objects and victims of that 'understanding'. In imagining the Pacific, Europeans imagined from a reality that they had to come to terms with, not a fancy or a fantasy that might eventually disappear.

The first chapter, 'Art in the Service of Science and Travel', outlines the development in Europe of those kinds of artwork within which the Pacific was imaged and imagined. It is a survey designed to place the cultural achievement of Cook's Pacific voyages within an historical perspective and owes much to the work of other scholars, particularly those who have concerned themselves over many years with the earliest European pictorial representations of the Americas, such as Paul Hulton, P.J.P. Whitehead, M. Boeseman, Rüdiger Joppien and Hugh Honour. This introductory chapter could not have been written, brief as it is, considering the nature of the subject, without their basic research.

The second chapter, 'The Intellectual and Artistic Framework of Captain Cook's Voyages', constructs the context within which 'scientific' art played its significant but subordinate role in the European penetration of the Pacific. In the third chapter, 'Art as Information' (a theme introduced in the first chapter), the impact of science, topography and travel, upon the genres of the academy is developed further by considering the effects of empirical naturalism upon the long-standing conventions of classical naturalism. The fourth chapter, 'Portraying Pacific People', considers the consequences that flowed from the imposition of an alien European *genre*, portraiture, upon the peoples of the Pacific, and its consequence for both Europe and the Pacific in terms of empathy and power. The fifth chapter, 'William Hodges and English *Plein-air* Painting' discusses the impact of Pacific light and atmosphere upon the art of Hodges and assesses his place in the history of *plein-air* landscape painting.

Chapter six differs from the others in two ways. It is concerned with the literary rather than the visual imagination and was written thirty-five years ago, whereas most of the other essays have originated during the past decade. It appears again here substantially unaltered because its crucial significance for the understanding of the imaginative origins of *The Rime of the Ancient Mariner* and for Coleridge's personal poetics has been disregarded by a generation of Coleridge scholars.

I am not a 'Coleridge scholar'. Nor was Livingstone Lowes, the greatest of them, when he stumbled upon the Gutch memorandum book that provided clues to what the poet was reading in the years immediately prior to his writing *The Ancient Mariner*. Lowes was studying Chaucer. I came upon the manuscript log of William Wales, Coleridge's mathematics teacher at Christ's Hospital, when I was studying the paintings of Hodges. Examining that log soon made it clear to me that it provided a missing clue to the genesis of the poem. Because Lowes was unaware of William Wales and his influence upon Coleridge he developed, despite his masterly investigation of *verbal* sources of the poem, an untenable account of Coleridge's imaginative processes in writing it; one that did not accord with the poet's own views about the poetic process.

The last word will never be said about the meaning of *The Rime of the Ancient Mariner*. Readers will continue to discuss its moral, allegorical, symbolic, supernatural and metaphysical components. That is in the nature of great poetry. Yet there is a very special sense in which chapter five can provide the first word about the poem; for it is not possible to appreciate the depths of its imaginative roots and ignore the influence of William Wales upon Coleridge.

After publishing the essay in its original form in 1956 I sent offprints to three of the most eminent Coleridge scholars of the day: Edmund Blunden, himself a Bluecoat boy with a special interest in Coleridge's schooldays at Christ's Hospital;[1] Kathleen Coburn, the editor of the poet's notebooks;[2] and E.L. Griggs, editor of his letters.[3] Blunden, in a characteristically warm and appreciative letter, wrote to say that my thesis was 'sound and good'; Coburn agreed that I was 'right in general'; and Griggs that I did 'have something'. Griggs also suggested that I strengthen my 'anti-Lowes' thesis. He felt that his explanations did not accord with the poet's own views on the morphology of the poetic process.

I sent an early draft of the essay to the poet A.D. Hope, who is also a distinguished critic and student of eighteenth-century English literature. Hope replied:

I feel that you really have added the missing link to Lowes' argument. In spite of the overwhelming evidence I never quite believed Lowes. I could not fault his evidence but I felt that something was missing and something essential. Lowes' case, as you point out, almost comes down to the vindication of the Hartleyean doctrine of mechanical association. Now I have no doubt you could do the same with the flattest of Coleridge's poems or the most rhetorical. What is it that sets the *Ancient Mariner* and *Kubla Khan* and parts of *Christabel* apart from the rest? It is the peculiar quality of that esemplastic power which Coleridge analysed so brilliantly and the essential ingredient of esemplastic power is the operation of the *Transcendental Will*. One needn't accept all the German metaphysical scaffolding. One has merely to recognise that a conscious and total organisation of the powers of the mind, of the whole man, is involved under a deliberate direction of the will, that a sort of organising perception is at work *transcending* that involved in the pursuit of consciously conceived practical ends. When you recognise that Coleridge was right about this you can never be happy about Lowes' picture of an unconscious coupling of verbal images in a mental snake-pit. You demand an *organising* principle and I think you have found it.[4]

All that was thirty-five years ago. Since then, apart from a few comments, my essay has been ignored. A generation of Coleridge biographers do not appear even to have heard of William Wales. It is timely, therefore, that the 'old navigator' (as Coleridge called *his* Ancient Mariner) should reappear here. In his letter to me, Edmund Blunden wrote, 'I think you have a book to complete'.[5] There is no need for a book; the evidence is in the essay.

In the seventh chapter, 'Constructing "Pacific" People', the ways in which an apparently documentary art can be fashioned to suit ideological concerns is investigated. In the eighth chapter, 'Style, Information and Image', some of the concerns of the earlier chapters are drawn together in order to test the relevance of Edward Said's concept of 'orientalism' for an understanding of European perceptions of the Pacific.[6] The ninth chapter, 'Greece and the Colonisation of the Pacific', discusses what is one of the underlying assumptions of the book as a whole, that the source of Europe's own imaginings of the Pacific lies in its own original 'primitivism', the civilisation of ancient Greece and the enduring cultural model which that civilisation produced. The final chapter returns to the question of ideology and surveys the ways in which Cook's posthumous reputation has been put to use to serve a variety of ends that he himself could never have imagined.

Although each chapter has been arranged to follow a sequence that is broadly chronological, proceeding from an emphasis in the early chapters on the events of the early voyages and the problems of imaging, towards an emphasis in the later chapters on the ways in which such imaging is transformed in response to the powers of the imagination, of tradition and of ideology, the book itself does not follow a firm narrative line. Instead, it addresses the problem embodied in the title from ten different but related aspects. In this way it is hoped that many of the facets of that complex chain that links imaging to imagining, art to science, original to reproduction, art to past tradition and to contemporary ideology, and the insular British mind to the vast ocean spaces of the Pacific, will be revealed not so much as a simple chain of causation but as so many aspects of an indissoluble, yet changing community of ceaselessly interacting human experience.

ACKNOWLEDGEMENTS

MUCH OF CHAPTER TWO, 'The Intellectual and Artistic Framework of Captain Cook's Voyages', first appeared in *Terra Australis the Furthest Shore* (Art Gallery of New South Wales, 1988); chapter three, 'Art as Information', was first published by the Australian Academy of the Humanities (Canberra, 1979); one section of chapter four was first published as 'The First European depictions of Australian Aborigines' in *Seeing the First Australians*, edited by Ian Donaldson and Tasmin Donaldson (George Allen and Unwin, Sydney, 1985); and another section, as 'Cook's artists and the portrayal of Pacific Peoples', was developed from a lecture given to the International Commission for Maritime History, at the Museum of Mankind, Burlington Gardens, London, 25 September 1979, and later published in *Art History*, vol. 7, no. 3, September 1984. Chapter five, 'William Hodges and English *Plein-air* Painting', was developed from a lecture given at the Paul Sandby Colloquium held in the Hamilton Art Gallery, Victoria in October 1981, and published in *Art History*, vol. 6, no. 2, June 1983; chapter six, 'Coleridge's *Ancient Mariner* and Cook's Second Voyage', was first published in the *Journal of the Warburg and Courtauld Institutes*, vol. 19, 1956; chapter seven, 'Constructing "Pacific" People', first appeared as 'Depicting Pacific Peoples', and was developed from the inaugural Founder's Lecture, National Library of Wellington, New Zealand, on 15 September 1987 and later published in *The Turnbull Record*, vol. 21, no. 1, May 1988; chapter eight, 'Style, Information and Image in the art of Cook's Voyages', was developed from the Harkness Lecture 1987, School of Fine Arts, University of Canterbury, Christchurch, New Zealand; chapter nine, 'Greece and the Colonisation of the Pacific', was developed from a lecture given at the conference on 'Ancient Hellenism: Greek Colonists and Native Populations', First Australian Congress of Classical Archaeology, held at Sydney University in July 1985. It was published in a slightly abbreviated form in J.-P. Descoeudres (ed.), *Greek Colonists and Native Populations*, Oxford, 1990. Chapter ten, 'Cook's Posthumous Reputation', was developed from a lecture given at the conference 'Captain James Cook and his Times' held at Simon Fraser University, British Columbia, in the spring of 1978, and later published in *Captain James Cook and his Times*, edited by Robin Fisher and Hugh Johnston (Vancouver 1979).

I want to express my profound gratitude to John Nicoll of Yale University Press and his anonymous but erudite reader who encouraged me to rework some disparate essays into a book that I believe now possesses its own unity and coherence. The book has been edited and designed by Gillian Malpass. On both counts it owes much to her good sense and her good taste. Emma Hicks provided me with invaluable assistance on a number of points that required research and checking at the last moment, and helped in hunting down many illustrations.

I have a duty also to acknowledge and thank the Literature Board of the Australia Council for the award during 1990 and 1991 of a Category A Fellowship which has enabled me, among other things, to defray expenses involved in preparing the book for publication.

Detail of pl. 123.

xiii

1 ART IN THE SERVICE OF SCIENCE AND TRAVEL

IN ONE OF THE MOST INTERESTING BOOKS ever written about the visual arts, William Ivins reminds us that Einstein's hypothesis concerning the action of gravity upon light was verified by photographs taken in Brazil and the Gulf of Guinea in 1919. Photography provided the evidence that the scientific world required in order to test the validity of the theory of relativity (pl. 1).[1]

The use of visual representation in the service of science began, of course, long before 1919. No one knows when a graphic record was first used as evidence for the occurrence of an event, but it is likely to have been one of the earliest uses, though far from the first, to which the visual arts were put. Yet it was not until the invention of photography that a means for recording visual phenomena became available which was demonstrably superior to words as testimony of an event. We all know that photographs have to be interpreted carefully in order to obtain accurate information; know too that photographers exercise choice as to what shall be photographed and the way it shall be photographed. They, or others, decide upon the process by which the photographic negative will be developed and printed. We may agree that photographs may be misleading and yet maintain that there are sound reasons for the acceptance of photographic evidence in law, science and other situations wherein accuracy of representation is crucial as evidence superior to the evidence of words.

Drawings do not achieve the degree of objectivity that may be obtained by photography. They are executed within the conventions of a personal and period style, or of one or more styles available to the draughtsman, and they are executed within the conventions of particular categories of art, such as portraiture or landscape. Furthermore, until the nineteenth century, the reproduction of drawings was limited almost entirely to the capacities of woodcuts, etchings and engravings. So that drawings come to us, even when executed for ostensibly scientific purposes, with the temperament and dispositions of the artist embedded within the information they contain, and they convey also something of the artist's own social, cultural and intellectual inheritance. Reproduction adds to this mixed bundle of skill, style, perception and temperament the historicity of its own particular technical processes. We must, therefore, when interpreting the information contained in drawings, be constantly alert for the level of skill, the nature of the style or styles involved, the quality of the perception present in a drawing or painting made apparently with an informational intent only, if we are to decode it accurately.

Consider the situation in the eighteenth century. It is common knowledge that at that time members of the privileged classes of Europe, and others who could afford it, undertook a grand tour of Italy. Such tours provided an appropriate conclusion to a classical education, served as an introduction to adult life and laid the foundation of a 'correct' aesthetic taste based largely upon classical precedent.

1. A photograph taken in 1919 to confirm Einstein's hypothesis concerning the action of gravity upon light. *Philosophical Transactions* (of the Royal Society), vol. 220, 1920, series A, pl. 1, fp. 292.

Detail of pl. 131.

The use of drawings as a record of such tours was widely practised. If he were fortunate, a young traveller would have had some training in drawing. Its importance in the education of a gentleman had been stressed by the philosopher John Locke in 1693 in his *Thoughts concerning Education*:

> When he can Write well and quick, I think it may be convenient not only to continue the exercise in his Hand in Writing, but also to improve the use of it farther in Drawing, a thing very useful to a Gentleman in several occasions, but especially if he travel, as that which helps a Man often to express, in a few Lines well put together, what a whole sheet of Paper in Writing would not be able to represent and make intelligible. How many Buildings may a Man see, how many Machines and Habits meet with, the Ideas whereof would be easily retained and communicated, by a little Skill in 'Drawing'; which being committed to Words are in danger to be lost, or at best but ill retained in the the most exact Descriptions? I do not mean that I would have your son a 'perfect Painter'; to be that to any tolerable degree, will require more time, than a Young Gentleman can spare from his other Improvements of greater Moment; but so much insight into 'Perspective' and skill in 'Drawing', as will enable him to repeat tolerably on Paper anything he sees except Faces, may, I think, be got in a little time.[2]

Locke was but one of many who at that time were beginning to recognise and assert in England the value of drawing for the retention and transmission of information. The fact that drawing of the kind recommended by Locke, commonly referred to as topographical, should be endorsed as a skill appropriate to the education of a gentleman helped to raise its social status from its lowly place in the academic hierarchy of fine art, one that it had occupied from the beginning of the sixteenth to the end of the seventeenth century.[3]

If the grand tourist possessed little skill in drawing (and sometimes, even if he were skilled), he usually included a professional artist among the members of his party. The artist might be expected to draw architectural monuments and the sculpture of antiquity seen and studied in Italy, take views and prospects of places, draw curious plants and animals, and at times make sketches of friends and acquaintances encountered on the tour. An important and influential early example of the practice was when Thomas Howard, Earl of Arundel, employed Wenzel Hollar (1607–77) in 1636 during his ambassadorial mission to Germany. Hollar made topographical drawings of many of the places through which the mission passed (pl. 2). Later he settled in England and greatly advanced the practice of topographical art there.

Travel exercised an obligation upon the draughtsman, whether amateur or professional, to complete his work with speed and an economy of means. It shifted emphasis from the care and finish of the studio to the flair and brevity of the field sketch completed on location. In the traditional studio situation the sketch occupied a crucial but relatively anonymous role. It was essentially a tool of workshop practice. For most clients and collectors it was the finished effect of the portrait, the view of one's house, or of scenes participated in and enjoyed that mattered. The amateur who made his own drawings, or watched them being made on tour, gained a closer awareness of the drawing process; and since the draughtsmanship of travel was devoted largely to the provision of faithful visual documentation, an increased importance came to be attached to field sketches and studies of things of interest such as curious plants and animals encountered.

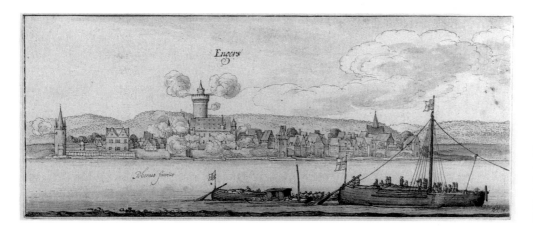

2. Wenzel Hollar, *View of Engers with the Rhine*, pen and watercolour on paper, 11 × 27.1 cm., 1636, Devonshire Collection, Chatsworth.

Under such circumstances the point put upon accuracy of documentation became an increasingly significant aspect of taste and aesthetic pleasure. Like the photographic transparencies and home videos of our own day, drawings made on tour were intended not only to instruct but also to be admired and to entertain.

With less time available to the artist-traveller, drawings were got down with expedition by pencil, pen or brush, often with sepia and washes of watercolour for tones and tints. Produced under such conditions, pure line, clear transparent washes, executed with skill, spirit and flair, came to be much admired. They captured essentials, suggested what they did not detail. The successful solution of the problems that confronted the itinerant draughtsman exercised an influence on the development of eighteenth-century art. Although the taste for pure outline drawing is rightly regarded as one of the distinguishing features of the neo-classical style, it has not been fully appreciated how the taste for purity of line was enhanced by the very exigencies of the travelling-artist's situation and the increasingly documentary function that he served.

Consequently, a new respect for drawings emerged during the eighteenth century, deriving partly from the increased recognition of their value as records and partly from a related development in the appreciation of a good drawing as a work of art in its own right. In 1757 Edmund Burke expressed a preference that was becoming increasingly common: 'In unfinished sketches of drawing, I have often seen something which pleased me beyond the best finishing.'[4]

The heightened appreciation of drawing was paralleled by an increased interest in the value of watercolour painting. It too was a response to the growing use of artists by travellers. Wherever mobility was important, watercolour techniques gained in value. It was the handiness of watercolour, its comparative speed of execution, the smallness, lightness, compactness of the tools and equipment compared with media such as oil that made it so useful a medium. Even its early history is linked with travel, for it was greatly favoured by limners, the painters of miniatures, an art that might well be called the art of portable portraiture.

* * *

Traditional art was based upon the copying of pre-existing art. Traditional European art was based also upon skills that had been learned in drawing the human body deduced from norms derived from proportion theory. Art in the service of science began, by contrast, in drawing empirically (that is to say, from

3

direct observation) animals pursued in the hunt, for the table. Perhaps the earliest set of drawings, now in the Vatican, that reveal an incipient scientific attitude are those that were drawn to illustrate a revised edition of Frederick II's book *The Art of Falconry*, prepared by his son King Manfred during the mid-thirteenth century. Frederick II (1194–1250), of Sicily and Southern Italy, in many ways a characteristic medieval despot was also a man who promoted learning and fostered the study of nature. His book on falconry is said to have been based on his own research. The birds that illustrate his son's edition of it have all the appearance of being drawn directly from life, or at least directly from dead specimens (pl. 3). It is the use of art for the conveyance of information and thus to instruct.

There was a special need for rare and unusual animals to be drawn directly from life. There was a greater need for accurate information about them than, for example, about cattle and sheep, which could be seen daily. For common animals there were plenty of copies available and everyone knew what they looked like anyway. But with exotic animals it was different. Were they like normal animals or were they like monsters, such as unicorns? The unicorn may have derived originally from the Indian rhinocerus, but it had established an impregnable mythical place in traditional art. For the curious, for men of Frederick II's stamp, the exotic had to be portrayed accurately.

There is no evidence that Frederick's scientific interests were continued in the years after his death. It is not until the latter part of the fourteenth century that an empirical naturalism based upon animal and plant studies from nature emerges as a continuing tradition. It is associated with the creation of botanical gardens and menageries by princes such as the Medici of Florence, the Visconti of Milan, and the Gonzaga of Mantua. Even human menageries were created. Burckhardt describes one formed by Cardinal Ippolito Medici that included Moors, Indians, Negroes, Tartars and Turks. Collecting exotics, whether animal, plant or human, was an expression not only of a wide-ranging curiosity, of a proto-scientific attitude, it was an assertion of prestige and power. The lion was not a European animal, but it was the most popular of those adopted by

3. Bird studies from *The Art of Falconry* (*De arte venandi*) by Frederick II, folio 36 × 25 cm., mid-thirteenth century, Vatican, Rome (MS Pal. Lat. 1071, f. 22r).

European princes and kings to symbolise their power. Yet the exotic, simply because it was rare, also encouraged an empirical naturalism in art. The *maniera greca*, proportion theory, the human body, were not of much use when confronted by exotics. Better to draw the strange as best you could when it was there before your eyes. One did not get a chance to see it often. This seems to have been the decision made by a few exceptional artists of northern Italy during the late fourteenth century. One such was the Monk of Hyeres.

The monk was from Genoa, and the Latin treatise on the vices that he illustrated, now in the British Library, originally belonged to a Genoese familly, the Cocharelli (pls 4, 5). It is a richly coloured miniature, the borders decorated with drawings of a great variety of animals, many of them exotic. He probably drew the exotics from available menageries. But he also made brilliantly naturalistic drawings of insects. There is a sense in which the insect world was akin to the exotic worlds of Africa and Asia. 'It lay', as Otto Pächt has put it, 'on the fringe of the medieval cosmos ... free from symbolic ties and therefore more accessible to unhampered curiosity. The human figure was the last of nature's creations from which the medieval ban on analytical observation was lifted.'[5]

During the late fourteenth century animal studies from nature became a feature also of artists of the Lombard School, such as Giovannino de' Grassi and Michelino da Besozzo, both of whom worked for the Visconti of Milan and Milan cathedral. Giovannino produced a book of animal studies from nature, drawn

4. A page from the Cocharelli Manuscript, showing animal borders, folio 26 × 18 cm., British Library, London (Add. MS 27695, f. 3v).

5. A page from the Cocharelli Manuscript, showing animal borders, folio 17 × 10.9 cm., British Library, London (Add. MS 28841, f. 3).

6. Pisanello, studies for an Epiphany, silverpoint, pen and bistre, 27.3 × 20.4 cm., early fifteenth century, Graphische Sammlung Albertina, Vienna.

7. Pisanello, studies of stags' heads, pen and ink, 27.3 × 20.4 cm., 1455, Graphische Sammlung Albertina, Vienna.

in silver point or with the point of a brush and sometimes painted in water-colour (pl. 8). Their static quality suggests that they were drawn from dead specimens, the products of the hunt. We know from the authority of Pier Candido Decembrio, writing about 1400, that Michelino also made animal drawings from nature. He influenced the work of Pisanello, who is well known for his animal studies, such as his sketches of horses and exotic animals: camels, leopards and cheetahs, drawn to illustrate religious narrative paintings. There can be little doubt that drawings of the quality of his study of a stag were made from life, or shortly after the death of the animal (pls 6, 7).

Unlike animal drawing, plant drawing possesses a continuous tradition in Europe from the Hellenistic era. From the time of Dioscorides (c.AD 40–c.90), physicians needed *materia medica* in the form of illustrated herbals that might help them to identify in nature plants of medicinal value. Until the end of the

8. Giovannino de' Grassi, *Hoopoe*, watercolour, 25.5 × 20 cm., late fourteenth century, Biblioteca Civica, Bergamo.

thirteenth century such illustrations were copied from herbals of classical or Arabic origin. Again, as a result of the proto-scientific interests promoted at the court of Frederick II, it is in southern Italy that the move from copying to sketching from nature is best observed. Predictably, there is a transitional phase. For example, the early fourteenth-century illustrator of *Nigella* (the Love-in-a-Mist plant of medicinal value) has drawn its flower and seed-pods directly from nature but added them to a traditional diagram copied from an earlier herbal. Organic relationships of whole to parts are neither grasped nor drawn (pl. 9). Not until the end of the fourteenth century are herbals found to contain illustrations sketched directly from life. Such are the beautfiul drawings that illuminate the herbal prepared for Francisco Carrara the Younger, Lord of Padua (pl. 10).

Drawings by artists such as Giovannino, Michelino and Pisanello are workshop drawings, to be used as aids in the production of their finished, public commissions. They were normally used for producing conventional designs and the decorative or religious narrative art of the time. Nevertheless, their drawings from life do reveal a new sensibility and a new sensitivity towards nature that is present also in Italian literature and theory of art during the early Renaissance. But in Italy nature did not achieve an aesthetic art genre of its own.[6] That was achieved with the emergence of landscape as an independent genre in the Netherlands and Germany. It was a secular art that did not require the support of rel=gious subject-matter. Stimulated by the Reformation, aesthetic value in the form of landscape began to emancipate itself from religious contexts.

South of the Alps, in Italy, the situation was somewhat different. Although the production of direct studies from nature continued unabated throughout the sixteenth century, encouraged by naturalists such as the Bolognese collector, Ulysse Aldrovandi (1522–1605), nature studies and landscape remained subordinant genre in the academic hierarchy of fine art. For despite the deep interest in nature revealed in the work of Leonardo and Dürer, the high art of the Renaissance was predicated upon the ideal. Indeed, this was intensified by the central scientific achievement of the Renaissance, the discovery born of both observation and geometric theory, of the rules governing centralised perspective.

9. Illustration of *Nigella* (Love-in-the-Mist) from the *Compendium Salernitanum*, folio 36 × 24.5 cm., early fourteenth century, British Library, London (Egerton MS 747, f. 68v).

10. Illustration of a violet from the *Carrara Herbal*, folio 35 × 24 cm., late fourteenth century, British Library, London (Egerton MS 2020, f. 94).

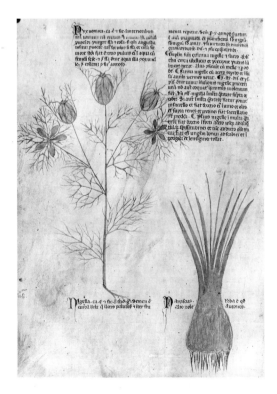

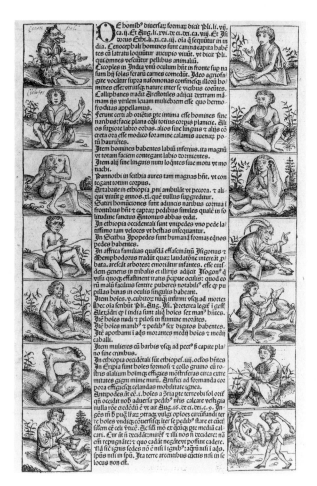

11. A page from the *Nuremburg Chronicle* (*Liber Chronicarum*), 1493, depicting and describing the fabulous race at the limits of the known world.

Centralised perspective provided a new, rational base for the pictorial representation of three dimensions on a flat surface; in effect the rationale of that kind of representation to be provided later by the photographic camera.[7] Centralised perspective enhanced the ideal in art, providing a rational (though illusory) space wherein the representations not only of actual persons, as in portraiture, could be idealised, but imaginary beings such as angels could be given a heightened pictorial reality. Furthermore, perspective was implicit in the naturalism of Greek art (according to Vitruvius, the Greeks had apparently been on the brink of discovering its principles), and its realisation in the fifteenth century may be seen as fulfilling a potential latent within Greek classical naturalism.

Such a cultivation of the ideal, related as it was so closely to the legitimation of Church and State and the aristocracy of taste and power, was bound to relegate an art that served science and curiosity (and the recording of information) to a subordinate role. Even so, science, like charity, began at home. Despite the advances made in empirical observation by artists during the fifteenth century, the world beyond Europe remained a region of marvels and wonders inhabited by monsters. At the end of the century Hartmann Schedel in his *Nuremburg Chronicle* (1493) could publish the monsters, the many-limbed and the one-eyed men, the skiapods and antipodes that inhabited the limits of the *oecumene*, the known world of antiquity and medieval Christendom (pl. 11). The *Chronicle* also provided the reasons why such monsters existed at the limits of the known. In its world map, based upon that of Ptolemy (*c.*AD 160), the three sons of Noah (Shem, Ham and

8

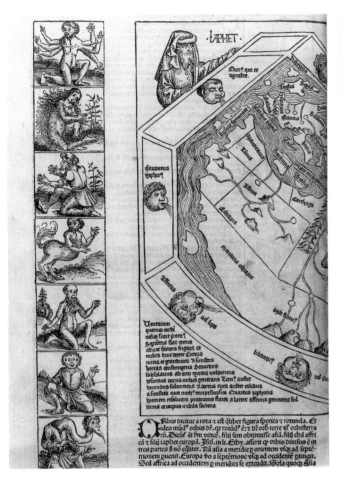

Japheth) were shown dispersing their descendants into the three known continents. Those of Japheth were believed to have inhabited Europe; those of Shem, Asia; and the less fortunate descendants of Ham, Africa. Beyond those limits dwelt dragons and monsters. So the *Chronicle* depicts its monsters in the margins of the map (pl. 12). It was still believed in the fifteenth century that, as the descendants of Noah had moved further from Christendom, they had degenerated steadily until they produced monsters like those depicted in the *Chronicle*.

But did such monsters actually live in the distant parts of the world? To postulate such was to offer a challenge to be taken up by the curious, the sceptical and the intrepid traveller. In the fabulous fourteenth-century travels of Sir John Mandeville lay the challenge for the scientific voyaging of Columbus in the fifteenth. In the year that Schedel published his monsters in his *Chronicle*, Columbus brought back nine Indians from the New World for baptism. A year later the young Dürer on his first journey to Italy made brilliant watercolour studies of nature in the Alpine passes.

Monsters or men? There is an historical dialectic of acquaintanceship at work here that may help us to understand the nature of the exotic. The exotic was what the European was not and so helped Europe to define itself. In the visual arts exotic representations acquired a tenuous and shifting quasi-aesthetic character, opposed to the beautiful, in a spatial sense, as the ugly and the grotesque were opposed to the beautiful in more direct, qualitative senses. The exotic is a fringe dweller among the aesthetic categories. It may reveal any visual qualities

12. The world map from the *Nuremburg Chronicle* (*Liber Chronicarum*), 1493, showing Japheth (Japhet), Shem (Sem) and Ham (Cam) dispersing the peoples.

9

except that ideal beauty derived from classical naturalism, the central norm of European aesthetics. It may be bizarre, extraordinary, marvellous, queer, weird— anything but beautiful. Nor could the exotic stand for the real. It could never represent those others, the non-Europeans, as they viewed and valued themselves. It was a category of accommodation by means of which the European perceived and interpreted the Other according to the limits and constraints of European understanding. What Edward Said has called 'orientalism' is but one of the ways the European has sought to come to terms with the diversities of the non-European.[8] A central function of the exotic is to conflate and reduce those diversities into an exotic polarity that may be conveniently opposed, in a geographical sense, to the beautiful. The exotic is thus the spatial antinome of the beautiful.

We must be clear about this. The sense in which exotic, as when we speak of an exotic plant or animal, simply means foreign is not helpful in understanding it as an aesthetic category or an aesthetic genre. An exotic plant originates in a non-European place. The exotic as aesthetic category or aesthetic genre originates in Europe, or at least in the European mind when it is seeking to perceive and understand the non-European. In this sense the exotic is an essential part of the parent culture: a hybrid constructed from a vision of the non-European. Consider Chinoiserie, Japonisme, orientalism. It is a fantasy bridge between the homely and the foreign. As such it has lived a discontinuous half-life as a sub-genre of European art, mainly in the decorative arts.

However, the exotic was not always to be found in distant parts. It could be found, as William Eisler has stressed, within the confines of Europe: 'On its islands, in its mountains and amongst its rural peasantry, Europe contained many "savage" peoples with "strange" customs, viewed as equally "exotic" by the upper strata of European society in the sixteenth century.'[9] For ideal beauty, the norm of classical naturalism, was the privileged possession of an aristocracy, an elite of wealth, power, intellect and taste. There were 'others' within Europe who were exotic.

The discovery of the Americas gave new impetus to art in the service of science and travel, though both science and travel were subordinated to the demands of commerce, power and ideology. Drawings made on location in the New World were not immediately endowed with the historic and aesthetic value they are now recognised to possess. That which is valued is treasured; valuation implies conservation. Sketches made in distant lands were not treasured in the way art masterpieces are. So the record of the European 'discovery' of the rest of the world from the fifteenth to the eighteenth century is, to say the least, discontinuous and possessed of many agonising gaps. That which has been preserved is to a large extent secondary information, when it is not pure fantasy. Here the exotic flourishes. For the object of the exotic was to transform first-hand information, such as field studies, processing it for the diverse needs of European audiences. That is another way of saying that the exotic was the aesthetic mode by which first-hand records were given an ideological function.

However, even first-hand accounts of the non-European were not devoid of the exotic. It was present in the very act of perception; the unknown being interpreted naturally enough in terms of the known. But there is a great difference in degree here between the first- and second-hand. Columbus, who thought that he had discovered islands off the coast of China, described those islands in terms that evoke the Gardens of the Hesperides, the Isles of the Blest of antiquity. Such

10

13. Jan Mostaert, *West Indian landscape*, oil on oak panel, 86.5 × 152.5 cm., *c*.1542, Frans Hals Museum, Haarlem.

perennial tropes of the European imagination did colour all visions of landscape, but it did not prevent Columbus bringing back basic, new information about America to Europe. The transformation of the metaphors of Columbus into fine art and graphic reproduction could serve quite a different purpose. Jan Mostaert's *West Indian Landscape* (*c*.1542) is the earliest known painting of a New World subject (pl. 13). It is probably based upon an incident in the life of the Spanish explorer Coronado, who was stoned by the inhabitants when he attacked a village at Cibola, Arizona in 1540. As Hugh Honour has pointed out, it is best viewed 'as a visual parable on the innocence and peace of unspoilt nature and the destructive urge of civilised man'.[10] Here the Arcadian metaphor is not used to colour and sweeten new information but set up to support a gentle critique of European civilisation itself.

The new knowledge could be adapted to re- ligious contexts. In the early sixteenth century a Portuguese artist painting the *Adoration of the Magi* presents one of the Magi in a Brazilian headdress carrying a Brazilian arrow and offer- ing, appropriately enough, a pot full of pre- sumably Brazilian gold to the Christ Child (pl. 14). Some years later another Portuguese painter depicts the Devil in an *Inferno* paint- ing (*c*.1550) as an American Indian (pl. 15). Brazilian Indians, one carrying a macaw and another ears of maize, were incorporated into a series of woodcuts representing the Triumph of Maximilian I, the Emperor of the Holy Roman Empire (1459–1519), curiously enough among the *People of Calicut* section of the Triumph—an admirable example of the conflation of imagery and ideas to which the exotic is prone as it functions as a spatial antinome of the beautiful (pl. 16).

14. Attributed to Vasco Fernandes, *The Adoration of the Magi*, oil on panel, 134 × 82 cm., *c*.1505, Museu de Grão Vasco, Viseu, Portugal.

11

15. Artist unknown, *Inferno*, oil on panel, 119 × 217.5 cm., *c.*1550, Museu Nacional de Art Antiga.

16. Hans Burgkmair the Elder (after), *People of Calicut*, woodcut, 41 × 58.5 cm., 1517–18. One of the series of woodcuts of the Triumph of Maximilian I. Department of Prints and Drawings, British Museum, London.

In the four examples discussed above we see novel first-hand information from the New World turned to the ideological usages of European primitivism, European religion and European power. This is a far cry from art in the service of science. Yet those images are relevant to our considerations. To the extent that it misled, the exotic stimulated criticism from humanists, virtuosi and collectors possessed of an enquiring and sceptical cast of mind. From the sixteenth century onwards such people encouraged travellers embarking on far voyages to collect specimens and make drawings of things seen, such as unusual plants and animals, native peoples and their dress, adornments and artefacts. But such interests remained subordinate to those who sponsored the voyages, the courts of Portugal, Spain and England, and the trading companies of Holland. Their main concern

12

was the acquisition of territory from the local inhabitants to establish colonies and to accumulate wealth by exploiting the natural or human productions of the new territories 'discovered' and settled.

The ways in which an early ethnographic interest in native Americans—and Europe's desire to dominate them—were fused in exotic representation are demonstrated vividly in the work of Jacques Le Moyne de Morgues (1533–88), probably the first professional European artist to work in the New World.[11] A Huguenot, he was associated with the attempt to establish a French Huguenot settlement in Florida. Organised by Coligny (1519–72), the Admiral of France and himself a Huguenot, and strongly supported by Charles IX of France, it was intended both to be a French challenge to Spanish claims to the southern regions of North America and to provide a place where Huguenots might live free from persecution. The first expedition, which left Le Havre in 1562, under Jean Ribaut, was a complete failure. Le Moyne, a native of Dieppe, was attached to the second expedition of 1564 under Laudonnière. This fared little better, because of sedition within the settlement and a Spanish attack. Le Moyne, who appears to have been trained in the tradition of manuscript illumination that still flourished in Dieppe, at that time also one of the great centres for cartography, was charged with mapping the Florida coast, its rivers and harbours. He was also expected to make drawings of 'the houses of the people and anything new there might be in that province'.[12] During his eighteen months in Florida, Le Moyne made many drawings, most of which were acquired after his death by Theodore de Bry in 1588 from Le Moyne's widow. De Bry, a publisher of Frankfurt, was the first to make the peoples of the New World widely known in Europe by means of his lavishly engraved, multi-volumed *America*.

Le Moyne was able to show Charles IX his drawings upon his return to France in 1566. The King urged him to write an account of the events he had lived through in Florida. This he did, and his narrative was published in Latin by De Bry, together with Le Moyne's textual notes to the illustrations. The notes and illustrations constitute the first comprehensive ethnographic account of a North American society—the Timucuans of Florida. Modern anthropological opinion places more weight on the accuracy of Le Moyne's notes to his drawings than to their engraved versions as published by De Bry.[13] This is not surprising. At this stage of its development the art of visual information was less reliable than verbal accounts. The engravings are composed and proportioned within the stylistic mannerist conventions prevailing at the time. That does not necessarily involve the conveyance of false information, but when the engraver was confronted with the absence of both a written description and a field sketch he turned to a European prototype to fill out his exotic depictions. Specific cases of this, noted by W.C. Sturtevant, include the representation of European pack baskets, hoes and shell vessels. De Bry's engraver, confronted with a paucity of field sketches, made considerable use of conflation, using Le Moyne's drawings of Florida artefacts to represent those of the peoples of other regions of the Americas.

This is not to say that De Bry's exotica conveyed no new information. There was a little, mixed in with the more dubious depictions. Sturtevant noted that De Bry gained from Le Moyne's field sketches his depictions of Timucuan bird-leg ornaments, oval metal pendants, their small bowls with handles, and their long-stemmed tobacco pipes. Such information could not have been found elsewhere.

It is likely that after De Bry had made use of Le Moyne's originals he discarded them as of little value, for they have never been recovered and were prob-

17. Jacques Le Moyne de Morgues, *Athore shows Laudonnière the marker column set up by Ribault*, watercolour and gouache with touches of gold vellum, 18 × 26 cm., after 1566, New York Public Library.

ably destroyed. Significantly enough, the one known illustration by Le Moyne that relates to his time in Florida refers to the French attempt to gain territory there (pl. 17). It is an elaborately finished drawing in water and body-colour with touches of gold on vellum. It was probably completed after Le Moyne's return to France in 1566, possibly as a presentation drawing either for Coligny or Charles IX. It represents the Indian Chief Athore with Laudonnière standing by the marker column set up as a sign of French sovereignty by Jean Ribaut in May 1562, on the south side of the St Johns river. Ribaut had brought with him from France the very stones, especially for the purpose, inscribed with the arms of the King of France. When Laudonnière arrived in 1564, Athore took him with his men to the place. Le Moyne in his explanatory note describes the occasion:

> Drawing close they noticed that the Indians were worshipping this stone as if it were an idol. For when the chief himself had saluted it and shown it the sort of reverence he was accustomed to receive from his subjects, he kissed it; his people copied him and encouraged us to do the same. In front of the stone were lying various offerings of fruits of the districts and roots that were either good to eat or medicinally useful dishes full of fragrant oils, and bows and arrows; it was also encircled from top to bottom with garlands of all kinds of flowers, and with branches of their most highly prized trees. After witnessing the rites of these poor savage people they returned to their comrades with the intent to search out the most suitable site for building a fort.
>
> The chief Athore is an extremely handsome man, intelligent, reliable, strong, of exceptional height, exceeding our tallest men by a foot and a half, and endowed with a certain restrained dignity, so that in him a remarkable majesty shone forth.[14]

Paul Hulton, in his description of the drawing, notes that the baskets, the fruits in them, and the quiver are most probably based upon European prototypes, not

Florida originals.[15] The gold and bright colours of the tattoos do not truthfully convey the grey or blue Indian tattoos and are probably owing to the conventions of manuscript illumination in which Le Moyne was trained. On the other hand, the two small basins with handles to our left of Athore, and the pendants hanging from his belt have been confirmed by archaeological evidence as belonging to the region. Appropriately enough, the whole intention of the drawing is to convey the impression that the Frenchmen have been received by the Timucuans in peace and amity, and that they worship the symbol of the French appropriation of their land as if it were a god.

Although the ideological intent of such a composition is obvious enough, De Bry, within the technical limitations of engraving and the drawings he had at his disposal, sought to provide as objective a description of the French occupation of Florida as possible—its main events together with a graphic account, verbal and visual, of the physique, dress, adornment and rituals of the Florida Indians. His great multi-volumed work provided Europe with its first comprehensive visual presentation of the New World. Furthermore, the life of the Indians evoked speculation as to the nature of life in Europe in early times. As John Locke put it much later, 'Once all the world was America'. De Bry was interested in such comparisons. It appears that one of Le Moyne's last commissions came directly from De Bry, the *Young daughter of the Picts* (pl. 18), which was engraved in *America*, part one, 1590. It is a brilliant example of exotic conflation. Le Moyne seems to have had in mind the drawings he made of an Indian chief's wife carried on a litter (pl. 19). Like the Indian, her hair is long and centrally parted, and she is adorned with a necklet and girdle. In place of the Indian tattoos, he adorns her body with flowers, for he was highly skilled as a flower painter, using not only flowers common to European gardens such as hollyhocks and columbine but also two flowers recently introduced into western Europe, the tulip from Asia Minor and the Marvel of Peru (*Miribilis Jalapa*) from South America. So here the exotic as the antinome of the beautiful achieves a triple conflation, the spatial exotic is combined with the temporal exotic and both with the erotic.[16]

Nothing is known of Le Moyne's activities between 1566 (when with Laudonnière he reported to Charles IX at Moulins on the outcome of the expedition to Florida) and 1581 when he fled to England from the persecutions that had followed the massacres of St Bartholomew's Day, 24 August 1572. He was

18. Jacques Le Moyne de Morgues, *A Young daughter of the Picts*, watercolour and gouache on vellum, 25.6 × 18.4 cm., c.1585–8, Yale Center for British Art, New Haven, Paul Mellon Collection.

19. *The Chief's chosen wife carried in procession on a litter*, engraving after Le Moyne, in De Bry, *America*, part two, 1591, pl. 37.

20. John White, *A Festive Dance*, watercolour over pencil touched with white, 27.4 × 35.8 cm., *c*.1585, British Museum, London.

allowed to remain in London and there became acquainted with John White (fl. 1585–90) through whom he met Sir Walter Raleigh, then seeking to establish a British settlement in North America. White, who appears to have been trained as a limner, was appointed to Raleigh's 1585 expedition to Virginia as its artist. It was this expedition that was responsible for the ill-fated settlement at Roanoke. Although the actual documents describing White's commission have not survived, they may be deduced, as Hulton has pointed out, from those given to Thomas Bavin, the artist appointed to Sir Humphrey Gilbert's expedition to Newfoundland in 1582:

> ...draw to lief one of each kind of thing that is strange to us in England, all strange birds, beasts, fishes, plants, herbs, Trees and Fruites ... also the figures and shapes of men and women in their apparell as also the manner of weapons, in every place, as you shall find them differing.[17]

White was more fortunate in Virginia than La Moyne had been in Florida. He worked with Thomas Harriott (1560–1621), a mathematician and astronomer, sent by Raleigh, whose mathematics tutor at Oxford he had been, to survey in Virginia. Scientist and artist, working closely together, described and drew whatever they encountered, noting economic value, whether of clothing, housing, food or medicine. White produced an unprecedented set of drawings depicting the life, dress and customs of the Algonquin Indians. The co-operative association of the two men established a new standard in ethnographic description. A fine example of that co-operation is White's illustration of a ceremonial dance of the Algonquin Indians of Virginia (pl. 20), which Harriott described in detail in his *Brief and True Report of the new found land of Virginia*, published in part one of De Bry's *America* (1590):

16

At a certayne tyme of the yere they make a great and solemne feast. The place where they meete is a broade playne, abowt the which are planted in the grownde certayne posts carved with heads like the faces of Nonnes covered with theyre vayls. Then being sett in order they dance singes, and use the strangest gestures that they can possibly devise. Three of the fayrest Virgins, of the companie are in the midds, which imbrassinge one another doe as yt wear turn abowt in their dancinge. All this is donne after the sunne is sett for the avoydinge of heate.[18]

Not all White's drawings survived. Much was lost when the survivors of the Roanoke settlement were being shipped aboard by Sir Francis Drake in June 1586, under extremely stormy conditions.

It is possible that on that voyage home with Drake, White met Drake's artist, Baptiste Boazio, who had been recruited to Drake's West Indian voyage (1585–6) to draw maps and plans of the coastal Spanish towns attacked. There is evidence that Drake himself kept sketchbooks in which he drew 'birds, trees and sea-lions', and that during his circumnavigation of the globe (1577–81), his cousin John Drake drew and painted with him.[19]

This use by the English of artists on voyages of piracy, exploration and settlement was stimulated by Spanish example. Richard Hakluyt, the elder, when writing his *Inducements* for voyages to Virginia between 1583 and 1585, included among the kinds of men who should be recruited for such voyages, 'A skilful painter . . . which the Spaniards used commonly in all their discoveries to bring the descriptions of all beasts, birds, fishes, trees, townes etc.'[20] Indeed, it was Philip II of Spain, the patron of Titian and builder of the Escorial, who instigated what was probably the first large scientific expedition to the New World, in which the visual arts were given an important role. This was the voyage of the physician Francisco Hernandez to Mexico (1571–6). Hernandez was able to compile as a result of his voyage no less than fifteen volumes of descriptions and illustrations of plants and animals collected and observed. Many of these drawings were used to produce decorative paintings for the King's antechamber in the Escorial. During the sixteenth and seventeenth centuries the exotic flourished most freely in the decorative arts where it created powerful impressions of the encompassing outreach of imperial power. Unfortunately, both the decorations of Philip's antechamber and Hernandez' great collection of drawings were destroyed in the 1671 fire in the Escorial.

One small set of Spanish drawings, of special interest to historians of the Pacific, has survived. These are the four rather crude drawings made by Diego Prado de Tovar, the deputy commander to Torres on his voyage from what is now Vanuatu to Manila through Torres Strait. They are rather rudimentary drawings of the people of Vanuatu and of southern New Guinea and are accompanied by descriptions of their skin colour, dress, weapons and artefacts. They are probably the earliest surviving drawings of peoples of the Pacific (pl. 21).

Soon after the Dutch established their independence from Spain in the early years of the seventeenth century, they rapidly became the world's dominant sea power, and Holland became the world centre for cartography and the publication of maps. The Dutch East India Company (VOC) challenged Portuguese supremacy in the East Indies, and between 1630 and 1654 the Dutch West Indian Company held a small section of north-eastern Brazil. Both companies kept a close guard upon information that might be of commercial value to competitors.

estaxente delas yslas que stan a la parte del sur de la nueba guinea,
son corpulentos, sus armas pesadas, son maças de piedra lanças
largas y flechas ≈

21. Diego Prado de Tovar, *The Natives of the islands off the southern shores of New Guinea* (Torres Strait), watercolour, 28.7 × 42.8 cm., 1606, Archiveo General de Simancas, Mapas, Planos y Dibujos (Caja XVIII, f. 83).

Now recording and collection became not so much the prerogative of princely courts but of powerful commercial monopolies and of the rich individual patrons and collectors associated with them. The most important of all was Johan Maurits van Nassau-Siegen (1604–79).

Maurits was Governor of the Dutch colony in Brazil for eight years (1637–44). Born of an illustrious Dutch family, he arrived in Brazil with a deep interest in and an enlightened knowledge of both the arts and the sciences. While there he commissioned the building of the Mauritshaus back in The Hague (now the home of some of Holland's finest art treasures) to house his Brazilian collection; and to Brazil he took two able scientists, Willem Pies (1611–78) and George Marcgraf (1610–43). Pies was a physician who was able to make from his studies in Brazil a major contribution to tropical medicine. Marcgraf was an astronomer, cartographer and naturalist. Their researches were published by Maurits at his own expense in 1648 in their great book *Historia naturalis Brasiliae*. It remained the authoritative source on the subject until Humboldt's work in the nineteenth century.

Maurits also took to Brazil two highly talented artists, Frans Post (1612–80) and Albert Eckhout (1610–64). Together they produced an unprecedented number of drawings of the plants and animals of the country. A great many of the drawings have been preserved, as have the copies made after the originals: some eight hundred or so, of Brazilian plants, animals and people, are now located in the Jagiellon Library, Cracow. It was from these drawings that the woodcuts that illustrated the *Historia* so lavishly were made, though their quality for scientific purposes leaves much to be desired.

Frans Post, a landscape painter, was born in Leiden. His work relates to the topographical tradition within Dutch landscape painting that emerges in the drawings of Hendrick Goltzius at the beginning of the seventeenth century and reaches a fulfilment in the work of Hercules Seghers and Philips Koninck. These artists raised 'mere' topography to the status of landscape art. Svetlana Alpers

18

has argued that the emergence of this kind of highly naturalistic landscape in Holland developed more readily in the Netherlands than elsewhere because surveyors and travellers were not impeded by the constraints and prohibitions of seigneurial possession.[21] Now although the political and social conditions of land ownership may well be of little moment in the development of the naturalistic landscape *within* the Netherlands, economics, land possession and politics are certainly not irrelevant to the depiction of landscape in Maurits's Brazil. As Rüdiger Joppien has remarked, Post's Brazilian landscapes feature the forts, towns and strongholds of the colony, and the sugar mills that provided its cash-crop.[22]

However, from a formal point of view, what is of special interest about Post's Brazilian landscapes is the sharp clarity with which the local plants, trees, flowers, insects and animals were introduced into the foreground of his panoramas (pl. 22). The fact that such things were little known in Europe meant that they should be delineated as clearly and as accurately as possible.

So it was that the special interests of naturalists began to affect the art of landscape. Post's work has sometimes been compared with the 'naive' art of Henri Rousseau (1844–1910). But one of the main sources of Rousseau's inspiration was not his own 'naivety' but the popular nineteenth-century oleographic illustrations of tropical scenery stimulated by Alexander Humboldt's writings. The so-called 'naivety' of both Post and Rousseau reveals the difficulties that modernism and modernist criticism have had in coming to terms with the exotic as a sub-genre of European art.

When he returned to Holland, Post settled in Haarlem and specialised in Brazilian landscapes, producing 130 or more of them. They are important for understanding exotic landscape as a European sub-genre. On the one hand, Post

22. Frans Post, *Sao Francisco river and Fort Maurits*, oil on canvas, 62 × 95 cm., 1639, Louvre, Paris.

23. Frans Post, *Landscape in Brazil*, oil on canvas, 282.5 × 210.5 cm., 1652, Rijksmuseum, Amsterdam.

makes every endeavour to subsume his Brazilian material within a sensibility system appropriate to European landscape art by evoking universalising modes: the arcadian, the romantic, the heroic, the nostalgic, drawn ultimately from literary precedent. On the other hand, there is an equal need to stress the novelties of Brazil, so much use is made of juxtaposing as foreground repoussoir elements a jumble of images representing the plants, animals, negro labourers and Tapuya Indians of the Dutch colony. Things themselves are drawn with realism and clarity but their relationships are arbitrary. In this Post anticipates the typical landscapes of the nineteenth century (pl. 23).[23]

Albert Eckhout, who was charged with drawing native peoples, animals and plants, avoided the exotic fusions of Post's post-Brazilian landscapes. The realism of the life drawings that he executed in Brazil is quite remarkable. 'There is no attempt', as Joppien has put it, 'to eschew ethnic truth or to compromise it for

20

the sake of European taste and feeling for decorum.'[24] His life drawings of Tapuyas are executed with a sympathetic sensitivity that is rare in the European portraiture of indigenous people, even during the eighteenth and nineteenth centuries (pl. 24). Eckhout retained the naturalism of his drawings in the close-focus realism of his paintings, probably owing to the fact that he seems to have been trained as a natural-history draughtsman. His *Tapuya dance*, in the National Museum of Denmark, Copenhagen, is his masterpiece, the recreation of a cere-monial act based on field sketches and magnificently objective (pl. 26). His portraits, for all their objectivity, are more stage-managed. Despite their frank-ness of presentation they project the look of slaves offered for sale at a colonial slave market (pl. 25).

In his awareness of the need for scientific description to be accompanied by field drawings – artist and scientist working in co-operation – Maurits foreshadowed the work of Joseph Banks on Cook's first voyage to the Pacific. Yet, as Whitehead and Boaseman have noted, it is remarkable how uncommon it was for a pro-fessional artist to voyage to and work in the New World prior to the eighteenth century.[25] And contemporary scientists rarely made the best use of what was available. Little value was placed on original drawings as visual evidence. After they had been reproduced they were often lost or forgotten. The systematics of the natural descriptive sciences had not yet been developed; the specimens in the cabinets of virtuosi were regarded as non-descript curiosities, valued only for their rarity.

24. Albert Eckhout, *Tapuya woman seated*, crayon, 33.2 × 21.6 cm., *c*.1637–44, Kupferstichkabinett, Staatliche Museen, Berlin.

25. Albert Eckhout, *Negro woman and child*, oil on canvas, 273 × 176 cm., Ethnography Collection, National Museum of Denmark, Copenhagen.

26. Albert Eckhout,
Tapuya dance, oil on
canvas, 168 × 294 cm.,
c.1645, Ethnography
Collection, National
Museum of Denmark,
Copenhagen.

The 'Mauritsian' drawings and the many copies that were made from them thus came to serve the needs of baroque art far more than they did the needs of 'baroque' science. Maurits, we have noted, was deeply interested in both art and science, and on his return home he made the fruits of his collecting in Brazil available to a number of the most powerful princely courts in Europe. He gave whole collections to the major towns of Holland: The Hague, Haarlem, Delft, Rotterdam and Leiden. To the Elector of Brandenburg he gave many drawings, paintings and specimens of natural history. To Frederick III of Denmark, his cousin, he gave twenty-six paintings by Eckhout and probably many specimens. To Louis XIV of France he gave cartoons of Brazilian subjects derived from Eckhout's and Post's work to be woven as tapestries at the Gobelins.

Yet paradoxically enough, though Holland was at the centre of all this distribution of visual information about the unfamiliar, it did not become a place where the exotic, in the sense defined and described above, flourished. Joppien has pointed out that there was little cult of the exotic in Holland.[26] This was probably largely owing to the fact, as Svetlana Alpers has argued convincingly, that the central tradition of Dutch art (particularly during the seventeenth century) is an art of describing, dedicated to seeing and depicting what is out there in the world rather than, as in Italy and the south, illustrating a narrative text.[27] The art of Eckhout certainly reinforces such a view.

Baroque exotica flourished most congenially in the decorative arts of the Catholic south, in ceramics, mural paintings and tapestries of the cabinets of virtuosi, and in the courts, garden pavilions and hunting lodges of princes. One of its most favoured subjects was the Continents, sometimes three, sometimes four (Asia, America and Africa, occasionally Europa as masterly mistress of them all). It provided a sumptuous opportunity to commingle and conflate the animals, plants, artefacts and indigenes of the non-European worlds within highly colourful, decorative schemes.

22

The decorative exotica embodied in such themes as the Continents was doubtless intended to indicate the global interests of those who commissioned them. They also expressed obliquely the social, intellectual, commercial and cultural supremacy of Europe over the descendants of Shem and Ham who inhabited the less fortunate regions of the world. This is nowhere better exemplified than in the two great series of tapestries produced by the Gobelins from the forty cartoons given to Louis XIV by Maurits, the *Anciennes Indes* (1687–1730) and the *Nouvelles Indes* (1740–1800), each of eight pieces (and known collectively as the *Tenture des Indes*). As Joppien has noted, both the content and the composition of these tapestries are unusual for their time: 'There is no coherent "story"... even their location is confused: the worlds of Africa, Brazil, Chile and Peru are fused into an entirely imaginative, uncultivated and irrational view of nature.'[28]

At this point it is advisable to remind ourselves that in academic art, history painting–narratives of events in the lives of gods, heroes and saints–retained the beau role; the decorative arts remained subordinate. The illustration of the sacred texts reiterated the central myths and legends of European culture. History painting asserted Europe's cultural ethnicity, traced its origins, guarded its identity, conserved its continuity. It was the art of European time.

It was in decoration that the dominance of narrative was first seriously challenged. That is understandable when we recall that the decorative artist is faced continually with a spatial problematic, the covering of a variety of shaped surfaces. So it was that in the decorative arts of the baroque, a compositional ordering in opposition to narrative and historical art began to insinuate itself, a form of ordering that invoked a pre-Renaissance past and heralded the modernist future of European art. The flatness of decorative borders and edges, the foliations and arabesques of framings challenged the illusionist centre of narrative paintings, those windows into a self-contained, rational but illusory world made possible by the discovery of perspective, and within which the dramas of the European tribes were played out. It was into these ordered spaces that the decorative arts began to introduce exotic *disjecta membra* culled from the fringes of the *oecumene*. Though baroque artists sought to give each strange, exotic thing a realistic presentation, out of respect for the reports of natural history draughtsmen, they found it impossible to present them within the rationally ordered space of centralised perspective, or any form of rationally ordered deep space. So they came to be depicted less like objects seen through a window occupying their natural settings and dispositions in space, and more like objects on a map or in a bazaar, in which the wealth of the world was spread out for Europa's admiration and delectation.

These formal transformations may best be remarked in the Gobelins' *Tenture des Indes*. Consider the *Le Cheval rayé* tapestry (pl. 27): the sources of its iconography are examined in detail in Whitehead and Boaseman: 'it is a rich exotic mix owing much to Maurits, a little to Dürer'.[29] What is of great interest, however, from a formal point of view is the degree to which the 'foreground', if we must call it that, has been flattened out to cover most of the pictorial space into which the assorted exotics have been introduced and juxtaposed. Though realistic enough in their individual representation, they are squeezed into tonal niches that have been hollowed out of a flat, illogical space.

If such spaces are irrational, so also are the relationships obtaining between the exotica. They are presented in a confused jumble, like animals hunted into a corner of a wood or fish caught in a net. They are presented as the spoils of a

27. Albert Eckhout, *Le Cheval rayé*, from the *Tenture des Indes* Gobelins tapestries, 475 × 375 cm., 1687–1730, Mobilier National, Paris.

European triumph: its dominance over all that is non-European. Here we may discern in baroque decorative art yet another source of that 'typical' landscape art which under the pressure of empirical naturalism began to supersede (during the nineteenth century) the pastoral and heroic landscapes of Renaissance and ultimately of classical and literary origin, as European artists came to grasp more fully the diversity of the global landscape. This was a change that was to be theorised later in the writings of Carus, Humboldt and Ruskin.[30] In typical landscape what was once perceived as exotic came to be ordered according to ecological principles rather than according to those derived from a great chain of theological being.

It would be grossly misleading, however, to suggest that such great changes, both formal and iconographic, happened with uniformity. That which was strange was always vulnerable to fantasy. Even the Dutch, those masters of the art of

24

describing, could revel on occasion in exotic fantasies. In 1718 Louis Renard published in Amsterdam a book containing 460 engravings of fish and crustaceans after specimens collected, it was said, around the Molluccas and the shores of Terra Australis.[31] Many were of quite fantastic shape. One extraordinary creature appeared to be a siren (pl. 28). It was described thus:

> Monster representing a Siren caught on the coast of Borne or Boeren in the province of Ambon. It was 59 inches long, and of eel-like proportion. It lived on shore in a tub for four days and seven hours. It occasionally uttered cries like those of a mouse. It did not wish to eat, even though small fishes, molluscs, crabs, crayfish etc. were offered. After its death a few feces, similar to those of a cat, were found in the tub.

A second edition of Renard's book was published in 1754. Little monsters, similar to those of the *Nuremburg Chronicle*, were alive and well in the European imagination even at the height of the Enlightenment.

Nevertheless, the Enlightenment did effect a major change in Europe's reception and understanding of its Other—the non-European. Scientists began to organise themselves increasingly into institutions, such as the Royal Society of London, established in 1662, and archaeologists began to apply empirical techniques to the study of the past. Artist-travellers and their patrons became as interested in examining, as objectively as they were able, human history as well as natural history.

None of them was a scientist in the full professional sense that we use the word today. But they were intensely curious, proto-scientific in their attitudes—and they used drawings to collect information as well as they could about the past and about whatever was strange, curious or unusual in the present. Their interests ranged from natural history to the monuments of antiquity and the middle

28. *Monster representing a siren*, hand-coloured engraving, in Louis Renard, *Poissons, Ecrivisses et Crabes . . . que l'on Trouve Autour des Isles Moloques, et sur les Côtes des Terres Australes*, Amsterdam, 2nd edn, 1754.

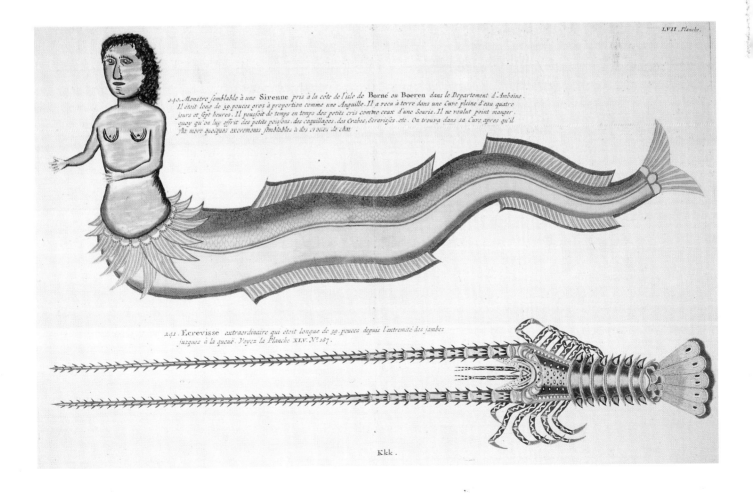

ages, from historic sites to exotic peoples. It is misleading to make any firm distinction between the growing interest in history and the growing interest in the natural sciences. Historical interest impelled artists to make measured drawings of classical monuments in Italy, later in Greece and the near East, while other artists throughout Europe were making equally careful drawings of plants and animals. The abiding concern was to record accurately and systematically the human and natural world as it had never been recorded before: the subject matter was interchangeable.

It was in this spirit that Joseph Pitton de Tournefort (1656–1706) employed Claude Aubriet (1665–1742) as his draughtsman on his voyage to the Levant and Egypt (1700–2). Although Tournefort is remembered today as a botanist and physician, he was equally interested in archaeology. His 'passion', as he said, 'was for the Discovery of Plants and antient Monuments'. For such interests he required an able draughtsman. In his account of his voyage he wrote, 'It frets a man to see fine Objects, and not to be able to make draughts of them; for without this help of *Drawing* 'tis impossible any account thereof should be perfectly intelligible.'[32]

In a similar spirit the Society of Dilettanti of London commissioned James Stuart and Nicholas Revett to visit Athens and make what turned out to be superb measured drawings of the classical buildings they found surviving there. The whole enterprise of eighteenth-century exploratory travel was at once scientific and historic: one aspect was concerned with the oldest 'science' of civil society–history; the other, with the science of the history of nature.

The unity of human history and natural history was stressed in one of the most influential books of the century, the comte de Buffon's *Histoire naturelle*:

> Just as in human history one consults documents, examines coins and medals, and deciphers ancient manuscripts in order to determine the revolutions and epochs in the intellectual life of man, so in natural history one must search the archives of the world, unearth the oldest relics, collect remnants, and unite all signs of physical changes which are traceable to the various ages of nature into one corpus of evidence.[33]

Buffon, of course, gave to style perhaps its best-known definition: *Le Style est l'homme même*. The literary style that he himself preferred was one in which the clear-headed expressed themselves with order, precision and clarity. For Buffon, as for Thomas Sprat who pleaded on behalf of the Royal Society of London for a 'naked, natural way of speaking',[34] a cool rhetoric was essential to scientific advancement. This new rhetoric for scientific literature is closely linked with the new interest, earlier advanced by Locke, in the use of drawing for the collection and transmission of information. Both helped to nourish an aesthetic that reached out towards the unknown instead of celebrating the traditional values and heroes of the past.

The close tie between scientific and aesthetic attitudes is at this time present wherever one looks. Consider the case of John Ellis (1710?–76). Carl Linné (Linnaeus) (1707–78), the famous founder of the binomial system of taxonomy, considered Ellis to be 'the main support of natural history of England'. In his *Essay towards a natural history of the Corallines* (1755), Ellis established the fact that coral polyp was not plant but animal. Yet his scientific interests had developed deviously, almost playfully. Here is his account of the events leading up to his discovery:

26

In the autumn of 1751 I received a curious Collection of Sea-plants from the Island of Anglesey in North Wales and another from Dublin. In order to preserve some Specimens of the most rare kinds, particularly those that were remembered for their Colours, I expanded them on Paper in fresh water, laying out their Ramifications with some Exactness... These when properly dried, I dispersed on thin Boards covered with clean white paper, in such a manner as to form a kind of Landscape, making use of two or three Sorts of *Ulva, Marina,* or Sea Liverwort, in designing a Variety of Hills, Dales and Rocks which made a proper ground work and keeping for the little trees which the expanded plants and corallines not inaptly represented.

My ingenious and Reverend Doctor Hales paying us a Visit, was pleased to express great Pleasure in viewing these natural lively Landscapes; and desired me to make some of the same kind for her Royal Highness the Princess Dowager of Wales, that the young Princesses might amuse themselves, in disposing the beautiful Productions in the like Picturesque Manner, and for that Purpose, further requested me to collect all the Varieties our Sea-Coasts offered; which I did, with the help of my worthy friend, George Shelvocke Esquire, Secretary of the Post Master General, and some of my acquaintances in Ireland.[35]

Ellis then proceeded to study his 'marine landscapes' under the microscope and enlisted the services of the marine painter Charles Brooking (1723–59) when he made a visit to the Isle of Sheppey. Here it was possible to make drawings of corallines while they were still alive in sea water 'by the Help of a very commodius microscope of Mr Crofts, the optician of Fleet Street'. As a result of this investigation Ellis became convinced finally 'that those apparent plants were ramified animals' (pl. 29).[36] This was a discovery of importance, and it may be noted that it was published a year after Louis Renard's *Monster representing a Siren* appeared in print for a second time.

29. *Groupes of different Corallines growing on shells, supposed to make this Appearance on the Retreat of the Sea at a very low Ebbtide,* engraving after Charles Brooking by A. Walker, in John Ellis, *An Essay towards the Natural History of the Corallines,* 1755, frontispiece.

The methods used in making field drawings varied with the character of the subjects recorded. The emphasis was upon the conveyance of the kind of truth appropriate to an understanding of the object. To see this new eighteenth-century delight in field studies and sketches simply as an expression of emerging romantic sensibility is to beg the question, though that no doubt is what, among other things, the delight became. But it is a consumer's way of considering the problem. The source of the new delight lay in the change in the relationship of the artist to his subject matter. His business now, as a draughtsman on location, or as one who had been on location, was not so much to invent as to inform; and if because of the artist's skill, sensibility and flair the information could retain something of the old delight in an art of free fancy, so much the better.

This point is fundamental to our understanding of the effect of scientific attitudes upon art at this time. The role of the artist was shifting steadily from its traditional Renaissance base. For Leonardo, drawing, which he certainly used for observing and recording, was an art best employed in the service of the freely ranging imagination. He advised artists composing subject pictures not to 'articulate the individual parts...the determinate outline' but to follow the practice of the poets and 'attend to the movements appropriate to the mental state of the creatures that make up your picture.'[37] To express the free play of the imagination, stimulated by natural form but not controlled by it, was the crucial role of drawing, of *disegno* in the Renaissance sense. The true role of the draughtsman was to be 'creative', to invent new forms with the assistance, if need be, of the known forms of nature. The new scientists of the eighteenth-century sought from the artist a more humble role, but they deeply respected the artist's capacity to record the truth more fully and completely than words—at least, where objective, spatial description was required. This was an aspect of Renaissance drawing, of Leonardo's own repertoire, that had lain relatively undeveloped from the sixteenth to the eighteenth centuries because of the low status that had been accorded to drawing as a tool in the discovery of the actual world as compared with drawing as a tool in the creation of the imagined and illusory wonders of the baroque imagination.[38]

By contrast, the romantics of the later eighteenth and early nineteenth centuries felt an increasing need to establish new connections between the imaginative process and the strangeness of things not European. They came to realise that so-called 'exotic' objects should not only be described with truth and clarity in themselves but that they should also be represented within a credible frame of relationships. This was one of the issues at the heart of Coleridge's poetics. With the publication of his *Species Plantarum* (1753) and *Systema Naturae*, Linnaeus revolutionised the study of natural history. Although still Aristotelian and Creationist in its theoretical assumptions, his new binomial taxonomy, based on the description of sexual organs, provided a ready index for the classification of the productions of the natural world. Its very existence stimulated new questions concerning the relationships between life and environment, anticipating the study of ecology. It became, in consequence, that much more difficult for the European imagination to fantasise about monsters at the ends of the earth or to present exotics in the decorative arts as the desirable trophies of a European triumph.

During the eighteenth century, too, art in the service of travel, like science and power, its masters and employers, began to institutionalise itself. It came increasingly to be realised that drawing was required for the more direct pursuit of scientific knowledge and imperial power. As we have already noted, drawing as an aid to the acquisition of accurate and useful information, had never been a central concern of the academies of fine arts. For them, skill in drawing was preparatory to the higher levels of art wherein invention was given pride of place, and where the painter aimed to rival the poet.[39] What Locke sought from drawing was at once more prosaic and yet more radical: an art for conveying accurate visual information. If this kind of drawing, of value to all, was to be fostered, it had to be developed as a skill acquired as part of a general education. It is not surprising, therefore, that the teaching of drawing for such practical purposes developed first in institutions whose graduates were professionally concerned with the security and imperial expansion of the realm, that is to say, in the naval and military schools.

Topography came to exercise a commanding influence upon landscape as a fine art because of its continuing importance to army and navy. Skills taught for highly practical purposes flooded out into the fertile fields of taste. As early as 1693 a drawing school was established in the Mathematical School of Christ's Hospital, which trained its boys for the navy. Earlier that century Wenzel Hollar, under the Earl of Arundel's patronage, gained favour at court and made maps and plans for the royalist cause during the early days of the Civil War before being captured at the seige of Basing House by Parliamentary forces. Escaping, he left England for Antwerp and did not return unitl the Restoration to work under Charles II, for whom he provided surveys and drawings of the fortress and naval base of Tangier, which had been transferred to Britain as part of the marriage dowry of Catherine of Braganza to Charles.

From the outset, artists with the topographical skills of a Hollar were in ready demand when military and naval information was required. Drawings and surveys for the army were carried out in the Drawing Room of the Board of Ordnance at the Tower of London. Later, drawing schools were established at the military academies at Woolwich, Marlow, Sandhurst and Addiscombe. Both Thomas and Paul Sandby were trained as draughtsmen at the Tower of London and both served in Scotland as military draughtsmen. Following the suppression of the Jacobite rebellion of 1745, it came to be realised that the most effective way to subjugate the Highlands was by means of a major programme of road and bridge building. This involved a comprehensive survey of northern Scotland, the first ever undertaken in the kingdom. At the age of sixteen Paul Sandby was sent from the Tower to serve under Colonel David Watson in the Highlands survey and worked as chief draughtsman there for four years. Basic techniques of survey and topographic description were developed in the Scottish Highlands that served Britain well in its preparations for the home defence of southern England during the Napoleonic wars, during the Peninsular war, and later during the British colonial expansion of the first half of the nineteenth century.

Six teams were assembled for the Highlands survey. Each contained a surveyor accompanied by a non-commissioned officer, with five or six soldiers as assistants. Paul Sandby depicted such a party at work by Kinloch Rannoch (pl. 30). During the winter months fair copies of the sketches that had been made on-site during the previous summer were drawn in the Ordnance Room of Edinburgh Castle. Sandby was responsible for showing relief: aligning brushwork in the direction of

30. Paul Sandby, *Surveying party by Kinloch Rannoch*, 17 × 24 cm., 1749, Map Library, British Library, London.

the slopes and using tonal gradations to describe steepness and height.[40] In Scotland he developed those skills that led him to become a key figure in British art in the shift towards naturalism that floursed towards the end of the eighteenth century and made it possible for Sandby himself to become a founding member of the Royal Academy, Chief Drawing Master at the Royal Military Academy at Woolwich, and personal drawing master to the royal princesses.

Predictably, there was academic resistance to topographic art. Henry Fuseli, speaking as Professor of Painting at the Academy (1799–1825), poured scorn on topographers: they were 'unworthy of their profession's high calling'. As Nicholas Alfrey has rightly insisted, topography and survey pursued traditions quite distinct from that of landscape painting. Yet in practice artists like Sandby found it increasingly convenient to move between the two traditions. Empirical naturalism came to exercise an over-arching influence upon these traditions because of the desire of both 'to come to a fuller understanding of the physical world'.[41] The defence of the realm encouraged drawing techniques that were able later to encompass an emotional appropriation of landscape in terms of the beautiful, the picturesque and the sublime–not only the landscape of one's own culture, but that of others, too.

The schools in which drawing was taught for the purpose of recording information provided the traditions and background for the drawing that was encouraged and carried out by Captain Cook during his voyages to the Pacific, especially those aspects of the schools' drawing lessons devoted to charting and the taking of coastal views for navigational purposes. Furthermore, the drawing schools raised the status of drawing in the community and did much to create a class of gentlemen amateurs who drew both for the practical purposes adverted to by Locke and others, and for their own pleasure.[42] Beyond the ateliers of the portrait painter and history painter, drawing came to serve the needs of science and technology. It was this widespread movement that as much as anything challenged and eventually destroyed the ordered hierarchy of academic art.

Although the academies of fine art placed a low value upon drawings intended to be no more than faithful copies of nature, the practice of drawing itself was always treated with great respect. For the Renaissance humanists who invented and developed the theory of fine art, the role of the draughtsman was crucial. It was *disegno*, drawing in its widest sense, the creative skill of the draughtsman in delineating and shaping his representations and configurations, that separated him from the craftsman and identified him as an artist. If professional draughtsmen should come to be engaged increasingly upon pursuits other than the creation of beautiful portraits and historic representations, it followed that the nature of *fine* art itself might change. During the eighteenth century such a shift, due to the changing role of the draughtsman, began to occur. Natural historians, archaeologists, geographers and engineers began to compete with the academies of art for the services and the loyalties of draughtsmen.

At the heart of the change lay the improved status accorded to science. During the second half of the eighteenth century the biological sciences, led by botany, which were once the preserve of dedicated savants and their noble patrons, began to acquire a large lay public. The change occurred when the crucial relationship between scientific method (which involved careful and systematic observation, accurate description, controlled experiment and the publication of results) and the utility of science for the improvement of agriculture and technology began to be understood. This, as is well known, first occurred in England, but the prestige of science and its developing connections with industry was coming to be realised throughout Europe. The encouragement of science was seen to be fundamental for the growth of trade and industry; it could assist the search for new markets, adapt and exploit new products found in distant and little-known lands. The support of science, therefore, became an increasingly important aspect of civic polity and attracted support from both the public and the private purse. This was the situation prior to the onset of the Industrial Revolution. Cook's three voyages, it must be emphasised, occurred in the decade that immediately preceded the full 'take-off' of that Revolution. Cook, in the event, provided a global stage for its ultimate operations.[43]

In earlier centuries the academies of fine arts had developed a hierarchy of categories based upon the conviction that it was the artist's concern to depict nature not in all her particularity, but in her perfect form. At the top of the ladder rested *istoria*, the practice of history painting, that category within which the deeds of the heroes of European culture, whether sacred or secular, were celebrated. Paintings upon the walls of churches, upon civic buildings and ancestral homes depicted the lives and deaths of the heroes of European culture. For such things, as for the illustrations in books containing similar subject matter, the visual forms appropriate to *istoria* were used. The purpose of such paintings and illustrations, as the theorists of academic art made clear, was primarily moral. By such means the young were taught the kinds of life they should emulate, the kinds of moral values they should embrace, if they aspired to leadership.

Portraiture, the second category of the academic hierarchy, provided a visual record not only of the appearance, but also of the role and class of the person portrayed by such means as costume, stance, attributes and setting. It provided links with the past, sustained tradition, revivified ancestral memories. History painting and portraiture were the esteemed categories of academic art within which most of the great masterpieces of European painting were executed between the sixteenth and the eighteenth centuries. This academic tradition, it must be stressed, was humanist at heart. It delineated the lives and activities of leaders in an appropriately dramatic and charismatic fashion, perpetuated their memories and continuously proposed new candidates for veneration. Yet towards the end of the eighteenth century the tradition began to be eroded by naturalistic art in the service of empirical science.

Change was possible because the academic tradition, though deeply conservative, was not a closed one. The delimitations of its categories were not barricaded by impassable sanctions, such as the proscription upon the figure in Islamic art. Indeed, one of the greatly respected doctrines of the academy insisted that artists could become aware of the ideal only by a sustained and continuous study of nature. In this doctrine lay a heel of Achilles. A history painter who set out to depict an ideal portrayal of an event in a hero's life might find himself involved more and more deeply in the naturalistic portrayal of the events and the setting. He might not succumb to naturalistic pressure, but to the extent that he did, his art moved from the ideals of the academy towards the conveyance of information. The category of portraiture, likewise, under pressure from naturalism could move from the ideal dignity of a Van Dyck towards the individual humanity of a Hogarth or the immediacy of a Gainsborough sketch. Pressure of this kind, to show the event as it actually occurred, to represent the appearance and disposition of a person at a particular moment of life, though it varied from time to time and from place to place, has of course, always been present in

European art. But from the mid-eighteenth century until the end of the nine-teenth the pressure on the representational arts to move in the direction of naturalism was stronger than it had ever been, or would be again.

The academic tradition was open in another way. New categories were estab-lished in practice and admitted–albeit reluctantly–into the hierarchy at its lower levels, long before the triumph of science and technology. The most important of these were landscape painting, genre and still life. They did not develop in full opposition to the academy but rather as an extension of the humanist impli-cations of its traditions. The character of an heroic action implied some account of the terrain across which it had occurred. The heroic landscapes of Poussin were implicit in the Sistine ceilings of Michelangelo. Emerging as a setting for heroic activity, landscape became an important category with its own conven-tions; sub-types, such as heroic, pastoral and picturesque landscape, emerged. Once the independence of landscape had been established, it could be pulled, like the academic tradition as a whole, either towards idealism or towards naturalism–yet its origins lay in naturalism. To the extent that the pressure was naturalistic, it was exerted upon landscape from still lower in the hierarchy, that is from topographic art. Botanical illustration, with its capacity to identify plants of medicinal and dietetic value, likewise exerted a pressure upon landscape art.

The push and pull upon landscape as a category caught between the idealism of history painting and the particularities of topography and botanical illustration is beautifully illustrated by the criticism that Sir Joshua Reynolds made of Francesco Algarotti in his eleventh *Discourse* (1782). Algarotti was a connoisseur with a European reputation which, if anything, was greater than that of Rey-nolds. Yet Algarotti's reading of Titian's famous painting (now destroyed) of St Peter Martyr was a 'botanist's' reading; Reynolds's reading was that of the British defender of the grand style.

For Algarotti, Titian was 'the Homer of Landscape':

His scenes have so much truth, so much variety, and such bloom in them, that it is impossible to behold them, without wishing, as if they were real, to make an excursion into them. And perhaps the finest landscape that ever issued from mortal hands is the background of his Martyrdom of St Peter, where by the difference between the bodies and the leaves of the trees, and the disposition of their branches one immediately discovers the difference between the trees themselves; where the different soils are so well expressed, and so exquisitely cloathed with their proper plants, that a botanist has much ado to keep his hands off them.[44]

To which Reynolds replied:

When Algarottie speaking of this picture [*St Peter Martyr*] praises it for the minute discriminations of the leaves and plants, even, as he says, to excite the admiration of a Botanist, his intention was undoubtedly to give praise even at the expense of truth, for he must have known, that this is not the character of the picture; but connoisseurs will always find in pictures what they think they ought to find: he was not aware that he was giving a description injurious to the reputation of Titian ... Such accounts must be very hurtful to young artists.[45]

Genre also was implicitly present in the humanistic conventions of the academy. The depiction of heroes and leaders invoked the presence of the led, and the distinction between the two was vital. The slave, the foreigner, the servant, the stranger within the gates, was distinguished clearly by physiognomical character, by costume and adornment. And here, as in the case of *genre*, where particularity rather than perfection is intrinsic to the category, naturalism readily asserted its presence. The case of still life was similar, for its aesthetic strength lay not in a rendering of the ideal but in depicting the palpable presence of the object in all its particularity. Yet it was confined largely, by the nature of its origins, to the pleasures of the hunt and the table, and its iconographic range was therefore limited to natural productions long domesticated to human use. The natural-history draughtsman could put severe pressure on such a tradition, both at a conceptual and a naturalistic level, by vastly multiplying the types of natural production available to be depicted.

The pressure of empirical naturalism did not operate, of course, with equal weight across all the categories of academic art. It operated most powerfully upon the lower categories. It operated, as we have seen, on landscape through the increased demand for accurate topography, on still life through the increase in the number of visual types of nature's productions made available by the illustrator of natural history; it acted upon *genre* through the identification of social classes within a society, and of the many peoples, both civilised and primitive, that lay outside the society. But pressure could be exerted on the higher categories also: in portraiture, for example. Primitive people could be portrayed as though they were objects of natural history, seen as plants or animals to be classified. Conversely, they could be seen and drawn as individuals who were also representative of humanity in a 'natural' state and so be endowed with an intrinsic ideality. Even at the level of *istoria*, the portrayal of events as they had actually occurred could become a matter of practical importance, particularly if they represented events within living memory. Accurate accounts of significant events were invaluable, for example, for the whole strategy of exploration and imperial expansion. Governments naturally insisted on knowing why some voyages failed where others succeeded. Naval officers attached to voyages of exploration were required to keep accurate logs which recorded information of potential value and for the purposes of naval intelligence to hand them over prior to disembarkation. Here it must be stressed, despite the value set upon visual records from the time of Locke until the time of Joseph Banks, the initiative and the responsibility lay almost entirely with those who compiled the written records.

In the portrayal of *events* as they had actually occurred, the draughtsman was at a distinct disadvantage. Not until the invention of the cinematograph towards the end of the nineteenth century did visual methods of recording and documenting events achieve a technology that could challenge written records. In the eighteenth century the best that could be done was to make on-the-spot field sketches of relatively small groups of people taking part in an event, and then, by assembling them later with the aid of memory and the visual conventions of pictorial composition, provide some record of what actually occurred. Such retrospective compositions, even at their best, cannot be taken as reliable records. They cannot be given the same status as information that we may wish to give to the drawings of plants, animals, artefacts and even landscape made in the presence of the object. Yet taken in combination with the extant written records, the contemporary visual documentation of events provides us with the best evidence we possess not only of what happened but how it happened. In such instances it must always remain an empirical question whether the drawings are wholly illustrative of an already existent text or whether they contain additional information drawn not from words but directly from the event as it was observed by the artist on the spot. It is, of course, in the visual and spatial components of an event, such as the costume and position of the participants, rather than in the temporal components that contemporary visual records can be most useful as information.

For the visual portrayal of the contemporary event there was an allied difficulty. The transference of a written to a visual account is not a simple process of translating a sequence of verbal propositions into a parallel sequence of images. The linguistic and the visual coding of information possess a different syntax and differing conventions. What is appropriate to language is not always available to the visual image, while, as Locke and later Banks asserted, the visual image was often superior to words. But the representation of an event visually brought out the complex relationship between visual and verbal codes. As Lessing (James Cook's exact contemporary) insisted, because of the nature of their medium, the painter and the sculptor, in seeking to record a significant event, must seize on the most telling moment of the event and use it to represent the full sequence of the action by providing an intimation of the events that led up to the moment and the events that succeeded it.[46]

However, the pressure of empirical naturalism on the academic hierarchy of categories was not simply to render existing categories more naturalistic. True, in the long run, that certainly occurred. But the process itself was more complex. Empirical naturalism, as we have seen, tended to create new categories, not only at the lower levels of the hierarchy but also between existing categories. Thus the emergence of the conversation piece during the eighteenth century may be seen as a product of the naturalistic pressure that *genre* was placing upon *istoria*.[47] Compositional modes native to *genre* were given something of the dignity of history. Likewise, the pressure of topography on landscape led to the creation of picturesque landscape which blended the compositional modes of the classical and pastoral landscape with the new demands for specific topographical information. It was this continuing pressure of topography on the picturesque which led in the nineteenth century to the emergence of *typical* landscape.

This discussion of the pressure exerted by empirical naturalism upon the academic hierarchy of pictorial categories provides a context suitable for the understanding of the long-term impact that the art of Cook's voyages (and the kind of art that those voyages subsequently, by their example, promoted), came to exercise on the traditional visual conventions of European art. For though the art of Cook's voyages did not attain the quality of the works that were Reynolds's concern when he wrote his *Discourses*, we should not confuse the preservation of conventional *standards* and traditional *qualities* with the erosive *challenge* of new problems for the visual arts—especially in a period like the last third of the eighteenth century. The art of Cook's voyages provided a model, championed by Herder, Humboldt and many other influential persons, for the visual description of the world. The problems inherent in the use of art as an efficient means of documentation set the stage for the invention of photography: Daguerre, we should keep in mind was a panorama painter; Fox Talbot, an amateur watercolourist.[48]

The growth of interest in the descriptive, natural sciences during the second half of the eighteenth century created a need for professional draughtsmen who

34

could put their talent to the service of natural historians. Young men, usually of humble origin, with a flair for drawing and some personal initiative, often found an opening to a modest but satisfying career as natural-history draughtsmen. The normal alternative for talents of this kind was apprenticeship to a portrait painter; but as such openings were few, especially to those from the provinces, talent began to flow in the direction of the new enthusiasm—the study and description of nature. By offering premiums to young artists, the [Royal] Society of Arts, founded by the provincial drawing master William Shipley, did much to help locate and encourage such talent as that of Sydney Parkinson, who exhibited with the Free Society of Artists in 1765 and 1766, with drawings of flowers on silk. William Hodges, Cook's artist on his second voyage, first studied at Shipley's school in the Strand and won a premium at the Society of Artists for a bas-relief in clay in 1759. Later he turned to landscape.

The career of George Edwards (1649–1773), whose important book *History of Birds* was included by Banks and Solander in their library on the *Endeavour*, may be considered in this context. Born at Stratford in Essex, he came to London as an apprentice and appears to have developed a talent for drawing and a passion for natural history. At the end of his time there he set out on a series of tours, walking most of the time, which took him to Holland and Norway (1718) and then to France (1719–20). Directing his attention to subjects of natural history, mainly birds and animals, on his return to London he made drawings that fetched good prices among Fellows of the Royal Society. Some of the Fellows, such as James Theobald and Sir Hans Sloane, became his patrons; it was through the latter's recommendation that he became Librarian to the Royal College of Surgeons. Edwards began his *History of Birds* in 1743, completing it in 1764 (pl. 31). For his scientific work he was awarded the gold medal of the Royal Society and later became a Fellow. In 1752 he became a Fellow of the Society of Antiquaries.

Several aspects of Edward's life illuminate our discussion. First, his primary talent was that of a draughtsman; he never set himself up as a scientist, but his drawings won the gratitude of the scientists of his day, and his book, which he had dedicated to God, became an authoritative text. That he should also have been elected a member of the Society of Antiquaries supports the view that the study of human history and of natural history were at this time much more closely related than at present.

In his book, Edwards discussed the importance of drawing for the pursuit of science and recommended that it be taught as an accomplishment:

31. George Edwards, frontispiece to his *History of Birds*, 1743–64.

35

'No one need think it an amusement beneath his dignity, since our present Royal Family and many of the young Nobility have been instructed in that Art.'[49] Some forty years before Edwards's book appeared, Jonathan Richardson, in his influential *Theory of Painting* (1715), also recommended that drawing should be part of the education of an English gentlemen and recognised, too, the importance of drawing for the 'useful sciences'. But Richardson, himself a portrait painter, was no advocate of naturalism. The object of his book was to encourage patrons to be capable of appreciating the higher categories of academic art, history and portraiture, where the ideal reigned. 'Common nature', he wrote, 'is no more fit for a picture than plain narration is for a poem. A painter must raise his eyes beyond what he sees.'[50]

George Edwards, at the middle of the century, though still appealing to the nobility and gentry for support, shifts the emphasis firmly away from the traditional view of the artist as a visual poet towards the view that the artist should serve the requirements of science:

> Those who draw after Nature, on account of Natural History, should represent things justly and according to Nature, and not strive to extoll her above herself; for by so doing, instead of instructing, they will lead the World into Errors.[51]

Edwards was well aware of the influential presence of the ideal theory of art among the artists of his time, though it had still to be given its classic expression in England by Sir Joshua Reynolds in his early discourses to the Royal Academy (1768–71). Edwards reluctantly admitted that the ideal theory, which equated poetry and painting, was suitable enough for the history painter to subscribe to, but he himself was opposed to it and longed for the day when draughtsmen might be held in as much respect for their perfection in the drawing of plants and animals as the sculptors of ancient Greece had been accorded for their studies of man:

> The historical painter, especially those who would represent the Fictions of the poets, may take greater liberties, and study all Methods to elevate his Subject by adding the highest Strokes of Art, in order to please the Eye, and raise in the Mind Ideas equal to the Historian or Poet he would represent. Yet everyone who reads Natural History, and sees Figures and Descriptions of things in Nature, supposes they are, or ought to have been immediately drawn and described from Nature. But no experienced Man when he beholds an historical piece, supposes the figures there drawn, are like to those they are intended to represent either in Feature or Person, any farther than in general the Historian and Poet may have told us, that one man was a graceful person, another a little crooked or deformed, which Accidents a Painter has liberty to carry to what degree of Perfection or Imperfection he can conceive, provided they do not contradict the letter of the Historian. But in drawing after Nature a most religious and Scrupulous Strictness is to be observed and by this means only can we demonstrate that Nature is, or is not the same at all times. If Natural Historians, or they who draw for them, would carefully observe these Rules, some of them might perhaps produce Figures that would be deemed perfect by the knowing Naturalists of these times, and escape their Censure; then might they, like the celebrated Statues of the Ancient Greeks and Romans, pass down as models to future Ages, as things justly and truly representing Nature; but these things are rather to be wished for than expected.[52]

Edwards's call to natural-history draughtsmen to produce figures that would be deemed perfect by naturalists exposes a central paradox of naturalism. He was not advocating a neutral naturalism which simply represented what was seen—if, for a moment, we assume that to be possible—but the depiction of animals and birds as perfect in their own way as representatives of their kind as were statues of men and women by Polyclitus and Phidias. The object of the natural-history draughtsman was to draw the *type* rather than the individual specimen with all its imperfections. Yet how was the artist to decide upon those characteristics that were typical of a particular animal and those that were accidental? To achieve this the draughtsman, like his colleague the history painter, required a conceptual framework to give order to his observations. Empirical naturalism had need of a conceptual ordering of the world no less than academic idealism. Edwards was not invoking artists to draw in a different way, but to turn their attention from the study of man to the study of the natural world. The paradox is neatly symbolised in the allegorical engraving that served as a frontispiece to Edwards's book in which the draughtsman, with the approval of appropriate attendant gods, is to be seen drawing the portraits of leading members of the animal kingdom (pl. 31).

Edwards's advocacy of the artist as a scrupulous recorder of the natural world was supported and developed by the antiquarian and naturalist Thomas Pennant (1726–98). Born at Downing, near Holywell in Flintshire, Pennant was deeply proud of his Welsh ancestry. He attributed his early taste for natural history to Francis Willougby's *Ornithology*, which was given to him as a boy by Willoughby himself, the father of Mrs Thrale. In 1746, while still an undergraduate at Oxford, Pennant visited Cornwall. In 1754 he toured Ireland; in 1769, Scotland, making after that a series of tours of the English counties: Northampton in 1774, Warwickshire in 1776, Kent in 1777, Cornwall in 1787 and Wales in 1778. His important *Tour of Scotland* appeared in 1769, and ran through several editions. This was followed by a standard text on *British Zoology* (1768–70), and a number of other important books, including an *Indian Zoology 1768–70*, a *Tour of Wales* (1773) and an *Arctic Zoology* (1784–7).

Pennant was an energetic and ever-curious traveller and a prolific writer. 'He observes more things', wrote Dr Johnson, 'than anyone else does', ard he illustrated his books at every possibility, claiming that 803 illustrations of his publications were drawn under his supervision. Many were drawn by Moses Griffith (1747–1819), whom Pennant took into his service in 1769 and who accompanied him on many of his tours.[53] Pennant employed the young Sydney Parkinson on illustrating some of the plates to his *Indian Zoology* shortly before Parkinson embarked on the *Endeavour* as one of Banks's artist.

Pennant believed in studying one's own country first. In the preface to his *British Zoology* he is mildly critical of those who remain ignorant of their native soil, 'while their passion for novelty leads them to superficial examinations of the wonders of Mexico and Japan'. Like George Edwards, he championed the role of the topographical and natural-history painters against the presumptions of the practioners of the highest categories. For they, too, he argued, have a significant role to play not only in the conveyance of accurate information but also in the formation of a sound taste and a good judgement. 'Painting', he wrote in the same preface, 'is an imitation of nature and who can imitate without consulting the original . . . animal and vegetable life are the essence of landscape, and are often secondary objects in history painting. Correct design is enough for the sculptor, but the painter should know their [i.e., animals' and vegetables'] different connections, manner of living, and places of abode, or he will fall into manifest absurdities.'[54]

Pennant is here suggesting that an awareness of *ecological* relationships is important for the painters of landscape and history. In nature, things are related in ways that the artist should be aware of. He should not substitute mere aesthetic relationships, 'good design', for his ignorance of them. It is to be noted that the artists who worked for Pennant depicted animals in settings that were ecologically suited to them. Pennant is one of the theoretical sources of *typical* landscape.

Pennant was critical of the view that taste has as its principal object the appreciation of works of art. He adopted Burke's sensationalist account of taste, since our sensory capacities are basically similar, but disagreed with Burke in confining the formation of taste to 'judgement of the works of the imagination and the elegant arts'.[55]

Arguing from the standpoint of naturalism and assuming a common sensory capacity, Pennant maintained that the source of taste lay in our judgements concerning the objects of nature, to which artists, like everyone else, must have recourse. 'Taste', he wrote, 'is no more than a quick sensibility of the imagination refined by judgement and corrected by experience; but experience is another term for knowledge and to judge of natural images, we must acquire the same knowledge, and by the same means as the painter, the poet or the sculptor.'[56]

A close knowledge of nature can be of assistance to the artist, Pennant insists, in quite practical ways. He should, for example, have a sound knowledge of the pigments that he uses to ensure that the colours he applies are permanent. Here, even the greatest artists have sometimes failed: 'the shadows of the divine Raphael have acquired an uniform blackness; which obscure the finest productions of his pencil, while the paintings of Holbein, Dürer and the Venetian School (who were admirably skilled in the knowledge of pigments) still exist in their pristine freshness'.[57] At that time the Society of Artists was interesting itself in the chemistry of artists' pigments and offering premiums for the discovery of local sources of pigment, particularly of those pigments that were obtainable only expensively by import.

Pennant's criticism of Raphael is revealing. The blackness of his shadows is unacceptable, for general aesthetic reasons—he is oblivious to the fact that they were acquired largely from the work of later varnishers—because they obscure 'his pencil'. Even when we allow for the fact that Pennant is using 'pencil' in the generalised eighteenth-century sense, the point of his objection is directed at shadow as an obscurer of detail. Holbein and Dürer are preferred. This is precisely the kind of preference one should expect from a natural historian exercising his taste, on this occasion not upon nature but upon works of art. Here is another example of the naturalist imposing on fine art his preference for a clear, detailed and linear style.

The increased use of drawing, then, by travellers, archaeologists, natural historians and the like during the second half of the eighteenth century, set up complicated processes in the visual arts, not only at the level of documentation, but also at the level of taste. The traditional role of draughtsmanship, of *disegno* and *invenzione* as the Renaissance art theorists had understood them, was challenged and eventually exchanged by an increasing number of artists, for a role that directed their activities towards the accurate documentation of the objects of the empirical descriptive sciences. This change in the function of the draughts-man operated at all levels of the academic hierarchy from the representation of historic events to the depiction of landscapes, peoples and inanimate objects. But it would be profoundly misleading to assume that this increased use of art for the conveyance of relevant scientific information operated as a direct, unilinear process by which error and illusion were cast off and the *truth* progressively revealed—though that certainly was the way the scientific optimists of the day chose to regard it. Naturalism, like idealism, is a conceptualising enterprise. In moving from the ideal theories of the academies towards the empirical standpoint of science, artists did not thereby achieve an unvarnished truthfulness of the eye; they exchanged one conceptual master for another. The new concepts of natural-ism arose from the descriptive sciences, whereas the concepts of idealism had been engendered by metaphysics and religion; but like all concepts, the concepts of naturalism were vulnerable to criticism and revision.

Finally, it must be stressed that the interactive relationships between percep-tion and conceptualising with which we have been concerned are extremely complex. Just as empirical attitudes and the naturalistic assumptions built into the classical, Renaissance and baroque views of artistic practice had been deeply affected by the artistic tradition of Europe on many occasions prior to the eighteenth century, so, during that century, traditional views continually reassert themselves. The process whereby a particular item of information was recorded and modified from its beginnings in the field to its possible end in publication must therefore be studied, so far as possible, in the situation particular to it and not inferred from the general conceptualising conventions prevailing at the time. And in the present climate of critical theory it is also of great importance that conceptions developed retrospectively by historians and others, such as primitiv-ism, exoticism and orientalism, invaluable as they are in drawing *attention* to long-term trends, are not used as *substitutes* for understanding the infinite complexity and subtlety of historical change.

2 THE INTELLECTUAL AND ARTISTIC FRAMEWORK OF CAPTAIN COOK'S VOYAGES

COOK'S VOYAGES BEGAN a new chapter in the history of maritime exploration. On his *Endeavour* voyage (1768–71), the captain and his crew were able to determine for the first time tolerably well just where they were upon the surface of the globe. Latitude was computed by taking meridian altitudes of the sun with a quadrant or sextant; longitude, by means of 'lunar distances' and the use of Maskelyne's *Nautical Almanac*, published in 1767, the year before the *Endeavour* sailed. Using these observations, and taking running surveys from the ship with compass bearings or sextant angles on prominent shoreline features, Cook (pl. 32) was able to lay down a reasonably accurate chart of a previously unknown coastline in a comparatively short space of time.[1] In order to do this kind of work efficiently, he required broad, shallow-bottomed vessels of the 'cat-built bark' type used in the British North Sea coal trade. Such ships made it possible for him to sail close to shore lines in relative safety. Skill in the use of astronomical and navigational instruments, accurate computation and vessels suitable for survey purposes provided the theoretical potential for efficient maritime exploration.[2]

A practical prerequisite was the sustained health of the crew. Here, too, Cook began a new chapter in the history of exploration. Though he did not find, as is commonly believed, the best answer to scurvy,[3] he did appreciate the importance of fresh food and insisted on its consumption whenever it was available. But in order to gain fresh food and water for his crew and wood for his stoves, it was essential that amicable relationships be established with unknown peoples. This was achieved by gifting: discriminate gifting to the appropriate persons promoted friendly relations. Efficient voyaging, however, required the maintenance of not only the health but also the morale of the crew. Although Cook won great respect from his crew again and again by his capacity as a commander in conditions of extreme crisis, high morale demanded even more. In order to prevent mutinous behaviour among shiploads of young men deprived of female company, Cook found it expedient to allow a degree of sexual freedom between members of his crew and native women. The economic rewards of the market in sex which was rapidly established in the Pacific as a result of Cook's voyages made it possible for the people of the Pacific to move from the Stone into the Iron Age. For the most part, this market encouraged amity rather than discord; but it did lead to some unpredictable results, and one of the least attractive legacies of more efficient, more scientific voyaging was the transmission of European diseases such as syphilis.

When the conditions outlined above were fulfilled, it became possible for Cook to provide a physical and social space on his ships not only for the pursuit of those sciences essential to navigation, such as astronomy and meteorology, but other sciences also, such as botany and ethnography, that might provide knowl-

32. John Webber, *Captain James Cook*, oil on canvas, 114.3 × 91.4 cm., 1782, private collection.

41

edge of practical and economic value. The young Joseph Banks (1743–1820) (pl. 33) was the first independent scientist to grasp the new possibilities opening in the wake of this more scientific voyaging.[4] A member of the landed gentry, he possessed the means, the enthusiasm and the drive to extend by 'field' work systematic knowledge in natural history in a manner analogous to Cook's sys-

33. Benjamin West, *Joseph Banks*, oil on canvas, 234 × 160 cm., 1771, Usher Gallery, Lincoln.

42

tematic approach to navigation and cartography. Banks was an early English disciple of Carl Linné, and so that the new Linnaean system of biological classification could be applied to unknown plants and animals collected in the Pacific, he took along with him on the *Endeavour* the Swede, Daniel Carl Solander (pl. 34), a pupil of Linné. He also took the young Scot, Sydney Parkinson (1745–71) (pl. 35), to make drawings of specimens collected before they dried and the colours faded.

Scientific field work, if it was to be more than naive description, required a reference library. Banks therefore carried with him on board a small but comprehensive library of books relating to travel and natural science; indeed, in the eighteenth century, travel literature often contained a rich harvest of information relating to natural history. The sixty-odd titles that accompanied Banks included accounts of the major voyages to the Pacific prior to Cook, together with the histories of Pacific voyaging by Charles de Brosses and Dalrymple, major works on natural history, and the travels of natural historians to regions beyond Europe such as Brazil (Pies and Marcgraf) and Jamaica (Sloane). The work of Pies, Marcgraf and Sloane would clearly have provided Banks with a model of what needed to be undertaken and published for the Pacific.[5]

With such a library at hand, Banks and Solander were in a position to compare what was known in natural history with the new and mostly unknown specimens they collected on the voyage. In their work they were ably assisted by Parkinson, who also brought a collection of books with him, though more for his private pleasure than instruction. They included a good deal of poetry, the works of Chaucer, Spencer, Pope, Ossian, Gray and Dryden, translations from Homer and Virgil, the tales of Marmontel and La Fontaine, and the works of Shakespeare – all reading, no doubt, for possible idle moments on the voyage.[6] Not that he could have had many, for he also kept a journal – from which an invaluable independent account of his voyage, *A Journal of a Voyage to the South Seas* (1773), was later published by his brother – as well as producing over 950 botanical drawings. A younger contemporary of David Hume and Adam Smith, Parkinson was an admirable example of the Scottish Enlightenment: industrious, highly intelligent and obviously the intellectual equal of Joseph Banks. Parkinson died aged twenty-six of malaria and dysentery contracted towards the end of the voyage in Batavia.[7]

Indeed, all three young artists accompanying Banks died on the voyage, but not before producing, in addition to Parkinson's botanical works, approximately 200 drawings of coastal views, of much service to navigation, and another 200 drawings relating to the peoples of the Pacific, their artefacts and the places in which they lived. To return from previously unknown lands with such a huge corpus of drawings was something quite new to the history of science. Regrettably, however, very few of the drawings were published as engravings, so that the information they contained did not enter the public domain. But this is a story that repeats itself throughout the history of Pacific exploration: great interest and enthusiasm at the outset of the voyage; little sustained interest in the publication of the scientific results at the end of the voyage.

By comparison with astronomy and navigation, the science of ethnography was relatively undeveloped when the *Endeavour* sailed in 1768. However, Lord Morton (pl. 36), the President of the Royal Society, which had sponsored the voyage, gave Cook an important set of *Hints* which included, among other things, advice concerning the description of native peoples encountered. Cook was expected to

34. John Flaxman, *Daniel Carl Solander*, medallion bust designed for Josiah Wedgwood, 1775.

35. *Sydney Parkinson*, frontispiece to his *Journal of a Voyage to the South Seas*, 1773, engraved by James Newton.

36. Lord Morton. Detail from Jeremiah Davison, *James Douglas, 13th Earl of Morton, and his family*, oil on canvas, 241.3 × 284.7 cm., 1740, Scottish National Portrait Gallery, Edinburgh.

report on their natural disposition; their progress in arts and science (especially their mechanics, tools and manner of using them); the character of their persons as to features, complexion, dress, habitations, food and weapons; their methods of commerce; their modes of religion, morality and government.[8] For this work there was much less background reading on the *Endeavour* than there was for botanical studies, but the magisterial fourth volume of Buffon's *Histoire naturelle*, which concerned itself with the nature of man, would have provided an excellent summary of the Enlightenment's views on the subject. Furthermore, Banks did not possess artists capable of drawing the human figure with competence. Alexander Buchan, about whom little is known,[9] was taken to make drawings of the dress and adornments of peoples encountered, but he had obviously not been trained in life drawing. An epileptic, he died a few days after reaching Tahiti, after which the work of drawing native peoples and landscapes was shared between Herman Spöring, Banks's secretary and amanuensis, and Parkinson, neither of whom had been trained in figure drawing.

Because the first voyage had almost ended in disaster on Endeavour Reef, Cook was given for his second voyage (1772–5) two ships, the *Resolution* and the *Adventure* (under the command of Tobias Furneaux). The voyage was directed towards solving the problem of the possible existence of a still undiscovered southern continent in the waters towards the South Pole. Banks had hoped to join Cook but, when his ambitious accommodation requirements made the *Resolution* unseaworthy, he withdrew.

The Admiralty then selected Johann Reinhold Forster and his son George, aged seventeen (pl. 37), to go, as scientist and scientific draughtsman respectively, in Banks's place. The Forsters, Germans of Scottish descent, had come to Banks's notice because of their translation into English of books relating to travel and natural history. The elder Forster, though possessed of a difficult temperament, was the most widely read and best informed scientist ever to travel with Cook.[10] George became a man of equal but more varied brilliance. He later became Europe's first academic expert in Pacific matters.[11]

37. John Francis Rigaud, *Johann Reinhold Forster and George Forster in Tahiti*, engraving by D. Beyel, 1781.

38. *William Hodges*, engraving after a painting by Richard Westall, 1791.

The sciences of astronomy and navigation were greatly advanced by Cook's second voyage. Nevil Maskelyne, the Astronomer Royal, chose two of Britain's best astronomers to join Cook: William Wales, who served on the *Resolution* and had observed the 1769 transit of Venus at Hudson Bay, and William Bayly, who served on the *Adventure* and had observed the transit at the North Cape. Realising the great value of their work for navigation, the Board of Longitude published their jointly authored *Astronomical Observations* in 1777. On the voyage, Wales and Bayly also tested the two chronometers invented by John Harrison and John Arnold. The Harrison chronometer performed brilliantly, and as a result it replaced the older and more arduous method of determining longitude by lunar distances. Some years later in 1788, Wales, with assistance from the Board of Longitude, published the collated astronomical observations made on the voyages of Byron (1764–6), Wallis (1766–8), Carteret (1767–9) and Cook in the *Endeavour*. Once published, such information was of great value to seaman.

Although a list of books Cook carried on the *Resolution* has not been published, it is likely that it included many of those that were on the *Endeavour*, together with a copy of Bougainville's *Voyage*. This had been published in Paris shortly before the *Resolution* sailed, and probably Cook also had access to a copy of Johann Forster's as yet unpublished English translation of it. In any case, he would certainly have had access to the extensive collection of books that Forster carried with him on the *Resolution*; we know that Forster had these books with him because he refers to them in specific contexts in a journal that he kept on the ship.[12] Although Forster experienced considerable difficulty on his return in publishing his work, he did succeed with his *Observations made during a Voyage round the World* (1778), a book that magnificently united Forster's capacity for theory and speculation with his meticulous field observations. It gained high praise from the German philosopher Herder.

Cook's official artist on the second voyage was William Hodges (1744–97) (pl. 38), a landscape painter trained by Richard Wilson. Thrust among a company of astronomers and scientists of natural history, he found himself paying particular attention in his drawings and paintings to conditions of weather, light and atmosphere. There is evidence that he painted directly in oils from nature while looking through the window of the great cabin of the *Resolution*, thus developing the *plein-air* practice that his master had followed in Italy. In many respects, Hodges's experimental attitude to his work in the Pacific anticipates the interests of Turner and Constable. Though not trained as a portrait painter, he also produced memorable portraits of Polynesians and Maoris, seeking to portray the individual rather than the type, and he made a number of remarkable wash drawings from his experience in the Antarctic Ocean.[13]

George Forster, working in gouache, completed a fine series of paintings of natural-history specimens collected on the voyage, and in his *A Voyage Round the World* (1777) also gave what is, from a literary point of view, the best written account to issue from all three of Cook's voyages. It was undertaken when Forster was twenty-one and appeared only because his father was prevented by the Admiralty from taking part in the publication of the official account of the voyage.

During the second voyage, the *Adventure* under Furneaux became separated from the *Resolution* and returned some months earlier, bringing back with it Mai (better known as Omai), a native of Raiatea. In England Omai became something of a social lion and was feted wherever he went. Satirists used his presence

39. William Parry, *Omai, Banks and Solander*, oil on canvas, *c*.1776, private collection.

in England to compare the admirable life of the Society Islands with the corruption and decadence of European society. From 1785 to 1788 a pantomime entitled *Omai* played in London and the provinces to capacity audiences; but that was long after Cook, on his third voyage, had returned Mai to Huahine (pl. 39).[14]

The object of Cook's third voyage (1777–80) was to find a north-west passage, if it existed, from the coast of north-west Canada, or through the Bering Strait, back into the north Atlantic. He was a sick man, and it began to show more and more as the voyage progressed. His increasing practice of taking hostages to regain stolen goods or escaping crew members led ultimately to his own death in Hawaii.

Though this was a longer voyage, lasting four years, Cook did not possess the array of talent present on the second voyage. After its encounters with Banks and the Forsters, the Admiralty had cooled to the idea of independent scientists on its voyages of exploration. If there was to be science it would be carried out by naval men. No list of books relating to science or travel carried on the third voyage has been compiled, and it is likely that in this regard the third voyage was less well equipped than either the first or the second voyages. Yet a great deal of competent field observation was undertaken, particularly by Cook's surgeons,

William Anderson, who died on the voyage, and David Samwell.[15] But the ability to compare, analyse and generalise from empirical observation, initiated on the first and developed on the second voyage, was less in evidence on the third voyage. There was, however, undoubtedly one major advance. On this occasion greater interest was taken in making detailed records of the manners and customs of the peoples of the Pacific. If the first voyage is the botanical voyage, the second, the meteorological voyage, the third is the ethnographic voyage.

In this Cook was admirably supported by his official artist, John Webber (1751–93) (pl. 40), who had been equally well trained in both landscape and figure work. Highly industrious, he brought back more drawings of peoples and places than any of Cook's previous artists, and his work got better as the voyage progressed. It is quite misleading to say, as it so often is, that because he was European he painted the native peoples of the Pacific to look like Europeans. Indeed, it might well be said that he was Europe's first serious ethnographic artist in that he sought, with considerable success, to portray a wide variety of the ethnic types that he encountered, especially in the north Pacific.[16] It is important to realise, however, that ethnic variety was depicted within the overriding Enlightenment conviction that all nations were the members of one great human family, though some may have degenerated, as a result of dispersion and the effects of climate, from that perfection that had been attained by the European. So far as Cook's artists were concerned, the concept of race, which was to have such devastating effects on non-European peoples, had not yet emerged. Its effect upon artwork does not begin until the nineteenth century.

40. Johann Daniel Mottet, *John Webber*, oil on canvas, 67.2 × 55.2 cm., 1812, after a contemporary miniature, Historisches Museum, Bern.

After Cook's death the practice of taking professionally trained scientists and artists as supernumeries on voyages of exploration passed to the French, in equipping the voyages of La Pérouse, d'Entrecasteaux and Baudin. For some years the practice lapsed in Britain. No scientists or artists were included in the First Fleet which sailed for Botany Bay in 1787, though it might have been assumed from Banks's work there that the eastern coast of New Holland would provide a rich harvest for natural science.

Nevertheless, the naval practice whereby officers and midshipmen kept personal journals and gained some competence in draughtsmanship did yield positive results. Drawing, as we have seen, was taught to naval cadets at Christ's Hospital and the Royal Naval College at Portsmouth, and on board His Majesty's ships. There were several naval men on the First Fleet who were competent in drawing charts and views, notably John Hunter, William Bradley, George Raper and an unidentified artist known as the Port Jackson Painter.[17] During the first four years of settlement, these and other artists completed hundreds of drawings of plants and animals which, though at times charmingly naive, are of inestimable scientific value.

One of the most important voyages modelled on those of Cook was the Spanish one under the command of Alejandro Malaspina which set out from Cadiz in 1789. Despite their excellent work of collecting and describing, completed on the voyage itself, those on the expedition came home to Spain to confront a social and political situation highly unfavourable to the encouragement of the arts and sciences. The momentum of the French Revolution, with all its attendant excesses, threatened the values upon which the dynamics of Enlightenment science were based.

This threat was present in France itself, the home of the Enlightenment. There, from Le Havre in October 1800, the *Géographe* and the *Naturaliste*, under the command of Nicolas Baudin, set sail to charter southern Australian waters and to undertake studies in natural history and ethnography. Sponsored by the Institut Nationale and dispatched by Napoleon, then First Consul, this expedition set out with an ambitious retinue of astronomers, botanists, zoologists, mineralogists and artists. Baudin did not succeed in maintaining the health of his crew, and sharp political divisions arose among this scientific contingent. When the ships stopped on Mauritius, many of them remained behind. After this event, most of the scientific work fell to three young men, François Peron and the artists C.-A. Lesueur and Nicolas Petit. Baudin charted, in considerable detail, parts of south-east Tasmania and the southern coastline of south-east Australia. Highly important work was completed in marine zoology, by far the best then achieved on any scientific voyage, and the expedition came back with invaluable ethnographic records about the Aborigines of Tasmania. These remain the most important record of Tasmanian Aboriginal society prior to European settlement. But even before the expedition had returned, it had fallen into disfavour with Napoleon, and its scientific work was published, after great difficulty, only years later.[18]

Baudin and Matthew Flinders were responsible for charting the last uncharted portions of the Australian coastline, and with them, for all practical purposes, the maritime exploration of Australia comes to an end. Furthermore, Flinders's circumnavigation of Australia in the *Investigator* (1801−4) completes the series of English voyages that had begun with Cook. Nothing comparable is attempted until the voyage of the *Beagle* thirty years later. And, as with the *Endeavour* voyage at the beginning, so with the *Investigator* voyage at the end: again it is Banks (now Sir Joseph and President of the Royal Society) who is the guiding scientific mind. Flinders found favour with Banks, who took a prominent part in the organisation of the voyage, choosing Robert Brown as the botanist and Ferdinand Bauer as the botanical artist. Both men achieved complete mastery in their fields and produced magnificent results. Joseph Dalton Hooker, himself one of the greatest English botanists, described Brown's *Prodromus Florae Hollandiae* as 'the greatest botanical work that has ever appeared',[19] though it was published, because of the war, very economically. The work of Ferdinand Bauer has frequently been referred to in similarly superlative terms.[20] For many he is the supreme botanical draughtsman, the 'Leonardo' of natural-history painting.

As with so many earlier voyages to the Pacific, and despite the achievements in cartography and botanical science, the conclusion of the *Investigator* voyage was attended by disaster. Flinders himself was imprisoned for many years by the French on Mauritius and did not succeed in publishing his work, *A Voyage to Terra Australis*, until 18 July 1814, the day before he died.[21] Bauer's great work illustrating Robert Brown's *magnum opus*, the *Illustrationes Florae Hollandiae*, had to be abandoned after fifteen plates had been issued. He returned to Vienna and completed his drawings of Australian plants there.[22]

William Westall had been chosen by Benjamin West, the President of the Royal Academy, to accompany Flinders as his official artist. Much of his work is closely related to Flinders's meticulous survey work: his coastal profiles relate to Flinders's running traverses, and his panoramic views made from high points of land at King George's Sound and in other harbours, to Flinders's triangulation surveys. Westall also completed a good deal of landscape work. Here his meticulous drawing of foliage in mass reflects perhaps the botanical preoccupations of Brown and Bauer, with whom he was in constant contact. Westall's paintings of

48

the north Australian landscape reveal a similar desire to capture the overall high tonalities of tropical light that is characteristic of William Hodges's Tahitian landscapes of the mid-1770's. Westall, however, had to work for long stretches of time on barren coasts and did not gain the same stimulation from his novel environment that Hodges gained in Polynesia. He left the expedition a disappointed man and made for China in search of something more exotic.[23]

Flinders mapped the last remaining portion of Australia's unknown coastline from the head of the Great Australian Bight to what is known as Encounter Bay in western Victoria, where he met Baudin sailing west. His work included the charting of Spencer and St Vincent Gulfs. Although Flinders mapped relatively little of the coastline that had not already been charted, he carried out a series of masterly surveys around the continent, and the *Investigator* voyage may be seen, therefore, as bridging the gap between those late eighteenth-century scientific voyages of exploration inaugurated by Cook, and the nineteenth-century voyages of close coastal survey carried through by such commanders as Fitzroy on the *Beagle*.

In other ways the *Investigator* voyage was a fitting conclusion to those of Cook. It was, as noted above, under the patronage of Banks, who ensured that it was well equipped from a scientific point of view: not only did it have the best available scientist and a competent artist, but it also carried with it a comprehensive library of charts and relevant literature. Prior to sailing, Flinders requested from Banks a range of charts that included Laurie and Whittle's *Complete East India Pilot* and Arrowsmith's charts of the world and of the Pacific. He also sought material on the voyages of Dampier, Dalrymple, Cook, Hawkesworth and Bligh, and asked for Murdoch McKenzie's *Treatise on Maritime Surveying*. He requested a set of *Encyclopaedia Britannica*, presumably the third edition consisting of fifteen volumes, published between 1788 and 1797.[24] To go on a scientific voyage was to sail with a wide range of relevant, up-to-date knowledge ready at hand. Such equipment was not available to land travellers, who could not carry Buffon or the *Encyclopaedia Britannica* on a pack horse or in a camel train. The map of the world was charted while the interiors of the continents remained relatively unknown. In their time, the 'tall' ships acted as the world's first effective mobile laboratories, where new knowledge and past knowledge could be related to each other in the actual process of discovery.

In this regard it is worth noting that the *first* edition of the *Encyclopaedia Britannica*, a direct product of the Scottish Enlightenment, was published between 1768 and 1771, the years of Cook's *Endeavour* voyage. But the successful scientific voyaging that he inaugurated may best be seen and understood as a major achievement of the European Enlightenment as a whole, just as the discovery of the New World is best seen as one of the major results of Renaissance science. By such means Europe gained a mastery of the world. The discovery and settlement of Australia was a comparatively minor episode in that long historical drama. For five centuries Europeans, as a result of their achievements in art and science, sustained a hubris by which they convinced themselves that they had reached a higher state of human perfection than had the peoples they brought under their control.

3 ART AS INFORMATION

John Keats ends his 'Ode On A Grecian Urn' with the lines:

> 'Beauty is truth, truth beauty'–that is all
> Ye know on earth and all ye need to know.

The lines are well worn with much quoting, but I repeat them because they reach to the heart of my subject. It has been noted that they terminate the poem on a surprising note. Art, as Keats is saying for most of the poem, gives to the transient events of daily life a perfection that transcends time. But he has the Grecian Urn to say that beauty is an earthly truth, so thrusting us into another realm in which a different set of ideas hold sway, one where beauty takes on the form of information, and man-made beauty–art–is akin to the conveyance of correct information.

As several critics of Keats have noted,[1] the 'Ode On A Grecian Urn' embodies two views concerning the nature of art which it seeks to resolve. Both views hold that art is an imitation of nature; both, that is to say, are varieties of naturalism. The first is classical naturalism, which centred itself upon the human figure as the finest creation of nature. The second view, which we might call empirical naturalism, takes the spot-light from the human figure and directs it, in the first instance, towards plants and animals. An empirical naturalism was present, as we have seen, in the lower categories of the visual arts in Europe from the fourteenth century onwards,[2] but it did not begin to threaten the supremacy of classical naturalism in the high aesthetic realm until the eighteenth century, when it received considerable impetus from the work of Linnaeus. As a result of Linnaeus's influence, empirical forms of naturalism were developed in the visual arts to assist in the provision of a systematic account of nature and of man by means of a connected group of descriptive sciences: botany, zoology, meteorology, geography, geology, archaeology and anthropology. As empirical naturalism came to be preferred to classical naturalism, humankind came to be seen no longer as the measure of all things, as it was for the classical naturalists, but as one kind of animal among others, specially endowed unquestionably, but sharing with those others the same earthly environment and subject to similar laws.

The history of the visual arts in Europe between 1750 and 1890, give or take a few years either way, can best be understood as the steady, relentless and continuing triumph of empirical naturalism over classical naturalism. And at the starting point of that triumph there is no single more significant factor to be found than the graphic-arts programme that was developed in the course of Captain Cook's three voyages and the discussions that attended the publication of its results. During the twelve years from 1768 to 1780 something in the order of three thousand original drawings were made of things, mostly from the Pacific, not seen before by Europeans: plants, fish, molluscs, birds, coastlines, landscapes, unknown peoples, their arts and crafts, religious practices and styles of life. And Cook's voyages were not only fact-gathering phenomena, they deeply affected

Detail of pl. 47.

51

conceptual thought, and their influence penetrated deeply into the aesthetic realm. That need not surprise us. It would be much more surprising if the unveiling to European eyes of more than one third of the world within fifteen or so years had had a lesser effect.

Yet until recently the effects wrought upon European vision by Cook's voyages have been largely ignored by art historians.[3] For the two and a half centuries of European exploration, exploitation and colonisation of the Americas and both the Indies prior to Cook, the visual records are small–unbelievably small.[4] The little that did get drawn or painted seems to have been the product of fortunate accident. With the important exceptions noted in chapter one, little value was placed upon the acquisition of accurate graphic information by most voyages of exploration; no continuing tradition of visual documentation and publication was established; the emphasis was upon secrecy. European artists did not look, were not encouraged to look, beyond Europe.

That situation, long sustained, was changed dramatically by Cook. Under his command the value of visual records was for the first time fully recognised and adequately provided for. They had, however, been advocated by scientists and thoughtful travellers in England for over a century. An early advocate was the Royal Society itself, which sponsored Cook's first voyage so that the 1769 transit of Venus might be observed at Tahiti. In 1665, shortly after the Society's creation, it had prepared with the help of one of its founder members, Lawrence Rooke, the astronomer, a set of written instructions for seamen bound for long voyages. The fourth instruction required them 'to make Plotts and Draughts of prospects of Coasts, Promontories, Islands and Ports'.[5]

Such instructions, however, were at first more often honoured in the breach than the observance. George, Lord Anson (1697–1762), during his famous voyage of seizure and plunder against Spain in the South Seas (1740–4), was one of the first seriously to take note of them. 'No voyage I have yet seen', wrote Richard Walter, the chaplain of Anson's ship, *Centurion*, 'furnishes such a number of views of land, soundings, draughts of roads and ports, charts and other materials, for the improvement of geography and navigation'.[6] It was Walter himself who edited Anson's *Voyage Round the World*, and it became the most popular travel book of its time. In his introduction he stressed at considerable length the importance of keeping graphic records of exploration and maritime adventure in the way that Anson did: 'For they were not copied from the works of others, or composed at home from imperfect accounts, given by incurious and unskilful observers, as hath frequently been the case in such matters; but the greatest part of them were drawn on the spot with the utmost exactness, by the direction, and under the eye of Mr Anson himself.' It was Piercy Brett (1709–81), Anson's second-lieutenant on the *Centurion*, who made most of these drawings. Entering the navy as a midshipman, he rose to be a commander who saw much active service and was knighted in 1753, becoming an Admiral of the Fleet in 1778. Unfortunately, his original drawings have been lost.

Brett was not a professional artist; he had other things to do than make accurate charts and views. He was, for example, placed in charge of the landing party that sacked and burned the town of Paita in Peru in November 1741. The two activities were not unconnected. Accurate drawing was often a prerequisite for a successful sea-borne assault. This was one of the points that Walter had made in advocating the appointment of professional draughtsmen to men-of-war bound for far voyages and the value of training officers in charting and drawing skills. Walter's edition of Anson's *Voyage Round the World* ran through many editions prior to 1768, and his views influenced thoughtful men in the British navy. We know that a copy of Anson's *Voyage* was taken aboard the *Endeavour*, for both Cook and Banks refer to it in specific contexts in their journals.[7] Walter's emphasis, however, was upon the value of drawing as an aid to navigation and sea-borne assault, though he does allude to the more general value of drawing for providing accurate accounts of foreign peoples and places.[8] It was Joseph Banks who first attempted to realise the possibilities of Walter's programme and to give it a strong scientific bent.

Young, highly energetic and heir to a considerable fortune, Banks, before he sailed with Cook at the age of twenty-five, had already befriended Matthew Boulton, Josiah Wedgwood and other pioneer industrialists, had grasped the significance of the application of science to technology for the future of England and was already an experienced member of the small but increasingly influential circle of English natural-historians who had been inspired by the work of Linnaeus.[9] He had botanised extensively in the western counties and in Newfoundland. It was Banks and his circle who promoted the practice of making drawings of the plants they collected, in order to record the form, structure and colour before the specimen dried and withered.

In order to appreciate the problems and achievements of the graphic-arts programme developed on Cook's voyages, it is useful to keep in mind some of the characteristics of visual perception and its graphic representation. I would suggest that there are three principal means by which drawings may be said to represent: we might call them inventive drawing, illustrative drawing and documentary drawing. Inventive drawing represents forms drawn, at least immediately, from the draughtsman's mind, as Paul Klee, say, drew the *Snake Goddess and her Enemy* (pl. 41). Illustrative drawing represents things already expressed in words, as Sebastiano Ricci, say, represented *Achilles surrendering Hector's corpse to Priam* (pl. 42). Documentary drawing represents things that the draughtsman perceives out there in his world, as Rembrandt, say, saw and drew *A Beggar and his family* (pl. 43). Such theoretical distinctions as these are, of course, never so clear-cut in

42 (below). Sebastiano Ricci, *Achilles surrendering Hector's corpse to Priam*, pen and wash, 22.3 × 31 cm., Graphische Sammlung Albertina, Vienna.

41 (left). Paul Klee, *The Snake Goddess and her Enemy*, 1940. By permission of Benteli Verlag, Bern.

43. Rembrandt, *A Beggar and his family*, chalk drawing, Graphische Sammlung Albertina, Vienna.

44. Animal drawings in the main chamber, Lascaux.

practice. Witness the difficulties archaeologists have got themselves into at times in attempting to decide whether a painting that lacks supporting documentary evidence, as at Lascaux for example, is inventive, illustrative of myth, or documentary of hunting (pl. 44). Inventive, illustrative and documentary draughtsmen all require a stock of visual memories drawn from their worlds; for all draughtsmen who have learned the art of speech, language normally mediates powerfully at every act of visual perception. In one sense, all drawing is illustrative, a visualising of verbalisations; all drawing is documentary in its recording of memories; all drawing is inventive in its translation of neural activities into a graphic code. It is better, therefore, to think of inventing, illustrating and documenting as actual or potential components of all acts of graphic representation. Considered in this way, inventive draughtsmanship is of a kind that stresses invention but minimises the illustrative and documentary components of perception. A documentary draughtsman, on the other hand, will endeavour to suppress the inventive and illustrative components of his perception and do his best to draw what he sees. If we keep these points in mind it will assist us in understanding the problems confronting Cook's artists and the limited yet nevertheless portentous character of their achievement.

From the time the *Endeavour* left Plymouth on 26 August 1768, Banks put his artists, Sydney Parkinson and Alexander Buchan (and later, Herman Spöring), to the task of drawing fish or molluscs caught in the naturalist's casting nets (pl. 45), or birds shot or snared from the deck or from the boats put out on calm days. When the ship was running down a coast, both Buchan and Parkinson made coastal profiles of the shoreline. This extra duty may have been Cook's suggestion. The drawing of coasts and profiles normally fell to the master or the master's mate, but on *Endeavour*, most of the surviving profiles were made by Banks's artists, not Cook's officers. Cook was the kind of commander who made the best use of the talent available.

Occasionally, coastal profiles possessed a potential naval and military value. From 13 November to 7 December 1769 the *Endeavour* was anchored in Rio harbour taking on provisions. Despite Cook's protestations that he was engaged upon a voyage of a purely scientific nature, the Portuguese viceroy in Rio did not trust him. Had he been able to see Buchan and Parkinson making their drawings of the harbour with keys identifying the military and naval installations (pl. 46), and to read Banks's and Cook's comments upon the weaknesses of the harbour's fortifications, he would have felt justified in his distrust. The expedition may have been predominantly scientific in its overt intentions, but Cook, who had helped to chart the St Lawrence prior to Wolfe's successful siege of Quebec, was not likely to let such an opportunity pass. To use topographical art to document military installations was, as we have seen, a venerable practice. It was the traditional role of topography to provide practical information, without aesthetic pretensions, in this way. But things were not to remain like this.

On 15 January 1769 the *Endeavour* anchored in the Bay of Good Success in Tierra del Fuego to wood and water, and the first encounter was made with non-

54

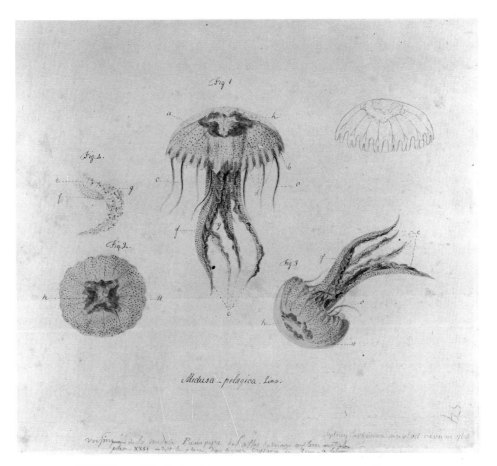

45. Sydney Parkinson, *Medusa-pelagica*, pen and wash, 23.5 × 28.5 cm., 1768, Zoological Library, British Museum, Natural History (Parkinson's drawings, iii, 54).

46. Alexander Buchan, *Part of a panoramic view of Rio de Janeiro*, 26.7 × 50.8 cm., 1768, British Library (Add. MS 23920, f. 7). Ill. in Andrew David, *Charts and Coastal Views of Captain Cook's Voyages*, London, 1988, vol. 1, 1.39.

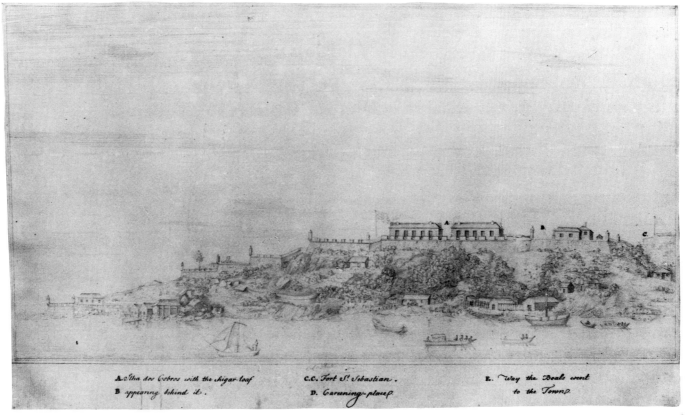

A VIEW of the *ENDEAVOUR'S* Watering-place in the Bay of GOOD SUCCESS

47. Alexander Buchan, *A View of the Endeavour's Watering-place in the Bay of Good Success*, gouache on vellum, 24.8 × 33.7 cm., 1769, British Library (Add. MS 23920, f. 11b).

European people; a tribe of the Ona Indians of Patagonia. Banks had taken Buchan in order to provide a visual record of the scenes of the voyage that would entertain his friends in England, and Buchan duly illustrated the event (pl. 47). Although not a skilled figure-draughtsman, his small puppet-like figures provide information better in some ways than an academically trained artist's drawings might have done. The watering place is shown as a grove sheltered from the south by banks through which a stream has cut a ravine. A tent has been erected and men are to be seen filling or caulking water barrels, supervised by marines. Two fires have been lit and there is a large pot over one. To the left a small party of Indians have met members of the *Endeavour*'s company, and in the foreground some trading is in progress.

Such depictions as this of encounters with indigenous peoples became a feature of the art of Cook's voyages. They were developed from studies in pencil, pen or wash made on the spot, sometimes immediately after the event, sometimes at the end of the voyage. This drawing must have been made shortly after the event; it is interesting to reflect that it must be one of the first, if not *the* first, in which an on-the-spot visual record was made by Europeans of their encounter with a non-European people at the moment of the encounter. It stands on the threshhold of recording contact at the time of contact, by visual means – the ancestor of the

56

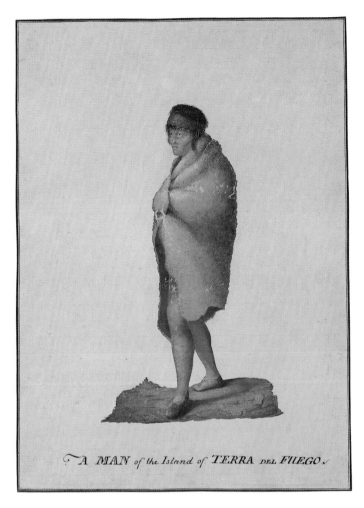

A MAN *of the Island of* TERRA DEL FUEGO.

A WOMAN *of the Island of* TERRA DEL FUEGO.

photographic, film and television documentary of cultural contact between European and non-European.

Banks also wanted faithful drawings of the Fuegian people and their manner of living. Towards this end, Buchan made a drawing of a man and a woman (pls 48, 49), and Banks wrote a detailed description in his journal:

> The inhabitants we saw here seemed to be one small tribe of Indians consisting of not more than 50 of all ages and sexes. They are of reddish Colour nearly resembling that of rusty iron mixd with oil: the men large built but very clumsey, their hight 5 ft 8 to 5 ft 10 nearly and all very much the same size, the women much less, seldom exceeding 5 ft. Their Cloaths are no more than a kind of cloak of Guanicoe or seal skin thrown loose over their shoulders and reaching down nearly to their knees; under this they have nothing at all nor anything to cover their feet, except a few of them had shoes or raw seal hide drawn loosely round their instep like a purse. In this dress there is no distinction between men and women, except that the latter have their cloak tied round their middle with a kind of belt or thong and a small flap of leather hanging like Eve's fig leaf over those parts which nature teaches them to hide; which precept tho she has taught to them she seems intirely to have omitted with the men, for they continually expose those parts to the view of strangers with a carelessness which thoroughly proves them to have no regard to that kind of decency.[10]

The relationship between Buchan's drawings and Banks's descriptions is of interest. Did Banks use the drawings to aid his memory when he wrote up his

48. Alexander Buchan, *A Man of the Island of Terra del Fuego*, gouache, 36.8 × 26.7 cm., 1769, British Library, London (Add. MS 23920, f. 16).

49. Alexander Buchan, *A Woman of the Island of Terra del Fuego*, gouache, 36.8 × 26.7 cm., 1769, British Library, London (Add. MS 23920, f. 17).

50. *Two Californian Women, the one in bird's skin, the other in that of a deer,* engraving by John Pine, in George Shelvocke, *A Voyage Round the World,* London, 1726, fp. 404.

description in his journal later? Or did he direct Buchan to include this or that feature of interest in drawing? Were the drawings made after, and to illustrate, Banks's verbal descriptions? We do know that Banks was committed to the view that pictorial descriptions were superior to verbal ones, but did he mean superior as independent records or as illustrations of description: was their function investigative or pedagogical? There is no obvious answer. But if the plant and animal drawings may be taken as a model, we might conclude that the verbal and visual descriptions were designed to be mutually supportive, each benefiting from the analytical techniques of the other.

But there is another problem. The way Buchan drew was affected by the way he had learned to draw. Clearly, he had not been trained in the skills of academic figure draughtsmanship. He appears to have been teaching himself to draw by copying engravings, which was the way most art students began at that time.[11] Compare Buchan's two drawings (pls 48, 49) with the engraving of *Two Californian Women* from George Shelvocke's *Voyage Round the World* (1726) (pl. 50). If we ignore the landscape setting in the engraving, it and the drawings will be seen to have much in common. Both establish volume by gradated shading in from sharp, dark contours. The stance of the figures and the treatment of the hair is similar and in both cases the feet cast shadows along a bare rocky shelving. It is likely that Buchan used this engraving as a general schematic model for developing some drawings in outline (pl. 51) which he probably made on 15 January 1769, when Banks and his party first encountered a small party of the Ona people, made friends with them and encouraged three of them to come aboard

58

51a and b. Alexander
Buchan, two drawings of
Tierra del Fuegans,
pencil on one sheet, 27 ×
10.1 cm., 1769, British
Library, London (Add.
MS 23920, f. 18a, b).

the *Endeavour*.[12] These drawings were the crucial acts of primary graphic draughtsmanship upon which a great burden of visual 'editing' later came to be hung. A
copy of Shelvocke was in Banks's *Endeavour* library and was in use at that time.
Banks had referred to it only three days before in comparing a marine inver-
tebrate he had fished up with a similar one mentioned by Shelvocke.[13] All this is
not to say that such a manner of developing a drawing renders the information
conveyed inaccurate, but that the information is coded through a drawing technique developed by imitating engravings.

If engravers' techniques could thus mediate between perception and representation in the secondary acts of draughtsmanship, the aesthetic conventions
adopted by engravers might also effect the tertiary elaboration and editing of the
visual material for publication. To illustrate.

Buchan made a drawing of a Fuegian village,[14] and both he and Parkinson
made drawings of individual habitations.[15] Some time before John Hawkesworth
published his *Account* (1773) of the voyage, the latter two drawings were handed

52. G.B. Cipriani, *A View of the Indians of Terra del Fuego in their Hut*, wash and watercolour, 20.8 × 28.5 cm., 1772, Dixson Library, Sydney (PXX 2, 43).

to the engraver Francisco Bartolozzi and his close friend, the history painter Giovanni Battista Cipriani, for the purpose of providing a suitable illustration for the *Account*. Cipriani made a composite drawing (pl. 52) based on Buchan's study of the hut, added extra figures from Parkinson but endowed them with a nobler grace and bearing than the original drawings possessed and furthermore gave them elegant proportions quite at variance with Banks's carefully written description. I have already discussed the transformation that thus took place in the context of Hawkesworth's interest in native peoples as examplars of 'hard primitivism' and also in the wider context of Renaissance and Enlightenment humanism.[16] But since I first drew attention to these changes, they have tended to be taken simplistically as conspicuous evidence that European voyagers to the Pacific during the eighteenth century tended to *see* Pacific islanders as 'noble savages'. Cipriani's alterations must therefore be considered here in another context.

First, it is clear that Banks and his artists did their best within the limits of their skills, techniques and materials to provide an accurate account of the Fuegians encountered. We might therefore want to say that the move from faithful reporting to false presentation occurred when the engraver took over the publication of the information. Yet even here we are on shaky ground. An alteration certainly took place, but there is no good reason to assume that this was due to either Cipriani or Bartolozzi having been converted, as John Hawkesworth may well have been, to the so-called Rousseauian belief in the nobility of savages. We must realise that both Bartolozzi and Cipriani had been trained as history painters in the Academy of Florence, and that it was the express business of history painters, proclaimed to academicians since Alberti's time onwards, that they should ennoble and dignify historic events. We must realise, too, that as fewer walls and more books became available for history painters to decorate

60

during the eighteenth century, artists like Cipriani turned increasingly to the preparation of designs for engraving and to the illustration of notable events for publication. They brought to this practice those processes of selection and elevation traditional to the history painter. Sir Joshua Reynolds, in response to comparable social changes, applied history painting's potential to elevate to his practice of portraiture. *Lady Sarah Bunbury sacrificing to the Graces* (pl. 53), which Reynolds exhibited in 1765, and Bartolozzi's Fuegian fisher-girl (pl. 54), published eight years later, were members, you might say, of the same neo-classical sisterhood. With this view of the matter, the nobility either of aristocrats or of 'savages' is not to be understood as a false kind of perception, but as an aesthetic grace which the sovereign artist bestows upon those whom he favours or the situation justifies. For in the same manner as the repertoire of motifs available to classical architecture, derived from arch, column and lintel, were adapted to suit a multiplicity of purposes whenever a touch of pomp or note of dignity was called for, so the classical repertoire of history painting was deployed whenever a sense of occasion was appropriate.

Yet on two points of Fuegian custom Banks's on-the-spot recording and Buchan's witness were accurately conveyed. The men exposed their bodies, Banks noted, without any sense of shame, and Bartolozzi ensured that one old man and a boy conspicuously display their penes. But the women were modest. The tiny girl held by her mother in the left-hand corner of the hut is therefore provided, as Banks recorded, with her 'small flap of leather hanging like Eve's fig leaf'. It is salutary to realize that the observations of travellers could be accurately conveyed within the conventions of neo-classical history painting; and also to remember that they could not be conveyed at all but within some kind of convention.

Let us view this whole matter, for a moment, from another angle. It is commonplace to regard the elevated, neo-classical sytle as a device appropriate for an artist of the stature of Reynolds to apply to the depiction of Europeans of rank, influence and power, but we implicitly accuse his minor contemporaries such as Cipriani or Bartolozzi of a false or 'Europeanised' perception should they apply the same device to the elevation of non-European people. It is important in this regard to realise that the ennobling of so-called Pacific savages contained a latent, but valuable, critique of Eurocentric attitudes. It enshrined a vestige of

53. Sir Joshua Reynolds, *Lady Sarah Bunbury sacrificing to the Graces*, oil on canvas, 242 × 151.5 cm., 1765, Art Institute of Chicago.

54. *A View of the Indians of Terra del Fuego in their Hut*, detail from the engraving by F. Bartolozzi after Cipriani, 1779, in Hawkesworth's *Account of the Voyages*, vol. 2, pl. 1, fp. 55.

that view, promulgated by Pico and the Renaissance humanists, of the dignity and potential godliness of all men, a view that remained an eminently respectable doctrine until Europe experienced its first real taste of popular democracy in action in the years that followed the outbreak of the French Revolution. As a result of the great fear that followed, notions about noble savagery and universal brotherhood became subversive, being replaced by theories more congenial to Europe's powerful, hierarchical societies during the age of colonial expansion. Such was Darwin's theory of evolution. It provided an empirical, secularised version of the theological dogma of original sin; God's election was replaced by nature's selection. That, surely, was one of the more sinister aspects of the triumph of empirical naturalism over classical naturalism. Those who had been portrayed like gods came to be portrayed like monkeys. Consider the simian-like proportions of the Melanesians who challenge Cook in Will B. Robinson's illustration in John Lang's *Story of Captain Cook*, written for T.C. and E.C. Jack's Childrens' Heroes Series and published in 1906 at the height of British Imperial power in the South Pacific, as elsewhere (pl. 55).

55. Will Robinson, *A few of the natives brandished spears*, from J. Lang, *Story of Captain Cook*, London, 1906.

*   *   *

As the *Endeavour* rounded the Horn and sailed slowly into the warmer waters of the Pacific, Banks's artists were at work daily drawing the life of the sea: the shearwater, albatross and frigate bird with its magnificent red tail (pl. 56). Parkinson became increasingly responsive to the changing colours of the sea. As they passed through the Tuamotus he noted on one drawing, 'the water in these lagoons a fine sea green',[17] and it may have been at this time that he made an extended colour note in his sketchbook, now in the British Library:

> the water within the reefs sea green brownish towards the edge of the Reefs the Breakers white. In many a bay have taken notice that the sea green colour with tops of the waves white, this stript and streakt with a dark colour of a purple cast occasioned by the intervention of clouds between sun and water. In a calm where there is a swell the water appears undulated with pale shadows and at other times it is quite smooth streakt here and there with dark colour occasioned by what sailors call catspaws on the water when there is a wind coming or rain it appears very black upon the water and when nigh it is full of poppling waves which spread themselves on the smooth water, the sky in general is very uniform often mottled with white clouds in a storm the sea is a dark bluish black here and there a pale blue, the tops of the billows white with a number of white streaks all near the surface of the water.[18]

The conventional wisdom of art history informs us that the French impressionists were the first to see and to paint the colour in shadows. Yet here, a century before, is a young artist describing with precision the purple he sees in shadows and the effects of broken colour on water that reads like a recipe for an impressionist painting. So we might naturally ask, why didn't he paint what he saw? The answer, surely, is contained in Heinrich Wölfflin's flat and enigmatic statement, 'Not everything is possible at all times. Vision itself has its history.'[19] Parkinson could not have painted such a picture successfully even if he had wanted to. A century of technical experiment with such problems lay between Parkinson's perception and their resolution into an adequate pictorial form. Nor would Banks, presumably, have allowed his precious pigments to be used upon such experiments. The purple in Parkinson's colour box was for the portrayal of such things as the tail of the frigate bird. His landscapes were always rendered in grey wash. Yet Cook's artists were being confronted with new problems. A new aesthetic stage was being set.

When Buchan died, Banks called upon Spöring to provide more drawings. He made one of a canoe that belonged to Purea, whom Wallis had described as the Queen of Tahiti (pl. 57). Spöring normally drew in ink; his eye was for construction; it is, you might say, an engineer's drawing. When he draws, Spöring does not look for the visual effect as Parkinson does, but for a linear description of the dynamic energy of a wave, as Leonardo had done in the fifteenth century. And this little drawing will serve to remind us how often it is that English art in the second half of the eighteenth century recalls the empirical, naturalistic interests of so much Italian art of the fifteenth century before it was folded over into the hard crusts of *grandeur* of the High Renaissance and baroque styles.

With Buchan dead, however, the great burden of the work fell to Parkinson. He was now required to provide drawings of landscape and people in addition to

56. Sydney Parkinson, *Red-tailed tropic bird* (*Phaethon rubricauda melanorhynchos*, Gm 1789), watercolour, 29 × 31.5 cm., 1769, Zoological drawings, British Museum, Natural History.

57. Herman Spöring, *Oberea's Canoe, Otaheite*, pencil, 18.7 × 32.5 cm., 1769, British Library, London (Add. MS 23921, f. 23a).

58. Sydney Parkinson,
*Otaheite. View up the river
among rocks*, wash
drawing, 241 × 295 cm.,
1769, British Library,
London (Add. MS 23921,
f. 7b).

59. Paul Sandby,
*Romantic landscape with
figures and a dog*, pen and
wash, 47.2 × 58.2 cm.,
Yale Center for British
Art, New Haven, Paul
Mellon Collection.

those of plants and animals. His study, the *Peaks of Orofena*, drawn in the morning from the deck of the *Endeavour*, gives one the impression that he was keen to become a landscape painter.[20] Some of his drawings, such as *View up the river among rocks* (pl. 58), are purely picturesque, but most contain information of human interest. Such drawings reveal, I believe, the influence of Paul Sandby, the first English artist of distinction to adopt a wholly naturalistic approach to the drawing of both landscapes and figures (pl. 59). Parkinson's life is closely comparable to that of the early life of Sandby, who, as we have seen, was attached as topographical draughtsman to Colonel David Watson's survey of the Scottish highlands from 1747 to 1751. As a young Scot, it is likely that Parkinson would have known Sandby's etched *Views of Scotland* published in 1751, and also likely that he saw Sandby originals at the exhibitions held by the Society of Artists in London during the 1760s. Although, as I have noted, the use of topographical artists for the recording of accurate naval and military information was a traditional one, with artists such as Sandby and Parkinson we reach a point, where art as information and art as taste meet with significance for the future direction of painting.

The catalyst was the picturesque. It served as the agent whereby topography, art as information, could be elevated to the level of taste. The reasons are varied and complex. At the social and political level, as Ann Bermingham has shown, the picturesque provided an aesthetic whereby the English countryside could be appropriated imaginatively by the new class of landowning squires (and a complicit traditional aristocracy) responsible for the enclosures of common land that proceeded throughout the century. It was in their interest to 'aestheticise nature and the natural'.[21]

But before that could happen, the practice and theory had itself to be created; and it was created, if it was created by anyone, we must remember, in the eye and mind of a landless parson who was an inveterate traveller, William Gilpin. Remember too, that Gilpin's father, Captain John Bernard Gilpin (1701–76), was for more than twenty years actively involved in the military occupation of Scotland. His passion for landscape sketching, which he passed on to his son, developed, as did Paul Sandby's, in the context of military topography.[22] It was

64

his son who began to provide the groundwork of a theory by which wild terrains, the coverts of outlaws and bandits, could be brought within the aegis of good taste. Spiritual possession followed and reinforced material possession. While Gilpin toured the mountains of Scotland, Wales and Cumberland, Cook's artists began the long process of 'aestheticising' the exotic landscapes of the Pacific Islands, New Zealand and Australia.

But as St Matthew informs us, 'if men put new wine into old bottles, the bottles break and the wine runs out'. Technically, something like that happened to picturesque painting. Picturesque composition traced its descent from the compositional methods of Claude Lorraine and Salvator Rosa, and through them back to the mannerist modes of Brill and Elsheimer and the classical modes of the Renaissance, in which harmonic geometry–poise and counterpoise–provides the essentially linear, framing structure. That, and the supporting use of tonal gradations, of closely related or sharply contrasted tones, by which a painting could be turned into a correlative of human feeling, of serenity, nostalgia, repose, fear or faith. Such landscapes were structured by a 'divine' geometry and united by human feeling; by what Constable speaking of Claude once called 'the calm sunshine of the heart', or Ruskin more critically described as 'pathetic fallacy'. Picturesque *composition*, I would argue, was one of the belated expressions of classical naturalism. It continued to influence Parkinson's treatment of landscape in the Pacific, particularly when he was called upon to record the funerary practices of Polynesia. By his disposition of branches and leaves, solitary waterbirds and isolated mourning figures or abandoned boats, he evokes a pervading melancholy for unredeemed pagan man which the engravers were quick to seize upon and enhance. In Parkinson's case it is more than a pictorial device, for it is clear that he was a devout young man despite his deep involvement in the science of his day. A disturbed Christian conscience is present in such drawings, explicitly enough for Chateaubriand many years later to recognise and seize upon it in order to attack the values of the Enlightenment.[23]

Where traditional feeling thus ran strongly, the old pictorial structures held. But it was not easy to stick all the new information being won for the emerging descriptive sciences together in views and landscape by means of the old glue; the pieces kept falling apart visually. They did not look well together. This, surely, is the root of the visual problem of so much nineteenth-century landscape painting. What was required was a new adhesive, a new compositional structure; one that belonged to the same level of enquiry as empirical science, an order grounded in time, not in timelessness.

The search for the new alternative form of composition was first undertaken, I would argue, in the depiction of weather, not merely as one of the substantial components among others in a painting, but increasingly as the compositional *modus vivendi* of the painting itself. The portrayal of weather became a catalyst by means of which colour and light–traditionally seen and painted as secondary qualities of the substantial and discrete objective components of a composition– were transformed into active manifestations that, in the long run, divested the discrete components of a painting of their conceptual substantiality. Now, it is true that this gradual triumph of light and colour over harmonic geometry and human feeling was a long time coming; that we should have to go back to the great Venetian colourists to do the subject justice. My point is that a compositional mode congenial to empirical naturalism was significantly advanced by the artists of Cook's voyages who had to front up as best they could to portraying–

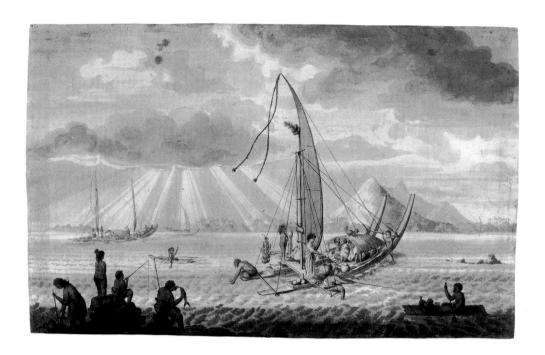

60. Sydney Parkinson, *Vessels of the Island of Otaha* (Tahaa), pencil and wash, 29.8 × 47.7 cm., 1769, British Library, London (Add. MS 23921, f. 17).

with scientists looking over their shoulders–the startling radiance of tropic seas, the drama of tropical weather, the half-light of antarctic seas–situations that were new to them all.[24]

In Parkinson we may gain only a faint glimpse of the coming change. His limited materials, pencil, pen and wash, were inadequate tools with which to face the challenge. But he was aware of it. Repeatedly, though he portrays the ethnographical information he was employed to portray, the real subject for him is the movement of the clouds in the sky, the shafts of light or rain, the effects of wind in the sky, as we may see in his study of *Vessels of the Island of Otaha* (pl. 60).

If the exploration of the Pacific itself encouraged these concerns, so did the interests of the *Endeavour*'s company. A capacity to forecast and interpret the weather was crucial to the art of navigation. Parkinson's attempt to depict weather patterns would have gained a larger and more appreciative audience among the ship's company than his more specialised work on plants and animals.

* * *

Let us turn now to Cook's second voyage and pursue some of the themes we have been considering. William Hodges, the artist employed on that voyage by the Admiralty, was better equipped than Parkinson. He had been trained under Richard Wilson as a landscape painter and took with him a wider range of materials. For coastal profiles he used pencil, ink, wash and watercolour and could, by his artistry, transform them into works of rare beauty (pl. 61). For his portraits of Pacific peoples he used red crayon exclusively, though occasionally he may have sketched heads in oils on canvas (pl. 62). For landscapes he used both watercolour and oil.

His use of red crayon for portraits is of interest. Richard Wilson, his teacher, favoured crayon for drawing, and Hodges probably picked up his skill with crayon from him. But there may be another reason. Soft-ground etching and stipple engraving, by means of which the qualities of drawings, with their informality and subtlety of line, could be effectively reproduced, had been developed in England during the 1760s and were very popular. I suspect that Hodges would have liked his portraits of Pacific Islanders reproduced by one of these new processes so that the intimacy of drawing might be preserved. Hodges had received no training in academic figure draughtsmanship and tended to avoid full-figure renderings, though he did develop an effective visual shorthand for rendering figures in land and seascapes.[25] This may have reflected his knowledge of the work of Alexander Cozens. Otherwise, he kept to portraiture. Not that his skill was here beyond question. He had trouble, for instance, with three-quarter views, sometimes getting the perspective of the face out of true.

As in the case of Buchan, there was one sense in which Hodges's lack of training in academic draughtsmanship served him well. The mental luggage that he brought to the Pacific did not include the visual models based upon classical statuary that were part of the equipment of every well-trained classical draughtsman. Hodges's portraits usually carry conviction: he does not see people as stereotypes, as noble or ignoble savages, as typical of this or that ethnic type, but as individuals in which character and temperament shine through with convincing clarity. Consider, for example, his portrait of that complex Tahitian Tu (pl. 64). Of Tu Cook wrote: 'he seems to avoid all unnecessary pomp and shew and even to demean himself, more than any of the other Earee's [arii]'.[26] Something of his intelligence, his nervous, apprehensive vitality, and perhaps even his cunning may be gleaned from this portrait, perhaps the finest Hodges ever drew. When we compare it with J. Hall's line engraving (pl. 63) in the official account of the second voyage published in 1777, we become aware of a loss in quality; we have

61. William Hodges, *In Dusky Bay, New Zealand*, wash and watercolour, 38.2 × 54.3 cm., 1773, Mitchell Library, Sydney (PXD 11, 31).

62 (above left). William Hodges, *Head of a Polynesian man*, oil on canvas, 10 × 6.4 cm., *c*.1774–5, Mitchell Library, Sydney (SSV, MAO, ib).

63 (above right). *Otoo [Tu] King of Otaheite*, engraving by J. Hall after William Hodges, in Cook, *Voyage towards the South Pole and Round the World*, 1777, vol. 1, pl. 38, fp. 254.

64. William Hodges, *Tu*, red chalk, 54 × 36.8 cm., 1773, National Library of Australia, Canberra.

moved back from the individual to the type. The presentation has become insensitive, the mouth thicker; the hair matted to a mop, the once-puzzled expression now vacuous: we feel that an individual has been reduced to the impersonality of an icon. What we are observing here, however, is probably nothing more than the deficiency of line engraving as a medium for the conveyance of subtle information, not necessarily the imposition by the engraver of his personal preconceptions upon the character of a man of the Pacific. It is to be regretted that none of Hodges's drawings was reproduced in the new techniques that had become available for rendering crayon.

Hodges's particular genius, however, lay in landscape. He succeeded on the second voyage in raising a documentary, informational art to a high level of creative achievement. An early test case is the masterly painting entitled *View of the Cape of Good Hope* now in the National Maritime Museum, London (pl. 122), which he probably painted from the great cabin of the *Resolution* during its three-week stay there in November 1772. There is little doubt, as I have argued elsewhere, that the naturalism he achieved on that occasion developed directly from a desire to provide an accurate visual record of the weather prevailing at the Cape at that time.[27] To gain such effects he painted broadly and sharpened his contrasts.

In the Antarctic, however, Hodges preferred the use of wash for capturing the special effects of light. In *The Resolution and Adventure taking in ice* (pl. 65), he records not only the water reflections in the cavernous interiors of the icebergs but also the curious effect of the low northern sun upon the ships' sails; working with economy he achieves sharp optical effects. Hodges is the first artist to capture the effect of a full flood of tropical light (pl. 66). In some landscapes he breaks up masses of foreground foliage by painting the innumerable faceted highlights upon leaves, as in his magnificent *View in the Island of New Caledonia*, (pl. 67) a technical device that came to be known some fifty years later, when Constable began to use it, as 'Constable's snow' (pl. 68). Even when Hodges paints a subject full of potential associations, such as a *fata tupa pau* in Tahiti, his approach is objective not literary.[28] His subject is weather and light even when he paints such evocative subjects as the *Monuments of Easter Island* (pl. 135).

65. William Hodges, *The Resolution and Adventure 4 Jan 1773 taking in Ice for Water. Lat. 61 s.*, wash and watercolour, 38 × 54.5 cm., 1773, Mitchell Library, Sydney (PXD 11, 26).

66. William Hodges,
*View from Point Venus,
Island of Otaheite*, oil on
panel, 24.1 × 47 cm.,
*c.*1775, National
Maritime Museum,
London, on loan from the
Ministry of Defence,
Navy.

The technical step that Hodges began to take to achieve such optical immediacy is of considerable interest. It is present in his oils but can be seen most vividly in his wash drawings, where he sharpens the contrasts between light and dark by virtually eliminating half-tone, a radical move which though quickly stated was one that painters struggled with for over a century. For shading in half-tone was a hallowed academic practice ever since Leonardo and his generation developed the principles and practice of chiaroscuro. Chiaroscuro provided a method whereby three-dimensional objects could be represented on a flat surface under conditions of controlled lighting. Hodges, seeking to represent the dazzling effects of uncontrolled tropic light, began to seek for an optical rather than a plastic representation of reality, by dispensing progressively with the use of half-tone and sharpening his contrasts. Manet, a century later, made precisely the same move in order to create an optically inspired mode of painting. He was, of course, able to proceed much further. But I would argue that the significant early move towards an optically inspired and empirical naturalism was made in the Pacific by Hodges working under the pressure of a geographic imperative to paint what Constable came to call, half a century later, 'a natural history of the skies'.

Hodges was before his time and knew it. In a letter to his friend the poet William Hayley a few years before his death, he wrote, 'I have sometimes secretly quarrelled with the world for allowing me the Character of a man of Genius in the display of fanciful representations than that of accurate observations'.[29] The comment goes to the source of his originality. For though one can find anticipations of his style in the works of earlier artists, particularly the more painterly artists of the Venetian baroque or the French rococo, in such cases the painterly flourishes are the individual gestures of highly expressive personalities.[30] Hodges's individuality developed as he struggled in turn to develop technical procedures suited to empirical naturalism. 'Everything', he wrote in his book on his travels in India, 'has a particular character, and certainly it is finding out the real and natural character which is required.'[31] And to Hayley he wrote, 'truth is the base of every work of mine'.[32]

Truth was certainly his base on the second voyage, where his associates, Cook,

70

67. William Hodges, *A View in the Island of New Caledonia*, oil on canvas, 135.2 × 193 cm., *c.*1777, National Maritime Museum, London, on loan from the Ministry of Defence, Navy.

68. John Constable, *Dedham Vale, Suffolk*, oil on canvas, 43.5 × 34.4 cm., 1802, Victoria and Albert Museum, London.

Wales and the two Forsters, were all of a strong scientific cast of mind. But upon his return he felt obliged in the paintings he executed for the Admiralty and exhibited in the Royal Academy to present his basic truths within conventional superstructures, constructed out of neo-classical, picturesque and romantic elements. In doing so he created some of the most evocative paintings of Tahiti as a South Sea Island Paradise that were painted before Gauguin, in which the memories of his feelings on location are mingled with his empirical vision.

Such imaginative recastings of visual information had already been attacked when Hawkesworth's *Account* appeared in 1773, and they were bound to be attacked again. When the attack came it came from one of Hodges's personal friends, the young and brilliant George Forster, the natural-history draughtsman on the voyage.

The object of Forster's attack was the engraving made after Hodges's drawings of the peoples of Eua which was published in the official account of the second voyage as *The Landing at Middleburgh* (pl. 69):

> Mr Hodges designed this memorable interview in an elegant picture, which has been engraved for captain Cook's account of this voyage. The same candour with which I have made it a rule to commend the performances of this ingenious artist, whenever they are characteristic of the objects, which he meant to represent, obliges me to mention, that this piece, in which the execution of Mr Sherwin cannot be too much admired, does not convey any adequate idea of the natives of Ea-oowhe or of Tonga Tabbo. The plates which ornamented the history of captain Cook's former voyage, have been justly criticised, because they exhibited to our eyes the pleasing forms of antique figures and draperies, instead of those Indians of which we wished to form an idea. But it is greatly to be feared, that Mr Hodges has lost the sketches and drawings which he made from *Nature* in the course of the voyage, and supplied the deficiency in this case, from his own elegant ideas. The connoisseur will find Greek contours and features in this picture, which have never existed in the South Sea. He will admire an elegant flowing robe which involves the whole head and body, in an island where women very rarely cover the shoulders and breast; and he will be struck with awe and delight by the figure of a divine old man, with a long white beard, though all the people of Ea-oowhe shave themselves with muscle-shells.[33]

The irony of it was that Hodges was not directly responsible for the engraving in question, though his name was on it. The drawing was probably made by a classicizing history painter such as Cipriani (we know that he made the drawing for the companion engraving, the *Landing at Erramanga*).[34] It was quite out of character with Hodges's work. Yet it must be stressed that even such an elegant composition as this could still convey accurate information. A close examination of the engraving will reveal that the Tongan ritual practice of amputating the little finger had been faithfully recorded.[35]

Forster's criticisms, however, were taken to heart. Never again did engravers depict Pacific peoples for an authoritative official publication as though they were actors in a Greek play in an English country garden. It came to be accepted that publishers of official voyages should do all they could to depict visual field work faithfully.

*　　*　　*

72

69. *The Landing at Middleburgh* (Eua), engraving by J.K. Sherwin after William Hodges, in Cook, *Voyage towards the South Pole and Round the World*, 1777, vol. 1, pl. 54, fp. 192.

For his third voyage, Cook, at Daniel Solander's suggestion, chose John Webber as his artist. Webber was more fully trained than any of the artists of the previous voyages, having studied first at Bern, then later at Paris, both as a landscape artist and as a figure draughtsman. Furthermore, Cook by now had a pretty clear idea of what he wanted from his artist and worked closely with him. In the introduction to the official voyage he explained Webber's duties:

> so that we might go out with every help that could serve to make the result of our voyage entertaining to the generality of readers, as well as instructive to the sailor and scholar, Mr Webber was pitched upon, and engaged to embark with me, for the express purpose of supplying the unavoidable imperfections of written accounts, by enabling us to preserve, and to bring home, such drawings of the most memorable scenes of our transactions, as could only be expected by a professed and skilled artist.[36]

There was an eye then, one notes, to publication from the beginning, and in many ways Webber provided the best and certainly the most comprehensive record of all three voyages. His art programme developed more or less as set pieces for each major landfall. First, he made studies for a large watercolour drawing which generally depicted Cook's first encounter with the local people (pl. 70). This usually included the accompanying wooding, watering and trading activities that proceeded more or less simultaneously. He then placed the whole scene in appropriate and (so far as they may be presently judged) remarkably accurate landscape settings.

In addition to such 'encounter' drawings, there is usually one or more of what we might call 'entertainment' drawings (pl. 71), in which Cook, and his men, are depicted being entertained by tribal elders at feasts or sporting engagements. The 'encounter' and 'entertainment' drawings, many of which were published in the *Atlas* to the third voyage with great care, both for artistic perfection and accuracy, constitute a new kind of historical genre more radical in its consequences for the

70. John Webber, *An Interview between Captain Cook and the natives in Adventure Bay – Van Diemen's Land*, pencil, pen and wash, 66 × 97.2 cm., 1777, Naval Library, Ministry of Defence, London.

71. John Webber, *A Boxing match before Captain Cook*, pen, wash and watercolour, 56 × 98.7 cm., 1779, Bernice P. Bishop Museum, Honolulu.

later history of art than Benjamin West's *Death of Wolfe* of 1771. Webber's drawings originated in the field and constituted a new visual source for the study of history and not, as in academic history painting, the retrospective illustration of a traditional text.[37]

Apart from such drawings designed to 'entertain the generality of readers', Webber also made careful studies of at least one man and one woman of the people encountered at each landfall, and frequently more (pl. 72). He also made studies of housing, sports, surfboard riding and dancing (pl. 73), dress and adornments, ritual and religious practices. These visual records relate closely to Cook's verbal descriptions and were obviously made to provide supportive visual evidence. Such was the material, as Cook had plainly said, drawn for the scholar. What Cook and Webber were engaged in, then, was nothing less than a well-thought-out programme to provide a systematic ethnographic account of the peoples encountered in the Pacific.

74

John Webber's achievement has not gained the recognition it deserves, for an odd reason—his use of mannerist proportions. John Beaglehole, for example, complains that he adopted 'a sort of modern fashion-artist's devotion to length of body and of leg, a manner rather than a style; and that, in a producer of documentary drawings, is rather dismaying'.[38] One must object that fashion art is an effective and influential form of documentary drawing. Rüdiger Joppien has recently shown that the illustrations of Cook's *Voyages*, and predominantly those based on Webber's drawings, provided the basic information about the Pacific which was published in the great Italian and French costume books that appeared during the first third of the nineteenth century.[39] It was through such books that Europeans gained a popular knowledge of the appearance of Pacific peoples.

The importance of Webber's use of proportion can be exaggerated. Proportion is largely an individual rather than an ethnic characteristic, and conventional proportions need not vitiate the conveyance of typical information. Sometimes, especially in an age of engraving, a tall figure had practical value when portraying figures in landscape; compare the case of the cartographer who chooses the projection best suited to the information he seeks to convey. Yet there was also, I suspect, a personal choice involved: mannerist proportions would have given Webber's portrayal of Pacific people elegance and dignity. This was the art in *his* information. At some stage during his student days in Bern, Paris or London—he was only twenty-four when he travelled with Cook—he had picked up the mannerist mode (this will be discussed in more detail in chapter seven). We must always remember that Webber was drawing people. He had to get them to stand or sit to him. Portrait drawing is a slower, more ceremonial affair than, for example, taking informal shots with a camera when the subject is not looking. That, incidentally, is a reason why portrait painters are the only kinds of painters notorious for exercising an influence upon heads of state and government; their trade immobilises when pride is vulnerable. Perhaps Webber felt that his subjects liked to be drawn in the tall, elegant way of mannerism. Europeans of birth and distinction had long approved the mode, as the portraits of Van Dyck and Gainsborough testify. Or he may have believed that the people he encountered possessed an innate human dignity and sought to make that dignity visible. If one

72. John Webber, *A Native prepared for hunting, Nootka Sound*, pen, ink and watercolour, 43.2 × 30.5 cm., 1778, Peabody Museum of Archaeology and Ethnology, Harvard University, Cambridge, Massachusetts.

73. John Webber, *Dancers of Owhyhee*, pen and wash, 30.5 × 48 cm., 1779, Bernice P. Bishop Museum, Honolulu.

75

were sensitive and intelligent, as Webber was, an adolescent of the 1760s in Switzerland and Paris, it is more likely than not that one would be predisposed to such an attitude. In any case, what has to be said is that Webber's ethnographic record of the peoples of the Pacific was a tremendous achievement that has never been equalled. It is invaluable; unique for our understanding of Pacific culture at the crucial moment of major European contact.

It is, then, upon the third voyage that we may witness a programme of empirical naturalism, which had begun with the portrayal of plants and animals on the *Endeavour* and was extended to the portrayal of weather and light on the second voyage, developed until it concentrated upon human beings, thus confronting classical naturalism on its own grounds. Classical naturalism had portrayed man as the master of nature and the measure of all things; empirical naturalism depicted him as one creature among others, subject to natural laws, at once the flower and victim of his environment.

I have been arguing that in seeking to develop an accurate informational art that was capable of supporting the expanding scientific programmes of Cook's three voyages, the leading artists, Parkinson, Hodges and Webber, were impelled by the social and environmental challenges that confronted them towards a pictorial mode of empirical naturalism which determined the course of the most progressive painting in Europe during the nineteenth century. It is true that they were not able to achieve, with the possible exception of Hodges, unquestioned masterpieces in this new kind of art. But they became aware of the problems and had begun to take the first steps in working out the technical methods necessary for its production. If we can, for a moment, imagine a hypothetical painter who, able enough to combine Hodges's technique for achieving a sense of direct optical presence by the elimination of half-tone, with Webber's ability to depict people not as heroes, but as members of communities who take on the colour and mood of their environment, and then transfer the scene from the Pacific back to a European setting, we shall find ourselves upon the threshold of impressionist painting. For in such paintings as Manet's *Concert in the Tuileries* (pl. 74), humankind is no longer presented acting out some heroic or sacred tale or raising monuments to its pride, but is seen as if it were so many frigate birds flying as best they can

74. Edouard Manet, *Concert in the Tuileries*, oil on canvas, 76.2 × 118 cm., 1862, National Gallery, London.

upon life's ocean. In such paintings, empirical naturalism is at last realised in a fully formulated aesthetic. But the change in perception that was necessary in order to make the new aesthetic, impressionism, possible, has as one of its earliest and most significant sources the use of art as information in the service of descriptive science, a use championed by the young Joseph Banks so effectively. If we agree with Wölfflin that 'vision itself has its history', then a precondition for the creation of that kind of vision that seeks an aesthetic reality in a sequence of impressions is the practice of art as an informational activity.

4 PORTRAYING PACIFIC PEOPLE

UNTIL RECENTLY THE ORIGINAL drawings and paintings completed during Cook's three voyages to the Pacific by the artists who travelled with him were little used as basic documents for the study of Pacific ethnohistory. For the greater part of the two hundred years that followed the publication of Hawkesworth's *Account of the Voyages undertaken . . . for making Discoveries in the Southern Hemisphere* (1773), historians and others were content with the engravings after the originals–used to illustrate official accounts of the voyages–as their sole visual resource in seeking to understand this crucial period of European contact with the Pacific. Even such an admirably researched work as A.C. Haddon's and J. Hornell's *Canoes of Oceania* (1936–8) drew exclusively upon the engravings. Yet it is only by studying the original works that we can assess the significance of the visual material generated by the voyages as either reliable information on the one hand or subjective, value-laden opinion on the other.

Let us consider one small aspect of that larger problem, that of ethnic portraiture. What kind of difficulties did the artists who travelled with Cook–Buchan and Parkinson on the first voyage, Hodges on the second and Webber on the third–face when they sought to depict the peoples of the Pacific?

We might begin by considering the role that artists in Joseph Banks's scientific team were expected to play on the *Endeavour*. Banks, as we have noted earlier, was convinced that drawings were often superior to words in the conveyance of information. But it was no simple matter. Drawings of individual objects–plants, animals, native artefacts–in order to be useful to scientists, had to be drawn in accord with received conventions. Thus, G.D. Ehret, probably the best-known and most influential botanical draughtsman of the eighteenth century, had collaborated with Linnaeus in determining the kinds of details that had to be collected (pl. 75) when drawing a plant for the purposes of Linnaean classification. With a certain degree of skill, the artist could record the details required in a fashion essentially diagrammatic, though a talented natural-history draughtsman like Parkinson could go far beyond diagrams and execute drawings of great beauty and sensitivity (pl. 76). But when it came to depicting people, Cook's artists faced much greater problems. First, and most importantly, people were not specimens to be cut, snared or shot, but persons who confronted you. It was difficult to draw them as specimens even if one tried. The situation, we might say, was an interaction. It was not a question of distinguishing between species, but of drawing a species, which was also one's own. How were the artists expected to draw man from a scientific viewpoint? Like Gainsborough working on a commission at Bath? Or as though portraying some fascinating, exotic animal? No one seems to have given much thought to that problem.

However, there were two long-standing conventions for the drawing of exotic peoples, to which, as likely as not, a travelling-artist's perception might conform, or by which it might be in part determined. These might be described as the allegoric convention and the ethnographic convention. The allegoric convention

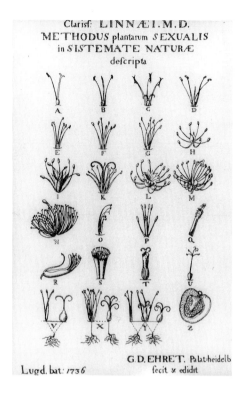

75. Illustration depicting the Linnaean system of classification, engraving after G.D. Ehret.

76. Sydney Parkinson, *A Brazilian vine (Serjania guarumina)* (Vell)C Martius, pencil and watercolour, 1768, 27.5 × 44 cm., British Museum, London, Natural History (Parkinson drawings).

77. *Tyche of Antioch*, Roman copy of a Greek work by Eutychides, Vatican, Rome.

78. Antonio Zucchi, *America*, from 'The Four Continents' eating-room, Osterley Park, Middlesex, 101 × 139.7 cm., c.1780. By permission of the Trustees of the Victoria and Albert Museum, London.

presented places as persons. It traced its origins back to antiquity. A famous example, perhaps the archetypal example, is the *Tyche of Antioch* (pl. 77), which personifies the city as a young matron seated, like Antioch itself, above the river Orontes, in which a boy, upon whom she rests a foot, is seen swimming. The allegorical mode maintained a lively existence in wall painting and book illustration, reaching its peak of perfection a few years before Cook sailed, in Tiepolo's great painting of the Four Continents around the ceiling of the staircase of the Residenz at Würzburg, completed in 1753. While Cook was in the Pacific disproving the existence of a fifth, southern continent, Antonio Zucchi (1726–95) was painting a Four Continents sequence as over-door panels for the eating-room at Osterley (pl. 78). But that was about the end of it. After Cook, no one seems to have painted such allegorical murals again.

79. John Webber, *A View in King George Sound*, pen, wash and watercolour, 57.2 × 36.8 cm., 1778, Department of Prints and Drawings, British Museum, London.

The convention did not materially affect the practice of Cook's artists. Yet there are reasons why we should not entirely ignore it. First, it may be noted that personified continents are surrounded by the animals, plants, peoples and even events typical of the continent depicted. They are the continent's attributes, definitional to its character, not merely contingent to it, as landscape settings are contingent to human action in classical landscape. In such cases, as in Poussin and Claude, it matters little if heroic action, originally set in Asia Minor or the Near East, is framed by a setting derived from the Roman campagna. Landscape is but a stage for gods and heroes whose movements are determined, if at all, by non-terrestrial influences. But the Four Continents allegories foreshadow a change in relationship between figure and landscape, a move from contingency to necessity. From Montesquieu at the beginning to Herder at the end of the eighteenth century, the theory of geographical determinism begins to give new significance to the relationship between figure and landscape. The empirical, naturalistic successors of the Four Continents allegories are the 'typical' landscapes of Hodges and Webber (pl. 79), in which people are depicted as the natural productions of natural environments.

The ethnographic convention is more relevant to our concerns. Its history also may be traced to classical roots. Unlike the *Tyche of Antioch*, the *Dying Gaul*

80. *Dying Gaul*, Roman
copy after a bronze
original, *c*.230–20 BC
from Pergamon,
Capitoline Museum,
Rome.

(pl. 80) makes no use of landscape attributes. He is defined as a Gaul by his
wild hair, his moustache and the torque about his neck. This is the nature of the
ethnographic convention. It defines by means of costume and adornment, and is
present in western art from Hellenistic times onwards, whenever the foreigner
needs to be specified. During the sixteenth and seventeenth centuries the allegoric
and ethnographic conventions were frequently combined, as in Cornelis Visscher's
engraving *America* (pl. 81). America is personified as a naked woman wearing a
feathered headdress. She rides an enormous armadillo, an exotic emblem for
America. Visscher has drawn upon Mostaert—they were both Haarlem artists—
for his warring scenes (see pl. 13), and on De Bry for the scenes of human flesh
being cut up and roasted. The engraving is an excellent example of that exotic
conflation discussed in the first chapter. In her right hand America holds a bow
more European than American, and in her left, a European halberd. On her right
are fat-tailed sheep and long-éared goats associated with Asia, and on her left,
maccaws and crocodiles associated with tropical America. Personification is here
assisted by attribution rather than description.

Buchan and Parkinson inevitably came under the influence of the ethnographic
convention. The *Endeavour*'s library contained several books with illustrations

81. *America*, engraving by
Cornelis Visscher
(*c*.1650–60).

conceived within the convention, notably Shelvocke's *Voyage* (1726), Pies and Marcgraf's *Natural History of Brasil* (1648), and Buffon's (then) fifteen-volume *Histoire naturelle* (1749–67). Moreover, the convention particularly suited Banks's extensive descriptions of Pacific peoples: they are wholly admirable compilations, and in many cases the first detailed and objective accounts of the physical appearance and the societies of the Pacific peoples. Banks is to be found thinking within the constraints of the convention when he wrote in his journal, on the occasion of the death of Alexander Buchan, 'no account of the figures and dresses of men can be satisfactory unless accompanied with figures'.[1] It is the figures and dresses that are to be described. People are to be portrayed in a manner similar to that of natural history, as type specimens, accompanied by detailed verbal descriptions. That is how Banks's programme for the portrayal of the peoples of the South Pacific began.

Consider Buchan's drawings of *A Man of the Island of Terra del Fuego* and *A Woman of the Island of Terra del Fuego* (pls 48, 49). These are well-developed drawings that illustrate closely a verbal description written by Banks in his journal about the same time as they were drawn. They fall entirely within the ethnographic convention. Although Buchan drew artefacts competently, he, clearly, had little training in figure drawing, and it is something of a mystery why Banks should have taken him as his figure draughtsman. While we might agree that Buchan has, in Locke's words, 'represented on paper tolerably well what he has seen', we might also want to qualify it by saying that the representation is conceived within the ethnographic convention and within the technical processes of engraving which have influenced the style of the drawing.

Like good fashion drawing, the ethnographic convention has its own charm and its own sophistications. Parkinson produced some particularly memorable drawings wholly within the constraints of the convention. Notably, his two fine heads of Maoris now in the British Library (pls 82, 83). Engraved and re-engraved, published and re-published from Cook's time to our own day, they have become the visual archetypes of the Maori warrior. Yet it is well to appreciate what Parkinson has done and what he has not done. Trained as a natural-history draughtsman, he has applied a visual analysis of component parts to the dress and adornment of the Maoris, seeing them, in a sense, as if they were plants. The parallel with drawing for Linnaean purposes is however, superficial; for Parkinson is not distinguishing between physiological characteristics to determine a species or even a variety, but distinguishing dress and adornment. These drawings were made well before the great age of physiological anthropology. Parkinson possessed no anxieties as to the unity of man as a species. In this he would have had the authority of Buffon, available on the *Endeavour* apparently both in the original French and in English translation. Buffon asserted that the basic questions concerning human proportion had been established by the sculptors of antiquity, and for that kind of information scientists and artists alike best had recourse to them.[2]

Parkinson's Maori heads obviously were not drawn in the field but in the cabin, from rudimentary field drawings (pl. 84). This brings us to a consideration of one of the central problems concerning the accurate depiction of people, that of interaction, to which I have already alluded. The eighteenth-century draughtsman faced a problem that differs from that of, say, the film crew of today which might be able to take frank shots with a telephoto lens from behind cover (though we need not doubt that they have their problems too). The eighteenth-century

82. Sydney Parkinson,
*Portrait of a New Zeland
Man*, pen and wash, 39.4
× 29.8 cm., 1769, British
Library, London (Add.
MS 23920, f. 54a).

83. Sydney Parkinson,
*Portrait of a New Zeland
Man*, pen and wash, 38.7
× 29.5 cm., 1769, British
Library, London (Add.
MS 23920, f. 55).

84. Sydney Parkinson,
*Sketch of a New Zeland
Man*, pencil, 37.5 × 27
cm., 1769, British
Library, London (Add.
MS 23920, f. 56).

artist-traveller needed to cultivate friendly relationships before anything like face or figure drawing became possible; and if he were one of Cook's artists, the actual prosecution of his calling meant that this need was more important and pressing for him than for any other member of the ship's company.

Friendship was an aspect of the artist's vocation. Native people were asked to stand or sit in situations often strange for both parties. On the second voyage there was the well-known case of Hodges and the young Maori woman, described by Anders Sparrman, who travelled on the *Resolution* as an assistant to J.R. and George Forster:

> Language difficulties at first gave rise to a misunderstanding between the girl and the painter, for she, having been well paid to go down into the saloon, imagined that she ought to give satisfaction, in the way she understood it, as soon as possible in return for her gift, perhaps she had previous experience with our sailors? She was astonished when signs were made for her to sit on a chair; such novel ways of doing things struck her as absurd, but she promptly volunteered a prone position on the chair for the painter and his companion. To her further surprise she was eventually put in a correct position, just sitting on the chair with nothing to do, whereupon, to the wonderment and entertainment of herself and the two savages with her, she quickly saw her likeness in a red chalk drawing.[3]

Even when a general tone of friendship prevailed, personal relationships had to be cultivated by the artist with courtesy and discretion; here is Parkinson's description of such an occasion, when in Tahiti he met Lycurgus, the playful Greek name that Banks gave a Tahitian chieftain, whose sense of justice he had had occasion to admire:

> we went round the point, and met with Lycurgus sitting on the ground, with his wife by his side . . . he gave us a hearty welcome; and, to divert us, ordered two boys to play on their flutes; while another sang a sort of melancholy ditty, very well suited to the music. Lycurgus is a middle-aged man, of a cheerful, though sedate, countenance, with thick black frizzled hair, and a beard of the same kind: his behaviour had something of natural majesty in them. I showed him some drawings, which he greatly admired, and pronounced their names as soon as he saw them.[4]

Unfortunately, the drawings referred to have been lost. But it was in such discreetly cultivated situations that Parkinson made drawings after which the engravings in his journal were executed. Consider the engraving (plate III in Parkinson's *Journal*) *A Native of Otaheite in the Dress of his Country* (pl. 85). Parkinson had the best of reasons for using such a classical pose—if, indeed, it is his, and not the engraver's. In Buffon he had the justification for using the sculpture of antiquity as a model, and measurement of the drawing reveals that he used Buffon's metric system, of ten faces to the length of the body, as his system of proportion. Again, it is a portrait of an 'arii', a nobleman, a member of the class of chieftains, to be distinguished from the 'manahune' (middling class) and 'toutou' (slaves); these were distinctions as apparent to the voyagers as that, say, between Banks and the agricultural labourers on his Revesby estate. Allan Ramsay had made an earlier use in Britain of a similar pose to give dignity to a member of the Scottish 'arii', Norman MacLeod, Chief of Macleod in 1748; and Reynolds used it for his well-known portrait of Omai at Castle Howard (pl. 153).

85. *A Native of Otaheite in the Dress of his Country*, engraving by R.B. Godfrey, from Parkinson, *A Journal of a Voyage to the South Seas*, 1773, pl. III, fp. 14.

It is important to realise that the so-called 'noble savage' mode of presentation was not a visual stereotype applied indiscriminately, a mis-perception of eighteenth-century European vision. It was, more often than not, the result of a conscious aesthetic decision to elevate where the artist felt that elevation was appropriate. Parkinson's *Journal* is admirable in the close relationship established between text and illustration; and the specific context of plate III reads, on the facing page, 'among the rest who visited us, there were some people of distinction in double canoes: their cloaths, carriage and behaviour evinced their superiority. I never beheld statlier men. They behaved courteously.' So, appropriately, the Polynesian chieftain is presented in the engraving as if he were a Roman magistrate, his flowing toga about him, delivering a speech in the Senate.[5]

My point that the cultivation of friendly relationships was essential to the success of the artist's mission is supported by the picture that Stanfield Parkinson draws, perhaps a little sanctimoniously but quite justifiably, of his dead brother:

> While many others, for want of a more innocent curiosity or amusement, were indulging themselves in those sensual gratifications, which are so easily obtained among the female part of uncivilised nations, we find him gratifying no other passion than that of laudable curiosity; which enabled him to employ his time, and escape those snares into which the vicious appetites of some others betrayed them. It doth equal honour to his ingenuousness and ingenuity, to find him protected by his own innocence, securely exercising his pleasant art amidst a savage, ignorant and hostile people, engaging their attention by the powers of his pencil, disarming them of their native ferocity, and rendering them even more serviceable to the great end of the voyage, in chearfully

84

Plate VIII

86. *Heads of Divers Natives of the Islands of Otaheite, Huaheine and Oheiteroah,* engraving by T. Chambers, from Parkinson, *A Journal of a Voyage to the South Seas,* 1773, pl. VIII, fp. 26.

furnishing him with the choicest productions of the soil and climate, which neither force nor stratagem might otherwise have procured.

By such honest arts and mild demeanour he, soon acquired the confidence of the inhabitants of most places, at which the voyagers went ashore, obtaining, thus, as I am well informed, with remarkable facility, the knowledge of many words, in various languages, hitherto little, if at all, known in Europe.[6]

In consequence, Parkinson was able to use the ethnograhic convention with skill, charm and a certain detachment, as the well-preened heads from the Society Islands and New Zealand engraved in his *Journal* testify (pl. 86).

Yet, at times, he moved a little beyond that convention and took a keen interest in facial gesture and expression. This interest was probably linked with his fascination with the Polynesian language. He made drawings of facial expressions adopted in dancing and in defiance by both Tahitians and Maoris (pls 87, 88). Facial expression was an object of current scientific inquiry. Physiognomy, the attempt to read character from the face and facial expression, was a pseudo-science of great antiquity, comparable to palmistry. But physicians, during the eighteenth century, were attempting to give it an empirical base by relating expression to the facial muscles. In 1745 Dr James Parson, a member of the Royal Society, gave the Croonian Lectures to the Society. They were published in the *Philosophical Transactions* in 1746 with a number of illustrations (pl. 89). One, figure 3, 'Shews a Countenance of Scorn and Derision, which is formed by the following muscles':

As soon as the Mind suggests a Contempt for Persons or Things, whether deservedly or not, the first muscles that begin to act are, the 'Elevator Labii superioris proprius Cowperi', and the 'Pyramidalis', on one side only; whereby

85

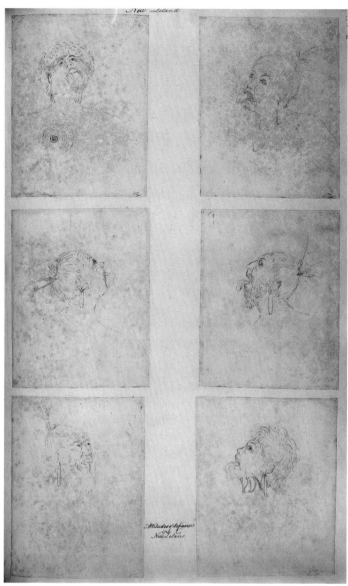

88. Sydney Parkinson, *Attitudes of defiance. New Zeland*, six pencil sketches, each approx. 20.3 × 16.8 cm., 1769, British Library, London (Add. MS 23920, f. 60).

87 (above left). Sydney Parkinson, *A Tahitian, shewing distortions of the mouth used in dancing*, pencil, 18.8 × 16.2 cm., 1769, British Library, London (Add. MS 23921, f. 51b).

89. Illustration of facial expressions, James Parson's Croonian Lectures, 1745, *Philosophical Transactions*, 1746.

the side of the upper Lip is pull'd up, so as to shew the Teeth, the other side only inclining a little to grin; and at the same time the 'Slip', which is an assistant to the 'Pyramidalis', wrinkles the skin of the Nose by its Contraction.

Parsons provides a similar muscular explanation for the movement of the eye and then proceeds:

There are several Gestures of the body, which consent to, and favour this villainous, ungenerous passion; as, looking back at the Object, with a Toss of the Head, and a Shrug of the Shoulders with this Countenance, upon being ask'd an Opinion of an absent Person; which is as keen as an Arrow, and stabs as deep, as even the slander of a base tongue; and sometimes it is attended with a grinning Laugh, which can have no real meaning, because there is no real Cause for it; and the Hypocrisy of the Mirth is easily distinguished upon the Face.[7]

If we compare Parkinson's original drawings of expressive heads with some of Parson's illustrations we might well suspect a link. There is no evidence that Banks took copies of the *Philosophical Transactions* with him on the *Endeavour*, though he was already a member of the Royal Society. Even so, the illustrations from Parsons might still have been available to Parkinson in Buffon (vol. 2), for the author, acknowledging his debt to Parsons, summarises his work on facial expression and reproduces the same plates.

In drawings of Maori in their war canoes, Parkinson combines his interest in dress and adornment with his interest in expressive gesture. Just how personal his approach is becomes evident if we compare one of his drawings (pl. 90) with one by Herman Spöring, of a similar subject (pl. 91). To Spöring they are an almost indistinguishable mass of pygmies; Parkinson, on the other hand, individualises the figures, draws dress and weapons with clarity and precision and gives each figure a set, almost statuesque position. It is a highly self-conscious composition. We know that Parkinson worked away at these drawings, relating the figures to one another, closing the groups like those on a Greek vase or pedimental sculpture. His use of pure line is possibly an early example of this neo-classical form of draughtsmanship, and one wonders which models might have influenced his vision (pl. 92). We do know, however, from a list of books written down in his sketchbook (British Library, Add. MS 9345) that he probably had his own copy of Hogarth's *Analysis of Beauty* on board the *Endeavour* with him, and it is possible that his highly sophisticated compositional groupings derive from Hogarth's discussions concerning pictorial composition, in which figures are reduced to geometrical shapes. Hogarth illustrated his discussion with his well-known plate of a country dance, in which he indicated how he made his figures change from the graceful curves made by the gentry down through the social scale to the robust angularities made by servants and country bumpkins. In the top left corner of his engraving Hogarth indicates how each pair of figures is based upon a simple geometric form. This kind of geometric reduction is obvious in Parkinson's drawings of Maori groups also, with the significant difference that he makes no use of the serpentine curve. It would have been quite out of place in depicting a Maori 'haka'. From the safety of the ship's side the war dance afforded a highly amusing spectacle. Here is Parkinson's description of it:

They gave us two Heivos, in their canoes, which were very diverting. They beat time with their paddles, and ended all at once with the word Epaah; at

90. Sydney Parkinson,
*New Zealand War Canoe
bidding defiance to the Ship*,
pen and wash, 29.9 ×
48.3 cm., 1770, British
Library, London (Add.
MS 23920, f. 50).

91. Herman Spöring,
*New Zealand War Canoe,
The Crew bidding defiance to
the Ship's Company*, pencil,
26.7 × 41.6 cm., 1769,
British Library, London
(Add. MS 23920, f. 48).

92. Sydney Parkinson,
*New Zealand War Canoe,
The Crew Peaceable*, pen,
27.9 × 42 cm., 1770,
British Library, London
(Add. MS 23920, f. 51).

the same instant striking their paddles on the thwarts: all of which afforded a truly comic act.[8]

Parkinson has sought to convey visually how, from the safety of the *Endeavour*'s side, the dance struck him as a comic act. To appreciate such drawings one must be aware of the reflexive and interacting character of the situation. Had Parkinson felt he needed support for drawing dancing Maoris by means of such brusque angular lines, he would have found explicit support in his copy of *The Analysis of Beauty*. 'The dances of barbarians', Hogarth wrote, 'are always represented without these movements [i.e., without serpentine lines] being only composed of wild skipping, jumping, and turning around, or running backward and forward, with convulsive shrugs and distorted gestures.'[9]

When Parkinson came to draw the magnificent carvings on Maori canoes he had plenty of opportunity to see and to use Hogarth's curve of beauty. But that is another matter.

By contrast with Parkinson's numerous depictions of Polynesians and Maori, his drawings of Australian Aborigines are few in number. From the *Endeavour* voyage there are only five sheets of drawings known that depict Aborigines: four are by Parkinson, and one by an unknown artist working in an untrained manner who may well have been Joseph Banks himself. There is also a drawing made by John Frederick Miller in 1771 of Aboriginal artefacts collected on the voyage. The main reason for this paucity of visual material is that Cook and his company had difficulty in making contact with Aborigines of a kind stable and amicable enough to permit detailed drawings to be made. Only the drawing by the unknown artist–almost certainly a copy from a lost original by Parkinson–suggests that an Aboriginal had actually posed for his portrait.

The problems of establishing contact are clear from the accounts of both Cook and Banks. The latter writes:

> That they are a very pusilanimous people we have reason to suppose from every part of their conduct in every place where we were except Sting Rays [Botany] bay, and there only the instance of the two people who opposed the Landing of our two boats full of men for near a quarter of an hour and were not to be drove away till several times wounded with small shot, which we were obliged to do so as at that time we suspected their Lances to be poisned from the quantity of gum which was about their points; but upon every other occasion both there and every where else they behaved alike, shunning us and giving up any part of the countrey which we landed upon at once ...[10]

There is another less important but not insignificant reason for the lack of drawings of Aborigines: Parkinson's first duty was to draw plants–for botany was Banks's first interest. It seems reasonably clear from the available evidence and from the behaviour of both Banks and Stanfield Parkinson after the conclusion of the voyage that Sydney took the view that his obligation to Banks–who had promised to pay him £80 per annum for the voyage–was to provide him with natural-history drawings only. Other drawings were made in his spare time as part of his personal record of the voyage; like his journal, these were to be regarded as his own property. Uncertainty concerning the delimitation of Parkinson's work and of his responsibility to Banks led to a complicated legal dispute after his death.[11] There can be no doubt, however, that Parkinson's main task was to draw sketches of plants collected on the voyage. In all, he made 955

drawings of plants, 675 of which were sketches and 280 finished drawings, usually in colour.[12] By the time the *Endeavour* left New Zealand in March 1770, the number of plants collected had become so great that Parkinson abandoned any attempt to provide finished drawings and concentrated instead upon sketches of the basic facts of structure and colour before the specimens withered and faded. In Australia, the backlog of plants to be drawn increased dramatically. In these circumstances Parkinson would have had little time to make drawings of Aboriginal people. Spöring, so far as we know, made no attempt at all to do so. He, too, as an assistant naturalist, was also most probably fully occupied in the collection and description of plants.

Parkinson's field sketches of Australian Aborigines are contained in a guard book in the Department of Manuscripts, British Library (Add. MS 9345). It binds together what were most probably two sketchbooks of different size kept by Parkinson on the voyage. The smaller (152 × 190 mm) contains drawings only of subjects related to the Society Islands. The larger (185 × 236 mm) contains drawings related to both the earlier (Madeira, Rio) and later (New Zealand, Australia, Batavia) sections of the voyage.

The first sheet (f. 14v) contains ten drawings (pl. 93). Two are of Aboriginal men, four of a bark canoe in various positions with one depicting an Aboriginal

94. Sydney Parkinson,
sketches of various
objects including a
Javanese house, pencil,
18.4 × 23.5 cm., 1770,
British Library, London
(Add. MS 9345, f. 20v).

paddling. There are also drawings of a bark hut, two of shields, and one of a paddle. These drawings were probably executed on or about 28 April 1770 when the *Endeavour* was at Botany Bay. Parkinson's sketches of the canoes and paddles accord closely with his journal entry for that day: 'Their canoes were made of one piece of bark, gathered at the two ends, and extended in the middle by two sticks. Their paddles were very small, two of which they used at one time.'[13] A more detailed drawing of a canoe and two views of a bark hut occur on a second sheet of drawings (f. 20v) (pl. 94). These seem to have been developed from the field sketches on f. 14v (pl. 93) and may have been completed after leaving the Endeavour River. Significantly, the same sheet contains a drawing of a fan palm and a 'Javanese house', both probably drawn on Savu.

The figure at lower right (pl. 93) of the man launching a lance from a throwing stick also suggests that f. 14v was drawn at Botany Bay. In his journal Parkinson recorded on 28 April: 'After we had landed, they threw two of their lances at us; one of which fell between my feet;[14] and he proceeded later to describe the body-paint worn by the men: 'some . . . were painted white, having a streak round their thighs, two below their knees, one like a sash over their shoulders, which ran diagonally downwards, and another across their foreheads'.[15] All these features can be seen on the figure except the second band below the knees. Parkinson also described the shields used: 'of oval figure, painted white in the middle, with two holes in it to see through'. This accords with the drawing he made of shields, except for the two holes. They are not there in the drawing, nor in Banks's description of Aboriginal shields, nor in the artefact drawn by Miller (pl. 95). Nevertheless, they are depicted in the engraving in Parkinson's *Journal* entitled *Two of the Natives of New Holland, Advancing to Combat* by Thomas Chambers (or Chambars) (pl. 96). This suggests that the engraver is following Parkinson's text, not his sketch.

Although the drawing of the man using a throwing stick in plate 93 is the first depiction of this subject, Parkinson does not describe it in the text of the *Journal*, though he refers to lances and a wooden sword. Banks, however, immediately understood the use of the woomera when he first saw a man in action at Botany Bay with 'a short stick which he seemed to handle as if it was a machine to throw the lance'.[16] Later, in his general description of Aboriginal weapons, etc., written after they had left the Endeavour River, Banks also wrote: 'these I beleive to be the things which many of our people were deceivd by imagining them to be wooden swords, Clubs etc. according to the direction in which they happned to see them'.[17] Parkinson may have been one of the people so deceived, being able to draw it accurately enough but unable to put a name to it. As a result of his confusion, Chambers, following Parkinson's text and without the field drawing at hand to correct him, drew the two famous defenders of New Holland advancing with dart and sword heroically but inaccurately (pl. 96).

The drawing of the man at lower left in plate 93 possesses some strange features. What looks like a pair of spectacles is most probably intended to depict the facial paint that Banks mentions in his general description ('They lay it on in circles round their eyes') and may be seen more clearly in Charles Praval's drawing (pl. 97). Neither Banks nor Parkinson mentions having noticed such facial marking while at Botany Bay. So that if f. 14v was executed at Botany Bay, as seems likely, this is the earliest record we have of such markings. The drawing upon the chest of the same man, however, raises large questions. The design on the man at lower right corresponds with Parkinson's observations in the *Journal* (already noted) concerning the body paint worn on shoulder and breast by Aborigines at Botany Bay. On the man at lower left, however, he has drawn a 'crucifix' figure as an integral part of the design across the man's chest. The simplest explanation is that the man's breast markings, when first seen, reminded him of a crucifix, and wishing to preserve the original perception, he drew them in that way. The fact that it was close to the Easter season while the *Endeavour* was at Botany Bay may also be relevant. The markings had reminded Banks of 'a soldiers cross belts'.[18]

These sketches, as mentioned above, were personal notes, not scientific records for Banks. Nevertheless, the drawing f. 14v is quite exceptional in Parkinson's oeuvre. On no other occasion did he produce a work of this kind in which his imagination is allowed free rein. It is true that we have several verbal accounts of preconceptions colouring vision on Cook's voyages. An amusing one is that of the seaman who at Endeavour River saw what was presumably a flying fox, but informed Banks that whatever it was it was 'as black as the Devil and had 2 horns on its head'.[19] On the second voyage J.R. Forster insisted that the colonial pines he saw on Norfolk Island were basaltic pillars similar to those on the Giant's Causeway:

all the military Men think them to be Trees, whereas the Experimental-Men are of the Opinion that they are Stone-pillars erected by Nature. We go by Analogy and judge from what we have seen and read before, but they think it impossible that such Rocks could be formed naturally.[20]

Whether Parkinson intended anything more than a visual metaphor with his crucifix figure must remain a matter of speculation. He was, however, the most devout of all the 'experimental-men'—to use Forster's phrase—on the *Endeavour*,

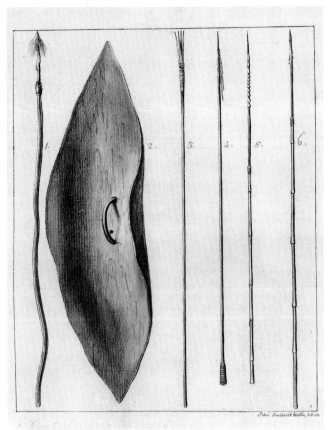

and the one who of all the ship's company, as his brother Stanfield rightly insisted, developed the closest rapport with the native peoples of the Pacific:

> engaging their attention by the powers of his pencil, disarming them of their native ferocity, and rendering them even serviceable to the great end of the voyage in chearfully furnishing him with the choicest productions of the soil and climate, which neither force nor strategem might otherwise have procured.[21]

It was also Parkinson who was most sympathetic to those peoples. This was apparent almost immediately. Only two days after the arrival at Tahiti he recorded his disgust at the way Tahitians were treated during an affray which developed after one of them seized a musket from a sentinel:

> A boy, a midshipman, was the commanding officer, and giving orders to fire, they obeyed with the greatest glee imaginable, as if they had been shooting wild ducks, killed one stout man, and wounded many others. What a pity, that such brutality should be exercised by civilized people upon unarmed ignorant Indians.[22]

Such a ready and sympathetic identification with native peoples unjustly treated rather than with his own companions may have been owing in part to Parkinson's Quaker upbringing. But it owed much also, as we have noted, to the artist's vocation and the necessity of cultivating amicable relationships in order to execute accurate visual records. The importance of the negotiations involved has never been fully appreciated. Although the act of drawing was itself a kind of

95. John Frederick Miller, *Five spears and a shield from New Zealand, Australia and New Guinea*, pen and wash, 20.6 × 16.5 cm., 1771, British Library, London (Add. MS 23920, f. 35).

96. *Two of the Natives of New Holland Advancing to Combat*, engraving by T. Chambers after Sydney Parkinson, from Parkinson, *Journal of a Voyage to the South Seas*, 1773, pl. xxvii, fp. 134.

assertion of European power, a pre-emptive acquisition of knowledge for the future, including future action, it could not be asserted, as other modes of power were, simply by the use of physical force. Drawings of the living not the dead were required, and these presupposed amicability and interaction. In this respect, the so-called 'scientific' drawing of people differed fundamentally from the drawing of plants and animals. Yet the cordial relationships upon which the artist's success depended, derived from the prior use of force. Just as Cook's friendly relationships with the Tahitians depended in no small measure upon Wallis's brutal use of force in the year preceding Cook's first visit (see pl. 180), so Parkinson's capacity to utilise the social space created by friendship relied considerably upon those raw assertions of power he found so distasteful. Art in this respect, like trade, followed the flag. However, even though Parkinson in the practice of his art was conducting a kind of second order of power relationship, we must realise that a redemptive process was already at work. The friendships that developed were valued on both sides. They were relationships not wholly of dominance and subordination; transfers of loyalty could occur.

Such general considerations provide a context for Parkinson's drawing. The crucifix is implanted on the unknown Aboriginal like the stigmata upon St Francis of Assisi. Here, as in Tahiti, Parkinson seems to have felt for the local people as victims. But he does not view them as the simple children of nature, 'far more happier than we Europeans'–Cook's phrase;[23] rather, they are 'ignorant Indians' for whom Parkinson's Christ died.[24] His drawing of the two Aborigines reveals a different kind of sympathy, that sympathy for the lost souls of pagan brothers that generated the missionary enterprise that was yet to come to the Pacific.

If such thoughts and feelings do indeed lie behind Parkinson's little drawing, then the engraving by Thomas Chambers presents a problem (pl. 96). None of the field drawings made by Parkinson bears any close relationship to the engravings published in his *Journal*, except the portrait of the Maori (engraved as plate xxi in the *Journal*) (pl. 82). Yet some of these drawings may well have provided information upon which more finished drawings (now lost) were developed and came later into the possession of the engravers who executed the plates for the *Journal*. It is probable that more developed drawings were later made from the two figures in plate 93, and that Chambers's engraved plate derives from these. But if so, the transformation effected is considerable. None of Parkinson's surviving field drawings resorts to the vocabulary of postures provided by classical statuary for presenting full-length figures, which is not to say that Parkinson was wholly immune to neo-classical influences. Although there is some evidence, discussed above, to suggest that he had read Hogarth on composition, his lack of training in figure drawing makes it likely that the two figures in the engraving owe their stance and posture to Chambers and not to Parkinson.

Chambers was an Associate of the Royal Academy who exhibited with the Society of Artists between 1761 and 1773 and also at the Academy. He was exposed to the influences of classicism far more fully than was Parkinson. It may be noted that the other two full-length figures that he engraved for Parkinson's *Journal* also adopt classical attitudes: *The Tahitian Woman* (plate v in the *Journal*) adopts a modified *Venus de' Medici* pose: *The New Zealand Warrior* (plate xv), a modified *Apollo Belvedere* pose. Engravings of this kind lent a certain elegance to the publication. They were essentially illustrations to words in the text rather than engravings developed from field sketches–even when such sketches played a part in the final result. This process of elevation was due in varying degrees to the high status of history painting, the currency of the grand style, the neo-classical taste of the engraver, and the conventions of fine-book illustration. What Chambers has done essentially is to draw an illustration expressive of true heroic courage based in part upon antique models, such as the *Borghese Gladiator*, the *Tyrant Slayers* and the *Horse Tamers*, and in part upon words chosen from Parkinson's text. For it was fundamental to the grand style that the general truths of action, not particularities of detail, should be seized upon in presenting historic events. Even so, ethnographic details such as nose ornaments and body-paint could still be included with a tolerable accuracy. But it was the heroic character of the act that determined the category of the depiction.

The stay at Endeavour River was much longer than that at Botany Bay, and a greater degree of contact was established with the local Aborigines. This is the clue to the problem surrounding a puzzling drawing which has been usually described as representing a Melanesian native (British Library, Add. MS 15508,

CH·PRAVAL DEL·

97. Charles Praval, *An Australian Aborigine from the Endeavour River*, pen, 26.7 × 21.6 cm., *c*.1771 (copied from a lost drawing by Sydney Parkinson), British Library, London (Add. MS 15508, f. 13).

f. 13) (pl. 97). It is drawn in ink and signed Ch. Praval. Without doubt this is Charles Praval, a seaman enlisted at Batavia and engaged to make copies of drawings by Parkinson and Spöring after the two artists died in January 1771. Cook required the copies in order to illustrate his Admiralty log. There seems little doubt that plate 97 is a copy of a lost drawing by Parkinson executed at the Endeavour River. There is no good reason for describing the man as Melanesian, for the drawing certainly comes from the *Endeavour* voyage in which contact with New Guinea was brief and such that no Melanesian could possibly have posed in this way for his portrait.

On the other hand, the drawing, despite its naivety, accords closely enough with descriptions of Aborigines seen at Endeavour River. They had, Parkinson informs us, 'flattish noses'; the hair of some was 'curled and bushy'; 'Their noses had holes bored in them, through which they drew a piece of white bone about three or five inches long and two round'; 'Some of them had necklaces made of oval pieces of bright shells, which lay imbricated over one another, and linked together by two strings'; 'Their bones were so small, that I could more than span their ancles; and their arms too, above the elbow joint.'[25] From Banks we have a description of the armbands: 'bracelets wore round the upper part of their arms, consisting of strings lapd round with other strings as what we Call gymp in England';[26] and it was Banks also, as noted earlier, who described the painted bands about the eyes. 'Their Beards', Cook informs us, 'which are generaly black they like wise crop short or singe off.'[27] Their shields were usually ovate in form.

However, the Aborigines at Endeavour River (as elsewhere) went naked, and the man in this drawing is clothed in some kind of garment and holds a small branch of a plant in his right hand. Can it be that the original drawing by Parkinson depicted an Aboriginal whom he had prevailed upon to pose in a garment given to him, holding a green branch as an emblem of friendship? Parkinson, as he himself tells us, was one of a party of three who gave a shirt to some Aborigines; this was 'found afterwards torn into rags'.[28] It may be that he prevailed upon one of them to pose for his portrait, dressed in the manner depicted. There is an element of prudery in Parkinson's sketches of the men in plate 93—the genitals are not drawn clearly—and the overall manner of composition in plate 97 suggests Parkinson's reluctance to show his subject in a state of total nudity. Here, too, one observes the beginning of a long tradition of Aboriginal acculturation in the ways of Europeans.

Another sketch (British Library, Add. MS 9345, f. 20) (pl. 98) supports this view. It, too, was probably drawn on the Endeavour River. The other drawings on the sheet—the shields, the head of the lance, the throwing stick, the palm tree and fish—were all drawn there. The figure beneath the palm tree is clothed in a shirt, a neckerchief and what looks like a short skirt of some kind. He holds a stick or lance in his right hand and some kind of object, possibly a small shield, in his left. Although the figure looks more European than Aboriginal, Parkinson is not known to have once depicted members of the *Endeavour*'s company during the three years of the voyage. Nor, so far as we know, did Hodges on the second, or Webber on the third voyage. To do so here would have been quite exceptional. Furthermore, it may be noted that the hair of the standing man is somewhat similar to that of the man seated in the canoe in plate 94. If plate 97 is indeed, as seems likely, a drawing of an Aboriginal dressed up for the occasion at Endeavour River, then plate 98 may be a field sketch preliminary to the execution of the lost drawing from which Praval's drawing was copied. Drawings of Pacific

96

98. Sydney Parkinson, studies of Australian Aboriginal artefacts and other drawings, pen, 18.4 × 23.5 cm., 1770, British Library, London (Add. MS 9345, f. 20).

peoples in European costume, though extremely rare, were made on other occasions on Cook's voyages. Thus, on the second voyage, Hodges depicted a young Tongan woman clothed in a blanket which she had apparently acquired from some member of the *Resolution*'s company.[29] Such drawings remind us that the depiction of native peoples took place in an interactive situation.

One last drawing of Australian Aborigines may be noted here. It is by the 'Artist of the Chief Mourner' (British Library, Add. MS 15508, f. 9). He was probably Joseph Banks.[30] The drawing has not been previously identified as depicting Aborigines because it is headed 'Otaheite' in the portfolio in which it is preserved (British Library, Add. MS 15508, f. 10) (pl 99), but it is obviously a drawing of Aborigines paddling bark canoes. The man in the canoe at right is striking a fish with a four-pronged lance (or fish gig) in his right hand, while holding a short paddle in his left. His nakedness and the cicatrices across his upper arm suggest he is an Australian Aboriginal. Though details do not exactly tally, the drawing may well be a record of a fishing party that Banks observed at Botany Bay on 26 April 1770: 'Under the South head . . . were four small canoes; in each of these was one man who held in his hand a long pole with which he struck fish.'[31]

*   *   *

Let us turn now to the second voyage. The scene is Dusky Bay, New Zealand, in April 1773, where the *Resolution* put in for wooding, watering and provisioning after four months in the cold Antarctic seas. Here is George Forster's description of the first encounter with a Maori family of the Bay:

97

99. Artist of the Chief Mourner (possibly Joseph Banks), *Australian Aborigines in bark canoes*, pencil and watercolour, 26.3 × 36.2 cm., 1770, British Library, London (Add. MS 15508, f. 10a).

Captain Cook went to the head of the boat, called to him [the Maori man] in a friendly manner, and threw him his own and some other handkerchiefs, which he would not pick up. The captain then taking some sheets of white paper in his hand, landed on the rock unarmed, and held the paper out to the native. The man now trembled very visibly, and having exhibited strong marks of fear in his countenance took the paper: upon which Captain Cook coming up to him, took hold of his hand, and embraced him, touching the man's nose with his own, which is their mode of salutation. His apprehension was by this means dissipated, and he called to the two women, who came and joined him, while several of us landed to keep the captain company. A short conversation ensued, of which little was understood on both sides, for want of a common knowledge of the language. Mr Hodges immediately took sketches of their countenances, and their gestures showed that they clearly understood what he was doing; on which they called him 'toa-toa', that term being probably applicable to the imitative arts.[32]

William Hodges established a close and friendly contact with this family. A few days later he made some delightful drawings (pls 100, 101) which he used later for his large landscape of a waterfall at Dusky Bay in the National Maritime Museum (pl. 124). It is in the presence of such fine drawings that we realise how much we have lost of Hodges's oeuvre and realise, too, that John Beaglehole was somewhat hasty in judgement when he wrote that Hodges 'was not given to the figure, and not very skilful at it'.[33] In these drawings Hodges is no longer working within an ethnographic 'schemata' but drawing figures as he might have done back home in England, and as his master Wilson had taught him to draw, with a feeling for the stance and living presence of the person.

It was not only a matter of skill. A new feeling of sympathy for the Maoris and for their society is discernible among the party of scientists and artists on the *Resolution*. The feeling is present in Cook himself. Here is an extract from his *Journal* in which he is reflecting on the introduction of European forms of commerce to New Zealand. It was written at Queen Charlotte Sound.

100. William Hodges, *A Maori holding a hatchet*, red chalk, 21.1 × 76 cm., 1773, Department of Prints and Drawings, British Museum, London (201. c.5 no. 282).

101. William Hodges, *A Maori woman carrying a child*, red chalk, 17 × 8.7 cm., 1773, Department of Prints and Drawings, British Museum, London (201 c.5 no. 283).

During our short stay in this Sound I have observed that this Second Visit of ours hath not mended the morals of the Natives of either Sex, the Women of this Country I have always looked upon to be more chaste than the generality of Indian Women, whatever favours a few of them might have granted to the crew of the *Endeavour*, it was generally done in a private manner and without the men seeming to interest themselves in it, but now we find the men are the chief promoters of this Vice, and for a spike or nail or anything they value will oblige their Wives and Daughters to prostitute themselves whether they will or no and that not with the privacy decency seems to require, such are the consequences of a commerce with Europeans and what is still more to our Shame civilized Christians, we debauch their Morals already too prone to vice and we introduce among them wants and perhaps disease which they never before knew and which serves only to disturb that happy tranquillity they and their fore Fathers injoy'd. If any one denies the truth of this assertion let him tell me what the Natives of the whole extent of America have gained by the commerce they have had with Europeans.[34]

Such sentiments as these were expressed more forcibly by the young George Forster in his account of the second voyage, as when he concluded a now much-quoted passage as follows:

99

If the knowledge of a few individuals can only be acquired at such a price as the happiness of nations, it were better for the discoverers and the discovered, that the South Sea had still remained unknown to Europe and its restless inhabitants.[35]

What we are in the presence of during the second voyage, then, is an attitude to the peoples of the Pacific distinguishable from the admirably detailed and objective but somewhat patronising anthropology of Banks, on the first. Even though there were personal tensions between the 'experimental gentlemen' on the *Resolution,* and though they quarrelled about matters of publication and the interpretation of facts later, Cook himself, the two Forsters, William Wales, Anders Sparrman were all touched in varying degrees by the moral and scientific fervour of the Enlightenment; nature, reason and humanity were the objects of their enquiries. It is in this context that we should seek to understand and to appreciate a fine series of portraits in crayon that Hodges drew in the Pacific.

George Forster has left useful accounts of the face-to-face situations in which this portraiture was carried out, and of the ways in which he himself assisted the artist. Here is his description of one such occasion, which occurred in May 1773 when a party of Maoris came aboard the *Resolution* as it lay at Ship Cove in Queen Charlotte Sound:

> Several of these people were invited into the cabin, where Mr Hodges applied himself to sketch the most characteristic faces, while we prevailed on them to sit still for a few moments, keeping their attention engaged, by a variety of trifles which we shewed, and some of which we presented to them. We found several expressive countenances among them, particularly some old men, with grey or white beards; and some young men, with amazingly bushy hair, which hung wildly over their faces, and increased their natural savage looks.[36]

It is likely that two drawings in the National Library, Canberra, were developed from sketches made at that time (pls 102, 103). It is noteworthy that Hodges has here escaped from the ethnographic emphasis upon dress and adornment and is seeking 'characteristic faces' and 'expressive countenances'. A search has begun for individual personality as distinct from the depiction of typical people and typical forms of expression that was Parkinson's concern. For though the Forsters came to the conclusion that Maori society had fallen from what they called an original state of philanthropy–there is much more than a touch of Rousseau in their thinking here–to a state of barbarism expressed in tribal wars and cannibalism, none the less, as empirical scientists, they tested their theories continually against specific cases. And Hodges, in this, worked closely with them.

The ethnographic record was, nevertheless, a matter of continuing importance. Hodges became quite skilled in presenting the dress and adornment, distinctive of a person of particular rank who played a particular role in tribal society. A fine example is the portrait of a Maori chieftain that Hodges drew on 22 October 1773 on the return visit to Queen Charlotte Sound. Forster describes this occasion:

> In the morning we were to the south of Cape Kidnappers, and advanced to the Black Cape. After breakfast three canoes put off from this part of the shore, where some level land appeared at the foot of the mountains. They came soon on board as we were not very far from land, and in one of them was a chief,

who came on deck without hesitation. He was a tall middle-aged man, clothed in two new and elegant dresses, made of New Zealand flag or flax-plant. His hair was dressed in the highest fashion of the country, tied on the crown, oiled and stuck with white feathers. In each ear he wore a piece of albatross skin covered with its white down, and his face was punctured in spiral and curved lines. Mr Hodges drew his portrait, and a print of it is inserted in Captain Cook's account of this voyage.[37]

If we compare the original drawing, now in Canberra (pl. 104), from which the engraving was made, with one of Parkinson's profiles of Maoris (pls 82, 83), we see the ethnographic convention humanised, Hodges provides the ethnography but also evokes a presence. He does not proceed by way of a diagram, a visual analysis equivalent to words, as Locke and Banks saw the role of the travelling artist. He proceeds by means of a sympathetic apprehension of the whole. Like all artists, he structured his work on a schematic model, but here the model is only a point of departure in a search for feeling rather than for the raw facts. The imagination, we might say, has entered scientific draughtsmanship.

From being what Thomas Hobbes had called 'decay'd sense', the imagination, as a mental faculty, had steadily gained respect throughout the eighteenth century. It came to be seen as the co-ordinator of those otherwise discrete sensations

102. William Hodges, *Old Maori man with grey beard*, red chalk, 54 × 37.7 cm., 1773, National Library of Australia, Canberra (R749).

103. William Hodges, *Maori man with bushy hair*, red chalk, 54.3 × 37.5 cm., 1773, National Library of Australia, Canberra (R751).

101

of our sensory organs; it was linked with sensibility, sensitivity, sympathy as a dynamic faculty for the apprehension of reality. The young Edmund Burke, in his highly influential *Enquiry into ... the Sublime and Beautiful*, published in 1757, located sympathy as the source of the imagination and defined sympathy as 'a sort of substitution, by which we are put into the place of another man, and affected in many respects as he is affected ... It is by this principle that poetry, painting, and other affecting arts, transfuse their passions from one breast to another.'[38] Hodges was aware of the importance of the imagination in art and sought to relate it to the requirements of scientific draughtsmanship. Years later in his own book, *Travels in India* (1793), he discussed the special demands placed on a travelling artist and made the significant point that 'the imagination must be under the strict guidance of a cool judgement, or we shall have fanciful representations instead of the truth'.[39] By using his imagination in drawing the Maori chieftain Hodges felt and portrayed something he could not have seen: the spiritual or psychic power known as 'mana', closely connected with rank, that every Maori chieftain treasured and believed himself to be invested with; the kind of hedging dignity of which, in another context, Shakespeare speaks.

We have but a few glimpses of Hodges at work, but what we have reveal an equable temperament that was suited, like Parkinson's, to the unpredictable human situations he had to face. We catch something of this from an amusing little story told by his close friend, the astronomer and meteorologist, William Wales, of an incident on Easter Island.

> Mr Hodges, the Draughtsman, & myself set out to Cross the Island, but had not proceeded far before the Natives became too troublesome to venture further, so we turned again for a Musket, which those People have by some persons or other been taught to pay a great deal of diference [i.e., deference] to, and we now walked ... without much molestation, all leaving us but one Man who would be very kind, and very officious, offering frequently to carry the Musket for us, which we on our part declined with proper Acknowledgements, to his great grief. He ever and anon called to such of his Countrymen, as he saw near the road we passed, and when they came to him they dropped behind and seemed to consult together concerning us; but as none of them had any weapons we walked on without the least regard to him or them, and they soon left him & picked up others. We continued our Course until we could see the greatest part of the South East side of the Island, and then sat down to take a sketch of it and rest ourselves. After we had done what we were about I got up to return and took up the musket, when the man walked past Mr Hodges snatched his hat off from his head and ran away with it. I cocked and pointed the Musket without thought of anything but firing at him; but when I saw a fellow Creature within 20 Yards of its muzzle I began to think his life worth more than a hat, *and as to the insult*, rot it! ...
> As to the owner of it
> He sat like Patience on a Monument
> Smiling at Grief.[40]

They were only three days at Easter Island. It may well have been the occasion of this walk with Wales that Hodges made the drawings, now lost, for his well-known painting of Easter Island (pl. 135), and some fine little field drawings of an Easter Islander, now in the Department of Prints and Drawings of the British Museum (pl. 105).

As might be expected, it was in the Society Islands that the most friendly and cordial relations were established with local inhabitants; and it was there that Hodges succeeded in completing some of his finest portraits. We must turn here to another extended quotation, this time from George Forster's *Voyage*, because it illustrates so well the need for the artist to promote easeful, cordial relationships if he were to produce good work.

It is August 1773, the place, Tahiti. Forster and his father have been at work most of the day drawing plants in the mountains:

after finishing our notes, and feasting our eyes once more on the romantick scenery, we returned to the plain. Here we observed a crowd of natives coming towards us, and at their near approach perceived two of our shipmates, Mr Hodges and Mr Grindall whom they surrounded and attended on their walk. We soon joined them, and resolved to continue our excursion together. A youth of a very promising countenance, who had distinguished himself by shewing a particular attachment for these gentlemen, was entrusted with Mr Hodges's portfolio, where he preserved the sketches and designs, which he had frequent opportunities of making on his walk. No favour, or mark of affection could I believe have given this youth so much real pleasure, as the confidence they had placed in him, upon which he seemed to value himself among his country men. Perhaps this circumstance, joined to the peaceable appearance of our gentlemen, who walked without arms of any kind, had a general effect upon all the people that surrounded us, as their familiarity and affection seemed much

104. William Hodges, *A Maori chieftain*, red chalk, 54.1 × 37.3 cm., 1773, National Library of Australia, Canberra (R747).

105. William Hodges, *Head of a man of Easter Island*, pen and pencil, 11 × 10 cm., 1774, Department of Prints and Drawings, British Museum, London (201 c.5 no. 275).

103

increased. We entered a spacious hut together, where we saw a large family assembled. An old man, with a placid countenance, lay on a clean mat, and rested his head on a little stool, which served as a pillow. His head, which was truly venerable, was well furnished with fine locks of a silvery grey, and a thick beard as white as snow descended to his breast. His eyes were lively, and health sat on his full cheeks. His wrinkles, which characterise age with us, were not deep; for cares, troubles and disappointment, cannot be supposed to exist in this happy nation. Several little ones, whom we took to be his grandchildren, and who, according to the custom of the country, were perfectly naked, played with their aged ancestor, while his actions and looks convinced us, that the simple way of living to which he had been used to, had not blunted his senses. Several well-made men and artless nymphs, in whom youth supplied the want of beauty, surrounded the old man, and as we came in seemed to be in conversation over a frugal meal. They desired us to sit down. Charmed with the picture of real happiness which was thus exhibited before us, Mr Hodges filled his portfolio with several sketches, which will convey to future times his beauties of a scene, of which words give but a faint idea. While he was drawing, all the natives looked on with great attention, and were highly pleased to find out the resemblance between his performances and different persons among them. Our acquaintance with their language, which we were at pains to improve, was as yet very imperfect, and deprived us of the pleasure which we might have received from a conversation with these good people. A few separate words, and an interlude of dumb mimickry, was all that we had to supply the place of a coherent speech. However, even this was sufficient to amuse the natives, and our docility and endeavours to please seemed to be at least as agreeable to them as their social temper and willingness to give instruction appeared to us.[41]

It was in such circumstances that Hodges was able to produce a number of little masterpieces of character interpretation, such as the portrait of Potatow (pl. 106): 'His features were so mild, comely and at the time majestic'. wrote George Forster, 'that Mr Hodges immediately applied himself to copy from them, as from the noblest models of nature.' Another example is the splendid portrait of Tu, or 'Otoo' as they called him (pl. 64). Tu was the 'arii nui', or leading chieftain, of the Pare region of Tahiti, which lay adjacent to Matavai Bay. He was so timorous as a young man that he could not bring himself to put in an appearance when the *Endeavour* visited Tahiti. But he was ambitious; and by a strange irony of history, and the assistance of a succession of British ships, it was Tu who succeeded in uniting the whole of the Society Islands under his own rule as Pomare I. The Pomare dynasty lasted for a period of seventy years before the French annexed the group, and it maintained its social and ritual roles for another forty years. At the time Hodges drew Tu he was just beginning to pass, to put the matter in our own quaint language, from prehistory to history. George Forster provided a verbal description of him: 'His head, notwithstanding a certain gloominess which seemed to express a fearful disposition, had a majestic and intelligent air, and there was great expression in his black eyes.'[42] Forster also tells us that he was 24 or 25 and was six foot three inches in height, the tallest man they had seen in the island. Cook thought him considerably older, about 30 or 35, and wrote that 'all his actions shewed him to be a timorous prince'. On another occasion, he wrote:

106. William Hodges, *Potatow*, red chalk, 53.9 × 37.1 cm., 1773, Mitchell Library, Sydney (PXD 11, N 17).

There is very little about Otoo's person or Court, by which a Stranger could distinguish the King from the Subject. I have seldom seen him dressed in anything but a Common piece of Cloth wraped around his loins, so that he seems to pay the same homage to his Subjects which is due to him from them; he seems to avoide all unnecessary pomp and shew and even to demean himself, more than any of the Earee's; I have seen him work at a Paddle, in coming and going from the ship, in common with the other Paddler[s] even when some of his Toutous, were seting looking on.[43]

*　　*　　*

The work of John Webber on the third voyage, will be considered in detail in chapter eight, but some points relevant here should be mentioned. He did not possess the same skill as Hodges in the rendering of individuality and temperament; but because he was more skilled with figure drawing and knew how to relate figure to landscape and social setting he was able to bring a more realistic, less schematic approach to ethnographic conventions. As with Parkinson and Hodges, this advance in cultural contact, in the aesthetic realisation of

Pacific people, was achieved only as a result of the establishment of amicable social relationships between the artist and his subjects. As might be expected, difficult situations were frequently encountered. Here is an account by Webber of an incident that took place on Monday, 20 April 1778 in a Nootka village on Nootka Sound on the Pacific coast of what is now Vancouver Island, North West Canada:

In the morning early we set out, the Pinnace and large Cutter to explore the Sound and Visit the Habitations we had seen on our entrance. These were at the bottom of a Bay some distance from where our ships Lay at anchor. At our arrival the Natives, what few were there, assembled about the boats, and brought such things with them they had to barter for. Capt. Cook distributed to them presents of beads and other trifles he had with him and with which they seem'd much pleas'd when our boats crews were sent to cut grass, finding it grew on a better soil than we had hitherto met with. The officers were employed to explore the Bay whilst Capt Cook and myself paid a visit to the Inhabitants. After having made a general view of their dwellings I sought for an inside which would furnish me with sufficient matter to convey a perfect Idea of the mode these people live in. Such was soon found: the people being employed in boiling their fish for a meal and semingly appear'd without any displeasure at my being present, this is done by filling a woden box with water and casting sucessively red hot stones into it, which so effectually answers the purpose that it instantaniously boils, when the fish are handed round to those present. While I was employ'd a man approach'd me with a large knife in one hand semingly displeas'd when he observed I notic'd two representations of human figures which were plac'd at one end of the apartment carv'd on a plank, and of Gigantic proportion: and painted after their custom. However I proceeded, and took as little notice of him as possible, which to prevent he soon provided himself with a Mat, and plac't it in such a manner as to hinder my having any further a sight of them. Being certain of no further oppertunity to finish my Drawing and the Object too interesting for leaving unfinished, I considered a little bribery might have some effect, and accordingly made an offer of a button from my coat, which when of metal they are much pleas'd with, this instantly produc'd the desir'd effect, for the mat was remov'd and I left at liberty to proceed as before, scarcely had I seated myself and made a beginning, but he return'd and renew'd his former practice, till I had dispos'd of my buttons, after which I found no opposition in my further employment.[44]

We might want to conclude from all this that the artists on Cook's voyages succeeded in portraying non-European peoples more successfully than they had ever been portrayed before, because, in the first instance, Cook himself always succeeded in maintaining control of the situation—until the fatal affair at Kealakekua Bay where he was killed; and that the artists themselves were able to establish an amicability and friendliness, because of the nature of their own vocation, within the controlled situation. This, no doubt, is true enough; but it is not the whole truth. A paradox lay at the heart of the process.

The Nootka Indian covered up his ancestral totem from the prying eye of the stranger; but the metal buttons on Webber's coat proved to be more attractive when put to the test than the urge to protect the household gods. Despite the peacefulness of his vocation, the artist, merely by practising it, weakened tribal bonds (pl. 107). The more he sought to break through conventional stereotypes in

107. John Webber, *The Inside of a house in Nootka Sound*, pen, wash and watercolour, 22.5 × 37.5 cm., *c*.1781–3, Dixson Library, Sydney (PXX 2, 24).

order to understand the people of the Pacific sympathetically and as individuals, the more those bonds were weakened. There was no art of portraiture in the Pacific. Portraiture was an individualising, Europeanising art. No one understood this better than Tu; he was well aware of the way in which portraiture could assist him to rise to power in Tahiti. So let us return to him for a moment. On the third voyage an interesting incident took place which John Webber related to the editor of the *Voyage of Governor Phillip to Botany Bay*, published in 1789:

> Otoo [i.e., Tu], by the Captain's [i.e., Cook's] particular desire, sat to Mr Webber, in order to furnish such memorial of his features, as might serve for the subject of a complete whole length picture, on the return of the ship to England. When the portrait was finished, and Otoo was informed that no more sittings would be necessary, he anxiously enquired of Captain Cook, and Captain Clerke, what might be the particular meaning and purpose of the painting. He was informed, that it would be kept by Captain Cook, as a perpetual memorial of his person, his friendship, and the many favours received from him. He seemed pleased with the idea, and instantly replied, that, for the very same reason, a picture of Captain Cook would be highly acceptable to him. This answer so unexpected, and expressed with such strong tokens of real attachment, made both Captain Clerke and Mr Webber, his advocates; and Captain Cook, charmed with the natural sincerity of his manner, complied with his request much more readily than on any other occasion he would have granted such a favour.
>
> When the portrait was finished it was framed, and with a box, lock and key, by which it was secured, was delivered to Otoo; who received it with inexpressible satisfaction. He readily, and, as the event has proved, most faithfully promised that he would preserve it always with the utmost care; and would show it to the commanders of such ships as might in future touch at the Society Islands.[45]

Tu's desire for an exchange of portraits may be seen within the context of Tahitian practice of exchanging names as a bond of friendship. Moreover,

107

108. John Webber, *Tu*, oil on canvas, 36.2 × 27.9 cm., 1777, Alexander Turnbull Library, Wellington, New Zealand.

possession of Cook's portrait was a visible reminder to other Tahitian chieftains of the supremacy of Tu's British connections and served as an influential visiting card to be presented to every ship's captain who entered Matavai Bay. Here is Lieutenant Watt's description of his meeting with Tu when he visited Tahiti in the *Lady Penrhyn* in the evening of Sunday 13 July 1788:

> a messenger came on board with a present from O'too of a small pig, a dog, and some white cloth, and intimated that he would be at Matavai the next day. Early in the next morning but a few canoes came off to the ship, and the natives were observed assembling on the shore in prodigious numbers: soon afterwards, a canoe came alongside and informed them that O'too was on the beach; on this, the Captain and Mr Watts went on shore immediately and found him surrounded by an amazing concourse of people, amongst whom were several women cutting their foreheads with the shark's tooth, but what surprised and pleased them very much, was, to see a man carrying the portrait of Captain Cook, drawn by Webber in 1777.

Notwithstanding so much time had elapsed since the picture was drawn, it had received no injury, and they were informed that O'too always carried it with him wherever he went. After the first salutations were over, Mr Watts asked O'too to accompany him to the ship, to which he readily agreed; but previously to his entering the boat he ordered the portrait in, and when he got alongside the ship he observed the same ceremony.[46]

Nothing is known of what happened eventually to Cook's portrait; presumably it rotted away in the humidity of the tropical atmosphere;[47] but Webber's portrait of Tu came to notice quite recently. It had long been in the possession of the family of Captain King, who took command of the *Resolution* after Cook's death in Hawaii. It is now owned by the Alexander Turnbull Library, Wellington (pl. 108).

We have been concerned primarily with one central problem: the artist's vocation and the problem of cultural contact. It may well be that the temperaments and personality of Parkinson, Hodges and Webber differed, because they were artists, in some degree from those of their shipmates. But if that is so, it is not my point. T.S. Eliot once observed that in his experience the only thing common to poets was that they all wrote poetry. It is the nature of the artist's vocation in an unknown world among unknown people with which we have been concerned. As an artist, it is difficult, we can assume, to work effectively with a musket across one's knees; or even to work effectively with a line of armed marines twenty-five yards to the rear. Such constraints were the prerogative of commanders and officers. The artist, to be effective, had to cultivate a different order of relationships. And I have suggested that however skilfully such relationships were established they still led, inevitably, to the promotion of individualism in the island societies of the Pacific. But we must not assume that the cultural trafficking was all one way. Parkinson and Webber, we know, and Hodges most probably, were great collectors of Pacific Island artefacts. These artefacts exercised a curious influence upon them. Both Spöring and Parkinson spent much time drawing the intricate designs upon Maori canoes and expressed their admiration for the craft skill with which they were designed.

No full account has yet been written of the process whereby the discovery of the arts and crafts of the Pacific, acting through the sensibilities of the collectors of Cook's voyages, provided a threshold for the development of the European taste for primitive art. The history of primitivism has never been fully written.[48] Any adequate history would have to take serious account, for example, of the ethnographical collections of Pacific material that were established in London, Dublin, Bern, Vienna, Leningrad and elsewhere in the wake of Cook's voyages and their eventual influence upon European sensibility and taste.

We cannot go into such matters here. I mention it because it seems to me that the strongest justification that can be made for the contemporary, non-mimetic art that swept Europe and the Europeanised world in our own century, consists in the fact that, as Meyer Shapiro once pointed out, it can trace its genesis back not to Rome and Greece only, but to sources that represent the diversity and plurality of humankind. So that whilst we have been concerned in this chapter in considering one of the ways in which the mimetic art of Europe promoted the 'cult of personality' and of individualism in the Pacific, it is well to remember that a contradictory process was also set in motion by those strange artefacts brought back by the voyagers, the aesthetic appreciation of which assisted the rise to prominence of non-mimetic art in twentieth-century Europe and North America.

5 WILLIAM HODGES AND ENGLISH *PLEIN-AIR* PAINTING

WILLIAM HODGES WAS the only one of Cook's artists on any of his voyages to paint in oils. He seems to have been exceptional in this during the whole period of pre-colonial exploration of the Pacific. Even the highly organised voyages of the later 1830s, such as Dumont D'Urville's second expedition (1837–40) and the United States Exploration (1838–42) under Charles Wilkes, employed artists who drew in pen, pencil or chalk and painted in watercolour. Why should Hodges have worked in oil? There were many disadvantages. The technical equipment required was more bulky and cumbersome than watercolour, the preservation of the pigments in a great variety of climates and weather, more hazardous. Oil paints were not normally used by topographers. It was the medium used for the painting of history, portraiture, arcadian landscapes in the manner of Claude, romantic landscapes in the manner of Rosa.

Yet, oddly enough, had it not been Hodges it might have been Johan Zoffany, painting in oils on the *Resolution* voyage. Before he withdrew from the voyage, Banks had included Zoffany as his figure painter in his retinue of thirteen. Zoffany, we may be sure, would have used oils. In England he had made his reputation in painting 'family' or conversation pieces in oils. He was just the kind of artist Banks needed to record the figures, costumes, artifacts and customs that would be encountered in the Pacific, in order to entertain his friends in England.[1]

Hodges not only painted in oils on the voyage; there are sound reasons for believing that he practised a kind of *plein-air* painting. Not *plein air* in the literal sense, for all the evidence suggests that he painted within the security of Cook's great cabin, but by looking through its suite of windows directly at the sea and shorescape spread out before his eyes. The security aspect was important. At ports like Madeira and Cape Town the authorities forbad the depiction of harbours, their fortifications and environs; in the Pacific islands and New Zealand, the natives had little respect for private property. The great cabin was about the only place where one's equipment might be reasonably safe.

Hodges's interest in *plein-air* painting must have come from his master, Richard Wilson. He joined Wilson's studio as his apprentice in 1758 shortly after Wilson had returned from a seven-year visit to Italy.[2] In Rome, the French painter Claude Joseph Vernet had encouraged Wilson to switch from portrait to landscape painting and appears to have encouraged him to sketch in oils in the open air.[3] The practice had already developed into something of a tradition at the French School at Rome, established in 1666. It may have been encouraged by Joachim von Sandrart's description, published in 1675, of Claude's practice of walking in the Roman campagna and preparing his colours in the field before returning to his studio to paint. Gaspar Dughet is believed to have developed similar practices. By the 1740s Vernet was advocating and practising oil sketching in the open air.[4]

Although the evidence for Wilson's painting *en plein air* during his Italian years is meagre, there is enough to place it beyond reasonable doubt. In his *Memoirs*, Detail of pl. 125.

109. Richard Wilson,
*Tivoli: the Cascatelli Grandi
and the Villa of Maecenas,*
oil on canvas, 50 × 66
cm., 1752, on National
Gallery of Ireland,
Dublin.

110. Richard Wilson,
*Tivoli: the Temple of the
Sybyl and the Campagna,* oil
on canvas, 50 × 66 cm.,
1752, National Gallery of
Ireland, Dublin.

Thomas Jones, Wilson's student, describes how in 1777 he sketched a large plane tree on the edge of Lake Nemi which had a great hollow in it. 'I was told', he added, 'that my old master Wilson when in this Country made use of it as a Study to Paint in'.[5] There are two paintings of Tivoli by Wilson in the National Gallery of Ireland, Dublin. One depicts a painter at work in the open air (pl. 109), the other, an artist hurrying away with the aid of an assistant apparently before the onset of a shower of rain (pl. 110). Whether the backgrounds of either or both of these two paintings were painted in the open air wholly or in part is an open question, but the paintings are more likely to represent a personal experience, that is of *sketching* in oils in the open air, than of conveying an ironic comment on other artists who did. Wilson is not known to have been given to irony. Nevertheless, he does not appear, either in Italy or back home in England, to have made a habit of sketching *en plein air*. It seems rather to have been an innovation that captured his interest, but not one that he adopted as a normal feature of his professional practice.

It is likely that he considered it appropriate to the training of young landscape painters in developing fine discriminations of tone and colour. This could be achieved more successfully in the open air, confronting the scene, than in the studio. It was also a practice suited to travelling. All his life Wilson sought to emulate Claude, but the increase in travel and in the topographical art that accompanied travel, together with contemporary developments in science–optics particularly–appears to have exerted pressure upon him that he was scarcely aware of, causing him to 'naturalise' further Claude's visions of Arcadia. Discussing Wilson's *Tivoli: the Cascatelli Grandi and the Villa of Maecenas* (pl. 109), David Solkin comments, 'it . . . lacks any overtly Claudean descriptive mannerisms, relying instead on a more realistic treatment of natural details'. Solkin supports his comment with another by Joseph Farington, Wilson's pupil: 'Wherever Wilson studied it was to nature that he principally referred. His admiration for the pictures of Claude could not be exceeded, but he contemplated those excellent works and compared them with what he saw in nature to refine his feeling and make his observations more exact.'[6]

On returning to London, Wilson encouraged three of his pupils, Thomas Jones, Joseph Farington and William Hodges, to practise *plein-air* oil sketching. There is evidence that all three adopted the practice in their earlier professional life. Later they abandoned it, painting more in conformity with the prevailing practice of the day. *Plein-air* sketching in oil was closely associated for all three

112

111. Thomas Jones, *View of Penkerrig*, oil on paper, 22.9 × 30.4 cm., 1772, City of Birmingham Art Gallery.

with travel—for making sketches and studies suited for developing finished work later in the studio.

Thomas Jones's oil sketches and studies are today the best known. They are the expression of an innovative but private sensibility. A good deal has been written recently that stresses their advanced character. In one sense, they are certainly advanced for their time.[7] What is still not sufficiently appreciated or understood is their links with tradition. Jones made his studies in oil on paper while on sketching tours during the late 1760s and early 1770s and again while on his tour of Italy during the early 1780s. We need not doubt that he made them, as was the practice of the time, as potential aids to his work intended for exhibition. That is not to say that they may not have given him much personal pleasure. He said himself that he 'painted mainly for my own amusement'.[8] Nevertheless, he exhibited some 40 pictures between 1770 and his departure for Italy in 1776. Of the few of these that are known, all are very much in the manner of his master Wilson. They reveal nothing of that freshness of vision that inhabits his oil studies and makes them so appealing to modern taste.

The one significant technical innovation Jones made was to paint in oils, rather than in watercolour, on paper—the preferred support for sketches and studies. It was particularly novel for British painting, though, as we have seen, it is likely that his master Wilson anticipated him in this. It is true that in such views as that of Penkerrig 1772 (pl. 111), he abandoned the use of the Claudean framing, 'coulisse' foreground. But that was not a device adopted by topographical artists anyway. Britain's earliest topographers, such as Wenzel Hollar and Francis Place (1647–1728), rarely used such a device, nor were they a feature of military or naval topography. In Britain William Gilpin adopted the Claudean frame as one of the components by means of which he elevated the topographical watercolour to the level of the picturesque and so to the level of good taste. But topographical art had already been elevated to the level of taste long before and without Claudean frames. The whole cycle is anticipated in the Dutch panoramic landscapes of the seventeenth century, from the pen drawings of Goltzius to the paintings of Koninck. Jones travelled a comparable path. Doubtless his position in society helped him to indulge in his painting as a personal pleasure rather than as a professional need. Because he did not have to paint views in watercolour for a living as a travelling artist, he was in a position to paint them in oils. His social status, as a member of the Welsh gentry, we might want to conclude, provided a space in his travelling for the emergence of an innovating private sensibility. In

113

112. Thomas Jones,
*Buildings in Naples with a
View of the Castel Nuovo,*
oil on paper, 22.2 × 28.6
cm., 1782, National
Museum of Wales,
Cardiff.

113. Thomas Jones,
Buildings in Naples, oil on
paper, 14 × 21.6 cm.,
1782, National Museum
of Wales, Cardiff.

that sense his oil paintings do herald a shift in sensibility towards naturalism. But though his sensibility was advanced, it was also hesitant. He was not ready to show in public exhibition the sensitivity for nature stirring within him. In the Society of Artists and Royal Academy exhibitions the models set by Claude and Rosa reigned supreme, and he followed them. If one aspired to be a professional, they were not to be challenged.

Recently, Richard Wollheim has advanced an interpretation of Jones's *plein-air* studies that were produced in the early 1780s on his Italian tour (pls 112, 113); it emphasises what he describes as their 'corporeality':

> Jones's achievement in these diminutive buildingscapes is that he gets timeless, discoloured buildings of great dignity and humble materials to revive the infant's perception of the body: the body, stretched out, close up, palpable, taken in through the eye of desire or destruction.[9]

If this view is a valid one, it implies a knowledge of Jones's childhood fantasies and perceptions, and his subsequent development as an artist of which I, at least, am ignorant. It is the concern of the art historian to recover, to the extent that it is possible, the cultural and aesthetic environments within which artists work— consciously, deliberately and professionally work. So an historian must question Wollheim's assertion that, because Jones described his Italian *plein-air* paintings as 'finished studies',[10] he intended them 'to be exactly what they seem to be: works of art in their own right'.[11] If by that Wollheim means that Jones gave his studies the same kind of public status that he gave work he exhibited, the contemporary evidence is all against him. I would not question that today we may view Jones's *plein-air* studies as works of art 'in their own right'. I would hope that today we might also be able to view work by naval and military topographers as works of art in their own right. But it seems clear that Jones never intended his studies to be displayed in contemporary public exhibitions. As Gere has pointed out, 'the fact that almost all of Jones's oil sketches were until recently in the possession of his family suggests that they were made not for sale but for the artist's own instruction and pleasure'.[12] Sketches, studies, even finished studies in oil were not meant for public display during the 1770s and 1780s. Wollheim, surely, is mistaken when he writes that Jones's oil studies in Italy were painted on primed canvas. Jones tells us that he painted them on primed paper, and all that have, to my knowledge, survived are on paper. Even if some were painted on canvas (and there is no evidence for this), it would suggest only that Jones intended them to be more durable, not that he intended them for public

114. Thomas Hearne, *Sir George Beaumont and Joseph Farington sketching a waterfall*, pen and brown and grey wash, 44.5 × 29.2 cm., *c.* 1777, The Wordsworth Trust, Dove Cottage, Grasmere, Cumbria.

115. Joseph Farington, *Richard Wilson painting from Nature in Moor Park*, pencil, 1765, Farington Sketchbook, Victoria and Albert Museum, London.

exhibition. All the present evidence suggests that Jones's *plein-air* studies in oil are the work of an advanced but also a private and hesitant sensibility.

Joseph Farington was a more conventional artist than Jones. He spent most of his professional life producing topographical views, in pencil, pen and wash, of town and country; compiling his famous diary; and acting as the 'dictator' of the Royal Academy.[13] Yet in his early years it would seem that he, too, made *plein-air* sketches and studies in the countryside, although none has yet come to light. A drawing by Thomas Hearne probably completed about 1777 when Farington was thirty (pl. 114), depicts the artist with his friend Sir George Beaumont painting in oils before a waterfall in the Lake District.[14] There can be no doubt that they are painting in oils, with brushes and mahlsticks on comparatively large canvases. Farington is known to have painted with his master, Wilson, on sketching excursions. On one such occasion he represented Wilson painting in oils from nature in Moor Park (pl. 115). It was drawn while Farington was still a pupil of Wilson, but, unlike his master, he did not, apparently, continue to paint for long in oils, making his name (for what it was) as an artist in the field of topographical views in pen and wash.

Farington came of a minor branch of the English gentry; Jones, of the Welsh squirearchy. Hodges was the son of a London blacksmith and was an apprentice, not an independent paying pupil, of Wilson. He was, therefore, more closely involved than Farington and Jones in assisting Wilson with his own work, for example preparing grounds. As a result, it has been very difficult to separate Hodges's early work, prior to his joining Cook on the *Resolution*, from that of his master's. However, Farington, who knew them both well, became quite skilled at it: on more than one occasion he identified a painting as by Hodges that had been given to Wilson.

115

Before he joined Cook, Hodges painted views in the Midlands, Wales, the north of England and the Rhineland, and it is likely that he, too, like Jones and Farington, painted in oils in the open air, at least occasionally, in the manner of his teacher. But if so, no such studies have come to light. As of the present, evidence for his special type of '*plein-air*' work comes wholly from his painting on the *Resolution* voyage.

Given the initial stimulus of Richard Wilson's *plein-air* teaching practices, it is possible to understand why it was that Hodges turned to a *plein-air* type of technique on the voyage. He was now painting landscapes not for gentlemen of taste, for whom Claude, Gaspar Dughet and Salvator Rosa represented the characteristic heights of achievement, but for, as they described themselves, 'experimental gentlemen', for whom the gathering of information, its classification and interpretation were matters of the first concern. The innovations that Hodges brought to British painting were made possible by the scientific milieu within which he worked for three years on the *Resolution*.

Much of the time of the *Resolution*'s voyage was taken up in sailing out of sight

116. William Hodges, *The Resolution in the Marquesas*, pen and wash, 28.9 × 23.1 cm., 1774, National Maritime Museum, London.

of land or along a coast with the object of laying down a chart. So it is not surprising that Cook made use of Hodges's ability for the provision of coastal views, and asked him to set up a little class in the great cabin to train his young midshipmen. One of them, John Elliott, records how 'myself, Mr Roberts and Mr Smith [Cook's nephew] were when off Watch, Employ'd in Capt Cooks Cabin either Copying Drawings for him, or Drawing for ourselves, under the Eye of Mr Hodges'.[15]

A fine wash drawing of the *Resolution* by Hodges (pl. 116), probably drawn in the Marquesas if the canoes are any indication, enables us to reconstruct the situation. It shows the great cabin aft with its seven large windows and two in each of the quarter galleries to port and starboard. From the cabin windows Hodges taught his pupils to observe passing coastlines, drawing the contours with a pencil and depicting shores and hills in perspective by means of a three-tone wash process. The tones were obviously laid down whilst the draughtsman was in direct visual contact with the object (pl. 117). This technique was adopted by his pupils: consider John Elliott's drawing of Savage Island (pl. 118). Hodges himself achieved some remarkably fine free work in this way, full of atmosphere (pl. 119). What we have here, then, are the rudiments of the *plein-air* practice, though the work was actually performed within a cabin and behind glass.

There were excellent reasons for working in the great cabin. It not only commanded extensive views aft and to port and starboard, it provided the best

120. William Hodges, *View of Funchal*, wash, 47 × 67.3 cm., 1772, private collection, Madeira.

space available on the ship–and, as mentioned above, security. The last was most important. When Cook arrived at Funchal, Madeira in July 1772, the Governor of the island permitted him to come ashore and take provisions, 'providing that no Plans or drawings might be made of any Fortifications', which Cook noted was 'a very reasonable restriction and very readily promised on my part'.[16] That the promise was not kept is revealed by a drawing of the bay of Funchal, Madeira, that recently came to light. It is clearly by Hodges and the ship is the *Resolution*, for the name can be seen on the stern (pl. 120). We need not doubt that Hodges drew it in Cook's cabin. He would never have been permitted off the ship to draw in an open boat or on the quay in defiance of the Governor's orders. Fort Pico is shown clearly to the left of the drawing. It is likely, therefore, that the ship was added later. Cook was well aware of the potential value of such drawings for attacks launched from the sea. On the *Endeavour* he had employed Alexander Buchan, as we have seen, to make detailed drawings of the fortifications of Rio whilst they were in the harbour.

There is good reason to believe that Hodges not only drew but painted the harbour of Funchal directly from the great cabin. In a letter that Cook sent to the Secretary of the Admiralty from the Cape of Good Hope on 18 November 1772, he says that he has left at the Cape to be sent on to England, 'One large painting of this place one Small one of part of Funchall and One of port praya all in Oyl Colours and some others in Water Colours of little Note.'[17] That the paintings were safely received is indicated by the fact that, as already indicated, paintings by Hodges, seven in all, were exhibited at the Free Society of Artists Exhibition of 1774, more than a year before the *Resolution* returned. Three of these correspond closely in their titles with Cook's descriptions: 'A View of the Cape of Good Hope taken on the spot from on board the Resolution. Capt. Cooke' (*sic*) (no. 342); 'A view of Fonchial in the island of Medeira' (no. 384); and 'A View of St Jago from the Bay of Porto Praya' (no. 383).

118

121. William Hodges, *View of Funchal*, oil on canvas, 36.9 × 48.9 cm., 1772, private collection, England.

The first is without doubt the large painting now in the National Maritime Museum (pl. 122); the last painting has not been identified. The Funchal painting is now in an English private collection. It was for many years attributed to Wilson but identified as a Hodges by W. G. Constable (pl. 121).[18] It does not include the *Resolution*, is not based on Hodges's Madeira drawing and may indeed have preceded it. The drawing possesses some of the features of a *capriccio* so far as the position of some buildings is concerned. Hodges, it must be stressed, even while on the voyage never regarded himself simply as a topographical artist. He was always prepared to select and combine. The Admiralty itself required him to 'give a more perfect idea . . . than can be formed from written descriptions only', and there were various ways in which 'a more perfect idea' could be interpreted by a young artist ambitious to advance in his profession. Even if Hodges had not attended some of Reynolds's early Royal Academy Discourses, he must have read summaries of them in the *Gentleman's Magazine* and elsewhere. Yet in the painting of Funchal it is the topographical view that prevails. The sharp precision of the tones suggests that Hodges was here painting with his eye on the object in the manner he had already put into use in training the young midshipmen to paint coastal views of Porto Santo as the *Resolution* approached Madeira.

At Cape Town the *Resolution* remained just on three weeks. Here Hodges painted the large view of Cape Town (pl. 122). This, too, despite its size, must have been painted in the great cabin. Any foreigners drawing or painting around a port were regarded as a security risk. In 1776, for example, Thomas Jones was not brave enough to make drawings in Lyons: 'Was it not for dread of the French police I should have, with great pleasure made several Studies.'[19]

In his Cape Town painting, pressure upon Hodges to develop a nascent *plein-air* vision increases. It was a first requirement of the voyage that it should return

119

122. William Hodges, *View of the Cape of Good Hope, taken on the spot, from on board the Resolution*, oil on canvas, 96.5 × 125.7 cm., 1772, National Maritime Museum, London.

with accurate records. Hodges not only sought to record the appearance of the town as he saw it through the cabin windows, but also provided a faithful portrayal of the turbulent condition of the sky caused by the continuous gusts and squalls that swept across Table Mountain during the three weeks that the *Resolution* was anchored in the harbour—conditions described in great detail by Hodges's close friend on the voyage, Wales.[20]

Nevertheless, paintings like *Funchall, Madeira* and the *Cape of Good Hope* are transitional pieces. They combine traditional methods deriving from Venetian *vedute* painting—such as the building up of a toned, topographical composition—with that freshness of touch we expect from the direct, on-the-spot observations of *plein-air* sketching. Hodges was combining traditional and *alla prima* methods, having the advantages of a mobile studio that provided a secure window upon what were new and often strange scenes.

He clung to traditional methods whenever these were the most convenient. Thus, when some time later the *Resolution* came up from three months' navigating Antarctic seas and took shelter in Dusky Bay, New Zealand, Hodges made drawings during his excursions and developed paintings from them in the great cabin as one might in a studio. On 12 April 1773 Cook recorded in his journal:

> Being a fine afternoon I took Mr Hodges to a large Cascade which falls down a high mountain on the South side of the Bay about a League higher up than the Cove where we anchord. He took a drawing of it on Paper and afterwards painted it in oyle Colours which exhibits at one view a better discription than I can give.[21]

No drawing has survived from this occasion. But a painting in the National Maritime Museum (pl. 123) may possibly be the oil painting he executed at Dusky Bay in the great cabin of the *Resolution*. Its dreamy evocation of the romantic scenery of the Bay anticipates in several ways the mood of early romantic painting and poetry, of Turner, Wordsworth and Shelley. From such

120

drawings and paintings made at Dusky Bay he developed the large *Cascade Cove, Dusky Bay* (pl. 124) on his return to England. If the imagery and mood of most of the Dusky Bay paintings look forward to the nineteenth century, the technical

123. William Hodges, *Waterfall in Dusky Bay, New Zealand with a Maori canoe*, oil on panel, 27.2 × 35.5 cm., 1772 or *c.*1776, National Maritime Museum, London.

124. William Hodges, *Cascade Cove, Dusky Bay, New Zealand*, oil on canvas, 134.6 × 191.1 cm., 1775, National Maritime Museum, London.

125. William Hodges,
*View in Pickersgill Harbour,
Dusky Bay, New Zealand,*
oil on canvas, 65.4 ×
73.1 cm., 1773, National
Maritime Museum,
London.

procedures are traditional enough: first the drawing, then the oil sketch, followed by the developed painting.

Yet he already seems to have been experimenting with prepared grounds and finishes *en plein air*. It was at Dusky Bay that he completed one of his most brilliant paintings, his *View in Pickersgill Harbour* (pl. 125). It indicates that he was beginning to realise the immediacy and freshness made possible by *plein-air* methods. The painting forms a link between the essentially tonal paintings completed at Madeira and the Cape and the colourism of his Tahitian studies. On this occasion, Hodges seems to have painted not from the great cabin but lodged within the confined space of a starboard quarter-gallery. This provided him with a sharply foreshortened view along the gunwhale of the ship as it stood inshore close enough for a large overhanging tree to be used as a gangway. Hodges is unlikely to have begun the painting before 28 March 1773, because the light breaking through the trees was the result of William Wales's heavy work with a team who cut down the primeval forest between 28 March and 2 April in order to erect his astronomer's tent. The tent itself, which is depicted in the painting, was not set up until the latter date. Hodges and Wales had become very close friends on the voyage and it is appealing to think that, while his older and more experienced friend was clearing the ground, the young painter began his painting as a record of the event.

Although we do not know for certain when Hodges began the painting, there is some evidence that he finished it on 11 April 1773, for that was the first sunny day since they arrived. Or, to put it in Cook's words:

> the Morning was clear and Serene which afforded an oppertuntiy for us to dry our linnen a thing very much wanting, not having had fair weather enough for that purpose sence we put into this Bay'.[22]

The brio with which Hodges has painted the clothes hanging out to dry, the sailor lad bringing back his catch, the vivid sparkle of light in the tree foliage, the yardarms and cordage of the ship, all strongly suggest that Hodges has here painted *en plein air* upon a traditionally prepared ground, in a successful attempt to capture the mood of a felicitous day, one of the first they had all experienced on a long arduous voyage.

However, it was in Tahiti that he began to depend less and less upon dark toned grounds–except when confronted with cliffs and promontories in deep coloured shadow. It is upon a series of small paintings executed there that his claim to being a pioneer of English *plein-air* painting must largely rest.

The first is a painting that has long been known as a 'View Taken in the Bay of Oaitepeha (Vaitipeha), Tahiti', but that, as Dr Steube has pointed out, is a *View of Point Venus and Matavai Bay, looking east* (pl. 126).[23] No preliminary drawings for this painting have been found and the freshness and directness of the work lead

126. William Hodges, *View of Point Venus and Matavai Bay, looking east*, oil on canvas, 34.3 × 51.4 cm., 1773, National Maritime Museum, London.

127. William Hodges, *View of Fare Harbour, Huahine*, oil on canvas, 34.3 × 51.5 cm., 1773, National Maritime Museum, London.

128. William Hodges, *View of the part of the Island of Ulietea* (Raiatea), oil on canvas, 33 × 48.9 cm., 1773, National Maritime Museum, London.

129. William Hodges, *View of the Islands of Otaha and Bola Bola* [Tahaa and Pora Pora] *with part of the Island of Ulietea* (Raiatea), oil on canvas, 33 × 48.9 cm., 1773, National Maritime Museum, London.

one to doubt whether any were ever made. It was most probably painted directly from the great cabin during the first visit to Matavai Bay between 26 August and 1 September 1773. Painting into the eye of the light, Hodges has produced a fine effect of tropical sunlight as it silhouettes hills and palm trees against a rose-pink sky. Sun-rays break through a cloud of smoky magenta blue to reflect the warm colours of the sky in the still water of the bay. A blue mist covers the tops of the hills. The whole object of the study, it would seem, has been to capture a colour effect of tropical light at sunrise.

The second painting, *View of Fare Harbour, Huahine* (pl. 127), also appears to have been painted from the great cabin when the *Resolution* was anchored at Fare between 2 and 7 September 1773. The palette employed is similar to the one used for the previous study but the contrast between light and dark tones is stronger. It is probably a study of a later part of the morning, the light harsher and deep shadows still clinging to the hills. Hodges's pictorial strategy has been to key his dark tones down to the very deep green-blue shadows of the promontory to provide a firm contrast against which to paint the fine nuances of colour in the sunlit areas.

The third painting is a *View of part of the Island of Ulietea* (Raiatea) (pl. 128). It was probably painted from the great cabin as the *Resolution* lay at anchor in Haamanino Harbour between 8 and 17 September 1773, looking towards the north-east. This, too, seems to be an effect of early morning, the pale blues and cool ochres painted over a dark ground.

The fourth and last of the group is the *View of the Islands of Otaha and Bola Bola* [Tahaa and Pora Pora] *with part of the Island of Ulietea* (Raiatea) (pl. 129). It was

124

probably painted in Haamanino Harbour, and judging from the technique and colours used probably painted about the same time as the *View of part of the Island of Ulieta*.

Although there are substantial grounds for believing that these four paintings were completed in the Society Islands during late August and mid-September 1773, the problem of distinguishing Hodges's voyage paintings from those he completed later in London is a difficult one. If we turn to the small painting *View from Point Venus, Island of Otaheite* (pls 66 and 130) there is, as Dr Steube has observed, 'the *plein-air* feeling of the sketch',[24] and this might lead us to conclude at a first glance that it was executed in Tahiti. But the fact that it is painted upon a panel of the same size (24.1 × 47 cm) as some that were, we may say confidently, painted in London after the *Resolution*'s return as illustrations to be engraved for the official account of the voyage, must give us pause. The painting certainly does provide a splendid impression of sunlight filtered through clouds on a dull overcast day, but the high quality of the observation recorded in the small panel is, on the evidence before us, more likely to be the product of a vivid perception, modulated and harmonised by memory.

But if this is indeed so, then we are confronted with a fusion of the freshness and directness developed by a *plein-air* technique with a *plein-air* vision developed away from the motif. This raises the whole question of the character of Hodges's post-voyage paintings. There are, of course, several large paintings that take the Society Islands for their subject and that were painted in London by Hodges either for the Admiralty or on his own account, which are clearly distinguishable from his voyage paintings by the elaboration of their foreground staffage and their late-baroque amplitude of gesture. Such a painting is the well-known *Resolution and Adventure in Matavai Bay* (pl. 131), which certainly recaptures faithfully much of the colour Hodges observed in the tropics but not the freshness

130. Detail of pl. 66.

131. William Hodges, *The Resolution and Adventure in Matavai Bay*, oil on canvas, 137.1 × 193 cm., 1776, National Maritime Museum, London.

132. William Hodges, *View of Fare Harbour*, oil on canvas, 30.1 × 45.7 cm., *c.*1775, private collection, England.

133. William Hodges, *View of part of Fare Harbour*, oil on canvas, 45.7 × 61.5 cm., *c.*1775, National Maritime Museum, London.

and spontaneity of his *plein-air* work, though there is spirit enough in the handling of the paint.

There is also a group of smaller paintings in a private collection that seem to be oil sketches painted in London as studies for larger paintings. These preserve the breadth if not always the vivacity of his voyage paintings. With such paintings before him, Hodges seems to have been able to recapture much of the spirit of his on-site *plein-air* work.

Let us return again to his *plein-air* study of Fare Harbour (pl. 127). From it Hodges seems to have developed a small oil sketch (pl. 132) from which he in

128

134. William Hodges, *Province of Oparee* (Pare), oil on panel, 76.2 × 123.2 cm., *c*.1775, National Maritime Museum, London.

135. William Hodges, *Monuments of Easter Island*, oil on panel, 77.5 × 121.9 cm., *c*.1775, National Maritime Museum, London.

turn painted the *View of part of Fare Harbour*, in the National Maritime Museum (pl. 133). In this painting the viewpoint is from the shore and the canvas is larger than the four *plein-air* sketches described above. I don't think Hodges painted on-shore oil sketches during the voyage if for no other reason than that his small store of oil pigments was most precious to him and the islanders were known to be great thieves. Furthermore, the detail and precision with which the habitations and canoes have been painted suggest that this is not a study made on location or at one sitting but one developed from drawings now lost or, as is more likely, from the paintings discussed above. Yet the spirit and sense of immediacy of the painting give the impression of an artist in direct contact with his subject. Hodges has not softened his contrasts but has given the impression of a sunny tropical day. In such paintings he combines his vivid visual memories with the technical skills of Venetian 'di tocco' painting, inherited through Wilson and Canaletto.

In other words, Hodges achieves in such paintings precisely what Philip

129

136. William Hodges, *View of Resolution Harbour, Vaitahu Bay, Marquesas,* oil on canvas, 47.6 × 62.9 cm., 1774, National Maritime Museum, London.

Conisbee claims was not achieved prior to the generation of Constable and Corot, 'a fusion of the landscape sketch and the finished work, where as far as possible and increasingly so, the pure sensation of the first response to nature could be carried over into a grander scale'.[25]

Relevant to this question are two large paintings, *Province of Oparee* (Pare), Tahiti and the *Monuments of Easter Island,* both in the National Maritime Museum (pls 134, 135). They are of approximately the same size (77.5 × 121.9 and 76.2 × 123.2 cm) and both on panel–quite big panels–and one is patched-up. They present real problems, for they possess the breadth and directness of the voyage work but have been conceived on a scale of Hodges's post-voyage work. The Easter Island painting could not possibly have been painted on the island, for the ship was there only three days and on two of them Hodges joined extensive excursions when he made drawings, most of which have disappeared. Since both paintings are of the same size and possess the same kind of paint quality, surface and liquidity, it seems reasonable to conclude that they were conceived as pendants. Both lack the heavy tonality and the repoussoir staffage of Hodges's post-voyage paintings. A further complication is that his paint stocks were exhausted well before the end of the voyage. As a supernumerary who was provided with victuals only, until Cook managed to sign him up as a seaman, we may assume that he was required to provide his own painting materials for the voyage. The last painting executed on the voyage seems to have been the *View of Resolution Harbour, Vaitahu Bay* in the Marquesas (pl. 136). Its thick, viscid drag of paint suggests that Hodges was coming near the end of his stock. After that, for fifteen months, he was reduced to drawing in crayon, pencil for wash–and a good deal of indian-ink work.

The only suggestion that I can offer concerning the Pare and Easter Island

130

paintings is that Hodges was able to acquire some pigments and two big panels at Cape Town on the voyage back (the panels, of course, may be ship's timber) and painted the pictures either at the Cape or during the voyage home. If this is so, or even if they are post-voyage paintings (possible but unlikely), they support the claim that Hodges was seeking 'to carry over the pure sensation of the first response to nature to a grander scale'.

There is evidence that he was aware of this. On the second visit to Tahiti, Hodges, Cook tells us, made drawings of the Tahitian war fleet drawn up for its projected attack on the neighbouring island of Moorea. Only two of the drawings have survived; one of which, now in the Mitchell Library, Sydney, is one of his finest (pl. 137).

It was from such drawings that Hodges painted a small picture (pl. 138) on his return which was engraved as an illustration for the official account of the voyage. The brilliant sparkle of the brushwork in the painting, the flash of the highlights, indicate that Hodges was seeking to recapture the colour and light of the original occasion. When, however, he turned to his largest known painting, the *War boats of the Island of Otaheite* (pl. 139), the brilliance and sparkle have gone. Hodges is now seeking epic grandeur; a painting that would provide visual evidence of those Homeric analogies that Johann Reinhold Forster and his son George had already developed in their accounts of the voyage.[26]

Yet even in this painting Hodges's experience of the light of the Pacific and the *plein-air* sketches that he executed in response to it had wrought a great change in his technique since the time he was a pupil of Richard Wilson. The painting was exhibited in the Academy of 1777 and the critic of the *London Packet or New Lloyd's Evening Post* commented:

> Mr Hodges, who in last year's Exhibition had several views of bays etc about the Island of Otaheite, had this year a large piece exhibiting the war boats of that Island ... The public are indebted to this artist for giving some idea of scenes which before they knew little of. It is surprising however, that a man of Mr Hodges's genius should adopt such a ragged mode of colouring; his pictures all appear as if they were unfinished, and as if the colours were laid on the canvas with a skewer.[27]

Such was the kind of criticism, as we all know, that artists who attempted to preserve the immediacy of the *plein-air* sketch in large-scale finished paintings had to face in the late nineteenth century. In 1777 men of genius were not expected to behave in that way; the whole weight of classical idealism opposed them.

Hodges was no hero. He took the hint. When he exhibited an equally large painting, *A View in the Island of New Caledonia in the South*, in the Royal Academy the following year, he worked the surface in a thin, smooth style in marked contrast to the big painting of the previous year (pl. 67). And though he painted many interesting paintings in later years in India and elsewhere, never again did he attempt the proto-*plein-air*-ism that emerged in the best of his Pacific paintings.

It was not only his painting technique but also his exotic imagery that was far in advance of its time. Truth to nature was as much a maxim for him as it was for his master Wilson,[28] but like Wilson, like any professional landscape painter aspiring to academic acceptance, he had to find images and themes that were agreeable and comprehensible to the cultivated taste of the time. Wilson had found, in Italy, a way. 'When he was not physically there, the cultured Englishman cherished a dream of Italy as a pastoral paradise of sunshine and shepherds:

137. William Hodges,
The Otaheite fleet at Appany
[Pare] *Bay*, pen and wash,
37 × 54.5 cm., 1774,
Mitchell Library, Sydney
(PXD 11 N 14).

it was the patrician's spiritual homeland, his mental refuge from the troubled world around him. What Wilson's public demanded above all was that he make this a believable fantasy, by tying it down to recognisable sites.'[29]

Hodges aspired to the production of an alternative dream – of Tahiti as a tropical paradise of sunshine and sensuous, liberated women – even more beautiful, more tempting than Italy. The public already knew about it from reading John Hawkesworth, a national best-seller. But it was a thorny theme to handle. Tahiti certainly was not the cultured Englishman's spiritual homeland; it hinted, rather, at the licentious opinions of that French radical Rousseau. Tahiti was a centre of pagan rites not of the Christian religion. So Hodges tempered his theme: he introduced the image of a pagan god (*tii*) towering over his bathing girls, and behind them an elevated platform (*tupapau*) with a shrouded corpse. These motifs of death and transience might possibly lull the anxieties aroused by such exotica (pl. 140).

But his Tahitian paintings did not meet with approval. In order to exist, Hodges was obliged to return to painting local scenery, as he had done before he

138. William Hodges,
Review of the war galleys of Tahiti, oil on panel, 24.1 × 47 cm., 1776, National Maritime Museum, London.

embarked with Cook. When he was offered the opportunity to paint in India, he took it and left. It would be left to John Webber to cultivate, more cautiously and in a more promising situation, the small but growing English market for Pacific exotica.

I must now return for a moment to Thomas Jones. There is quite a possibility that Hodges's work and advice may have encouraged him to continue experimenting with *plein-air* methods during his Italian tour; that they were not the result of a 'habit he had stumbled into' as Wollheim suggests. As we noted,

139. William Hodges, *War boats of the Island of Otaheite*, oil on canvas, 177.8 × 301 cm., 1777, National Maritime Museum, London.

140. William Hodges, *Tahiti Revisited*, oil on canvas, 97.7 × 138.4 cm., 1776, National Maritime Museum, London.

three of Hodges's voyage paintings were exhibited in the Free Society of Artists' exhibition of 1774. Cook had sent them back by a returning vessel from the Cape. Jones would certainly have seen them, for he exhibited six of his own paintings in the same exhibition. For an artist who proved to be so sensitive to the rendering of surface and texture within the broad guidelines of naturalism, we cannot doubt that Jones would have responded to the highly innovative qualities of Hodges's Cape of Good Hope painting, with its magnificently direct evocation of the weather conditions prevailing at the time at the Cape. The brilliance with which the town, the fort and the *Adventure* riding at anchor had been painted under conditions of direct sunlight could not have escaped him. At any rate, after the *Resolution* returned in July 1775 he made a point of going to see Hodges. On 22 August he noted in his *Memoirs*: 'Called on my old fellow Pupil *Hodges*, who has just returned from a Voyage to the South Seas with Captain Cooke [*sic*]'.[30] We need not doubt that on that occasion Hodges would have shown him some of the *plein-air* studies of tropical light he had painted in Tahiti. He would also have seen the Tahitian and Dusky Bay paintings that Hodges exhibited at the Royal Academy exhibition of 1776, prior to Jones's own departure for Italy in the October of that year. Indeed, Jones might have been tempted to embark with Cook as his professional artist on the last voyage. We know that he was approached by James (Athenian) Stuart in the name of the Dilettanti Society when Cook was seeking an artist to accompany him. It was the thought of their son going on such a perilous adventure that enabled Jones's parents to overcome their initial aversion to his undertaking a tour of Italy.[31]

It was in Italy, of course, that Jones painted those studies of buildingscapes, as Wollheim aptly calls them, that have finally made him, after two hundred years, so famous. He painted most of the time by looking out of the windows of his temporary studios. It was not in a literal sense *plein-air* painting. He was repeating precisely Hodges's method of painting from the great-cabin window of the *Resolution*. Both used the security and seclusion of a room from which to paint a view directly before them. It was not so much painting *en plein air* as painting *de la fenêtre*, a significant transitional method, useful for obvious reasons, at a time when even European audiences had not yet become accustomed to seeing their artists' painting *in oils* in the open air. It was a method that made it possible for Jones to develop a new sensitivity for *alla prima* painting and that Hodges exploited in the service of the 'experimental gentlemen' of science.

6 COLERIDGE'S *ANCIENT MARINER* AND COOK'S SECOND VOYAGE

> 'I sometimes wonder whether, germinally, the Ancient Mariner is
> not one of his Christ's Hospital poems.'
>
> Edmund Blunden, 1934.

WHILE STUDYING THE PREVAILING IDEAS whereby Europeans interpreted the peoples and landscapes of the South Pacific during the late eighteenth and early nineteenth centuries,[1] I came upon a clue that led me to suspect that it might be possible to say something new concerning the genesis of *The Rime of the Ancient Mariner*, despite all that Livingstone Lowes has already said.[2] I noted that William Wales, the astronomer and meteorologist on the *Resolution*, Cook's own ship on his second voyage, taught mathematics at Christ's Hospital when Coleridge was there. This led me to Wales's manuscript journal kept on the voyage, a previously unknown source for the study of Coleridge, which is now located in the Mitchell Library, Sydney.[3]

All who have felt the haunting and dreamlike power of the poem know well enough that *The Ancient Mariner* is not a room to be entered by means of one key; and the intention here is not to offer any new explanation for the profound moral and spiritual experience that Coleridge, on this occasion at least, was able to resolve into adequate poetic form; it is confined to an examination of material that throws new light upon the naturalistic elements that frame this allegory of the soul in its wanderings. However, Wales's journal also makes it possible to trace more completely than hitherto the growth of the poem in the poet's mind and makes it necessary for us to re-examine Livingstone Lowes's explanation of the way in which Coleridge's memory and imagination assembled the material that went to the making of the poem.

A study of the journal suggests firstly, that the course of the Ancient Mariner's voyage, as it is presented in the first two parts of the poem, was influenced to a large extent by Coleridge's recollections of accounts of Cook's second voyage either as they were told to him by Wales, or read in books available at Christ's Hospital; secondly, that a good deal of the imagery of the poem was germinating in the poet's mind from the time he was at school; and thirdly, that the precision and clarity of Coleridge's atmospheric imagery derived much from the precision and clarity of Wales's astronomical and meteorological observations.

Wales (pl. 141) was born in 1734, probably in Yorkshire, of parents in humble circumstances[4] and first came to notice as a contributor to the *Ladies Magazine*, which has been described as 'that very useful little journal which has formed most of our eminent mathematicians'.[5] His work was sufficiently well thought of by 1769 for the Royal Society to send him to Hudson's Bay to observe the transit of Venus while Cook was at Tahiti. On his return, Wales published his results in the *Philosophical Transactions*,[6] and in 1772 he joined Cook on the *Resolution*. On his return in 1775, the Board of Longitude asked him to prepare his observations for

141. John Russell,
William Wales,
pastel, oval 38 cm.
wide, 1794, in the
possession of H.O.
Stafford Cooke,
Esq.

publication, and in the same year he was appointed master of the Mathematical School at Christ's Hospital. In November 1776, he was elected a Fellow of the Royal Society. From the time of his appointment to Christ's Hospital in 1775 until his death in 1798 he edited and published a considerable amount of material relating mainly to mathematics and navigation.[7] Such work did not, however, prevent him from becoming a splendid teacher. His grandson, William Trollope, gives an excellent account of him as a teacher in his *History of Christ's Hospital*, published in 1834:

> When Mr. William Wales was elected to the mastership in 1775, he found the school [i.e. the Mathematical School] in the most desperate state of anarchy and confusion; the boys were a terror to the whole community; and it required the most determined perseverance of that able mathematician, and strict disciplinarian, to establish authority over his new pupils. Under his judicious and effective care, however, the school attained to that high reputation, in which it has since been effectually upheld. The vices and immoralities, which had taken deep root in this branch of the establishment, were speedily eradicated; the duties of the school rigidly enforced; and sixteen was the age, beyond which he seldom allowed a boy's continuance at the school.
>
> Mr. Wales, was, indeed, precisely the man for the station, which he was called upon to fulfil. A practical sailor himself, and the co-navigator of Captain Cook, he knew the requisite qualifications of a seaman; and his whole aim was to fit his boys for the profession in which they were destined to embark. At the commencement of his labours he had to battle it hard for the mastery; and severity for a time was the order of the day. He was not long, however, in

136

subduing the spirit of insubordination; and his whole soul was thenceforward engaged in the improvement of those committed to his charge. Strict and punctual in his discipline, he was frank and open in his temperament; and he was more loved for the goodness of his heart than feared for the heaviness of his hand. There was a fund of genuine humour about him, and a joyous expression of countenance, which took at once a strong hold upon the affection; and his ready wit, expressed in a pleasing provincial dialect, frequently elicited the hearty mirth of his juvenile auditors. Many are the living witnesses to the success of his instructions; while it will be readily acknowledged, that by his energies the Royal Mathematical School of Christ's Hospital was first seen to realize the objects of its foundation, and gave the promise of becoming one of the first naval seminaries in the world. He died on 29th December, 1798; and lies buried in the south cloister of the Hospital.[8]

Trollope's description of Wales echoes in part an earlier one given by Charles Lamb in *Recollections of Christ's Hospital*. Writing of the King's Boys, as the pupils of the Mathematical School were known, Lamb observes that

they were the terror of all the other boys; bred up under that hardy sailor as well as excellent mathematician, and co-navigator of Captain Cook, William Wales. All his systems were adapted to fit them for the rough element they were destined to encounter ... To make his boys hardy, and to give them early sailor habits, seemed to be his only aim ... There was in William Wales a perpetual fund of humour, a constant glee about him, heightened by an inveterate provincialism of North country-dialect, absolutely took away the sting from his severities.[9]

How did Wales establish discipline and gain the affection of the riotous King's Boys? A successful teacher would probably hazard the guess that he told the boys tales of the days when he travelled with Cook. But there is no need to speculate on the point, for Leigh Hunt in his *Autobiography* writes:

among those masters [i.e., at the school] in my time, the mathematics master was William Wales, a man well-known for his science, who had been round the world with Cook, for which we highly venerated him. He was a good man, of plain simple manners, with a heavy large person and benign countenance. When he was at Otaheite, the natives played him a trick while bathing and stole his small-clothes; which we used to think a liberty scarcely credible.[10]

Doubtless Wales told of other incidents that occurred on the voyage, and there was one pupil at the school who, possessing a prodigious memory, was not likely to forget them. Coleridge joined the school in August 1782, at the age of ten. Wales had been there for seven years, was forty-eight and was, at the time, assisting Canon Douglas to edit the official account of Cook's third voyage. Coleridge remained at Christ's Hospital for nine years and was taught mathematics by Wales when he was a member of the Upper Grammar School between the ages of fifteen and nineteen. On the evidence of Trollope's *History of Christ's Hospital*, it seems unlikely that Coleridge was taught mathematics as a member of the Lower Grammar School between the ages of ten and fifteen. Even so, the Grammar and Mathematical Schools were housed under the same roof,[11] and as Coleridge remained at the school during many of the vacations, it is likely that he saw a good deal of Wales from the beginning. Even when Coleridge went up to

Jesus College, Cambridge, in 1791, he retained connexions with the school. There was a circle of former Christ's Hospital pupils at Cambridge with whom he associated. It was some Grecians[12] who first informed Coleridge's friend Tuckett of Coleridge's enlistment in the 15th Light Dragoons. One of the reasons given by the Almoners of Christ's Hospital when they cancelled Coleridge's scholarship in April 1795 was that his example 'may be highly detrimental to the welfare of the Youth of this House'.[13] The decision is not altogether surprising. During the previous September he had lodged at the Angel Inn close to Christ's Hospital, and spent most of his days with the Grecians, to whom he talked of his scheme of pantisocracy with considerable success.[14] Thus, for nine years of his life Coleridge was in close contact with Wales, and occasional contact with him was quite likely during a further four years, that is until 1795. It is not unreasonable to suppose that during those thirteen years Wales told Coleridge of many of his experiences when he sailed with Cook.

Wales's personality as drawn for us by Lamb, Hunt and Trollope suggests that he would enjoy telling a good story. Furthermore, he gave some thought to the question of travellers' tales himself. As early as 10 May 1774, he had reflected upon the plight of the honest *raconteur* when faced with an unbelieving audience:

> I have always thought the situation of a Traveller singularly hard. If he tells nothing that is uncommon he must be a stupid fellow to have gone so far, and brought home so little; and if he does, why–it is hum–aya–a tap of the Chin;–and–, He's a Traveller.[15]

That was in Tahiti. The very next year Wales, as master of the Mathematical School, was provided with a perfect audience. Coleridge scholars have not paid much attention to the fact that Christ's Hospital was also a naval seminary. Even Edmund Blunden, the only writer to associate the *Ancient Mariner* with the school, does not make anything of this point:

> I sometimes wonder whether, germinally, the Ancient Mariner is not one of his Christ's Hospital poems. I mean, partly that the superstitions and tales of wonder current among the Blues gave encouragement to the tendency of his own faculty; partly that he became conscious of certain mighty and ancient images of beauty and marvel; and also that he had to travel through a long period of haunted solitariness.[16]

Blunden's comment will, however, serve to remind us that whatever Coleridge did not hear about Cook's second voyage from Wales himself, he may well have heard at second- or third-hand as tales were passed through the school from one boy to another. There was plenty of time for such stories to spread as Wales had been at the school for seven years before Coleridge arrived. More than one writer has reflected upon the effect of the strange tales that passed from boy to boy in the dormitories and cloisters of the school. Gordon Hake, who was a pupil there in the early years of the nineteenth century, writes:

> After we reached our beds at night the boys were wont to coze in literary cliques round some favourite tale-teller, who would recite marvellous stories of knights and ladies, with much about genii, fairies and witches. Though I have never heard anything to that effect, I have always thought that Coleridge must have lent himself to such delights for the pleasure of others, and that Christabel was an outcome of these romantic adventures.[17]

Gordon Hake's evidence can be backed by Charles Lamb's account of the character of the Blue-coat boy:

> This religious character in him is not always untinged with superstition. That is not wonderful, when we consider the thousand tales and traditions which must circulate with undisturbed credulity, amongst so many boys, that have so few checks to their belief from any intercourse with the world at large; upon whom their equals in age must work so much, their elders so little. With this leaning towards an over-belief in matters of religion . . . may be classed a turn for romance above most other boys. This is to be traced in the same manner to their excesses of society with each other, and defect of mingling with the world. Hence the peculiar avidity with which such books as the Arabian Nights Entertainments, and others of a still wilder cast, are, or at least were in my time, sought for by the boys. I remember when some half-dozen of them set off from school, without map, card or compass, on a serious expedition to find *Phillip Quarll's Island.*[18]

It may be assumed, then, that whatever tales of wonder William Wales chose to tell concerning Cook's second voyage would circulate through the school. There were, however, many occasions, before Coleridge was fifteen, when he might have heard the mathematics master himself speak of the wonders and adventures to be met with in seafaring life. Coleridge tells us, in one of his letters to Thomas Poole, how,

> Two or three times a year the mathematics master beats up recruits for the King's Boys, as they are called, and all who like the navy are drafted into mathematical and drawings schools, where they continue till sixteen or seventeen and go out as midshipmen and schoolmasters in the navy.[19]

Now since Wales had to train his boys and have them out of the school by the age of sixteen, such recruiting forays would be obviously directed at the younger boys in the other schools, such as the Lower Grammar School. Wales had never been in a naval battle, but he was a specialist on nautical mirabilia particularly in high latitudes, his naval career having been confined to scientific expeditions; and of his own experience, presumably, he would speak in his recruiting forays.

There was, of course, a close connexion between mathematics and navigation in the eighteenth century, and the mathematics that Wales taught the King's Boys had a strongly nautical flavour. Wales himself revised the mathematics syllabus when he came to the school, and it was virtually the same syllabus that Trollope, as he tells us, recorded in his history of the school in 1834. Here is a typical item drawn from it:

> The use of instruments proper for observing the altitudes, azimuths, and angular distances of the sun, moon, and stars; such as the quadrant, and amplitude of azimuth compass: with the use of the observations in finding the variation of the compass, the latitude a ship is in, as well as from the meridional altitudes of the sun, moon and stars, as by means of two altitudes of the sun, and the time which elapses between the observation; also in finding the longitude of the ship by a time keeper and by the observed distances of the moon from the sun or a fixed star.[20]

Even when it is conceded that the mathematics course provided by Wales for the Upper Grammar School might not have been identical with that which he provided for the Mathematical School, having regard for the different future vocations of the pupils concerned, the fact remains that any mathematics taught by Wales would be bound to possess a strongly nautical bias. He taught the Grecians one afternoon a week, the course covering four years. It is likely that, even if he provided separate courses for Mathemats[21] and Grecians, there would be much of nautical interest common to both courses, and—in light of the evidence contained in Wales's journal, to be discussed later—it is probable that the weekly afternoon mathematics lesson with the Grecians was punctuated from time to time by the most vivid descriptions of waterspouts, phosphorescent seas and the perils of navigating the polar ice.

Having regard for Wales's position as mathematics master at Christ's Hospital, his position as Secretary to the Board of Longitude and the amount of material he published, it is reasonable to assume that he assembled a good, up-to-date library at Christ's Hospital in his own fields of navigation, astronomy, meteorology and travel. All that he wrote gives the impression of wide reading in these fields. A Christ's Hospital minute of 1786 reveals his complaining to the Governors that several of the books and charts given to the King's Boys at their going out were useless 'on account of the great improvements in the practice of navigation'.[22] Now there was, according to Trollope, a special mathematical library at Christ's Hospital which the context suggests may well have been formed by Wales himself and used by the boys:

> In the mathematical school there is also a library, considerably dilapidated indeed, but well worthy of preservation; and devoutly is it to be hoped, that it may not, for want of due attention, meet the same fate as the valuable astronomical apparatus, with which the observatory over the old school was furnished. Under the inspection and care of Mr. Wales, not only the more common instruments were there fixed for the use of the boys; but he accustomed them to make the most nice and delicate observations; and they once assisted in observing the transit of Venus over the sun's disc.[23]

If any boy was likely to make use of such a library it was Coleridge, for Coleridge devoured books. When he was given a free ticket in 1785 to the circulating library in Cheapside, he started at the beginning of the catalogue and worked through until he had read all the books in the library. It would be interesting to reconstruct the library in the Mathematical School at Christ's Hospital which Trollope describes, for it is noteworthy that most of the books that Livingstone Lowes has shown Coleridge to have consulted between the years 1795 and 1798 are just the kind of books Wales would be likely to place in the mathematics library. We can be reasonably certain, for instance, that Wales had his own copies of the *Philosophical Transactions*, since he was a member of the Royal Society and his own papers had been published therein. He would certainly have had the voyages of Byron, Wallis, Carteret and Cook, George Forster's *Voyage round the World*,[24] John Reinhold Forster's *Observations made during a Voyage round the World*, and probably held such books as Joseph Priestley's *History and Present State of Discoveries Relating to Vision, Light and Colours*, since his own writings show an intense interest in all forms of meteorological phenomena, and David Crantz's *History of Greenland*, which he cites in his own writings.[25] Livingstone Lowes, in *The Road to Xanadu*, has shown how Coleridge's reading of the *Philosophical Transactions*, Cook, Forster and Crantz played an important part in the genesis of *The Ancient Mariner*.

140

It is reasonable to suppose, then, that Wales, by talking to his pupils, by means of stories passed on by other boys, or by means of the library in the Mathematical School, was able to bring to Coleridge's knowledge many incidents of Cook's second voyage. This is rendered even more likely when we realise that Coleridge had the deepest respect for his mathematics teacher and remembered him long after Wales's death. This is revealed in one of Coleridge's essays in *The Friend*. To appreciate the reference we must be aware that Wales was also a demographer, and his attempt to come to some conclusion as to the population of England was published in 1781, under the title *An Enquiry into the Present State of the Population in England and Wales*. Coleridge, in his essay, is attacking the notion that England's population is decreasing, and writes:

Challenging Dr. Price's argument that the island was in a rapid state of depopulation, that England at the Revolution had been, Heaven's knows how much! more populous: and that in Queen Elizabeth's time or about the Reformation (!!) the number of the inhabitants in England might have been greater than at the Revolution, my old mathematics master, a man of uncommonly clear head, answered this blundering book of the worthy doctor's, and left not a stone unturned of the pompous epitaph in which the effigy of the still living and bustling English prosperity lay interred. And yet so much more suitable was the Doctor's book to the purposes of faction, and to the November mood of (what is called) the public, that Mr. Wales's pamphlet, though a masterpiece of perspicacity as well as perspicuity, was scarcely heard of.[26]

Coleridge also recalled his teacher in another context, one in which he regretted deeply his neglect of mathematics:

what bitter neglect, and in the conscience of such glorious opportunities, both at School under the Janus Mathematician, Wales, the companion of Cook in his circumnavigation, and at Jesus College, under that excellent Mathematical Tutor, Newton, all neglected, with still greater remorse . . .[27]

One can only guess why Coleridge thought of his old maths teacher as Janus-headed. Janus was, of course, the door-keeping god of the Romans; and Coleridge might well have been recalling the famous occasion in 1780, two years before he himself arrived in the school, when Wales single-handedly defended the School by standing at its gates and defying the enraged mob of Gordon rioters that threatened to enter the school and burn it down. It was an incident that made Wales both feared and venerated among the boys. But Janus, of course, possessed two heads, and it is possible that here the poet is referring to the many interests of his old teacher: mathematician, astronomer, meteorologist and demographer, Wales was also interested in poetry. That there was poetry in the man is clear from his journal kept on Cook's voyage. As a young man he, like Coleridge, had written verse, and in 1762 published an 'Ode to William Pitt'. He was well acquainted with Thompson' *Seasons*, for on seeing a remarkable waterfall in Dusky Bay, New Zealand, he was able to quote seventeen lines more or less verbatim from it,[28] and there is a great deal of much human interest in his account of the native peoples he encountered on the *Resolution*'s voyage.

Is Wales's influence discernible in the poetry that Coleridge wrote while still a pupil at Christ's Hospital? In 1791, during his last year at school, Coleridge produced 'A Mathematical Problem', a patently humorous attempt to combine the merits of poetry with the merits of Euclid. The letter, however, which Coleridge sent with the poem to his brother George, is couched in a somewhat more serious vein:

> Dear Brother,
>
> I have often been surprised that Mathematics, the quintessence of Truth, should have found admirers so few and so languid. Frequent consideration and minute scrutiny have at length unravelled the cause; viz. that though Reason is feasted, Imagination is starved; whilst Reason is luxuriating in its proper Paradise, Imagination is wearily travelling on a dreary desert. To assist Reason by the stimulus of the Imagination is the design of the following production.[29]

Reason assisted by the stimulus of the imagination became one of the great achievements of Coleridge's critical scholarship in later years. That he was able to hold the balance between these basic qualities of mind may well have been due in no small measure to the influence of a most able and sympathetic teacher. But there is no better evidence of the influence of William Wales's teaching upon Coleridge than the fact that the poet is said to have read mathematics for three hours a day when he went up to Cambridge.[30] The influence, however, was not confined to mathematics; it appears to have sharpened the poet's interest in scientific inquiry in general.

Three years before he wrote 'A Mathematical Problem', Coleridge had written 'Quae Nocent Docent'. In this poem he laments with the guilty intensity not uncommon to early adolescence his 'ill-past hours'. If only they might return again he would use them to a much better purpose:

> . . . o'er the midnight Lamp I'd love to pore,
> I'd seek with care fair Learning's depths to sound,
> And gather scientific Lore.

In 1789 Coleridge still had three more years at Christ's Hospital in which to put his hours to a better purpose and carry out the resolution implied in the poem, and the obvious place to gather 'scientific lore' at the school would be from the books of the mathematical library, presided over William Wales.

In his capacity as astronomer and meteorologist to the *Resolution*, Wales kept an hourly account of wind and weather throughout the voyage and a detailed astronomical log.[31] The astronomical and meteorological observations were closely interrelated, since weather conditions obviously affected the observation of heavenly bodies. Indeed, the refraction of light from such bodies under conditions of mist, haze and cloud became an absorbing scientific problem for Wales. This is clear from a study of his journal and his published works. While in Hudson's Bay he observed how the ice and land on the horizon appeared to be lifted up as a result of 'the very great refractive power of the air in these parts'.[32] He realised that his calculation of the sun's altitude would be affected by the phenomena, and, consequently, the calculation of 'the latitude of the ship'. Wales mentioned the circumstance, upon his return, to the Astronomer Royal, the Reverend Nevil Maskelyne, who understood immediately how refraction would thus affect the computation of a shop's bearings.[33] Thenceforward, refraction appears to have become one of Wales's main fields of inquiry. Here is a typical description in which Wales's astronomical and meteorological interests are brought to bear upon his observation of the heavens:

This evening I staid upon deck till after midnight, in hopes to have observed the moon's distance from a star; but after trying for near an hour, I was obliged to give up, on account of the twilights, which are amazingly bright in these high latitudes. There is another great inconvenience which attends observation of this kind here, viz. a red haziness round the horizon, to a considerable height, rendering the stars very dim; but at the same time large, something like the nucleus of a comet.[34]

Wales's interest in refraction led him to take a particular interest in such phenomena as the mock-sun and the auroral phenomena in both hemispheres. Of the mock-sun he writes:

I have mentioned the haze which is continually found near the horizon here. This, I apprehend, is the cause why the sun's rising is always preceded by two long streams of red light, one on each side of him, and about 20 degrees distant there from. These rise as the sun rises; and as they grow longer, begin to be inflected towards each other, till they meet directly over the sun, just as he rises, forming there a kind of parhelion, or mock-sun.[35]

Wales had numerous opportunities when he travelled with Cook, as his journal reveals, of observing under the most varied conditions phenomena in which heavenly bodies were partly obscured by mist and cloud, and thus of extending his knowledge of atmospheric refraction. He records, for instance, that, when running along the north-east trade winds, the skies were not quite clear, yet not so cloudy 'but that we could almost always observe the sun's Altitude: other more delicate observations could not indeed be made to advantage as the heavens were almost always covered with a thin grey cloud.'[36] On 6 August 1773 he records: 'a thick haze began to rise in the eastern horizon, which by noon was become so thick, and had spread so far it was with difficulty we got the sun's meridion altitude'.[37] And on 31 December of the same year he records:

Whilst observing at Noon, a shower of snow came from the Westward and passed ahead of the ship during which I marked that a large island of Ice which was considerably within the horizon was entirely hid by it. When it cleared up again the sun was directly over the Island and I observed that it required to have the sun dipped something more than its whole diameter to bring the lower limb to the nearer edge of the Ice Island, which during the shower must have been beyond the visible horizon. Hence may be observed the uncertainty of Altitude observed in Foggy, or what seaman call Hazy weather.[38]

The observation, then, of the sun, moon and stars, under conditions of mist and cloud, rain and snow, at twilight, or in conjunction with the polar lights, raised interesting problems in refraction for Wales.

It is not unreasonable to suppose that he brought much of his interest in refraction to his teaching at Christ's Hospital. We have Trollope's evidence that he accustomed his boys to make 'the most nice and delicate observations', and Leigh Hunt tells us of a boy at the school who studied the weather and the stars and had a reputation for forecasting the weather.[39] One interesting aspect of Wales's teaching at Christ's Hospital appears to have been his capacity to awaken or strengthen in his pupils an awareness of the wonder and beauty of the heavens. This would account for Coleridge's statement in 'Frost at Midnight':

> I was reared
> In the great city, pent 'mid cloisters dim,
> And saw nought lovely but the sky and stars.

When these lines are read in conjunction with Wordsworth's picture of his friend as,

> a liveried schoolboy, in the depths
> Of the huge city, on the leaded roof
> Of that wide edifice, thy school and home,
> Wert used to lie and gaze upon the clouds
> Moving in heaven.[40]

we are led to suspect that Coleridge's interest in clouds and stars may be connected with Wales's specialised interest in atmospheric phenomena. But whereas the sight of the sun, moon or stars hid in mist or cloud became for Wales a problem in the refraction of light, for Coleridge it became an image of the wonder and mystery of the universe. For no image recurs more frequently in his poetry nor is so typical of his romantic genius; and it first occurs in his Christ's Hospital poems. It is in 'The Autumnal Moon', written at Christ's Hospital in 1788, that we glimpse the earliest, unmistakable stirrings of Coleridge's future poetic powers, and the whole poem is based upon a vision of the moon seen glimmering 'through a fleecy veil'. For Coleridge the moon became an emblem of hope, the cloud, an emblem of despair, and he continued to weave the image into the tapestry of his poetry throughout his life. Repeatedly, the embodiment of this image into appropriate verbal form evoked many of his finest lines, as in 'Lewti' or in the 'Dejection Ode':

> For lo! the New-moon winter-bright!
> And overspread with phantom light,
> (With swimming phantom light o'erspread
> But rimmed and circled by a silver thread)
> I see the old Moon in her lap, foretelling
> The coming-on of rain and squally blast.

As we have seen, he first used the image in 1788; a year later he uses it again in 'The Nose–An Odaic Rhapsody', on this occasion evoking a sense of the ludicrous:

> I saw when from the turtle feast
> The thick dark smoke in volumes rose!
> I saw the darkness of the mist
> Encircle thee, O Nose!
> Shorn of thy rays thou shott'st a fearful gleam
> (The turtle quiver'd with prophetic fright)
> Gloomy and sullen thro' the night of steam:–
> So Satan's Nose when Dunstan urg'd to flight,
> Glowing from gripe of red-hot pincers dread
> Athwart the smokes of Hell disastrous twilight shed!

When considered in the light of Wales's teaching, 'The Nose' becomes one of Coleridge's most interesting Christ's Hospital poems for the wealth of astronomical

144

imagery contained in its four stanzas. The red nose of the Lord Mayor of London, William Gill, was not a subject that one would expect to evoke astronomical metaphors, but Coleridge did, in fact, adorn it with a whole cluster of them: 'Sirius', 'the focus of the sun', 'comets', 'fire-clad meteors' and the 'torrid zone' all find a mention in the poem. Here, surely, either directly or indirectly, is the influence of Wales's teaching. And Coleridge writes in one line of the poem:

> In robes of ice my body wrap!

Here it is possible that he was recalling an account of the great cold experienced by the *Resolution*'s company in high southern latitudes. In his account of the voyage, John Marra, one of the gunner's mates on the *Resolution*, recorded how he had 'seen the men in frozen snow as if clad in armour'.[41]

There is a fourth poem written at Christ's Hospital in which the influence of Wales may be inferred. This is 'Dura Navis', written in 1787, when Coleridge was fifteen years of age and near the time when he transferred from the Lower to the Upper Grammar School. The poem opens with the lines:

> To tempt the dangerous deep, too venturous youth,
> Why does thy breast with fondest wishes glow?

The answer to this poetic questioning that immediately leaps to mind is: because William Wales has been round on one of his recruiting forays again. And even if we refuse to identify the 'too venturous youth' with Coleridge himself, despite the poet's own remark that this, 'like most school poetry is a *Putting of Thought into Verse*',[42] the poem remains one long argument against joining the navy by one who is sorely tempted to do so. Six years before, his elder brother Frank had joined the navy, and Frank's life, in its own way and at a different level of experience, may have had as deep an influence upon the *theme* of *The Ancient Mariner* as the influence of Wales did upon its structure and imagery. In the particular case of 'Dura Navis' it is possible that the images of clouds, waves, lightnings, famine at sea, etc., may owe something to descriptions of sea voyages related by Wales, but they are all much too general to be specifically attributed to his influence. All, that is, with the exception of one. The fourth stanza begins:

> Yet not the tempest or the Whirlwind's roar
> Equal the horrors of a Naval Fight

When Coleridge referred to the 'Whirlwind's roar', he was most probably thinking about a marine phenomenon that was exciting considerable attention in his day. Benjamin Franklin had ascribed the formation of waterspouts to the action of whirlwinds over the sea, and this view had not been seriously disputed.[43] When Coleridge refers to whirlwinds at sea we may be reasonably certain that he is thinking of waterspouts. This identification of whirlwinds and waterspouts in Coleridge's mind is also indicated by a more precise description of a waterspout which he included in his tragedy *Osorio*, written in 1797. In Act III a sorcerer is calling up the spirits of the departed which are said to provide energy and motion to the most diverse natural phenomena, they girdle the earth 'in dizzy motion', 'toss high the desert sands' and

> build up on the becalmed waves
> That whirling pillar, which from earth to heaven
> Stands vast, and moves in blackness. Ye too split

142. *Waterspouts in Cook's Straits, in New Zealand,* engraving after William Hodges in Wales and Bayly, *Astronomical Observations, made in the course of a Voyage towards the South Pole,* 1777, pl. 4.

> The ice-mount, and with fragments many and huge,
> Tempest the new-thaw'd sea . . .

Now the whirlwind-waterspout image, like the image of heavenly bodies obscured by a mist or cloud, is an image that, after first appearing in Coleridge's Christ's Hospital poetry, recurs frequently in his later verse. It would be difficult, perhaps, to pin Coleridge's initial interest in whirlwinds to any single source; it may have arisen, for instance, from his reading of Falconer's *Shipwreck*—that is, if we assume Coleridge to have read the poem before he was fifteen—for in his second canto of the poem a waterspout—named as an 'angry whirlwind'—is described in great detail. A more likely source, however, for his *initial* interest in the image is to be found in his association with Wales. One of the most exciting of all the many wonders experienced on the second voyage was the meeting on 17 May 1773 with waterspouts in Cook's Straits, New Zealand. Every detail of their formation and dispersal was recounted in Cook's *Voyage towards the South Pole*,[44] in George Forster's *Voyage round the World*,[45] Wales's manuscript journal[46] and in his *Astronomical Observations*.[47] Coleridge was in a position to consult three of these books, if not the journal, in the school's mathematical library. If he did not at some time or other hear a vivid description of the waterspouts in Cook's Straits from Wales himself, he might well have read of the incident in Wales's *Astronomical Observations* in which the phenomenon is described as 'one of the most curious and perhaps the most extraordinary and powerful of Nature's productions'.[48] That was a sentence not likely to be overlooked by a poet who years later decided to write a hymn to the 'Sun, moon and the Elements' that would sublimely enumerate 'the tremendities of nature'.[49] Wales appended to his description a double-page engraving—the only engraving in the book—from an original drawing by William Hodges, an eye-witness of the event. The dramatic nature of Hodges's presentation of it could well have left a permanent impression on Coleridge's mind (pls 142, 143). And it is important to stress at this point that deep imagery,

146

143. William Hodges, *A View of Cape Stephens in Cook's Strait with Waterspout*, oil on canvas, 137.2 × 193.1 cm., 1776, National Maritime Museum, London.

as in dreams, tends to take on a visual rather than a verbal form. I am not at any point seeking close verbal parallels between Wales's writings and Coleridge's poems, but rather the creation of a substantial repertoire of imagery, as in dream formation, from tales of the *Resolution*'s voyage told in the school, either by Wales himself or in garbled form by the boys.

Evidence that Wales's description and Hodges's engraving of the whirlwind-waterspout image did influence Coleridge while still at Christ's Hospital has been provided by Edmund Blunden. Coleridge's contribution on 6 June 1788 to Dr Boyer's *Liber Aureas*, the album into which his boys were asked to copy their best pieces of poetry and prose, was an essay on temperance in which he compared the intemperate man to 'a ship driven by whirlwind'. In another essay in the same album he wrote of uncontrolled passion as 'some great sea-vortex, every moment we perceive our ruin more clearly, every moment we are impelled towards it with greater force'.[50]

Another indication that the whirlwind-waterspout image owes something to Coleridge's association with Wales may be found in the fact that the passage from *Osorio*, quoted above, is followed by a description of the formation of icebergs. This was a subject on which Wales had formed his own opinion. He disagreed with Crantz, and later with George Forster (who was no doubt speaking for his father) when they suggested that icebergs could be formed in the open sea, and with the belief that they took hundreds of years to dissolve. He insisted that icebergs were formed from fresh ice splitting off from ice- and snow-covered shores.

Both in his 'Journal of a Voyage to Churchill River'[51] and his *Remarks on Mr. Forster's Account of Cook's Second Voyage*,[52] Wales provided a detailed account of his views on the formation and dispersal of icebergs. It must have been a subject that he would have enjoyed talking about with his boys.[53]

There is, then, a wealth of evidence that Wales exercised an influence upon the imagery that Coleridge used in his school poetry. But Kathleen Coburn has offered a gentle caveat: 'I confess I think you strain a bit in attributing to Wales so much, e.g. Coleridge's interest in the starry heavens in which we know old John Coleridge had interested him even earlier. And some uses of sun, moon and stars, mist etc. are so general, and so common, and so natural to a Devonshire boy who grew up only a few miles from the sea coast, that I cannot think that either books or schoolmasters are needed to explain or even gloss them.'[54]

The answer, of course, is that not all Devonshire boys write poems like *The Ancient Mariner*. One need not question a primal influence from both father and environment in developing the poet's love of the sky and the heavenly bodies. But Coburn ignores the vital principle that reinforcement plays in the memory process. Wales reinforced childhood interests, gave them new fascinating intellectual, scientific, travelling and exotic contexts.

May we not conclude, then, that the Reverend James Boyer was not the only teacher at Christ's Hospital who had a hand in Coleridge's development as a poet? Yet all his biographers have ignored the fact. For them William Wales does not exist. Even one so sensitive and stimulating as Richard Holmes (*Coleridge, Early Visions*, 1989) not only ignores Wales, he quotes but one image from Cook's *third* voyage to stand in, presumably, for that vast constellation of atmospheric and marine imagery that began to invade Coleridge's mind at school.

To the banal question, if we must reluctantly address it—why then did Coleridge not confess that Wales was one of the major inspirational sources of *The Ancient Mariner?*—there are two rather obvious answers. Firstly, poets, that is to say great poets, even loquacious and intellectually curious ones like Coleridge, are not in the habit of discoursing upon the inspirational origins of their own work. Least of all the British romantic poets. They did not regard the unweaving of their rainbows as in their line of business. And rightly so. The interpretation of creativity is for others. The most powerful gods hide themselves. The danger of such undertakings when attempted by the creators themselves is that the explantion of a source will be taken by the dull-witted as a substitute for the quality and power of the poem itself. Perhaps that is why, for so many centuries, poets have taken heart and refuge in the Greek theory of inspiration: creativity is in the hands of the gods. Better to not meddle there.

The second answer is that, in all probability, Coleridge was not himself aware that Wales was the effective *fons et origo*, not, of course, of the poem itself, but of that flood of Pacific Ocean imagery that in the fullness of poetic time flowed into the earlier and greater sections of *The Ancient Mariner*. To appreciate the situation we must attempt to reconstruct Coleridge's intellectual climate as a schoolboy at Christ's Hospital when his poetic powers were beginning to sprout tender and vulnerable shoots.

With Cook and his little company, Wales had travelled further south into antarctic waters than anyone had ever travelled. When he became mathematics master at Christ's Hospital, it was as if Neil Armstrong, a few months after standing on the moon, had taken to teaching physics and astronomy at Smith Academy, St. Louis, six years before T.S. Eliot had come to school there and was still teaching there when Eliot went off to Harvard. The analogy is stronger if we acknowledge that Wales was also a man given to poetry and possessed of a remarkable store of imagery about the sea, sky, ice mist, cloud, watersnakes and phosphorescent seas, such that might inspire boys to join the navy, images that would lodge deeply in a potentially poetic mind not merely as words remembered from reading but as the most vivid visualisations, the stuff of dreams, upon which à highly volatile and poetic will would later, in its own time, work so creatively.

148

It is Wordsworth who tells us that Coleridge called his ancient mariner the 'old navigator'. Wales was the closest person the poet knew in real life who answered that description.

It is not, interestingly, in Coleridge's Christ's Hospital poetry, but in the remarkable series of parallels that may be drawn between Wales's journal and *The Ancient Mariner* that the stimulus of Wales's teaching is to be most fully observed.

In *The Road to Xanadu*, Livingstone Lowes revealed a great many verbal correspondences between selections from Coleridge's reading (chiefly between the spring of 1795 and the summer of 1798) and the text of *The Ancient Mariner*. Upon the implications of these correspondences he erected a theory that sought to explain the mode of operation of Coleridge's creative imagination. My intention here is to suggest the presence not of *verbal* correspondences but *substantial* correspondences of pattern, events and imagery subsisting between accounts of Cook's second voyage and the natural setting of the poem, more especially as recounted in its first and second parts. The Wales journal will be the main source for providing the parallels, but since the intention is to recover, so far as possible, something of the accounts of the second voyage that Coleridge heard or read of at Christ's Hospital, it will be useful to use other accounts from time to time.

The argument of *The Ancient Mariner*, as published in the *Lyrical Ballads'* version of 1798, reads:

> How a Ship having passed the Line was driven by storms to the cold Country towards the South Pole; and how from thence she made her course to the tropical Latitude of the Great Pacific Ocean; and of the strange things that befell; and in what manner the Ancyent Marinere came back to his own Country.

Now this is, in broad outline, a fair description of the *Resolution*'s voyage, if we are prepared to neglect its intricate weavings in search of the Great South Land. For the *Resolution*, having passed the Line, was, as we shall see, driven by storms; and she was one of the few ships that up to that time did, in fact, reach the cold country towards the South Pole.[55] Indeed, the very words, 'towards the South Pole' occupy pride of place in the title of Cook's official account of the voyage which Coleridge certainly read, namely, *A Voyage towards the South Pole and Round the World*, and the words also occur in the title of Wales's own book, *The Original Astronomical Observations made in the course of a Voyage towards the South Pole and Round the World*. And later, the *Resolution* did, in fact, make her course to the tropical latitudes of the Pacific Ocean. Finally, it must be said that, while having due regard for the fact that the events of the one occurred in the real world and the events of the other, in the realm of the imagination, the strange things that befell the *Resolution*'s company and that many of them recorded, frequently bear a striking likeness to the strange things that befell the Ancient Mariner himself. This is revealed by a detailed study of the poem.

The Ancient Mariner's vessel at the commencement of its voyage made a good passage south to the equator:

> The Sun came up upon the left,
> Out of the sea came he!
> And he shone bright, and on the right
> Went down into the sea.

And the accompanying gloss records: 'The Mariner tells how the ship sailed southward with a good wind and fair weather, till it reached the line.' The *Resolution* was subject to similar conditions as she sailed southwards. On 21 September 1772, William Wales recorded in his journal:

> It is remarkable that in running along the N.E. Trade winds on the north side of the line we found them always uniform and steady, with very fine weather:– not quite cloudy but that we could almost always observe the sun's Altitude.

Having crossed the Line, conditions quickly changed for the Ancient Mariner's vessel:

> And now the STORM-BLAST came, and he
> Was tyrannous and strong:
> He struck with his o'ertaking wings,
> And chased us south along.

And the gloss tell us: 'The ship driven by a storm toward the south pole.' The *Resolution* encountered similar conditions as soon as she, too, crossed the Line: Wales's entry for 21 September, already quoted, continues:

> On the contrary since we crossed the line, and got the south-east Trades, we have found them very unequal, blowing in strong gusts, and attended with squalls of rain.

The passage records, however, not only that the *Resolution* had a squally southing, but also that the weather was very unequal, that is to say, freakish and unreliable. It is notable that the first version of *The Ancient Mariner*, as published in the *Lyrical Ballads*, records the freakish as well as the squally nature of the voyage south of the Line:

> Listen, Stranger! Storm and Wind,
> A Wind and Tempest strong!
> For days and weeks it play'd us freaks–
> Like chaff we drove along.

Wales wrote the comment quoted above before the *Resolution* reached Cape Town. After leaving the Cape the weather became worse. George Forster wrote after leaving the Cape, 'The Wind blew in hard squalls'; on 5 December, 'the stormy weather continued, intermixed with frequent rains and fogs'.[56] On 8 December he wrote, 'the wind still continuing very high, the sea very turbulent'.[57]

The Ancient Mariner's vessel proceeded to move down into the regions of mist, snow and ice, under the pressure of the storm:

> And now there came both mist and snow,
> And it grew wondrous cold:
> And ice, mast-high, came floating by,
> As green as emerald.

The *Resolution*, too, moved down under very squally conditions into the ice (pl. 144). On 9 December 1772 Forster recorded:

> Towards night it grew colder again, and at half-past ten, we found the thermometer on deck very near 32 degrees . . . This great cold preceded the sight of ice floating in the sea, which we fell in with on the next morning.[58]

150

144. William Hodges, *The Resolution passing a large island of ice*, wash and watercolour, 32.4 × 47.2 cm., 1773–4, Mitchell Library, Sydney (PXD 11, N.27a).

Cook, on the following morning, recorded:

At eight o'clock saw an island of ice to the Westward of us . . . The weather becoming hazy, I called the Adventure by signal under my stern; which was no sooner done, than the haze increased so much, with snow and sleet, that we did not see an island of ice, which we were steering directly for, till we were less than a mile from it. I judged it to be about fifty feet high.[59]

And on 10 December Wales wrote in his journal:

Passed very near to large Island of Ice, which we mistook for land, at first, as did the Adventure. This island, I conceive, was at least twice as high above the Water as our Top-Gallant mast head.[60]

The poem continues:

> And through the drifts the snowy clifts,
> Did send a dismal sheen.

The image is of high cliffs or ridges of ice reflecting a sheen of light from behind and beyond a field of drift ice. Such a phenomenon is carefully described by Wales in a lengthy passage which he entered in his journal on 29 January 1774:

Discovered a large field of Ice ahead, extending east and west beyond our sight from the mast-Head. At a distance it appeared very high, and like a fixed solid Map with many high mountainous parts in it but when we came nearer it we found its edge was scarce higher than the water and composed of small pieces close jambed together and the high parts very large Islands which were amongst it; but farther in it still appeared high, and as if one solid piece; though this, I conceive, was a deception as well as the other. Along way within the field (which we could not see over) was the appearance of a long ridge of

151

very high mountainous Ice: but I am of opinion this was nothing more than a strong Fog bank, illuminated by the rays of light which were reflected from the Ice.

Wales here provides us with a picture of drift ice in the foreground, backed by what is apparently high mountainous ice in the background, emitting rays of light (pl. 145). It is questionable whether Coleridge was referring, either directly or indirectly, to the phenomenon known as the ice-blink when he wrote, 'the snowy clifts/Did send a dismal sheen', since the ice-blink, in its particular meaning, refers to a reflection seen in the sky before the ice itself is met with, whereas in the stanza the image of the ice itself is clearly present together with the sheen it emits. If, however, some recollection of this peculiar phenomenon of Polar regions did enter into the creation of the poetic image, it is quite likely that Coleridge first heard of it through the agency of Wales. For Wales was something of an authority upon ice-blink, which was, after all, only a particular case of atmospheric refraction, his great interest. While at Hudson's Bay, Wales had noted the optical illusion created by light reflected from ice:

> I had often admired the singular appearance of the ice in these parts, which I have seen lifted up 2 or 3 degrees at a distance of 8 or 10 miles, although when we came to it, we have found it scarcely higher than the surface of the water.[61]

Experience with the ice in the northern fields made it possible for Wales to understand the true character of the phenomenon better than other members of the *Resolution*'s company when it was encountered in the Antarctic. On 16 December 1772 he recorded:

> about 3 o'clock we began to discover a whitish haze in the horizon extending from about S.E. to S.W. which I described to a field of Ice, having always found it so in the Northern fields, and was laughed at for my information; however, at 4 o'clock such a field was discovered from the mast head extending without opening from S.S.w. to S.E.

145. George Forster, *Ice islands with ice-blink*, gouache, 35 × 54.5 cm., *c*.1772–3, Mitchell Library, Sydney (PXD 11, N.30).

146. William Hodges, *The Resolution and Adventure among icebergs*, wash and watercolour, 36.7 × 54.6 cm., *c.*1772–3, Mitchell Library, Sydney (PXD 11, N.28).

The ice-glint was subsequently noted in the published accounts of George Forster,[62] and John Reinhold Forster,[63] both of whom were, of course, on board the *Resolution* with Wales.

The stanza with which we have been concerned concludes:

> Nor shapes of men nor beasts we ken—
> The ice was all between.

On 31 January 1775, the *Resolution* reached the southernmost land discovered on the whole voyage; Forster senior called it Southern Thule, a name Cook adopted. It appeared utterly wretched and forsaken. George Forster described an island nearby in the following terms:

> The whole country had the most desolate and horrid appearance which can possibly be conceived; not a single grass could be discerned upon it, and it seemed to be forsaken even by the amphibious and lumpish animals which dwelt on Southern Georgia. In short we could not help applying to it, that remarkable expression of Pliny.

> *Pars mundi damnata a rerum natura, et densa mersa caligine*
> *Hist. Nat. lib. xc. c. 36.*[64]

The poem continues with the lines:

> The ice was here, the ice was there,
> The Ice was all around.

This was a common experience of the *Resolution* voyage. Two years before reaching Southern Thule, comments that the two vessels were surrounded by ice islands are quite common in Wales's journal. Thus, on 13 December 1772, he records: 'found ourselves quite embayed by low ice', and on 19 February, 'all this forenoon passing by exceedingly large islands of Ice, so that the sea had a truly tremendous appearance' (pl. 146).

The Ancient Mariner continues with a description of the ice breaking, which is mentioned in three ways by Coleridge. In the gloss we read of 'the land of ice, and of fearful sounds'; in the poem we read how the ice 'cracked and growled, and roared and howled' and that it 'split with a thunder-fit'. The sound of the ice splitting was mentioned by most of the *Resolution*'s company who had occasion to write about the voyage, and it obviously left a lasting impression upon them all. John Reinhold Forster in his *Observations* emphasised both the great noise of the ice splitting and the fearful nature of the situation for the voyagers:

> We had frequent opportunity of seeing the effect of sea-water upon ice, in dissolving and crumbling large masses to pieces, with a crash not inferior to the explosion of guns; and sometimes we were scarce out of reach of the danger of being crushed by an ice-rock splitting in pieces, which were oversetting, each of them having gotten new centres of gravity.[65]

And on 5 March 1773 William Wales recorded:

> Saw the large Island of Ice to the Westward; but found that in the night many large pieces had broke from it. During the night many great reports had been heard from the quarter on which it was, which some of the People thought was Thunder; but I now conceive were occasioned by those Pieces breaking off.[66]

The same phenomenon was described with greater feeling by John Marra: 'This day . . . passed by a great island of ice, and heard many dreadful cracks, as if the whole earth was cleaving asunder.'[67]

The gloss of the poem now describes how 'a great sea-bird, called the Albatross, came through the snow-fog, and was received with great joy and hospitality'. In his official account of the voyage Cook wrote: 'We began to see these birds [i.e., albatrosses] about the time of our first falling in with the ice islands; and some had accompanied us ever since.'[68] Albatrosses are mentioned quite frequently by Cook, Wales and George Forster in their accounts of the voyage. It was Wordsworth, of course, who suggested the theme of the Ancient Mariner as Coleridge and he walked across the Quantock hills one autumn evening in 1797. As Wordsworth said later, 'the idea of shooting an albatross was mine; for I had been reading Shelvocke's Voyages'.[69] But why, we might well ask, did Coleridge react so favourably to the suggestion, and why did it produce such poetry? Did Wordsworth on this occasion touch upon the chords of older and deeper memories? For albatrosses were both taken and shot on Cook's second voyage. Wales recorded on 8 January 1774 how an albatross was 'catched with a hook and line',[70] Cook recorded for 23 October 1772; 'Mr. Forster shot some albatrosses',[71] and on 12 January 1773, 'Mr. Forster shot an albatross' (pl. 147).[72]

In Shelvocke, and in the poem, the albatross was, of course, first regarded as a bird of ill-omen; and we have some evidence that albatrosses were regarded with superstition by seamen on the *Resolution*. In his account of the voyage, Anders Sparrman records an incident that occurred on 8 June 1773, shortly after the vessel had left New Zealand on her winter work in the Pacific:

> Concerning the three large albatrosses of a large species that floated around us above the sea on this day, several of the ship's company who had made extensive and more agreeable voyages in East Indian waters, were joking over

154

147. George Forster, *Wandering Albatross Diomedea exulans*, Linn, watercolour, 33.2 × 48 cm., 1758, British Museum, London, Natural History, Zoological Library (Forster's paintings, f. 99).

the East Indian's belief in the transmigration of souls, and about the hardships of our voyage. They suggested that the Captains and Chief Mates who had enjoyed a very indolent and lazy time in their cabins in warm and calm East Indian waters, were banished as a punishment to these cold regions to cheer up the albatrosses and stormy petrels, always restlessly hunting for food.[73]

Certainly, the incident is reported as a joke; but this is a joke that gains point against the background of superstition associated with albatrosses. Though it would be rash to infer that Wales, a most objective thinker, regarded the albatross with superstition, he certainly disliked the wanton slaughter of living creatures. We may consider, for example, the incident recorded in his journal which occurred on Easter Island on 14 March 1774, already noted above (p. 102), in which he refrained from shooting at an islander who had stolen William Hodges's hat.

Did Wales's feeling for fellow-creatures ever include wounded and suffering birds? We have no explicit evidence that it did, but there is a hint of something very like it in a reflection written at Dusky Bay, New Zealand, on 10 May 1773:

It appeared odd enough at least to me to see Birds here so familiar with us, as if they had not the least Idea of our being their Enemies. It was not uncommon for them to perch on the barrel of the Gun in our hands already loaded for their destruction. This makes either for or against the Doctrine of Inate [*sic*] Ideas: for either they were possessed of none, and so perched there indifferent, or else they were, and knew there was less danger to be apprehended whilst there than when a few yards from the muzzle.[74]

Wales's trite remark about innate ideas leaves the distinct impression that he has recorded a scrap from a discussion among some of the *Resolution*'s scientists at Dusky Bay. Assuming such a discussion to have taken place, did it include a discussion of the moral issue involved in shooting birds merely for sport? The

155

moral issue involved in the New Zealand practice of killing and eating one's enemies was almost certainly discussed at Dusky Bay; and one of the naturalists, at least, saw a connexion between the two issues. There may well be a connexion between Wales's comments about the birds of Dusky Bay and the remarkable moment of moral illumination that his shipmate Sparrman experienced there, when, like the Ancient Mariner himself, he suddenly felt a sense of guilt and horror as he reflected upon his wanton slaughter of defenceless birds:

> To this hour I remember one of my shots in Dusky Bay as a dark reflection on the bad effect which hunting as a habit and extreme passion, pursued without the object of providing food or any other justifiable reason, could and did have on the human mind. I had waded after two duck I had killed with one shot, with the moderate zest of the ordinary hunter; but when I had recovered them the blood from these warm birds which were dying in my hands, running over my fingers, excited me to a degree I had never previously experienced while shooting in Sweden or New Zealand. This filled me with amazement, but the next moment I felt frightened. I reproached myself for being a harsh and calculated tyrant to nature, and acknowledged that hunting resembled not a little the murder and cruelty of the New Zealand savages.[75]

On another occasion during the voyage, a friendly swallow developed the habit, according to George Forster, of visiting the ship and of passing some part of the morning in Wales's cabin. One day it disappeared mysteriously. Forster suggested that it was 'more than probable that it came into the berth of some unfeeling person who caught it in order to provide a meal for a favourite cat'.[76] There is some evidence, then, that, on the *Resolution*, three persons at least, Wales, George Forster and Sparrman, expressed uneasy feelings about the wanton destruction of birds.

If Wordsworth provided Coleridge with the albatross theme, need more be said? I would insist that if we are seriously concerned about the imaginative *sources* of the poem, then we must pay attention to those foundational areas of interest, whether verbal, visual or oral, that could provide fertile ground for Wordsworth's explicit suggestion. The question is not only why Coleridge adopted Wordsworth's suggestion so readily, but why the adoption yielded such a magnificent poem? Did Wordsworth stir 'relics of sensation' latent in his friend's unconscious memory processes? It is just possible that some such story about wanton destruction and the subsequent revulsion of some of the more sensitive souls on the *Resolution*, including Wales, might have gained currency among those other tales of superstition and wonder current among the Blue-coat boys.

What we do know is that Coleridge did hear some such tale of guilt and wonder while at Christ's Hospital, for he virtually tells us so in his poem 'To a Young Lady With a Poem on the French Revolution' (1794), addressed to his young wife, Sara.

> Much on my early youth I love to dwell
> Ere yet I bade that friendly dome farewell,
> Where first, beneath the echoing cloisters pale,
> I heard of guilt and wondered at the tale.

We cannot assume that the poet is here referring to the story of Prince Lee Boo (recounted in George Keate's *Account of the Pelew Islands* (1788)) that he refers to a few lines later. This pathetic tale of the young Palau islander who was brought to

156

England to be civilised and died of smallpox there cannot, on Keate's telling of it, be described as a tale of guilt. Coleridge may have been referring to some other story he had heard at school which led him on to Lee Boo, whose grave he may have visited in Rotherhithe churchyard on one of his leave days or truant excursions from the school. Keate ended his story by printing the full inscription on Lee Boo's tomb:

> Stop, Reader, stop!–Let NATURE claim a Tear–
> A Prince of *Mine*, Lee Boo, lies bury'd here.

It appears to have inspired the lines a little later in the poem:

> Where'er I wander'd, Pity still was near
> Breath'd from the heart and glisten'd in the tear:
> No knell that toll'd but fill'd my anxious eye,
> And suffering Nature wept that *one* should die.

If a bird is wantonly destroyed, if Lee Boo, an innocent prince of nature, dies by civilisation's hand, all nature weeps. Here is the conflated theme of guilt and innocent suffering that will become central to *The Ancient Mariner*. If, according to the poet's account, its source was in his schoolboy experiences, who was the ultimate agent of those experiences? Again, all the evidence points to Wales. Any story about the wanton destruction of birds on the *Resolution* voyage would have come to the poet from Wales. Keate's *Account of the Pelew Islands* would have been one of the obvious books for Wales to have in his library. It was a highly sentimental account of a voyage to the South Seas that would hold an enormous appeal for his boys and might well inspire them to join the navy and see the world. In any case, he would have had need of it for its account of the voyage and its accompanying chart.

If then some such tale of guilt and suffering circulated at Christ's Hospital as a result of Wales's presence there, it would have fallen upon fertile ground in the young poet's mind. As a child, years before he came to Christ's Hospital, he read the fictitious tale of *Philip Quarll*. Written in the Robinsonade tradition, it tells of a man who lived for more than fifty years on an uninhabited island in the South Seas. On one occasion Philip shot a beautiful bird with a home-made bow and then immediately regretted it: 'I have destroyed that as was certainly made for Nature's diversions with such a Variety of Colours...'[77] We can only conclude that Wordsworth's suggestion, on that walk across the Quantock hills, encountered a mind that had been richly prepared for it.

*   *   *

Navigation of the antarctic ice was fraught with great peril, and Coleridge emphasises the responsibility of the helmsman on these occasions in his lines:

> The ice did split with a thunder-fit
> The helmsman steered us through.

Now William Wales had to train the boys in his charge to be navigators, and he had himself revised Robertson's *Elements of Navigation*. It is not likely, therefore, that he would refrain from telling the boys at Christ's Hospital something of the dangers and excitements of polar navigation. He might have told them, for

157

instance, of the exciting incident that occurred on 20 December 1773 and that he recorded in his journal:

> Discovered a very large Island of Ice directly ahead and scarce more than 100 yards distant: the ship luckily wore clear of it; but before she was half round, another large one was discovered, at about the like distance on the Lee bow. The Lieut, had therefore no reason but to put the helm up again, and endeavour to drive her through a large field of loose ice which lay betwixt them, and as soon as she was clear of them Tacked and stood Northward.

Critics tend to assume that in *The Ancient Mariner*, Coleridge intended it to be understood that the Mariner's vessel doubled Cape Horn, the two lines 'the Sun came up upon the left' and 'the Sun now rose upon the right' being cited in support. A moment's reflection, however, will make one realise that as soon as the vessel began to move north instead of south the sun would rise upon the right. Now the action of the poem clearly suggests that the Mariner's vessel was among ths southern ice for a considerable time, this being indicated in such lines as '*At length* did cross an albatross', '*And every* day for food and play' and 'It perched for vespers none.' Immediately following upon the lines:

> The ice did split with a thunder-fit;
> The helmsman steered us through! [Plate 148]

we have the line:

> And a good south wind sprung up behind.

Such a wind in the region of the prevailing westerlies would drive a ship eastwards. When this is read in conjunction with the accompanying gloss, which tells us how the albatross followed the ship 'as it returned northwards through fog and floating ice', a more feasible interpretation than the doubling of the Horn is that the vessel is moving into the southern Indian Ocean. It is to be noted that although the line 'The sun now rose upon the right' opens part two of the poem there is no mention of the Pacific until we come to the gloss accompanying the fifth stanza of part two in which it is clearly stated: 'The fair breeze continues; the ship enters the Pacific Ocean, and sails northward, even till it reaches the Line.' This gloss accompanies the lines:

> We were the first that ever burst
> Into that silent sea

And Lowes himself noted the similarity here to George Forster's description of their entry into the Pacific:

> We were the first Europeans, and I believe I may add, the first human beings, who have reached this point [in the Southern Seas], where it is probable none will come after us.[78] [Pl. 149.]

Before this point is reached in the poem, however, we are informed, in the first line of the second stanza of the second part of the poem:

> And the good south wind still blew behind.

This reiteration suggests a prevailing wind which in high southern latitudes would drive the ship eastwards so that she would enter the Pacific from the south-west.

158

148. William Hodges, *Ice islands*, wash and watercolour, 42.9 × 30.5 cm., *c*.1773–4, Mitchell Library, Sydney (PXD 11, N.27).

149. William Hodges, *Ice islands*, wash and watercolour, 27 × 38 cm., *c*.1773–4, Mitchell Library, Sydney (PXD 11, N.29).

The *Resolution* followed such a course. After working among the ice from early December 1772, moving southwards and, for the most part, to the east, in the track of the prevailing winds, Cook passed the Antarctic Circle in mid-January 1773. A few days later he was prevented from further progress south by the extent of the ice. This phase of the *Resolution*'s voyage may be compared with the Ancient Mariner's as described in lines 55–62 of the poem with their accompanying gloss, 'The land of ice and fearful sounds where no living thing was to be seen.' Then from 17 January until 3 February, Cook sailed northwards into the southern Indian Ocean. This phase of his voyage may be compared with the gloss that describes how the albatross followed the ship 'as it returned northwards through the fog and floating ice.' Reference to Wales's journal between 17 January and 3 February 1773 reveals that the *Resolution* encountered a good deal of fog and floating ice during their passage northwards. After 3 February, Cook struck south-east again, continuing along the 60 degree latitude until he entered the south Pacific in the region of the 145th meridian on 16 March, and then began to sail in a north-easterly direction for New Zealand. This phase of the voyage may be compared with the course of the Ancient Mariner's voyage as described in the early stanzas of the second part of the poem. The continuance of the south wind is repeated twice, first in the line:

> And the good south wind still blew behind,

and in the gloss, 'The fair breeze continues . . .' Only then do we come to the first mention of the vessel entering the Pacific Ocean; a phase of the Mariner's voyage that may be compared with Cook's entry into the Pacific from the south-west.

There is no need to insist that Coleridge had in mind all the details of the *Resolution*'s voyage when he came to write *The Ancient Mariner*. All that needs to be maintained is that the common assumption that the Mariner's vessel doubled the

159

Horn does not rest upon any firm foundation in the text, and that, on the other hand, there is nothing in the text which cannot be shown to agree, in outline, with the course of the *Resolution* in southern waters.

There was also a powerful personal reason why a voyage round the Cape of Good Hope and not round Cape Horn should have lodged deeply in Coleridge's unconscious mind. In his psychobiography of Coleridge, *His Brother's Keeper*, Stephen Weissman argues convincingly that the central theme of *The Ancient Mariner* is intimately connected with the poet's feelings of guilt and responsibility for his brother Frank's death. As a child of seven, Coleridge threatened Frank, aged nine, with a knife; a deeply traumatic experience that remained with Coleridge for life. At the age of eleven Frank joined the navy, voyaged round the Cape of Good Hope to India, later joined the British army there and committed suicide after his involvement in the seige of Seringapatam had induced a delirious fever. News of Frank's death reached Coleridge shortly after he had left Cambridge to join the King's Fifteenth Light Dragoons under the assumed name of Comberbache. Frank's suicide and the sense of personal guilt associated with it probably provided Coleridge's imagination with the unifying drive that he was later to describe as the co-adunative or esemplastic power so essential to the imaginative process and so distinct from the associationist mechanisms of fancy. It was a voyage around the Cape of Good Hope rather than one around Cape Horn that would have burnt its way into his mind, thus reinforcing, under conditions of guilt and remorse, those stories of the *Resolution*'s voyage he had gained as a schoolboy through the agency of Wales. Weissman's argument is convincing as far as it goes. But it does not go far enough. He accepts the conventional, but unwarranted, view that the Ancient Mariner's voyage was a westerly one around Cape Horn, for which, as we have seen, there is no internal evidence provided by the poem. Nor does he pay sufficient attention to the history of the discrete images of sun, mist, snow and ice, etc. built into it. He accepts, as Lowes does, that their origin lies largely in the poet's reading between 1795 and 1797, but he also speculates that some of the images may have come from Frank's letters home, though none that are known contain any such.[79] This point is crucial. It is, after all, not the story-line of *The Ancient Mariner*, though scholars may argue endlessly about its meaning and moral burden, but the brilliance of its imagery that gives the poem its enduring quality.[80] Now, as we have seen a great number of discrete images were already present in Coleridge's schoolboy experiences and associated with south-sea voyaging. We can assume that such images would gain an additional emotional resonance and be reinforced on the occasion of Frank's death and become associated, if we accept Weissman's thesis, with a sense of guilt. All this well before Wordsworth mentioned Shelvocke and the albatross motif.

* * *

Towards the end of the first part of the poem we have the lines:

> Whiles all the night, through the fog-smoke white,
> Glimmered the white Moon-shine.

We have already seen why the moon partly covered by mist and fog was a subject of special interest to Wales. Such a phenomenon was frequently observed on the second voyage in high latitudes. J.R. Forster noted that

160

When the air is charged with dense vapours, and often when they are frozen into snow or sleet, there appears a HALO about the sun or moon, which is by no means remarkable upon the whole; but that it has been observed that Halos precede high winds, squalls and often rain or snow . . . On Feb. 25, 1774, we saw a large Halo about the Moon, and that very night came on squalls with rain.[81]

This is just the kind of phenomenon that Wales might have discussed with Forster on board the *Resolution*, and with his pupils at Christ's Hospital.

The second part of the poem opens with the picture of the Mariner's vessel moving up from the ice northwards:

> The sun now rose upon the right:
> Out of the sea came he,
> Still hid in mist, and on the left
> Went down into the sea.

A brief study of the remarks in Wales's journal reveals, as might be expected, a great many days experienced on the voyage that might be described by just these lines. Here is one such example. Throughout most of July 1773, the *Resolution* had been moving steadily northwards as she wintered in warmer waters; the sun, of course, rising on her right. By 7 August the ship's company were waiting expectantly for the Trade Winds, and Wales wrote for the day in his journal:

The much wished for, and long-excepted Trade-Winds seem now to have joined us. Our hopes began to grow very sanguine yesterday forenoon for about 10 o'clock A.M. a thick haze began to rise in the Eastern quarter, and by noon was so thick that I could not see the sun at times.

In the fourth stanza of the second part of the poem the mariner's shipmates are so pleased at the sun's return that they justify his shooting of the albatross. Wales records the joy which he and his shipmates experienced after weeks of stormy weather south of the Cape of Good Hope. On 3 December 1772 he wrote:

I remember to have read in some Author or other, how that 'After a storm the sun more bright appears' and he adds 'That joy is greatest which is rais'd from fears.' The latter may be true for aught I know to the contrary; but I am certain the former is so: for never did sunshine and moderate Weather appear more delightful than now to us, after near a week of the most turbulent weather than can be well imagined.[82]

The Mariner's vessel moves northwards till it reaches the Line, where it is becalmed:

> Down dropt the breeze, the sails dropped down,
> 'Twas sad as sad could be;
> And we did speak only to break
> The silence of the sea!
> All in a hot and copper sky,
> The bloody Sun, at noon,
> Right up above the mast did stand,
> No bigger than the Moon.

All through March and April 1774, the *Resolution* experienced very little wind and very hot weather. The maximum daily temperature began to rise steadily from 71 degrees on 1 March, was in the 80s through most of April and reached 93 degrees at noon on 8 May. On 1 March, Wales wrote in his journal:

> Little Wind and Clear weather. Omnium rerum Vicissitudo, say my brother Star-gazers and though they have worn the expression threadbare I am fully convinced by experience it is not a jot the less true for it is scarcely 3 weeks ago we were miserable on acct of the cold we are now wretched with the heat: the latter is I think, less supportable of the two.

In the poem the heat is accompanied by calms:

> Day after day, day after day,
> We stuck nor breath nor motion;
> As idle as a painted ship
> Upon a painted ocean.

And Wales, too, follows his description of the heat with many descriptions of the calm. Thus, the entry for 2 and 3 March, 'Little wind and clear'; for the 4th, 'For several days past we have not had the least swell from any quarter, but this forenoon the swell has begun to come from the s.s.w., ' and he writes, later in the day, 'Calm, ships head all Round the compass. The South-west Swell considerably increased, which gave us some hopes of a wind from that quarter. We have need of it, for the heat, this calm weather, is almost insupportable.'

The poem now mentions 'God's creatures of the great calm' which are to play such an important part in the action of the poem:

> The very deep did rot: O Christ!
> That ever this should be!
> Yea, slimy things did crawl with legs
> Upon the slimy sea.

And at a later stage in the poem we have the lines:

> Beyond the shadow of the ship,
> I watched the water-snakes.

On 8 March, only a few days after he had mentioned the calm, Wales records: 'Passed by a sea-snake: it was speckled, black and white; and in every respect like those we used to see at Tonga Tabu and the Society Islands,' and the printed version of his journal has for the same day: 'sea-snakes, sponge, leaves and birds'.[83]

It is apparent, too, that the peculiar phenomenon of 'the rotting sea' was something that excited the interest of the *Resolution*'s company, for J.R. Forster discusses it at length when dealing with the general question of phosphorescent seas:

> It is likewise a well established fact, that the ocean itself after a long continued calm, becomes stinking and highly putrid, arising probably from the putrefaction of a great many animal substances, that die in the ocean, float on it, and in hot days frequently and suddenly putrefy. That fishes and mollusca contain oily and inflammable particles is equally well known. The acid of phosphorus disengaged by putrefaction from its original mixture in animal bodies may closely combine with some of the just mentioned inflammables, and thus

162

produce a phosphorous on top of the ocean, and causing that luminous appearance, which we so much admire[84]

The 'rotting' sea, therefore, in Forster's view, was a reason for phosphorescent seas; and it is to be noted that Coleridge proceeds directly from 'the very deep did rot' to,

> The water, like a witch's oils,
> Burnt green, and blue and white.

Coleridge first made poetic use of the phenomenon, described by Forster, in 'The Destiny of Nations', a poem that relates such a wealth of exotic natural phenomena to the world of morality that it is, in this respect at least, a forerunner of *The Ancient Mariner*. At the beginning of the poem Coleridge claims that the visible world is a symbol and key to the invisible:

> . . . all that meets the bodily sense I deem
> Symbolical, one mighty alphabet
> For infant minds.

And in keeping with this belief he proceeds in one of the fragments of this unfinished poem to use the image of slime in a rotting sea creating its own beauty upon the surface of the dark ocean as symbolising the defeat of Chaos by the power of Love:

> 'Maid beloved of Heaven!
> (To her the tutelary Power exclaimed)
> Of Chaos the adventurous progeny
> Thou seest; foul missionaries of foul sire,
> Fierce to regain the losses of that hour
> When Love rose glittering, and his gorgeous wings
> Over the abyss fluttered with such glad noise,
> As what time after long and pestful calms,
> With slimy shapes and miscreated life
> Poisoning the vast Pacific, the fresh breeze
> Wakens the merchant-sail uprising. Night
> An heavy unimaginable moan
> Sent forth, when she the Protoplast beheld
> Stand beauteous on Confusion's charméd wave.'

Here, clearly, Love, as a life-giving breeze, not only wakens 'the merchant-sail' but, moaning upon the waters, makes what is rotten beautiful on the charméd wave. So it is that the moral ideas associated with the image of the rotting-phosphorescent sea in *The Ancient Mariner* are already adumbrated in 'The Destiny of Nations'. Only when a 'spring of love' gushes from the Ancient Mariner's heart is he able to appreciate the beauty of the water-snakes (which have mingled their beauty, as Lowes has shown, with the phosphorescent animalculae) and refresh his anguished spirit. Just as the energy contained within the natural order can transform slime to radiance, so Love, the energy of the moral order, can transform moral ugliness to moral beauty.

Phosphorescent sea was encountered on several occasions during the second voyage, and detailed accounts of the phenomenon were published by Cook,[85] and the two Forsters.[86] One of the passages that Lowes quotes as a source for

Coleridge's lines on phosphorescent sea is to be found in Cook's official account of the third voyage. Wales doubtless knew the passage well, for he assisted Canon Douglas in the editing of the account, and the passage itself is not from Cook's journal but is an editorial addition from the journal kept by William Anderson, surgeon on the *Resolution* during the third voyage. Wales, however, knew the phenomenon well enough from his own experience. His entry for 29 October 1772 reads:

> This evening we amused ourselves with enquiring into the Cause of a very odd Phenomenon. The sea all round the Ship, as far as we could see was perfectly illuminated by the number and brightness of those shining particles which are usually seen in a ship's Wake. We took up several Buckets full of water and found it full of small Insects which when laid on a piece of paper were much like a bit of Jelly; but excepting those the water was perfectly clear. When the water was at rest in the Buckets, it ceased to be illuminated; but as soon as it was disturbed became as bright as that in the sea.[87]

All the accounts of this experiment stress the fact that the animalculae ceased to be radiant when at rest but became radiant when the water was agitated. J.R. Forster writes: 'it became dark as soon as it was free from motion: but at each violent agitation of the water, it appeared luminous'.[88] His son George writes:

> . . . on being stirred again, the whole became as luminous as before. Again, as the water gradually subsided the sparks were observed to move in directions contrary to the undulations of the water, which they did not before, whilst the agitation was more violent, and seemed to carry them along with its own motions. We suspended the bucket, to prevent its being too much affected by the motion of the ship; the bright objects by this means betrayed more and more voluntary motion, independent of the agitation of the water caused by our hands, or by the rolling of the vessel. The luminous appearance always gradually subsided, but on the least agitation of the water with my hand, the sparkling was renewed, in proportion as the motion was encreased. As I stirred the water with my hand, one of the luminous sparks adhered to my finger.[89]

It is generally agreed that Coleridge was indebted to *Macbeth*, I.iii.32–4, when he came to write the lines:

> About, about, in reel and rout
> The death-fires danced at night;
> The water, like a witch's oils,
> Burnt green, and blue and white.

Lowes points out that the association with Macbeth was probably brought about because the First Witch, a few lines earlier in the play, is cursing another mariner placed in a similar predicament to the Ancient Mariner. Assuming, however, that Coleridge's *first* acquaintance with the phenomenon of phosphorescent seas came either verbally from Wales or from accounts of the second voyage, it is reasonable to suppose that the bucket-stirring experiment with the slimy animalculae was associated in the poet's mind with phosphorescent seas from the beginning. This would give further point to the association with the lines in Macbeth, since the stirring of oily substances in a bucket to create a fiery liquid would lead naturally enough to the idea of 'a witch's oils'. Furthermore, there is both here, and in the

164

later reference to the phosphorescent sea in part four, a clear suggestion that the agitation of the water was necessary for its illumination.

J.R. Forster also provides us with a detailed description of the effect of the passage of the vessel and of fish through phosphorescent waters:

> Scarcely had night spread its veil over the surface of the ocean when it had the appearance of being all over on fire. Every wave had a luminous margin on top; wherever the sides of the ship came in contact with the sea, there appeared a line of phosphoreal light. The eye discovered this luminous appearance everywhere on the ocean; nay, the very bosom of this immense element seemed to be pregnant with this shining appearance. We saw great bodies illuminated moving in the sea; some came alongside the ship and stood along with her, others moved off with a velocity almost equal to lightning. The shape of these illuminated bodies discovered them to be fishes. Some approached near one another, and when a small one came near a larger, it made all possible haste to fly from the danger.[90]

Forster's account should be compared with the stanza:

> Beyond the shadow of the ship,
> I watched the water-snakes:
> They moved in tracks of shining white,
> And when they reared, the elfish light
> Fell off in hoary flakes.

Forster's graphic description compares well with the descriptions from Bourzes[91] and from Cook's third voyage[92] quoted in Lowes as among the sources upon which Coleridge's imagination drew when he created his picture of phosphorescent sea. But its particular significance for us is that it derives directly from the experience of a man who travelled with Wales on board the *Resolution* and so helps us, albeit indirectly, to gain a more complete picture of the knowledge of phosphorescent seas that Wales himself brought to Christ's Hospital. There is also the very strong likelihood that Forster's *Observations* was in the mathematics library or in Wales's personal library, and that Coleridge had access to it there.

In this connexion, another passage may be cited from the same book. When the mariner's vessel is in the tropics we have the line:

> From the sails the dew did drip.

Forster, in his discussion of atmospheric conditions met with on the voyage, raises the question of the formation of the dew on ships in tropical latitudes:

> The climate within the tropics being very warm, and the nights rather long, the vapours raised in the day time by the heat of the sun, are condensed towards night, and fall frequently as dew on every part of the ship.[93]

Two lines further on in the poem we have the image:

> The horned Moon, with one bright star
> Within the nether tip.

Lowes, in his discussion of these lines, shows that Coleridge almost certainly read Maskelyne's 'Account of an Appearance of Light, like a Star, seen in the dark part of the Moon, on Friday 7th of March, 1794.'[94] Here is further evidence of Coleridge's interest in curious astronomical phenomena; and it should be noted here that Wales was a close acquaintance and probably a friend of Nevil Maskelyne. The earlier version of the poem read:

> The horned moon with one bright star
> Almost atween the tips.

Lowes has quoted a number of possible sources for this image, including one from Cook's third voyage, 'an immersion of [a star] behind the moon's dark limb'.[95] Observations of a similar nature were, however, made by Bayly at Queen Charlotte Sound on 12 May 1773, where the immergence of Aquarii behind the moon's bright limb, and its emersion from the dark limb of the moon about an hour and a quarter later, was observed and recorded. The comment on the emersion reads: 'These observations also very good, the air being very clear, and the objects distinct and well defined; the same magnifying power was used as at the immersion.'[96] And it is well to keep in mind in our consideration of this image that recording the distance of the moon from a fixed star was one of the ways used by Wales to determine longitude during the voyage, and that the mathematics syllabus at Christ's Hospital reveals that he taught this method to the pupils of the Mathematical School.

Being a meteorologist, Wales was particularly interested in the appearance of the aurora borealis. He had observed it both in northern England and in Hudson's Bay. Coleridge's first reference to the phenomenon occurs in his sonnet to William Godwin:

> In Finland's wintry skies the Mimic Morn
> Electric pours a stream of rosy light.

The poem was probably written at the Salutation and Cat Inn at a time when Coleridge was still maintaining fairly close contact with his old school. A year later the aurora borealis is described more fully in 'The Destiny of Nations', a poem in which clouds veiling the sun, and rushing 'with whirlwind speed', 'meteorlights', 'the rotting sea', the 'sporting Leviathan' and 'the white bear, drifting on a field of ice' all reveal Coleridge's growing interest in 'the tremendities of nature' at this time, and suggest the continuing influence of Wales's teaching in the growth of the poet's imaginative powers.

Having seen and described the aurora borealis, Wales was keen to ascertain whether a similar phenomenon was visible in high latitudes in the south. The scientists on board the *Resolution* claimed to be the first who saw and described the aurora australis: 'I never heard or read of any who had seen the Southern Lights (Aurora Australis) before us,' wrote J.R. Forster.[97] Wales, however, suspected that the phenomenon would be observed during the voyage and asked his companions to keep a sharp look-out for its appearance:

> At leaving the Cape of Good Hope I had desired that Lieut, and other officers who kept the Watch to be so obliging as to tell me if they saw [an] extraordinary appearance in the Heavens and this Morning Mr Pickersgill told me that he had seen something like the Aurora Borealis; but he had not time to appraise me of it before the clouds returned and covered it.[98]

Subsequently, however, there were many opportunities of observing the southern lights and Wales's journal contains several accounts of their appearance in the southern heavens. Each appearance is carefully described, and Wales is fond of making comparisons between the southern and the northern lights. It is clear that he considered himself one of the leading authorities on auroral phenomena. It is most likely, therefore, that, from time to time, he gave the boys at Christ's Hospital some of the benefits of his knowledge.

From the beginning of the third part of *The Ancient Mariner* until the conclusion of the voyage, the geographical location of the vessel becomes increasingly vague as the supernatural element takes charge of the action of the poem. It is pointless, therefore, to discuss whether Coleridge had the aurora australis or the aurora borealis in mind when he wrote:

> The upper air burst into life!
> And a hundred fire-flags sheen,
> To and fro were hurried about!
> And to and fro, and in and out,
> The wan stars danced between.

Quite likely, recollections of the auroral lights of both hemispheres have entered into the composition of the stanza. Indeed, the five stanzas following line 305 of the poem are obviously an attempt–a remarkably successful attempt–to assemble a composite picture of several of the 'tremendities of nature' in simultaneous operation as a setting for the supernatural drama in operation. However, if Coleridge drew so heavily upon accounts of the *Resolution*'s voyage, it is reasonable to suppose that descriptions of the aurora australis played their part in the imaginative construction of the poem. And this is borne out by a comparison of the stanza, quoted above, with some of Wales's descriptions of the phenomenon. On 15 March 1773 he recorded:

> . . . southern lights very bright at times, and exceedingly beautiful, the Colours being as varied and vivid as I have ever seen, the Motion also very quick and curious.[99]

and on 18 March:

> . . . These Lights were once so bright we could discern our Shadows on the Deck.[100]

The first note, with its description of the variety and motion of the lights, finds an effective poetic equivalent in the poet's imaginative presentation of the phenomenon; but it is the second note that, though finding no precise parallel in the poem at all, does contain in its simple and precise diction something of that peculiar blending of reality and unreality that constitutes the unique atmosphere of *The Ancient Mariner*. No other entry in the whole of Wales's journal so powerfully conveys the suggestion that Coleridge's old mathematics teacher provided the initial and perhaps the most lasting stimulus to the growth of the poet's imagination. And this suggestion is further borne out by the fact that in one of Wales's many descriptions of the phenomenon, the image of the wan stars dancing behind the aurora australis is distinctly foreshadowed. In his entry for 17 February 1773 we read:

> When I got up in the night, the natural state of the heavens except a little of the S.E., and about 10 degrees high all round the horizon was a whitish haze through which Stars of ye 3rd degree magnitude were just discernible all round

ye horizon was covered with thick clouds out of which arose Streams of a Pale reddish light that ascended towards the Zenith.[101]

When we reflect upon the course taken by the *Resolution*, the events associated with the voyage, and the many natural wonders described by its remarkable company of scientific travellers, it is clear that no other voyage in the whole realm of travel literature affords so many parallels with the voyage of the Ancient Mariner as does Cook's second voyage, the very voyage that, on the evidence, Coleridge would get to know better than any other, while attending Christ's Hospital.

*   *   *

If we agree that Coleridge first encountered much of the material from which he later fashioned the setting of *The Ancient Mariner* as a result of his association with William Wales at Christ's Hospital, it will be necessary to relate our findings to the explanation of the genesis of the poem provided by Livingstone Lowes. It was Lowes who first realised the value of the Gutch Memorandum Book for the study of Coleridge's creative imagination. By using this notebook he was able to identify a great number of the books read by Coleridge between the spring of 1795 and the spring or summer of 1798 and was able to demonstrate how, times out of number, striking phrases that Coleridge met with in his reading were completely refashioned by his imagination to emerge in a new poetic form in *The Ancient Mariner* and *Kubla Khan*. Lowes's book has, deservedly, established itself as one of the most brilliant and influential pieces of investigative literary criticism written during the present century, and the great mass of evidence uncovered has been so convincing that there has been a tendency to assume that the last word has been said as to the creation of the poem.[102] The weight of the evidence provided by Lowes has also tended to obscure the fact that his explanation of the operation of Coleridge's imagination is unduly intellectualistic. It begins with words and ends with words and is based primarily upon a study of the poet's reading. For Lowes, the creation of *The Ancient Mariner* began with a conscious act, the act of highly discriminating reading, and ended with a conscious act, the act of writing a poem. Between these two acts lay a period in which recollections of things read were blended and associated below the level of conscious thought:

> The depths are peopled to start out with . . . by conscious intellectual activity, keyed, it may be, as in Coleridge's intense and exigent reading to the highest pitch. Moreover . . . , it is again conscious energy, now of another and loftier type, which later drags the depths for their submerged treasure, and moulds the bewildering chaos into unity. But interposed between consciousness and consciousness is the well.[103]

However, such an explanation does not accord with Coleridge's explanation,[104] nor with systematic studies in the psychology of memory,[105] nor with the material discussed in the previous sections of this chapter. Why, we must ask, did the words and phrases that Coleridge recollected from his reading in the three or four years prior to the writing of *The Ancient Mariner* cling so fast to his memory? Lowes provides no better explanation than the intrinsic quality of the words and phrases themselves, together with the associative links that they were able to establish below the level of Coleridge's conscious thought. Such an explanation pays insufficient attention to the role of *feeling* and *interest* in the operation of the memory. Lowes never seriously addresses himself to a crucial question for the understanding of *The Ancient Mariner*: why did Coleridge read science and travel with such passionate enjoyment? On the evidence presented above, it is clear that Coleridge's interest in such things was first awakened at Christ's Hospital. There he absorbed the story of Cook's second voyage, a voyage in which science, adventure and the strange wonders of the deep were blended in a marvellous unity; and from the rapture of his receptive enthusiasm, the seeds of *The Ancient Mariner* were sown. The course of the voyage itself traced a pattern in his mind never to be entirely forgotten—as was not forgotten the voice of the mariner who told the tale. The events of the voyage established *centres of interest* in Coleridge's mind which directed much of his later reading and helped to organise and give coherence to his recollections when he came to write his great poem.

The genesis of *The Ancient Mariner*, then, is to be found in Coleridge's schoolboy interests and enthusiasms. He was himself aware of the great importance of this early stage of growth of the imagination. In discussing the education of the child he wrote:

> We are aware that it is with our cognitions as with our children. There is a period in which the method of nature is working for them; a period of aimless activity and unregulated accumulation, during which it is enough if we can preserve them in health and out of harm's way.[106]

Then, when the mind has had the benefit of this early, fallow period, a second phase of creativity may ensue:

> Again, there is a period of orderliness, of circumspection, of discipline, in which we purify, separate, define, select, arrange, and settle the nomenclature of communication.[107]

Such a second period did, of course, ensue in the creation of *The Ancient Mariner*; it was this period that was analysed with consummate skill in Lowes's *The Road to Xanadu*. We know from the evidence of the Gutch Memorandum Book and Lamb's letters to Coleridge that from 1796 the poet was conscientiously preparing himself to write an ambitious sequence of poems to the Sun, Moon and Elements. Lowes points out that a great deal of Coleridge's reading between 1796 and 1798 was directed towards that end. It was a scholar's reading, engaged upon with a purpose in view, in which relevant information was harried down from footnote to footnote. At this time it is to be suspected that Coleridge often consulted again books first met with in the mathematics library of Christ's Hospital. Now, from this period of reading, as Lowes has shown, a great wealth of *verbal* material found its way into the fabric of *The Ancient Mariner*. This is not surprising; since Coleridge was reading in preparation for writing poetry and with half an eye to the value of words, he was, in fact, settling 'the nomenclature of communication'. But the words and phrases that did linger in his mind did so by attaching themselves to interests that had been laid down years before.

Coleridge, himself, was well aware that the memory had its own principles of organisation, an awareness that caused him to make his famous distinction between the Fancy and the Imagination. In one of his letters he speaks of a 'confluence of recollections' and states how:

> ... we establish a centre as it were, a sort of nucleus in the reservoir of the soul, and towards this needle shoots after needle, cluster points on cluster points, from all parts of contained fluid and in all directions.[108]

Such a 'confluence of recollections' was certainly established in Coleridge's own mind around both the whole pattern of Cook's second voyage and the many natural wonders recorded by the voyagers. Whenever his reading passed over the nodal points of these old interests, something was drawn off and stored away by the passionate, discriminating memory. But perhaps the most remarkable feature of all is the preservation in the poem of the broad pattern of the *Resolution*'s voyage, so that, to some extent, the order of sequence of events in the poem follows the order of sequence of the relevant events of the voyage. The fair passage of the north-east trade winds, the squally passage of the south-east trades, the mast-high ice, the glint of the ice, the noise of ice splitting, follow the same order in the poem as in Wales's journal; and later in both the poem and the journal, accounts of the heat, the calm and the sea-snakes agree in their sequence. Not that this is to be considered a special feat of memory. It was most likely, assuming the voyage to have made a deep impression upon Coleridge, that the broad pattern and the sequence of events should have impressed themselves firmly upon his memory, especially if he had heard Wales recount them orally. On this question, too, we have the poet's own testimony: 'Reliques of sensation may exist for an indefinite time in a latent state, in the very same order in which they were originally impressed.'[109]

In the case of *The Ancient Mariner*, the 'reliques of sensation' appear to have existed in a latent state for between seven and sixteen years. This long period of slow germination had a good deal to do, we may be sure, with the poetic *quality* of so many of the individual images of the poem when they eventually found adequate *verbal* forms.

In Coleridge's comparison of the growth of thought to the growth of children, from which we have already quoted the first two phases, Coleridge adds yet a third stage: 'There is also a period of dawning and twilight, a period of anticipation affording trials of strength.'[110] Now many of his poems we have discussed above are related to *The Ancient Mariner* in just this way, but more particularly 'The Destiny of Nations' and the unwritten 'Hymns to the Sun, Moon, and the Elements'. Such poems afforded 'trials of strength'. It was not until Wordsworth suggested the theme of the Ancient Mariner that Coleridge discovered a structural pattern fully congenial to his creative personality. For congenial it certainly was. We know that he had read *Robinson Crusoe*, *Philip Quarll* and the *Arabian Nights* by the age of six, and he has told us that he was a playless dreamer until he was fourteen years old and would get into a sunny corner and imagine himself upon Crusoe's island. Later, as we have seen, he appears to have been tempted to join the navy, later still he did, in fact, join the 15th Light Dragoons to escape his creditors at Cambridge, and even later he planned his pantisocratic settlement upon the banks of the Susequennah. Throughout life, Coleridge had the greatest difficulty in coming to grips with the irritations and responsibilities of daily living. There is reason to believe, then, that tales of far voyages satisfied something very close to his own nature, and that in imagination,

> He went on shipboard
> With those bold voyagers, who made discovery
> Of golden lands.[111]

170

In so doing he might have been unconsciously seeking, as Weissman has suggested, to be 'his brother's keeper.'[112]

If, then, Coleridge first read or listened to tales of far voyages in a state of rapt wonder and delight as a schoolboy, it is likely that when he recollected them years later he recovered not only the events but also the states of mind that accompanied his first acquaintance with the stories.[113] Perhaps, like his own Wedding Guest, Coleridge once listened as a child would, spellbound, to an old seafaring man tell his one truly wonderful story; and when the poet came to write *The Ancient Mariner*, he became by means of what he himself called 'the transforming witchcraft of early associations' a schoolboy again listening to William Wales. As Coleridge wrote years later in *The Friend*:

> To carry on the feelings of childhood into the powers of manhood, to combine the child's sense of wonder and novelty with the appearances which every day for perhaps forty years has rendered familiar, this is the character and privilege of genius, and one of the marks which distinguish genius from talent.[114]

It is curious to reflect upon what in the case of *The Ancient Mariner* the feelings of childhood carried on into the powers of manhood accomplished. The most carefully planned and the most scientifically and efficiently conducted expedition ever made up to its time in the realm of reality provided the poet with a world of wonder and a nucleus of recollections from whence emerged in its own good time the most romantic voyage ever undertaken in the realm of the imagination.

7 STYLE, INFORMATION AND IMAGE IN THE ART OF COOK'S VOYAGES

WHEN I WAS A BOY it was difficult not to be stirred by the full-blooded rhythms of Kipling. 'Oh, East is East, and West is West, and never the twain shall meet,' he wrote, and in a more serious vein reminded us constantly in a famous hymn that the God of Great Britain had given us, in a kind of trust, 'dominion over palm and pine' and 'lesser breeds without the law'.

In his now-famous book, *Orientalism*,[1] Edward Said examines critically a set of received western views about the Orient over a vast period, from the time of Aeschylus's *The Persians* to the present day. He concludes that these views, which he describes as orientalist, are consistent and relatively unchanging, and present a view of the East from Egypt to China that is addressed to the past and achieves a kind of timeless quality. He describes it as 'an internally structured archive'[2] and argues that it gives a profoundly false view of the East, but one by means of which Europe and, more recently, the United States, have been able to exert and maintain mastery over the East.

It should, therefore, be interesting to consider the emergence of a European imagery of the Pacific and its peoples in the small time span of Cook's voyages (no more than twelve years) along the lines of Said's vast canvas. Following his line of approach, we might ask to what extent was the imagery truthful, to what extent false, and, whether true or false, to what extent was it accessible to serve the purposes of European domination? I shall not promise to provide a conclusive answer to those questions; that would require an analysis as sweeping as Said's. I suggest it only as a promising line of enquiry.

John Locke once said that 'in the beginning all the world was America',[3] meaning that in the history of civil society all the peoples of the world were once hunters and gatherers. He could have said that once all the world, or most of it, was India. Because from the time of Columbus's misconception that he had reached India, the term 'Indian' developed a generic usage for all non-European peoples, apart from a few old-time exotics such as Arab and Chinese. In his journal of the *Endeavour* voyage, Joseph Banks calls the natives of Tierra del Fuego, the Tahitians, the Maori and the Australian Aborigines all Indians, though he is at pains to distinguish their physical and social differences. And as with the generic verbal concept, so with the visual concept: the earliest depictions of Pacific peoples appear to depend on models, particularly in the matter of dress, upon the peoples of the Indian sub-continent.

Compare the engraved depiction of a Buddhist procession from François Valentijn's *Oud en Nieuw Oost-Indien* (1724–6) (pl. 151) with the two illustrations used in the first volume of John Hawkesworth's *Account of the Voyages . . .* (1773) (pls 180, 152) to illustrate Captain Wallis's initial encounter with the Tahitians. Wallis possessed no professional artist with him on his ship *Dolphin*. The unknown draughtsman and the engraver of the illustrations in Hawkesworth have

150 (facing page). G.B. Cipriani, *A Dance in Raiatea*, oil on oval canvas, 33 × 73.7 cm., *c.*1772, Goodwood House, West Sussex.

151. *A Buddhist procession,*
engraving from François
Valentijn, *Oud en Nieuw
Oost-Indien,* 1724–6.

152. *Captain Wallis, on his
arrival at O'Taheite, in
conversation with Oberea the
Queen,* engraving from
Hawkesworth's *Account of
the Voyages,* 1773, vol. 1,
pl. 22.

turned wholly to Hawkesworth's text for their subject matter and to an Indian
(i.e., 'Orientalist') model, such as the engravings in Valentijn, to depict the dress
and demeanour of the Tahitians.

The dependence upon a text is a matter of the first importance towards
understanding representations purporting to portray events experienced on European voyages to the Pacific. The portrayal of events has long possessed an
immense academic prestige in the visual arts and reaches back to a time when the
only events depicted by artists worthy of the name were those crucial to the lives
of gods, heroes and saints. When Nicolas Poussin painted *The Crossing of the Red
Sea* (1635),[4] he depended upon the text of Exodus. The Israelites, needless to say,

174

possessed no travelling artist to make field sketches of the God of Israel drowning the hosts of Pharaoh.

Orientalist imagery was powerful enough to supervene even when an artist had a Tahitian in the flesh before him. As E.H. McCormick has noted, when Reynolds drew the young Tahitian Mai (universally known as Omai), brought back to England by Captain Furneaux, commander of the *Adventure* on Cook's second voyage, he gave us an excellent likeness of the man and 'the representative of a new race, a Polynesian'.[5] But when Reynolds painted Omai's full-length portrait for the Royal Academy of 1776, he effected a major 'poetic' transformation. As Joseph Burke has observed, 'his spurious Tahitian garb evokes the Rajah and the Roman Senator' (pl. 153).[6] The visual presence of the subject himself in England did not diminish the countervailing power of the orientalising image. Engravers also could orientalise original drawings of Pacific peoples who possessed little or no 'oriental' features. Note how John Hall orientalised William Hodges's classicised drawing of Potatow (pls 106, 154).

The orientalisation of the imagery illustrating Wallis's voyage and its persistence in Reynolds's portrait of Omai and Hall's engraving of Potatow suggest a fruitful line of enquiry that I cannot pursue further here. To what extent, it might be asked, was the pre-Cook imagery of the Pacific, the imagery that issued from the Portuguese, Spanish and Dutch voyages modelled on oriental prototypes? To what extent was the Pacific, as it became known to Europeans, a fringe-dweller beside the great orientalist stereotype?

Parkinson was the first artist who ever attempted to draw Tahitians from life.

153. Sir Joshua Reynolds, *Omai*, oil on canvas, 604 × 370 cm., *c*.1775, Castle Howard, Yorkshire.

154. *Potatow*, engraving by John Hall after Hodges, in Cook, *A Voyage towards the South Pole and Round the World*, 1777, pl. LVI, fp. 159.

175

He made slight, hesitant and rather perfunctory drawings of Tahitians or, to be more precise, Raiateans dancing, at Banks's request (pl. 155). In his journal Banks described the dancing in detail and doubtless desired some accompanying illustrations. Here we are confronted by a point of general interest. Which came first, Banks's textual record or Parkinson's drawings? It is most unlikely that the drawings are done from memory, for Parkinson was trained to draw what was before him. This means that the drawings were probably available to Banks as an *aide-mémoire* when he came to write up his journal. When such field studies were available, it is always possible that the text of Banks's journal was in part dependent upon them, and perhaps also other journals, such as Cook's.

Banks retained Parkinson's sketch-book after his death, and it was probably from Parkinson's little drawings that the Italian artist Cipriani developed his rather grand composition of Tahitians dancing that his close friend Bartolozzi engraved for the second volume of Hawkesworth's *Account* (1773) (pl. 156). Obviously, we have now moved some distance from the orientalist stereotype that determined the depiction of Tahitians illustrating Wallis's voyage that were used in the first volume of Hawkesworth.

Both Cipriani and Bartolozzi were foundation members of the Royal Academy that had been established in 1768, the year Cook left on his first voyage to the Pacific. Both were Florentines, and both belonged to the small but influential circle of Italian artists that supported the grand style of history painting championed by Reynolds, as first President of the Academy, in his Discourses, particularly the early Discourses delivered between 1768 and 1773 (the year Hawkesworth's volumes appeared).

In the fourth Discourse, delivered in 1771, Reynolds had a good deal to say about the grand style that determined the character of history painting:

> ... it is not enough in Invention that the Artist should restrain and keep under all the inferior parts of his subject; he must sometimes deviate from vulgar and strict historical truth, in pursuing the grandeur of his design.
>
> How much the great stile exacts from its professors to conceive and represent their subjects in a poetical manner, not confined to mere matter of fact, may be seen in the Cartoons of Raffaele. In all the pictures in which the painter has represented the apostles, he has drawn them with great nobleness, he has given them as much dignity as the human figure is capable of receiving; yet we are expressly told in scripture they had no such respectable appearance; and of St Paul in particular, we are told by himself, that his bodily presence was mean. Alexander is said to have been of a low stature: a Painter ought not so to represent him. Agiselaus was low, lame, and of a mean appearance: none of these defects ought to appear in a piece of which he is the hero. In conformity to custom, I call this part of the art History Painting, it ought to be called Poetical, as in reality it is.[7]

Cipriani clearly perceived himself to be working within the category of history painting when he developed Parkinson's field studies with the help most probably of Raphael's cartoons to give them a transforming, poetic nobility as Reynolds recommended. Compare his stately Tahitians with the apostles in Raphael's cartoon *Christ's charge to Peter* (pl. 157).

As we have already noted, such eighteenth-century representations of Pacific people are popularly described as 'noble savage' depictions. But that can be misleading. Cipriani and Bartolozzi did not set out consciously to ennoble Tahitians:

155. Sydney Parkinson,
*Sketch of a Dancing Girl,
Raiatea*, pencil, 28.7 ×
22.9 cm., 1769, British
Library, London (Add.
MS 23921, f. 37c).

156. G.B. Cipriani, *A
View of the inside of a house
in the Island of Ulietea
[Raiatea], with the
representation of a dance to the
music of the country*, pen and
wash, 21.2 × 33.7 cm.,
*c.*1772, Dixson Library,
Sydney (PXX 2, 14).

157. Raphael, *Christ's
charge to Peter*, cartoon for
tapestry, Victoria and
Albert Museum, London.

158. Sydney Parkinson, *Distortions of the Mouth used in Dancing*, pencil, 18.8 × 16.2 cm., 1769, British Library, London (Add. MS 23921, f. 51a).

they probably believed with Dr Johnson that 'one savage is very much like another'. They sought rather to conform to the principles of history painting as enunciated by Reynolds when portraying even contemporary events. The grand style was strongly supported by the Italian junta of artists in the Academy for whom painting in that style was a matter of national pride. Raphael, after all, was an Italian. So Cipriani, on Reynolds's advice, suppressed anything in Parkinson's drawings that seemed mean or peculiar.

However, Banks had taken pains in his journal to describe the facial distortions made by Tahitians while dancing, 'setting their mouths askew in the most extraordinary manner, in the practice of which they are brought up from earliest childhood'. In his field drawings Parkinson depicted the grimacing girls (pl. 158). But if we examine Cipriani's drawing and the engraving Bartolozzi developed from it, the grimaces have virtually disappeared; and when Cipriani painted his oval version of the scene, now in the Goodwood Collection (pl. 150) even the one vestigial grimace has been suppressed.[8] In order to give a poetic dignity even to recent events, particular truths, if ugly or mean, should not be shown.

This application of the grand style to the portrayal of events of Cook's voyages was largely a contingent matter that arose from the Italianate domination of English taste during the early years of the Royal Academy, not a general predisposition characteristic of late eighteenth-century depictions of Pacific people as a whole. Parkinson's little drawing was never engraved in Hawkesworth's *Account*. Perhaps the distorted gestures were regarded as being too mean to portray in such an official, up-market production. However, there were many in England who sought realistic portrayals of Pacific people. Stanfield Parkinson eventually succeeded in getting his dead brother's journal[9] published in 1773 in the face of the concerted opposition of Banks, Hawkesworth and the Admiralty, but it did not become readily available to the public until 1784. The reviewer of the *Gentleman's Magazine* spoke for those who sought the accurate portrayal of reality:

> ... by far the most valuable part of his labours [i.e., Sydney Parkinson's labours], and what was never before executed with equal judgement and fidelity, is that characteristic distinction observable in the portraits of his chiefs, their dresses and ornaments, which mark their originality ... It were needless to enlarge upon the accuracy of the drawings which embellish and illustrate the work, as they are universally acknowledged to be the resemblance of whatever they are intended to represent.

178

These are the important objects that give the work before us . . . a superiority over those contemporary voyagers who, being intent on gaining the character of fine writers and elegant artists, have departed from the simplicity of Nature to give scope to the decorations of Art.[10]

Both in his sketchbook and in his published *Journal*, Parkinson faithfully depicted the facial distortions used in Tahitian dancing.

At this point it will be useful to make a general distinction relevant for the voyage art of the late eighteenth and early nineteenth centuries in which on-the-spot drawings are known to have been made. In such cases we usually possess both field studies of Pacific peoples and developed drawings and engravings derived from them based more or less on the studies in which the people concerned are re-presented. In both cases, in the original field depictions and in the re-presentations, a European perception of things Pacific is in operation, but acting at different levels and in different ways. In the first case, that of field depictions, the demand for accurate information acts more powerfully, despite the conceptual luggage that each artist brought from Europe with him; and in the second case, that of re-presentation, though the original information is rarely subverted entirely, the canons of taste operate powerfully to transform the field studies into acceptable imagery—acceptable, that is to say, within the particular category of art within which the new information is being presented. Furthermore, it is probably in the tensions that developed between art in the service of taste and art in the service of information that the allied problem of the relationship of visual art to power and domination resides. Both art as taste and art as information could be adapted to the needs of power, mastery and domination, but they served in different ways.

William Hodges, on the second voyage, was somewhat better at portraiture than Parkinson, portraying people with a greater feeling for their individual personality rather than as simply ethnic types.[11] Yet an element of classicism persists in his portraits. His friends on the voyage, the two Forsters, were keen to draw parallels between ancient Greeks and Pacific peoples, Tahitians especially. But though a classicist vision frequently inhabits Hodges's on-site portraiture, an orientalist stereotype sometimes, as we have seen, intrudes when the subjects are transformed by engraving.[12] But they are not *invariably* orientalised. Other stereotypes begin to emerge. For example, Hodges's sensitive drawing of Tu, with its apprehensive, puzzled expression, is transformed by engraving into a wild-looking savage, the hair matted and thickened, the eyes popping (pl. 63).[13] It is an early example of the romantic savage stereotype, a being of unpredictable behaviour, incapable of constraining emotion—a type that will come to dominate nineteenth-century representations.

Yet the elaborate late-baroque classicism of the Cipriani/Bartolozzi circle persisted in the engravings associated with the second voyage. When Hodges was asked to supervise the production of the engravings chosen to illustrate the second voyage, he employed Cipriani to draw the figures for some of his more elaborate compositions, those depicting notable events of the voyage. We know that Cipriani drew the figures for Hodges's *Landing at Erramanga* (pl. 181),[14] and he most probably drew the figures for *The Landing at Middleburgh* (Eua) also.[15] It was engraved for the official account of the voyage by John Keyes Sherwin, a pupil of Bartolozzi (pl. 69). On this occasion, however, the use of the grand style of history painting for the portrayal of recent events in the Pacific produced a

179

much greater fracas than that created by Hawkesworth's *Account*. For, as we have seen, the veracity of the engravings was challenged by one of Hodges's companions on the *Resolution*, the young George Forster, who had been friendly enough on the voyage itself. The sting in Forster's attack may have been due to the fact that the Admiralty had refused to allow his father to edit the official account of the voyage, which was understood to have been part of his father's original commission; but it did not weaken its point. For its veiled sarcasm was a piece of invective that would be hard to improve upon, and it is not surprising that the young Forster later became a master of German prose.[16]

But poor Hodges, as was noted earlier, was hardly to blame. Home in London he was caught, as a potential aspirant to Royal Academy membership, between the rules of taste and the demands of ethnographic accuracy. And there may have been other reasons for the elevated style adopted for *The Landing at Middleburgh*. Cook had been quite shocked by some of the more salacious passages in Hawkesworth and had advised Dr Douglas, his editor for his account of the second voyage, that 'with respect to the Amours of my People at Otaheite and other places: I think it will not be necessary to mention them attall . . . my desire is that nothing indecent may appear in the whole book, and you cannot oblige me more than by pointing out whatever may appear to you as such.'[17] With such instructions in mind, Douglas may well have felt that an engraving that presented young bare-breasted Tongan women welcoming Cook's young sailors with open arms was something Cook might not have approved of. Hodges, too, may have been aware of such constraints when planning the engraving.

However, there is another aspect to the story. Hodges found a strong champion for the way he presented *The Landing at Middleburgh*, whatever the role of Cipriani may have been in its designing, in his old friend William Wales. Wales was incensed at the way George Forster had interpreted many of the actions of Cook and his men in his *A Voyage round the World* (1777). He assumed that the book had been written by the elder Forster, using his son's name as a cloak, after being prevented from writing the official account of the voyage. Wales's comments on Forster's book are of special interest because they provide an insight into the ways in which Hodges went about constructing drawings relating to events of the voyage and because they point to the strong probability that Forster had access to Hodges's engravings for the official account when writing his own and made good use of them to develop the descriptive passages of his narrative.

Wales stressed that he was authorised by Hodges himself to say that Hodges had lost none of his original sketches of the people who featured in *The Landing at Middleburgh*. Every figure, so far as is related to dress, manners and customs, was drawn from persons Hodges had seen, 'even the divine old man with a long white beard'. Wales then proceeded to draw verbal parallels from Forster's book to show how closely the engraving corresponded to Forster's own verbal descriptions of the people of Eua. Wales had a strong point here, because a comparison of Forster's descriptions and the engravings reveals that Forster made more use of them to develop his own account than Dr Douglas did for the official voyage.

Forster had also been highly critical, as already noted, of Hodges's depiction of the landing at Eromanga (pl. 181). In criticising Forster's comments, Wales provided an account of Hodges's working methods when confronted with the need to depict a specific event. He quoted from Cook's own journal, comparing it with Forster's version of the event, and then added that Hodges had transcribed the same extract from Cook's journal a few days after the incident for the express purpose of developing a visual description of the event. 'The manners and persons of the natives were copied chiefly from those of Tanna, as they were exactly alike.'[18]

Hodges had not been on the boats that attempted the landing at Eromanga. Not being an eye-witness, he resorted to the text of Cook's journal, acting as history painters had traditionally worked in constructing a visual representation of an event. What Hodges apparently did not tell Wales is that he had later employed Cipriani to provide the basic drawing representing the action.

* * *

The controversy sparked off by George Forster's book did not begin until months after Cook had left on his third voyage, so neither Cook nor Webber, his artist on the voyage, could have been aware of the issues debated between Wales and Forster. In the circumstances, Webber's approach to the portrayal of events was similar to that of Hodges, based upon academic convention. By 1777 Cook, more than ever before, was aware that he was making contemporary history and would have had the publication of the new voyage in mind from the time he departed. An important part of Webber's programme was to record remarkable events. So once again, an official artist on a scientific voyage was caught between the demands of taste and the need for accurate information. To grasp this problem we must remember that Webber, whose drawings will be discussed in greater detail in the next chapter, worked within several quite distinct categories of art, each possessed of its own conventions. He drew coastal profiles in association with the cartographers such as William Bligh, the master of the *Resolution*. Such views were wholly informational. He made drawings of plants and animals that were subject to the conventions of naturalists in their processes of classification. He drew portraits of native peoples in which he sought to record ethnic characteristics observed by Cook and others, such as William Anderson, the surgeon on the *Resolution*. At the other end of the scale, he constructed drawings to represent events. In the latter case, the conventions of the grand style still operated strongly.

But Webber's approach to history painting differed from that of the Cipriani/ Bartolozzi circle. In the place of their late-baroque classicism he substituted a mannerist style. Mannerism had come back into fashion along with the early Gothic Revival and the storm-and-stress phase of early romanticism, particularly in Switzerland. It is especially evident in the work of Fuseli.[19] But no direct links between Webber and Fuseli are known, and his style is quite unlike that of Fuseli in all respects, apart from the heightening and elongation of the figure. Many mannerists adopted a proportion of nine or even ten heads to the full figure. The most likely source for Webber's neo-mannerism is to be found in the work and teaching of Joseph-Marie Vien (pls 159, 160).[20] Webber studied in Paris with Johann Wille from 1770 to 1774 and attended classes at the Ecole des Beaux-Arts at a time when Vien was the most influential artist. Wille himself was a good friend of Vien and sent his son to study under him.[21] In the year that Webber sailed with Cook, Vien became the head of the French School at Rome.

In this connection it is interesting to note that a book on anatomy that had been prepared for use by the pupils in the French School at Rome was on board the *Resolution* when it sailed. This was Bernardino Genga's *Anatomy Improved and Illustrated with regard to the uses thereof in designing . . . demonstrated and exemplified from*

159. Joseph-Marie Vien, *Greek girl at the bath*, oil on canvas, 90.2 × 67.3 cm., 1767, Museo de Arte, Ponce, Puerto Rico.

160. John Webber, *A Night Dance by Women*, pencil and pen, 48.9 × 66 cm., *c.*1777, British Library, London (Add. MS 15513, f. 10).

161a and b (facing page top). *Borghese Gladiator*, two engravings by Jan van der Gucht from Bernardino Genga, *Anatomia per uso et intellegenza del disegno*, Rome, 1691, pls xxx and xxxiv.

162 (facing page bottom). John Webber, *A Boxing match, Friendly Islands*, pen, pencil and wash, 31.1 × 45.1 cm., 1778, British Library, London (Add. MS 15513, f. 9).

the most celebrated statues in Rome. The engravings in this book–and it was virtually a book of engravings–were by Jan van der Gucht, a friend and collaborator of Hogarth (pl. 161). The book first appeared in Italian in 1691 and an English translation was published in 1723. We do not know who owned the *Resolution* copy; it may have been Webber's–he certainly made use of it–or it may have been David Samwell's, the young Welsh surgeon's mate on the *Resolution*, who mentions the book in his diary.[22] It was the kind of book that could have been equally of value to an artist or a surgeon.

When we compare the engravings after the *Borghese Gladiator* in Genga's *Anatomy* with the drawings Webber made of Tongan boxers who helped to entertain Cook at his grand reception at Tongatapu (pl. 162) and of the boxers who entertained Cook on Hawaii also,[23] we realise that Webber used the book to help him with his figure work. Here, then, is further evidence for the source of Webber's use of elongated proportions and classical parallels. But this is relevant only for his portrayal of events. It is misleading to generalise indiscriminately, as John Beaglehole and others have done, that Webber elongated his figures invariably. To do this is to ignore the differing conventions that determined the use of style for the different categories of art that Webber practised. An artist even today rarely uses one style only, and in the eighteenth century artists varied their style to the category within which they were working. Furthermore, a personal style is subject to change and development.

On the voyage, the overriding requirements were that Webber should be specific and make distinctions in his drawings of plants, animals and people that reinforced the verbal distinctions made by Anderson, the surgeon, Cook, Samwell and others in their journals. As the voyage progressed, these requirements became a challenge and a stimulus: his work developed a greater sense of immediacy and freshness. He learned much during those four years. As Rüdiger

TAVOLA XXXIV.

50

TAVOLA XXX.

46

Joppien has put it, 'the voyage for him had been a school for seeing'[24] Contrast his drawing of *A Woman of New Holland* (pl. 179), made at the beginning of the voyage, with the one of *A Hottentot woman* (pl. 163), made at the Cape of Good Hope towards the end of it. The first is drawn within the firm, linear conventions he had learned at art school; the second uses line and brush with deftness and skill, with the confidence of an artist who had learned how to get down an effect quickly while the chance was offered. Or contrast the tall *Man of Hawaii dancing* (pl. 164) with his squat *Man of Kamchatka* (pl. 165). No mannerist conventions of elongation are employed here. Other artists had drawn the natives of the Pacific before Webber, but no other artist before him had been called upon to draw so many varied ethnic types. He is Europe's first serious ethnographic artist and his work stands at the threshold of ethnography as a science. It was his business not only to draw native peoples as such but also to distinguish as best he could the visual differences to be observed between one ethnic group and another. He was the first artist to make Europeans aware of the great variety of peoples who inhabited the Pacific.

It is sometimes forgotten that the presence of a dominant style or convention, whether 'orientalist', classicist or mannerist, does not preclude the conveyance of ethnographic information. Dr Adrienne Kaeppler has noted, as we have seen, that even in Sherwin's engraving of *The Landing at Middleburgh*, the butt of George Forster's criticism, the Tongan ritual mutilation of the small finger is recorded faithfully. An English sense of decorum may have precluded Webber from presenting the Fatafei Poulaho, who was the Tu'i Tonga, or sacred king, as the enormously fat man that we are assured he was; but he did depict the fae, or sacred feathered headdress, worn only by the greatest chieftains.[25] Before we dismiss voyage drawings or engravings as inaccurate or misleading, we should remind ourselves that all information is conveyed by a code of some kind, and the first thing to do is to learn to read that code.

One often hears the comment: eighteenth-century draughtsmen made Pacific Islanders look like Europeans. A counter question would be: which Europeans? Irish or Ukrainian, Spaniards or Swedes? Webber was capable of making clear ethnic distinctions, but we must realise that he was trained to draw the figure as artists are still trained today, within some kind of common human stereotype. Artists do not learn to draw the human figure by first drawing a Maori, a Scot or an Eskimo; they begin by drawing human figures as distinct, say, from cats and dogs. Then, as now, there were norms for drawing the human figure of one kind or another, and in the eighteenth century it was agreed by artists and scientists alike that the best models were provided by the sculptors of ancient Greece. Furthermore, this visual mode was reinforced by the universal view that all humankind was descended from a common family, and that after the Deluge the nations had been dispersed throughout the world and that many had suffered degeneration following their dispersion. Since all sprang from one family, all belonged to one species, and eighteenth-century voyagers did not expect to find major physical differences between one nation and another. Ethnic differences of a physical kind could be and were noted: the breadth of the nose of the Polynesian, the high cheek bones and plump faces of the Nootkans, the short necks of the Unalaskans, and so forth. But these were empirical observations based on the observation of individuals; they had not been conceptualised or theorised. For the greater part of the eighteenth century the concept of race, as it later came to be understood, was unknown, and the word little used. Webber's ethnic distinctions

184

163. John Webber, *A Hottentot woman*, pencil, pen and wash, 32.9 × 19 cm., 1780, British Library, London (Add. MS 17277, no. 49).

164 (below left). John Webber, *A Man of Hawaii dancing*, wash and watercolour, 24.1 × 17.8 cm., *c*.1781–3, Dixson Library, Sydney (PXX 2, 36).

165 (below right). John Webber, *A Man of Kamchatka*, pencil, chalk and wash, 27.9 × 20.3 cm., 1779, Francis P. Farquhar Collection, Berkeley, California.

are best understood as empirical and contingent observations based upon his observation of individuals. He drew a broad-nosed Polynesian as he might have drawn a broad-nosed European.

*   *   *

Concepts about native people were changing, nevertheless, while Webber was away on his four-year voyage. From 1775 onwards, Johann Blumenbach of Göttingen was developing the emerging science of comparative anatomy by his work on the human cranium. As the result of his investigations, he came to the conclusion that humanity was divided into Caucasian (white), Mongolian (yellow), Malayan (brown), Ethiopian (black) and American (red) races. His theory would profoundly affect the way native peoples were to be studied during the nineteenth century.

More importantly from a visual point of view was the contemporaneous work of Petrus Camper (1722–89), who had trained as an artist and later developed a special interest in anatomical studies, becoming Professor of Anatomy at Gröningen. Like most of the artists of his day, he believed that the ancient Greeks had provided in their sculpture the best models of human proportion and perfection, but his own anatomical studies led him to agree in principle with Blumenbach's theories. Racial distinction could be revealed by what he called the facial angle: the angle formed by a line let fall vertically from the hair line of the forehead and a line from the hair line to the line of the teeth (pl. 166). The smaller the angle, according to Camper, the higher the level of human development. A minus angle was the height of perfection.[26]

Camper's work on the facial angle was read by the young Georges Cuvier (1769–1832), one of the major pioneers of comparative anatomy. In 1800 he wrote an 'Instructive note on the researches to be made relative to the anatomical differences between diverse races of men'. 'Everyone knows', he wrote,

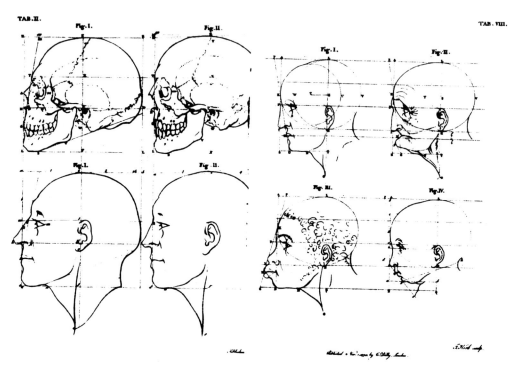

166. Illustrations from *The Works of the Late Professor Camper...*, trans. T. Cogan, London, 1794.

that the greatest painters have often badly portrayed the character of the negro and have only painted a white man smeared with soot. The drawings which are found in modern voyages, although made on the spot, show the effects more or less of the rules and proportions that the designers learnt in the Schools of Europe, and there is almost none of them on whom the naturalist can sufficiently rely to form the basis of subsequent research. Special studies for the type of portraits which we require are necessary, to the worth of ordinary portraits must be added that of geometric precision which can only be obtained with certain positions of the head, but which must be exact. Thus it is imperative that the straight profile should be joined with the frontal view . . . Drawings of all ages, and different sexes and of diverse conditions in each race must be taken. The clothes, the markings with which the majority of the natives disfigure themselves and which the ordinary travellers are at such pains to send us only serve to disfigure the true character of the face. It would be important that the painter should paint all his heads with the same hair style, the simplest possible, and above all, that which would least cover the forehead and which least changes the shape of the head. All strange ornaments, the rings, the pendants, the tattooing ought to be omitted. The designer should have studied the famous essay by Camper on the methods of portraying the characters of the various human races . . .[27]

What we have here are quite new proposals being projected for ethnic portraiture, proposals that would establish conventions suited to new needs of the science of comparative anatomy. The older empirical distinctions that included an interest in dress and ornament are to be ignored. A conceptual distinction is being drawn between the needs of physical and the needs of social anthropologists. Cuvier's views thus form a watershed between Enlightenment interest in native peoples and the new racial interests of the nineteenth century.

Cuvier's manuscript came into the possession of Charles-Alexandre Lesueur (1778–1846) and Nicolas Petit (d. 1805) who were together responsible for the drawings of Tasmanian and Australian Aborigines made on Nicolas Baudin's voyage (1800–4) to Tasmania and southern Australia. It is clear that they fashioned their drawings to accord with the new needs expressed by Cuvier (pl. 167).

The new science of comparative anatomy had no influence upon the drawings of native peoples made by the artists who travelled with Cook. J.R. Forster, however, knew Blumenbach well, and the latter corresponded with Banks. Furthermore, Captain James King, who took charge of Cook's third voyage after his death in Hawaii, brought back the skull of a young man from Nootka Sound, and Petrus Camper made a drawing of it when he visited Oxford in 1783.[28] In addition, William Anderson appears to have had some knowledge, even if indirectly, of Camper's theories. Consider his description of the Tasmanians encountered in Adventure Bay when the *Resolution* called there to wood and water:

Their features are not at all agreeable, and their noses though broad and full are not flat and their lips of an ordinary thickness. The lower part of the face projects a good deal, as is the case in most Indians I have seen, so that a line let fall from the forehead would cut off a much larger portion than in Europeans.[29]

167. Nicolas Petit, *Head of an Aborigine of Van Diemen's Land*, pencil and wash, 11.5 × 14.5 cm., probably 1802, Museé d'Histoire Naturelle, Le Havre, France, Lesueur Collection (2008.2).

168. John Webber, *A Native of Van Diemen's Land*, pencil and wash, 35.5 × 29.2 cm., 1777, Allport Library and Museum of Fine Arts, State Library of Tasmania, Hobart.

Webber worked closely with Anderson but his drawing of a Tasmanian man (pl. 168) is still presented within the empirical conventions of the Enlightenment. The prognathous face is not entirely ignored. Webber has drawn what he has seen, but he did not make a conceptual point about it as Anderson did. Had he wished to do so he would no doubt have drawn the Tasmanian in profile as Nicolas Petit was to do later when he came to draw Tasmanians in 1802 (pl. 167).

* * *

I want to turn now from the problem of particularising native types into racial concepts to a quite different problem: the convergence of the multiple imagery of the Pacific produced by Cook's artists into two sharply contrasting dominant images. I shall deal with them briefly because a good deal has been said about them already. The first depicted the Pacific, particularly its islands, as a southern Arcadia or paradise, as the lands of free love and easy living, where life could be lived without toil and labour. The other depicted these same islands as the abode of savages who performed ghastly rites in the fear of their pagan gods. These generalised images crystallised rapidly in the space of a decade or so, from 1773 to 1784, from the large variety of representations available, because they suited European needs at many levels: psychological, religious, political and so forth. The waters of the Pacific, it might be said, mirrored once again the old dualities at the centre of European culture: classical antiquity and medieval Christianity.

The idea of the Pacific as Arcadia was promoted by such images as Cipriani's picture of Raiateans dancing (pl. 150), Hodges's paintings of young Tahitian girls bathing (pl. 140) and Webber's idealised views of the Vaitepiha valley (pl. 169) and the Friendly Islands (pl. 170). The image of the Pacific as a nether world of pagan cannibals was promoted by the depictions of Polynesian funerary rites (pls

188

169. John Webber, *A View in Vaitepiha Valley*, oil on canvas, 58.4 × 80.4 cm., 1787, Honolulu Academy of Arts, Honolulu.

170. John Webber, *A View in Annamooka, one of the Friendly Isles*, coloured etching, 28.7 × 42.4 cm., 1787, Department of Prints and Drawings, British Museum, London.

171, 172), by images of death without the promise of salvation (pl. 173), and by representations of such rituals as that in Webber's *Human sacrifice at Otaheite* (pl. 174).

*   *   *

By way of conclusion, we might glance again at Edward Said's thesis. From what we have surveyed it would be false, surely, to conclude that the early visual imagery of the Pacific issuing from Cook's voyages is internally consistent in the way that characterises the orientalist imagery described by Said. For we have

189

171. Sydney Parkinson, *A Morai with an offering to the dead*, wash, 23.8 × 37 cm., 1769, British Library, London (Add. MS 23921, f. 28).

172. *A Toupapow with a corpse on it*, engraving by William Woollett after a drawing by William Hodges, in Cook, *A Voyage towards the South Pole and Round the World*, 1777, vol. 1, pl. XLIV, fp. 184.

seen in sequence Pacific peoples rendered according to oriental, classical and mannerist imagery and the beginnings of a racialist-type imagery emerging at the beginning of the nineteenth century. Yet there is a tendency for the representations to coalesce into two antithetical and yet mutually supportive images around which a high degree of internal consistency, in Said's sense, develops during the nineteenth century; that is to say, the Pacific as a kind of paradise in which Europeans might find a heavenly bliss on earth, and an opposing image of the Pacific as a kind of purgatory from which the poor children of nature might be won for a life of bliss in heaven. It was Dante who first placed purgatory in the southern hemisphere. European imagery of the Pacific does possess a durable though contradictory inner consistency.

Finally, there is the question of power. Here it seems images, representations, of two sharply different kinds were required. On the one hand, there was the need for highly specific images: charts, coastal profiles and so forth, by means of which ships could penetrate the Pacific with a degree of safety; and drawings of fauna and flora, by means of which Europeans could gain a knowledge of the natural productions of the Pacific and decide what was and what was not of commercial value. Such specific imagery acted at an intellectual, utilitarian, practical level; art in the service of science, commerce and the flag. The more generalised images, whether paradisal or purgatorial, acted at an emotional level. They helped to mobilise that great host of sailors, sealers, whalers, missionaries

190

173. *Monuments in Easter Island*, engraving by William Woollett after a drawing by William Hodges, in Cook, *A Voyage towards the South Pole and Round the World*, 1777, vol. 1, pl. XLIX, fp. 294.

174. John Webber, *A Human sacrifice at Otaheite*, pen, wash and watercolour, 42.2 × 62.5 cm., *c*.1777, British Library, London (Add. MS 15513, f. 16).

and colonial administrators who were to leave their old lives in the northern hemisphere for the anticipated pleasures of the southern, or, if they were made of sterner moral stuff, who were to risk their lives to save the souls of savages for God's eternal kingdom. In either case, the imagery was a component of the decision-making of those Europeans who would enter the Pacific in their thousands and eventually dominate it.

8 CONSTRUCTING 'PACIFIC' PEOPLE[1]

IT IS GENERALLY AGREED THAT Cook's three voyages greatly enhanced the economic and political power of Europe in the Pacific. But before such power could be fully exercised, certain basic sciences and technologies, the efficient maidservants of power, had themselves to be enhanced. Cook's voyages advanced astronomy, navigation and cartography or, as he might have put it, geographical science. But there were other sciences of less direct concern to the Admiralty enhanced by his voyages, and these contributed also in their time to European domination in the Pacific, namely natural history, meteorology and the emergent science of ethnography.

Important advances were made in all these sciences continually throughout the three voyages, but there were differences in emphasis. As we have noted, the first voyage is the botanical voyage, *par excellence*, the second is the meteorological voyage, and the third, the ethnographic voyage.

These changing emphases were owing largely, though not entirely, to contingent factors. On the *Endeavour* voyage, Banks, Solander and Parkinson, with their interests centred on botany, made a powerful team. On the second voyage, Cook himself, his astronomers Wales and Bayly, the two Forsters and William Hodges were all deeply interested in the changing conditions of wind and weather, light and atmosphere, as they traversed vast sections of the southern oceans. By the third voyage Cook had come to realise that both scientific and popular interest had shifted to the native peoples of the Pacific; to the nascent science of ethnography.

All these sciences were descriptive sciences and depended greatly upon the production of visual records. Historians, dazzled by the abilities of men like Cook and Banks, have not done full justice to the abilities of their supporting artists. Yet it was their work, in engraved reproduction, that fashioned the images of the Pacific that etched themselves deeply into the European mind. Words are often forgotten but images remain.

However, none of the three professionals artists, Parkinson, Hodges and Webber, who travelled with Cook was trained for the enormous task that confronted them. To have found and enlisted the versatility that the portrayal of the Pacific and its peoples required would have been impossible. Eighteenth-century art students were trained to fulfil special requirements: to draw plants and animals for natural historians; to draw maps and charts and topographic views for the army and the navy; or, higher up the social ladder, to paint landscapes and portraits or even history paintings of memorable deeds from scripture or the classics for Royal Academy audiences. But no one was trained to do all these things.

So the demands the voyages placed on their artists were quite unprecedented. It is surprising they coped as well as they did. The young Sydney Parkinson was probably as good a botanical draughtsman as anyone practising in England at that time. But with the death of the unfortunate Alexander Buchan, he had to

175. John Webber, *Poedua*, oil on canvas, 142.2 × 94 cm., 1777, National Maritime Museum, London.

193

cope with figure drawings as well, something that he had obviously no training in. Hodges had been trained superbly by Richard Wilson as a landscape painter, but on the voyage he had to train himself to produce portraits.

Hodges has not been given his due. He is one of the finest of all English eighteenth-century landscape painters. A greater, more varied painter than his master Richard Wilson, only Thomas Gainsborough, among his contemporaries, excels him. The quality of his work, unfortunately, has been largely ignored because of the abiding ethnocentricity of European taste that draws a firm distinction between the aesthetic and the exotic. So much of Hodges's life was spent outside of Europe, first in the Pacific, then in India, that the exotic character of his work has largely precluded an approach in terms of aesthetic assessment—at least among Europeans. Exotic content inhibits aesthetic judgement. Yet in the work of Hodges and Gainsborough, English landscape first released itself from its provincial domination by those classical Italianate models in which British artists were trained, and it is in the work of Hodges and the work of Joseph Wright of Derby that eighteenth-century landscape painting begins to confront the central interest of nineteenth-century landscape—the portrayal of light.

John Webber never succeeded in reaching the kinds of aesthetic quality that we find in the best of Hodges's work, but he was better trained for the job ahead of him than any of the others. He could, as we have seen, put his hand to anything. Navigational views, plants and animals, portraits, landscapes, and something rather new, a sequence of drawings depicting historical events of the voyage. 'We should be nowhere without Webber', John Beaglehole rightly observed, yet managed to do him less than justice.

They were all quite young men when they enlisted with Cook: Parkinson, twenty-three; Hodges, twenty-eight; Webber, twenty-four; and all in poor circumstances. Webber's father was an orphan of Bern who had been assisted by the Corporation of Merchants of that city to train as a sculptor. In his thirties he had gone to England in search of work and there married Mary Quant, an English girl, with whom he had six children. Life was difficult for the young family and John, who was the second son, was sent back to Bern where he grew up under the care and protection of his maiden aunt. The Corporation assisted John as it had assisted his father, and at the age of sixteen he was apprenticed to Johann Aberli, the most famous Swiss landscape painter of his day, the man who first made views of the Swiss mountains high fashion. No drawings by Webber from his time with Aberli are known to have survived, but he must have learned from him to give his landscapes that sense of breadth and height, and that feeling for atmosphere that served him in such good stead when he came to paint the icy landscapes of the north Pacific.[2]

After three years with Aberli, Webber proceeded to Paris, assisted by an annual stipend from the Bernese Corporation. There as already noted, he studied under Johann Wille, a German artist and engraver long resident in Paris, a respected teacher of and authority on art.

Wille was something of a *bon viveur*, entertained dealers and connoisseurs, and possessed the attractive habit of taking his students into the rural hinterland of Paris in search of peasant life. They were living through the autumnal days of the ancien regime when peasant life was *à la mode*, both in the sentimental rococo manner that Marie-Antoinette so loved, and in the more realistic style of the Dutch. Under Wille's influence Webber made drawings of French rural life (pl.

176). The training came in handy when he had to fill his Pacific landscapes with the peoples of Tonga, Tahiti or Nootka Sound.

In Paris, Webber also attended classes at the Ecole des Beaux-Arts, learned to paint in oils and probably took lessons in the life class. The *Portrait of a Sculptor* (Kunstmuseum, Bern), possibly Friedrich Funk, his cousin, was probably painted during his student days in Paris. After four years in Paris he returned to his family in London and was admitted as a student at the Royal Academy classes. He also did some work for a London architect, mythological scenes for interiors. They were probably similar to those overdoor panels one sees in Adam houses. He may also have painted the religious painting *Abraham and the three angels* (Landesmuseum, Münster) after his return to London. It is the only attempt, we know of, of a major figure composition completed before he embarked with Cook (pl. 177).

Webber exhibited a portrait of an artist and two Parisian views at the 1776 Royal Academy exhibition. Attracted by the quality of the portrait, which has never come to light, Solander recommended to Cook that Webber should accompany him on his third voyage. It seems to have been all somewhat last minute.

Indeed, one gains the impression that the Admiralty was not greatly interested in the appointment of professional artists to its ships. Had it not been for the continuing influence of men like Banks and Solander, professionals like Hodges and Webber might never have been employed. Webber's appointment was expressed in words identical to those used in Hodges's commission:

Whereas we have engaged Mr John Webber Draughtsman and Landskip painter to proceed in His Majesty's Sloop under your Command on her present intended Voyage, in order to make Drawings and Paintings of such places in the Countries you may touch at in the course of the said Voyage as may be proper to give a more perfect Idea therof than can be formed by written description only; You are hereby required and directed to receive the said Mr John Webber on board giving him all proper assistance, Victualling him as the Sloop's company, and taking care that he does diligently employ himself in making Drawings and Paintings of such places as you may touch at, that may

176. John Webber, *Rural landscape with drover and flock*, pen and watercolour, 20.1 × 27.9 cm., 1773, Stadelsches Kunstinstitut, Frankfurt.

177. John Webber, *Abraham and the three angels*, oil on canvas, 90 × 115 cm., c.1755–6, Landesmuseum, Münster.

195

be worthy of notice, in the course of your Voyage, as also of such other objects and things as may fall within the compass of His abilities.[3]

There is some uncertainty as to the length of time Webber had to prepare for the voyage. The Academy exhibition opened on 24 April 1776, and Solander is said to have gone to Webber's rooms with the invitation to join the voyage two days later. But Webber in a letter to his cousin states that the decision for him to go was not made until 'eight days before my departure'. Doubtless he did not get the official Admiralty letter until eight days prior to leaving. He also told his cousin why he had decided to go:

> This idea my dear Cousin, no doubt will seem rather strange to you, but to me it was enough to see that the offer was advantageous and besides, contained the matter which I had always desired to do most (to know, to sail and to see far away and unknown countries). The Admiralty appointed me for 100 Guineas per year and above that paid all the expenses of my work. This, together with the means which I hoped to receive on my return, in order to distinguish myself with images of novelties, gave me hope that my lot would be happier in the end, if God spared my life. All this was decided eight days before my departure, and I was in quite a hurry to pursue all matters that were necessary.[4]

It is pleasing to be able to record that in the end Webber succeeded in distinguishing himself with images of novelties he had seen and drawn in the Pacific, but it occurred only years after the voyage and only by his carefully cultivating the market for Pacific exotica that developed in Britain following the publication of the official account of the third voyage in 1784.[5] Webber's *Views in the South Seas* were the first of those etched or aquatinted series of prints put out independently by travelling artists to cater for the demand for scenes of the exotic picturesque that became so fashionable during the first half of the nineteenth century.

In our catalogue of the artwork of the third voyage, Rüdiger Joppien and I have itemised and described over four hundred drawings made by Webber that relate to the voyage. What I should like to do here is consider that body of work as a whole. What kinds of drawings were made? Is there a consistent programme of work being followed? Were there constraints on Webber, and how did they operate?

As to Webber himself there was the hope, innocent enough, as we have seen, that he would eventually be able to distinguish himself with 'images of novelties'. But he was in Cook's service, and it is to Cook's perception of the uses that he could make of Webber's skills that we must turn if we are to understand the visual programme of work undertaken.

Cook was above all a navigator, and coastal views were the most valuable drawings an artist could make for the purposes of navigation. So Cook asked Webber to make coastal views that were used to embellish the charts made on the voyage, largely by the young William Bligh. The late R.A. Skelton attributed these views to Bligh himself, but a comparison with the original coastal views by Webber now in the British Library indicates clearly enough that they are by Webber not Bligh. There is in them that feeling for atmospheric perspective that Webber probably gained from working with Aberli as a student in Bern.

196

Webber's coastal views have never been fully published, but they will be when the Hakluyt Society completes the three volumes of the Charts and Views of Cook's Voyages which has been designed to complement *The Art Of Captain Cook's Voyages*. Then, when the historians of science eventually get around to publishing all the *original* drawings relating to natural history, we shall have the full corpus of visual material, to complement the comprehensive verbal record compiled by John Beaglehole.

Cook's instructions certainly required him to make natural history drawings. 'You are . . . carefully to observe the nature of the Soil', they read, '& the produce thereof; the Animals and Fowls that inhabit or frequent it; the Fishes that are to be found in the rivers or upon the Coast, and in what plenty; and, in case there are any, peculiar to such places, to described them as minutely, and to make accurate drawings of them, as you can.'[6] Cook carried out these instructions with the assistance of his surgeons on the *Resolution*, Anderson and Samwell, and William Ellis, surgeon's second mate on the *Discovery*. The Print Room of the British Museum holds sixty-five drawings by Webber, mostly of birds and fishes. The British Museum of Natural History holds an album of drawings mostly of fish by William Ellis, and the Alexander Turnbull Library includes eight folios of natural-history drawings by Ellis.

What is of more than passing interest is that on neither the second nor the third voyage was Cook required by his instructions to make drawings of plants. Instead, he was told to collect specimens of the seeds of 'Trees, Shrubs, Plants, Fruits and Grains peculiar to those Places' visited.[7] Nevertheless, the Forsters, who to some extent were a law unto themselves, carried on Banks's excellent botanical work, George Forster making over 300 plant drawings, now in the British Museum (Natural History). But on the third voyage few drawings of plants were made. Perhaps the Admiralty felt that it would be quicker to bring home specimens than spend an inordinate amount of time on the voyage producing drawings of plants. Not that they were entirely neglected; Webber made a fine drawing of the Kerguelan cabbage (British Library, London), but his general practice was to incorporate curious plants within landscape settings.

For on the third voyage the emphasis moved firmly from drawing plants and animals towards drawing peoples and places. This was not because Cook's instructions had changed, and so far as people were concerned, they had remained constant for all three voyages:

> You are likewise to observe the Genius, Temper, Disposition, and Number of the Natives and Inhabitants, where you find any; and to endeavour, by all proper means to cultivate a friendship with them; making them Presents of such Trinkets as you may have on board, and they may like best; inviting them to Traffick; and shewing them every Civility and Regard; but taking care nevertheless not to suffer yourself to be surprised by them . . .[8]

There is no requirement here or anywhere else that the native peoples should be drawn, and if the instructions are taken literally, Genius, Temper and Disposition would have been difficult to render graphically, except by the most talented of artists and in conditions different from those that obtained on the voyages. Nevertheless, the depiction of indigenous peoples became an increasingly important concern with each voyage. Cook followed his instructions but, as John Beaglehole observed, never felt himself limited by them. 'A man would never accomplish much in discovery who only stuck to his orders,' Cook had advised his young French correspondent Latouch-Treville.[9]

Cook was forty-eight when he embarked on his third voyage in 1776. He had just completed preparing the text of his second voyage for Dr Douglas. His portrait had been painted by Nathanial Dance. He was already the most famous navigator in the world, and he must have been aware of it, knew that he had already made history, that on the present voyage he would be making more history and had in John Webber an artist capable of recording it.

It would also seem that he had developed a fairly clear idea how that history, the history of the third voyage, should be presented in publication. While at the Cape, returning to England on the second voyage, he had been mortified and distressed by the many inaccuracies in Hawkesworth's account of his first voyage and by the attitudes attributed to him that were not his.[10] Nor did he appreciate the controversies that had arisen from Hawkesworth's discussion of the sexual practices and freedoms of Tahitian society. On that issue, as we have seen, he had written to Douglas in quite unequivocal terms, concerning the second voyage: 'In short my desire is that nothing indecent may appear in the whole book, and you cannot oblige me more than by pointing out whatever may appear to you as such.'[11] This implies that Webber would not be expected to spend much time drawing naked savages in the Pacific, even though he may have spent time drawing nude men and women in the life class of the Ecole des Beaux-Arts.

The test came early. From 24 to 30 January 1777, the *Resolution* and the *Discovery* havened in Adventure Bay, Van Diemen's Land, to wood and water. Twice a party of Tasmanians came out of the woods to greet the woodcutters, 'without', Cook recorded, 'shewing the least mark of fear and with the greatest confidence imaginable, for none of them had any weapons, except one who had in his hand a stick about 2 feet long and pointed at one end. They were quite naked & wore no ornaments, except the large punctures or ridges raised on the skin . . .'[12] Webber appears to have made a drawing (pl. 70) to record the second meeting on 29 January:

> We had not be[en] long landed before about twenty of them men and boys joined us without expressing the least fear or distrust, some of them were the same as had been with us the day before, but the greater part were strangers. There was one who was much deformed, being humpbacked, he was no less distinguishable by his wit and humour, which he shewed on all occasions and we regretted much that we could not understand him for their language was wholly unintelligible to us . . . Some of these men wore loose round the neck 3 or 4 folds of small Cord which was made of the fur of some animal, and others wore a narrow slip of the kangaroo skin tied around the ankle. I gave them a string of Beads and a Medal, which I thought they received with some satisfaction.[13]

This was the first occasion on which native peoples had been encountered on the third voyage, and Webber's little-known drawing, now in the Naval Library of the Ministry of Defence, London, provides an insight into the subsequent visual programme that was closely followed during the whole third voyage (pl. 70). It is quite an ambitious composition for Webber to have begun so early in the voyage, but is obviously unfinished, and I suspect that it is unfinished because Cook felt that it would not be a suitable subject to be engraved in the official account. There seems to be little doubt that it was drawn on the voyage,

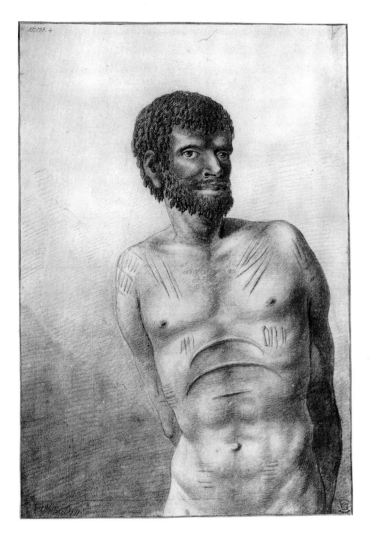

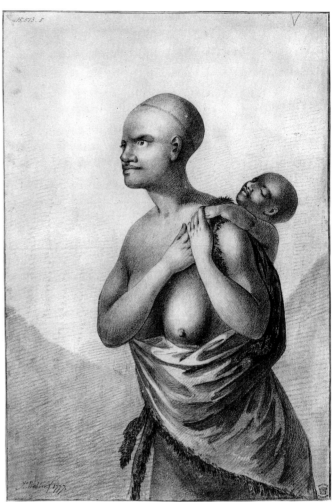

because Webber included a drawing, under the heading 'New Holland Van Diemans Land', in his catalogue of works submitted to the Admiralty on his return, entitled *An Interview between Captain Cook and the Natives*. What it would seem Cook did approve of was a drawing of a man and another of a woman of Van Diemen's Land which would indicate nudity without actually representing it (pls 178, 179).

Although the 'Interview' drawing was never completed or engraved, it does foreshadow what might be described as the official Cook/Webber visual-art programme for the voyage. Cook is shown meeting the local people in an atmosphere of peace and potential understanding, offering them gifts and the hope of friendship. And as he began, so he continued. All of Webber's developed compositions constructed on the voyage and for the official publication seem to be saying the same thing: the people of the Pacific are indeed pacific people.[14]

They had not always been depicted as being so peaceful. In Hawkesworth's *Account*, for example, the first engraving ever to depict Tahitians, though it renders them looking like orientals, shows them engaged in a violent conflict with Captain Wallis's ships, and his guns reducing them to submission (pl. 180). In Parkinson's *Journal*, two Australian Aborigines are depicted advancing to combat' as Cook landed in Botany Bay (pl. 96),[15] and in the official account of Cook's

178. John Webber, *A Man of New Holland*, pencil and red crayon, 47.3 × 32.4 cm., 1777, British Library, London (Add. MS 15513, f. 4).

179. John Webber, *A Woman of New Holland*, pencil, 45.7 × 32.1 cm., 1777, British Library, London (Add. MS 15513, f. 5).

199

second voyage, Hodges had published his painting depicting the violent reception
Cook received when he attempted to land at Eromanga in Vanuatu in 1774
(pls 181, 182).

Illustrations of this kind were bound to create controversy, and did. On the
second voyage the Forsters, father and son, had both been critical of the way in
which native peoples were frequently treated by the members of Cook's crews.
They saw themselves as independent, scientific witnesses who, though they
greatly respected Cook's abilities, were not prepared to turn a blind eye to
everything that happened. This itself caused resentment. Some of the tensions
that developed on the voyage are implicitly revealed in George Forster's *A Voyage
round the World*. After providing a detailed account of Cook's attempted landing at
Eromanga, he wrote:

From his [i.e., Cook's] account of this unhappy dispute, Mr. Hodges has
invented a drawing, which is meant as a representation of his interview with

the natives. For my own part, I cannot entirely persuade myself that these people had any hostile intentions in detaining our boat. The levelling of a musket at them, or rather at their chief, provoked them to attack our crew. On our part this manoeuvre was equally necessary; but it is much to be lamented that the voyages of Europeans cannot be performed without being fatal to the nations whom they visit.[16]

Comments of this kind aroused the anger of William Wales, who felt deeply loyal to Cook whatever the circumstance and was also Hodges's friend. In his *Remarks on Mr. Forster's Account of Captain Cook's last Voyage round the World*, he described Forster's description of the affair at Eromanga as 'one of the most singular pieces of misrepresentation and detraction that ever dropped from a pen'.[17] This was characteristic of the vitriolic attack that Wales launched on the book as a whole. It caused Forster in turn to publish his *Reply to Mr. Wales's Remarks* (1778). Concerning Eromanga he wrote in defence:

I had my information of this transaction from the mouth of Captain Cook and those who accompanied him, within an hour or two after the affair had happened. Suppose it disagreed with Captain Cook's written journal, and printed narrative, and contained some particulars not advantageous to seaman;–what then? What reasonable man will not believe that Captain Cook would exactly relate the matter in the same order as he meant to write it afterwards; or that he would not, upon cool reflection, suppress in writing the mention of such facts as were unfavourable to his own character, even tho' they could at most be construed into effects of unguarded heat... The officer's orders [i.e., to shoot] appeared to me unjust and cruel. Let every man judge for himself. So much I know, that the matter was discussed in my hearing, with much warmth, between the officers and Captain Cook, who by no means approved of their conduct at that time.[18]

Cook had sailed on the third voyage before Forster's *Voyage* and the resulting

201

controversy was in print. But the heat that had arisen on his own ship over the affair at Eromanga may well have discouraged him from permitting Webber to portray violent confrontations with native peoples on the third voyage.

Cook had good practical reasons to suppress images of conflict. Not only did his instructions require him to cultivate friendship with native people, but the representation of conflict with natives could have had at that time the most unpredictable results. For the contemporary political situation in England was volatile. A week before Cook sailed out of Plymouth,[19] the American colonies had declared their independence. Radical opinion seized upon Cook's voyages as yet another attempt by England to dominate weaker societies. Cook had been instructed to return Omai to the Society Islands; the social lion had become something of an embarrassment.[20] Satirists had seized upon his presence to lampoon the condition of English society. It would be surprising if Cook had not seen and read the most virulent of these satirical broadsides, entitled *An Historical Epistle, from Omiah to the Queen of Otaheite; being his Remarks on the English Nation*, which appeared in 1775 while he was resident in London between his second and third voyages. Omai is presented as a critic of European culture and attacks trenchantly those nations who:

183. John Webber, *Captain Cook in Ship Cove, Queen Charlotte Sound*, pen, wash and watercolour, 60.7 × 98.5 cm., 1777, National Maritime Museum, London.

> . . . in cool blood premeditately go
> To murder wretches whom they cannot know.
> Urg'd by no injury, prompted by no ill
> In forms they butcher, and by systems kill;
> Cross o'er the seas, to ravage distant realms,
> And ruin thousands worthier than themselves.

As a man of Empire, the representative of George III and the Admiralty in the South Seas, Cook it may be assumed, was reluctant to allow anything to occur in the visual record of the voyage that could give credence to these kinds of sentiments.

*　　*　　*

Let us turn to Webber's second major set piece of the voyage, *Captain Cook in Ship Cove, Queen Charlotte Sound* (pl. 183). Cook is presented shaking a Maori chief by the hand, a European mode of greeting that it is unlikely he would have proffered since he knew well enough that nose rubbing was the traditional Maori greeting. Nor does the scene confirm the written evidence of any of the journals. For, on entering Ship Cove on this occasion, Cook found the Maori afraid to come aboard, though many of them knew him well from his previous visits. They were afraid he had come to avenge the massacre of Furneaux's men, eight of whom had been killed and eaten at Grass Cove nearby, on the previous voyage. With Omai as interpreter, however, friendly relations were quickly established with the parties visiting the ships.

Yet there is no evidence that the obvious reading of this composition records an actual event. That is to say, Cook did not on this occasion come off his landing boat and go up and shake a Maori chief by the hand. By all accounts the portion of the beach they landed on was unoccupied – a natural precaution in any case – and it was not until a little later that a party of the Maori came and set up some temporary habitations nearby. It is indeed true that friendly relations were established on this occasion quickly enough, and this may be credited to Cook's

184. John Webber, *The Reception of Captain Cook at Hapee* (Lifuka, Tonga), watercolour, 22.4 × 38.1 cm., 1777, British Library, London (Add. MS 15513, f. 8).

202

185. John Webber,
Summer huts of the Chukchi,
pencil, pen and wash,
25.4 × 48.9 cm., 1778,
British Library, London
(Add. MS 17277, no. 26).

186. John Webber, *Two
Chukchi armed*, pencil,
pen, wash and
watercolour, 25.4 × 37.8
cm., 1778, British
Library, London (Add.
MS 17277, no. 27).

practical good sense; true, too, that all we should expect from a record of an historical event rendered in the mode of a history painting is the general spirit of the occasion, not evidence as to what actually occurred. But my point is that in staging the event in this way, Webber is addressing a British, indeed a European audience. Ethnographical information of great interest is being conveyed about the nature of the temporary habitations, the dress and adornment of the Maori, but it is conveyed within the framework of a potentially political message: Cook the friendly voyager meeting his old friends the Maori.

A few months later in Lifuka, Tonga, Webber began another large history set piece. Cook and his men intermingle freely with a great crowd of Tongans as they mutually enjoy the boxing and other entertainments prepared for them (pl. 184). The painting may be identified with the work in Webber's catalogue entitled *The manner of receiving, entertaining and making Captain Cook a present of the productions of the Island, on his Arrival at the Happi*.

So it continued throughout the voyage. Everywhere Cook goes in the Pacific his

arrival is celebrated by Webber in scenes of joyful reception, in dancing, boxing entertainments, gifting, trading. Nothing must disturb this sense of peacefulness. Even Cook's own death, the great trauma of the voyage, is not drawn, nor will it be included in the official publication.

Webber got better at it as the voyage progressed. One of the finest of all his drawings surely must be his record of Cook's meeting with the Chuckchi people of northern Siberia. They were only on that icy peninsula for between two and three hours, yet Webber managed to make a number of delightful drawings on the spot (pls 185, 186).[21] Naturally suspicious of the newcomers, the Chuckchi refused to put down their arms—except upon one occasion, when a few of them laid them down and danced for Cook and his men. It was that moment of friendship that Webber chose to record in a beautifully balanced composition (pl. 187).

This then is the implicit message of the Cook/Webber programme. Cook is the peacemaker, the philanthropist who is bringing the gifts of civilisation and the values of an exchange economy to the savage peoples of the Pacific. Later, after Cook's death, the same message is spelt out to all Europe, in the sixty-odd plates, upon which enormous care and attention was spent, that were included in the Atlas to the official account.

True, these grand peaceful ceremonies and occasions did occur, they were high points in a long voyage and, we might agree, deserved to be recorded for posterity. They were, moreover, the kinds of events that suited Webber's medium. Watercolour drawing and painting with its broad washes of transparent colour, its feeling of amplitude for the breadth and depth of space is an art surely suited to rendering peaceful scenes. So that in this instance we might want to

187. John Webber, *Captain Cook's meeting with the Chukchi at St Lawrence Bay*, pencil, pen, wash and watercolour, 64.8 × 99.1 cm., 1778, National Maritime Museum, London.

205

conclude with Marshall McLuhan that the medium is indeed the message.[22] Webber portrayed the truth, but it was a highly selective truth, from which all sense of violence and tension had been removed.

Consider for a moment what a modern television camera crew, with the right to film whatever they chose, might have selected, to send by satellite to Europe. They might have selected different events than the boxing and dancing receptions at Tonga for Europeans to remember the visit by. Consider, for example, these incidents recorded by the young midshipman on the *Resolution*, George Gilbert, concerning the stay at Tonga.

> These Indians are very dexterous at thieving and as they were permitted to come on board the ships in great numbers, they stole several things from us. This vice which is very pervilent [prevalent] here, Captain Cook punished in a manner rather unbecoming of an European viz: by cutting off their ears; fireing at them with small shot, or ball, as they were swimming or paddling to the shore and suffering the people (as he rowed after them) to beat them with the oars, and stick the boat hook into them where ever they could hit them; one in particular he punished by ordering one of our people to make two cuts upon his arm to the bone one across the other close below the shoulder; which was an act that I cannot account for otherways than to have proceeded from a momentary fit of anger as it certainly was not in the least premeditated.[23]

It was Cook himself who on the previous voyage had named Tonga the Friendly Islands.

Nothing delights a camera crew so much as a conflagration; so they would have been very busy on Moorea on 9 and 10 October 1777. When the *Resolution* had left the Cape it must have seemed like, as David Samwell described it, a 'second Noah's ark'.[24] Cook had on board 'two Horses, two Mares, three Bulls, four Cows, two Calves, fifteen Goats, 30 Sheep, a peacock and a hen, Turkeys, Rabbits, Geese, Ducks and Fowls in great plenty...for the purpose of distributing them among the Islands visited'.[25] This was Cook in the role of philanthropist of the Enlightenment bringing the blessings of civilisation to the Pacific. The livestock was to be distributed to the natives, either as gifts to appropriate chieftains or in the process of trade.

Not every Pacific person understood the conventions of hierarchical gifting or of a market economy. So when one of the *Resolution*'s fifteen goats was stolen in Moorea, Cook went on a violent punitive mission for two days burning the native houses and destroying all the native canoes his party came in contact with and did not cease until the goat was returned. 'The Losses these poor People must have suffer'd would affect them for years to come', wrote Thomas Edgar, the master of the *Discovery*.[26] 'I can't well account for Capt Cooks proceedings on this occasion; as they were so very different from his conduct in like cases in his former voyages', wrote young George Gilbert.[27]

Others since Gilbert have attempted to explain Cook's markedly changed behaviour on the third voyage. The best is that given by Sir James Watt in his masterly essay on the 'Medical Aspects and Consequences of Cook's Voyages'.[28] Watt brings strong evidence to show that Cook on the third voyage was a sick man and suggests that it may well have had the effect of changing his normal pattern of behaviour. I would not question this, but it must be said that his illness did not curb his aggression when his authority was threatened.

It is not my intention here to address the whole question of Cook's changed behaviour on the third voyage. I do not feel adequately equipped as an historian to attempt it. But I would suggest that those historians who feel they are might address themselves, without wishing to minimise the significance of Watt's findings (since historical causation is notoriously multiple rather than singular) to wider, more general, more countervailing forces acting upon Cook's behaviour and personality during the later months of his life. What I am getting at might be summarised in such phrases as 'the loss of hope', 'an increased cynicism', 'familiarity breeds contempt', 'power tends to corrupt and absolute power corrupts absolutely'. By comparison with his contemporaries there need be no doubt that Cook was a wise, extraordinarily gifted and humane commander. But his first duty was the survival of his crew and the success of his expeditions. That meant that his word must not be questioned, even when it could not be properly understood. When words were not understood, only brute action remained.

On setting out on his first voyage in the *Endeavour*, Cook had been given written advice by Lord Morton, president to the Royal Society. The Society, you will recall, had sponsored the voyage and Cook gave to Morton's *Hints* a respect second only to his Admiralty instructions. They contained the most detailed set of instructions he ever received on how to treat native peoples encountered. Morton's *Hints* enshrined the high hopes of the philosophers of the Enlightenment for an eventual universal brotherhood of mankind under the leadership, it need hardly be said, of European man. Allow me to quote:

> Have it still in view that sheding the blood of those people is a crime of the highest nature:–They are human creatures, the work of the same omnipotent Author, equally under his care with the most polished European; perhaps being less offensive, more entitled to his favour.
>
> They are natural, and in the strictest sense of the word, the legal possessors of the several Regions they inhabit. No European Nation has a right to occupy any part of their country, or settle among them without their voluntary consent.
>
> Conquest over such people can give no just title; because they could never be the Agressors.
>
> They may naturally and justly attempt to repel intruders, whom they may apprehend are come to disturb them in the quiet possession of their country, whether that apprehension be well or ill founded.
>
> Therefore should they in a hostile manner oppose a landing, and kill some men in the attempt, even this would hardly justify firing among them, till every other gentle method had been tried.
>
> There are many ways to convince them of the Superiority of Europeans . . .[29]

That, indeed, was an Enlightenment vision of hope. But by 1777 Cook was an old Pacific hand who seems to have grown tired in the use of the many subtle ways in which indigenous people could be convinced of the superiority of Europeans. By 1777 he could cut corners brutally if the occasion arose. There is a sense of disillusion, of a loss of hope. On the first voyage, rather in the spirit of Morton's *Hints*, he had, we have noted, expressed an admiration for the simple life of the Australian Aborigines, 'far . . . happier than we Europeans'.[30] And on the second, in Queen Charlotte Sound, he expressed a fear that his very contact with the Maori, since his first voyage, had degraded them: 'Such are the consequences of commerce with Europeans and what is still more to our Shame civilised Christians, we debauch their Morals already too prone to vice and we interduce among them wants and perhaps diseases which they never before knew and which serves only to disturb that happy tranquillity they and their fore Fathers had injoy'd.'[31] Yet on his third voyage, with his horses, cows, bulls and goats, etc., he was still playing the role of an official philanthropist of the Enlightenment seeking to raise Pacific people from their savage state to a higher level of civilisation. Did the growing realisation of the contradiction between the philanthropist role he was required to play and his actual experience make him increasingly cynical and brutalise his behaviour? By the third voyage he had become convinced that he and other European voyagers were bringing venereal and other diseases to the Pacific. In such cases of guilt it is not unusual to blame the victims. In Queen Charlotte Sound he wrote in his journal, 'A connection with Women I allow because I cannot prevent it . . . more men are betrayed than saved by having connection with their women, and how can it be otherwise since all their Views are selfish without the least mixture of regard or attachment whatever . . .'[32]

The point I wish to make is this: Cook, in his lifetime, had absorbed enough of the hopes and expectancies of the Enlightenment to become aware by his third voyage that his mission to the Pacific involved him in a profound and unresolvable contradiction. In order to treat native peoples in the enlightened way that Morton had exhorted and in order to survive, he had to establish markets among people who possessed little if any notions of a market economy. The alternative was to use force from the beginning as the Spaniards and Portuguese had done, and eighteenth-century Englishmen prided themselves that they could behave more humanely than Spaniards.

There was nothing new about the working methods used for establishing more or less humane contact with primitive people, even when they were, as the ancient Greeks said, stubborn. The Greeks had borne gifts all the way down the Red Sea Coast to the fish-eaters and others of the Arabian Sea.[33] It was the acknowledged way of expanding a commercial empire. And if you wanted wood, water and fresh food at each new landfall on a long voyage, without immediately resorting to violence, there was no other way. So you had to establish markets, at the side of the ship, or on the beaches, as in Webber's fine paintings of the market Cook established at Nomuka, in Tonga (pl. 188).

To establish one's peaceful intentions one began by gifting. The nature of gifting was more deeply embedded in primitive survival economies than the nature of property or the nature of a free market. So Cook took with him on his third voyage thousands of articles from Matthew Boulton's factory, Soho, in Birmingham–axes, chisels, saws, metal buttons, beads, mirrors etc.–as presents, and for trading.[34] The year Cook sailed (1776) was the year in which the principle of free trade, of the universal benefits of an international market economy was given its classic expression in Adam Smith's *Inquiry into the Nature and Causes of the Wealth of Nations*. Cook was Adam Smith's first and perhaps greatest global agent. He opened a new third of the world to free enterprise.

Smith, the theorist of perfect competition, argued that market prices established themselves by the natural laws of supply and demand; if there was any control at all exercised by this beautifully delicate mechanism it was best described as wrought by 'an invisible hand'.[35] But Smith drew his conclusions primarily from a study of developed market economies that had been in existence in Europe from ancient times. Cook, the practical man, had the grave problem of insisting upon the rules and conventions where they did not exist or existed at the

188. John Webber, *The Harbour of Annamooka*, pen, wash and watercolour, 44.8 × 100 cm., 1777, British Library, London (Add. MS 15513, f. 7).

fringes rather than the centre of the primitive polity. There were, of course, markets in the Pacific before Cook, but at various stages of development, from the complete non-existence of the concept among the natives of Van Diemen's Land[36] to the astute Indians of Nootka Sound, of whom Cook wrote in chagrin on one occasion that it seemed that 'there was not a blade of grass that did not possess a separate owner'.[37]

So in the Pacific Cook had to play at being, as best he could, Adam Smith's god. If the laws of property essential to a free market economy were transgressed and a goat stolen, an act of the god must descend upon the whole community. If a law is not understood as a natural law, the best thing to do, if you possess the power of a god, is to make it seem like one.

What I would suggest, then, is that Cook on his third voyage grew more and more aware in his grand role as Enlightenment Man that he was involved in contradictions that he could not resolve. He had come to the Pacific to spread the blessings and advantages of civilised Europe. What the locals most wanted was the ironware that for so many centuries had made Europe powerful; what Cook's young sailors wanted even more than they wanted fresh food was the bodies of the native women, and it was the one universal product most often offered, most readily available. So Cook increasingly realised that wherever he went he was spreading the curses much more liberally than the benefits of European civilisation. The third voyage records not only his death but, before that, his loss of hope. For what Adam Smith's free-market economy offered the South Seas was not really the difference between civilisation and savagery but the difference between exploitation and extermination. Those peoples who were sufficiently advanced to grasp the potential advantages of a market economy survived to become the colonial servants of their European masters; those who could not, because of the primitive nature of their societies, like the natives of Tierra del Fuego and Van Dieman's Land, in the fullness of the time of Adam Smith's invisible god, were exterminated–though in a few cases their part-European descendants lived on to cherish the sad tale.

The art of John Webber cannot, of course, speak to us of such things except by its very silences. And for what he does give us we should be grateful. It is an Arcadian Pacific and, for the most part, a pacific Pacific; a new region of the world to be desired by Europeans, sought out, converted to the true, Christian religion, rendered subservient, exploited. It is epitomised in Webber's portrait of Poedua, the daughter of Orio, chief of Raiatea (pl. 175). Here Webber builds upon that image of the Pacific that the proceeding voyages had so rapidly and so successfully fashioned. The Pacific as young, feminine, desirable and vulnerable, an ocean of desire. To her, during the next century, all the nations of Europe will come.

Now in all probability, though it cannot be established entirely beyond doubt, Webber painted Poedua's portrait during the five days during which she was held hostage in the *Discovery*. Raiatea was Cook's last port of call in the Society Islands before he sailed for the cold waters of the north Pacific. Two of the crew, enchanted by the island life, decided to desert. Cook, by now well versed in the art of taking hostages, had Orio, his daughter Poedua and his son-in-law lured into Captain Clerke's cabin and a guard mounted, holding them prisoner. They should not be released but taken to Europe, old Orio was informed, unless he activated himself in getting the deserters back to Cook. It took five days.

Captain Clerke, who like William Anderson, also secretly longed to stay in the Society Islands instead of going, as they did, to their deaths from tuberculosis in the cold northern seas,[38] describes what occurred:

> I order'd some Centinels at the Cabin Door, and the Windows to be strongly barred, then told them, we would certainly all go to England together, if their friends did not procure their release by bringing back the 2 Deserters. My poor frends at first were a good deal struck with surprise and fear, but they soon recollected themselves, got the better of their apprehensions & were perfectly reconciled to their Situation . . . The News of their Confinement of course was blaz'd instantaneously throughout the Isle; old Oreo was half mad, and within an hour afterwards we had a most numerous congregation of Women under the Stern, cutting their Heads with Sharks Teeth and lamenting the Fate of the Prisoners, in so melancholy a howl, as render'd the Ship while it lasted, which was 2 or 3 Hours, a most wretched Habitation; nobody cou'd help in some measure being affected by it; it destroyed the spirits of the Prisoners altogether, who lost all their Chearfulness and joined in this cursed dismal Howl, I made use of every method I cou'd suggest to get them away, but all to no purpose, there they wou'd stand and bleed and cry, till their Strength was exhausted and they cou'd act the farce no longer. When we got rid of these Tragedians, I soon recover'd my Friends and we set down to Dinner together very chearfully.[39]

Whether you view the affair as a Pacific farce or as a Greek tragedy it is not difficult to imagine how the camera crew of a not particularly friendly nation might have recorded the scene.

Everything points to the fact that so far as the visual events of the voyage were concerned, Webber was setting out quite deliberately to construct a peaceful image of the Pacific, and of the peaceable relations of its peoples with the voyagers. Even when he drew portraits—for example, just as they left the Society Islands Webber drew a portrait of a chief of Bora Bora, with his lance (pls 189, 190), but when he made the finished drawing he removed the lance.

210

After Cook's death, the apparent desire for a suppression of all scenes of violence and conflict continues in the engraving of scenes of the voyages published in the Atlas of the official account. Even a face that might recall a scene of great violence is not included. We know that Webber painted a portrait in oils of Kahura,[40] the Maori chieftain who was responsible for the killing and eating of Captain Furneaux's men at Grass Cove on the second voyage. Cook established beyond any reasonable doubt that Kahura was responsible for the massacre, but instead of taking revenge, he developed a respect for his courage and the confidence Kahura placed in him.[41] Dr Joppien has succeeded in identifying one of the portraits now in the Dixson Library, Sydney, as a portrait of Kahura (pl. 191).[42] It is of interest that a portrait of Kahura was among those omitted in the list selected for publication in the Atlas. Perhaps the portrait of a notorious cannibal, however much admired by Cook, was not considered suitable for the official account of the voyage.

Nor was a representation of Cook's own death. And when Webber made his famous drawing (pl. 199), which was later engraved by Bartolozzi and published separately in 1784, the great navigator was presented in the role of a peacemaker holding out a hand gesturing to his men in the *Resolution* pinnace to stop firing at the enraged Hawaiians.

If my analysis is correct, Cook on his third voyage, at least so far as the visual record was concerned, was constructing an image of himself as a man of peace in the Pacific, a man universally welcomed there by peaceable people.

189. John Webber, portrait sketch of a chief of Bora Bora, pencil and wash, 37.8 × 25.4 cm., 1777, British Library, London (Add. MS 17277, no. 10).

190. John Webber, *A Chief of Oparapora* (Bora Bora), pencil and wash, 31.4 × 48.6 cm., 1777, British Library, London (Add. MS 15513, f. 24).

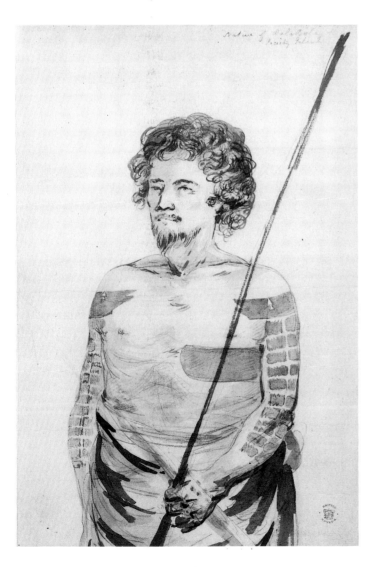

191. John Webber, *The Chief Kahura*, pen and wash, 43.8 × 31.3 cm., 1777, Dixson Library, Sydney.

Representations of violent encounters were suppressed or ignored. He could not have known as he left the island of Bora Bora that he would discover another great Polynesian society in the north Pacific unknown to Europeans, and that there he would be received as the very incarnation of a god of peace, as the returning god Lono, the god of carnival, of the Makahiki festival.[43] So it was that Cook was received, as few men have been, into an alien culture in a fashion that accorded with his own personal and most innermost desire; and the myth of Cook as the hero of peace and the harbinger of civilisation in the Pacific was sustained in Europe and the Pacific long after his death. But it was myth not reality. The reality lay in the hidden contradictions latent in establishing a free-market economy in the Pacific. To do that Cook had taken with him iron from a Birmingham factory that, when fashioned into daggers, was used to cut him down on Kealakekua beach. For when Cook, this man of peace, attempted for the last time to take a Pacific chieftain hostage—dealing once again in the coercive market in which captives are exchanged for stolen goods—the hidden hand of Kukalimoku, the Hawaiian god of war, struck down him and four of his marines. Cook had committed the fatal error of returning to the island when peace no longer reigned there, not even in myth. The course of history is littered with such ironies.

212

9 GREECE AND THE COLONISATION OF THE PACIFIC

REFERENCE HAS BEEN MADE from time to time in several of the preceding chapters to that varied bundle of mental luggage drawn from classical precedent that Europeans brought to their perception and interpretation of Pacific peoples and Pacific things. It may be of interest, therefore, to explore in a little more depth some analogies between the pre-colonial phase of Greek expansion in the Mediterranean and, in the wake of this expansion, the growth of naturalism in Hellenistic art on the one hand and nineteenth-century art on the other.

I hold no brief for cyclical or structural theories that impose seductive *a priori* patterns upon the complexities of history, but our perception of an historical event does assume a paradoxical form: we perceive an event, if we perceive it at all, as in part unique, in part a recurrence. There is an ultimate sense in which we employ analogy even in distinguishing a sherd from bedrock. Nevertheless, my foray here into the Greek side of this analogical exercise must needs be minimal. My hope is that the Pacific side of our enquiry may suggest other similarities with the Greek exploration and colonisation of the Mediterranean: that what Cook and his company of seamen, marines, scientists and artists experienced when they first confronted the indigenous peoples of Tahiti, Tonga. Hawaii, New Zealand and Australia, may once have been, in some manner at least, experienced by those Greeks who first brought their ambiguous gifts to Al Mina, Pithekoussai and elsewhere in the Mediterranean.

I shall also be thinking of Greece in another sense: the European memory of Greece. Four years before Cook first entered the Pacific, Gabriel Dumont first published the temples of Paestum and Winckelmann published his *History of Ancient Art*;[1] one year before, d'Hancarville and Tischbein published the Hamilton collection.[2] Sir William Hamilton was a close friend of Sir Joseph Banks, who began the process, if any one did, of publishing the Pacific. The Greek Revival in Europe is conveniently contemporaneous with the European pre-colonisation period in the Pacific, so that it is tempting to explore the role that the memory of Greece played in making the Pacific known to Europeans.

But I must first take account, however briefly, of the situation in the central Pacific before Cook entered it. It was there during the second and first millenium BC that, according to present knowledge, a neolithic culture possessed of a technology of stone adzes, chisels and bone fishing gear, and a root-and-tree-crop horticulture, moving eastwards, occupied the last of the islands to be inhabited. These Polynesian peoples, it would appear, originally inhabited an archipelago in Eastern Melanesia and evolved from diverse groups, while their language developed from an ancient language to which Fijian also belongs. Although their capacity for canoe voyaging cannot be supposed to have been markedly different during the early days of their development from that employed at the time of European contact, during the period of its expansion Polynesian culture spread from Samoa and the Society Islands to Hawaii in the north, Easter Island in the east and New Zealand in the south-west.

Each of Cook's voyages took three or more years to complete. To sustain his company he required wood for his stoves, fresh water and food, from landfall to landfall. To obtain these essentials, as discussed earlier, it was necessary for him to establish markets with the island people who confronted him at most of his landings. A condition for success depended on whether the concept of a market economy, or the rudimentary notion of a market, existed in the local culture. Even when some such notion was present, it was necessary first to establish communication by a process of gesture, charade and other appropriate symbolic forms that might hopefully bridge the cultural gap, for example, open arms, holding out a green branch (as at the landing at Tana) (pl. 192), or a sheet of white chart paper (as at Dusky Bay). If that were successful, names might then be exchanged and the names of things, such as water. The establishment of a useful market for commodities entailed the concomitant establishment of a linguistic market.

There was no developed market economy in Polynesia. In *Ancient Tahitian Society*, Douglas Oliver writes 'most food was consumed by members of a producer's own household',[3] and his book has no section on trading. But an intricate system of reciprocal gifting existed, and certain articles of ritual significance, such as the red feathers of the tropic bird, were much sought after. On his third voyage, Cook set up a highly successful market at Nomuka in Tonga, with the agreement of the local chieftain. It was presided over by a marine with a musket (pl. 188).

David Samwell described the scene:

We continued upon friendly terms with him [the chieftain] by making him Presents &c. & he encouraged his Subjects to bring Hogs & other Provisions to market which were our first object, tho' in a short time another article engaged our Attention from the highest to the lowest and was sought after with greater avidity than the Hogs or breadfruit, & tho' it was a contraband Trade it was prosecuted with the greatest Activity & Spirit in defiance of the severe

192. William Hodges, *The Landing at Tanna* [Tana] *one of the New Hebrides*, oil on panel, 24.1 × 45.7 cm., *c.*1775–6, National Maritime Museum, London.

Penalties with which it was loaded, & in Contempt of that Danger which attended the Prosecution of this fraudulent & lucrative Traffick. This article was no other than red Feathers. It must be remembered that at Otaheite red Feathers are prized above anything whatsoever, they being the most valuable offering they make to their Gods & very scarce at that Island as they have no birds with red Plumage . . .[4]

Cook had little difficulty in establishing such markets, though more difficulty in controlling them, because Polynesians desperately wanted iron, and the sharp European distinction between property and theft was not yet fully appreciated. Captain Wallis, the first known European to arrive in Tahiti, found to his alarm that his own men were pulling nails from the ship's timbers to exchange for the favours of the Tahitian women. Cook had similar problems on his first voyage. On his second and third he was better prepared, taking large quantities of nails and iron spikes, axes, hatchets and hammers mostly purchased, as remarked in the previous chapter, from Matthew Boulton of Birmingham. He also took mirrors, beads and a quantity of shirts, old sheets, hats and lengths of red baize, 'to exchange for Refreshments with the Natives of such New discovered or unfrequented countries as they may touch at, or to be distributed to them in presents towards obtaining their friendship, & winning over to our Interest'[5]

Ironware from Boulton's Birmingham factory rapidly transformed island technology, years before there were permanent European settlers in the Pacific. It could happen in a matter of months. On his second voyage Cook visited Matavai Bay, first in August 1773 and again in April 1774. He had visited Matavai, of course, on his first voyage and observed the transit of Venus there, but on that occasion he had little ironware for exchange. J.R. Forster noted the changes that had occurred between the *Resolution*'s first and second visits to Matavai: 'many new houses were erected & vast numbers of new Canoes were building & already built, chiefly owing to the facility they got to build them by the Assistance of our tools or Iron.'[6] In Hawaii the effects of iron tools upon local crafts, immediately after Cook's visits there on the third voyage went unnoticed until recently, when Dr Adrienne Kaeppler has been able to demonstrate that what has long been regarded as the high classic period of pre-Cook craftsmanship in Hawaii consists in fact of artefacts fashioned in the years immediately following Cook's visits. 'The introduction of metal tools [in the period prior to European settlement] stimulated', she concluded, 'an artistic efflorescence which resulted in a refinement of traditional techniques and an elaboration of indigenous aesthetic traditions.'[7]

Cook's need to provide food and maintain the health of his ships' companies had the effect of introducing the iron age and an international market economy to Polynesia. He was, as we noted earlier, Adam Smith's global agent. It was fitting surely, that, after publishing *The Wealth of Nations* in 1776, Strahan and Cadell should proceed to publish in the year following–the year in which Cook introduced Birmingham ironware to the Pacific–the official account of Cook's second voyage.

If we should now ask the larger question whether, in Cook's case, trade followed the flag, there is no single answer. On the north-west American coast, for example, Cook found that the Indians of Nootka Sound were well versed in inter-tribal trading and in the strategies of keen bargaining. Cook describes a typical situation:

The Inhabitants of this village received us in the same friendly manner they had done before, and the Moment we landed I sent some [i.e., of his crew] to cut grass not thinking that the Natives could or would have the least objection, but it proved otherwise for the Moment our people began to cut they stoped them and told them they must *Makook* for it, that is first buy it. As soon as I heard of this I went to the place and found about a dozen men who all laid cla[i]m to some part of the grass which I purchased of them and as I thought liberty to cut where ever I pleased, but here again I was mistaken, for the liberal manner I had paid the first pretended pr[o]prietors brought more upon me and there was not a blade of grass that had not a seperated owner, so that I very soon emptied my pockets with purchasing, and when they found I had nothing more to give they let us cut where ever we pleased.[8]

In most cases, however, the establishment and control of a market where the custom had not previously existed in the Pacific involved the demonstration, or at least a ready perception, of Cook's superior weaponry. In that sense 'the flag' was a vital prerequisite of trade. Pacific islanders were often deeply suspicious of these strangers bringing gifts. Cook recorded how at Eromanga, on his second voyage, while seeking, in the ship's boat, for a place to land, 'a few men came to us to whom I gave pieces of cloth, medals, etc. for this treatement they offered to haul the boat over some breakers to a Sandy beach, I thought this a friendly offer, but afterwards had reason to think otherwise'.[9] Cook found that he had to shoot himself out of a desparate situation (pl. 181).

His problems in establishing markets in subsistence economics recall those of that unknown Greek traveller who wrote the *Periplus of the Erithraean Sea*, though in his case trading along the Red Sea and Arabian coasts was much more developed. He, too, took presents, wine and corn, not 'for trade but for expenses in making friends with the Barbaroi'. He complains repeatedly 'the *barbaroi* who live in the place are . . . stubborn'.[10] We have been advised by economists that there is no such thing as a free lunch; from the Greek experience in the Indian ocean and Cook's experience in the Pacific, we might want to conclude that there is no such thing as a free market either.

Markets presuppose an assemblage, not only of commodities and agreed conventions about the nature of exchange, they presuppose also an acceptance of power relationships. Cook's equipment was his capital and it was severely limited. A boat stolen might affect the success of a voyage. So he ensured that the conventions he associated with his markets were adhered to meticulously even by those who barely understood them. In the Marquesas a man was shot dead for stealing a ship's stanchion.

Superiority in arms created a first order of power relationships. There was also a second order, a linguistic order that made for more conciliatory relationships, more amicability, than could be cultivated by the strangers under the ultimate authority and protection of the musket. It was this second order of power that Cook's scientists and artists had to cultivate much more assiduously than his seamen or marines in order to carry out their daily tasks. What was a strange plant called, where was it to be found in quantity, what was it used for? In order to draw an islander's portrait a measure of ease and friendship must first be established. It is not surprising that it was the scientists and artists on Cook's voyages who assembled the largest word lists, and were the keenest to establish friendly relations. This was not necessarily because they were the most intelligent or the most compassionate among Cook's company, but because the prosecution of their callings depended to a greater extent than those trained to the use of force upon the development of what Pierre Bourdieu has described as a linguistic market,[11] a market by means of which the social and spiritual cultures of the Pacific could be transformed into European forms and values.

There were places on the edge of the Pacific, however, where people lived so close to primal subsistence that it was impossible to establish markets. Cook describes how in visiting Adventure Bay, Tasmania, on his third voyage, his wooding party were:

> agreeably surprised . . . with a visit from some of the Natives, Eight men and a boy: they came out of the Woods to us without shewing the least mark of fear and with the greatest confidence immaginable, for none of them had any weapons, except one who had in his hand a stick about 2 feet long and pointed at one end. They were quite naked & wore no ornaments . . . They received every thing we gave them without the least appearance of satisfaction . . . They seem'd to set no value on Iron or Iron tools nor did they seem to know the use of fish hooks . . . nor did we see a Canoe or any Vessel in which they could go upon the water . . . it was evident that shel fish made a part of their food by the many heaps of Muscle shels we saw in different parts near the shore and about some deserted habitations near the head of the bay. These were little Shades or hovels built of sticks and covered with bark; we also saw evedent signs of them some times taking up their aboad in the trunks of large trees, which had been hollowed out by fire most probable for this very purpose.[12]

Cook was far more attracted to the austere innocence of such peoples than he was to the soft primitivism of Tahitian life.[13] Concerning the aborigines of the Endeavour River he had already written, 'they appear to some to be the most wretched people upon Earth, but in reality they are far more happier than we Europeans'.[14] What was impressive about the Tasmanians was their utter ignorance of firearms and the innocence of their friendliness. They acted like the penguins that the men of the *Resolution* had met with a month before on Kerguelan's Island (pl. 193): 'Each sort was so tame that we took as many as we pleas'd with our hands', Anderson, the surgeon, recorded.[15]

We find a classical parallel to Cook's description of the Tasmanians in the description that Agatharkhides has left of the fish-eaters (*Ikhthuophagoi*) who lived on the Arabian side of the Red Sea coast towards the end of the second century

193. John Webber, *A View of Christmas Harbour*, watercolour, 22.2 × 37.8 cm., *c.*1781–3, Dixson Library, Sydney (PXX 2, 1).

BC. Like the Tasmanians, they apparently possessed no village life, went naked and lived on fish, which they trapped with stones in tidal reaches. 'They have not', Agatharkhides explained, 'any of that knowledge and experience of the greatest evils which are common to most of mankind. For they have no occasion to flee from the drawn sword ... they are disturbed by no insults or injuries; unharmed, they bewail no adverse change of fortune; and should such by chance come to them from strangers, they gaze with intent face and many shakings and nods of the head, but they take not the slightest notice of the things which one man commonly does to another.'[16]

What is impressive about these descriptions of peoples living in a primitive subsistence economy is their innocence when confronted by technologies they cannot comprehend. One might well wonder whether those Greeks of the ninth and eighth centuries also encountered such innocence as they took the new wonders of the Iron Age to the limits of the Mediterranean world. It has often been noted that in Homer, as with Cook, the most virtuous of people live in the most distant, or most difficult climes, in places akin, in the Greek world, to Tierra del Fuego and Tasmania. The 'blameless' Ethiopians lived in the far south, the milk-drinking Abioi, in the far north, and Menelaus, we are told, will not die but will be sent to those Elysian fields, to the boundaries of the earth, where life is easiest for men.[17]

It is, of course, conventional wisdom to explain the admiration for the noble savage as one way in which Europeans have repeatedly perceived primitive peoples since classical times. But wherein lay the appeal of such comparatively simple societies for the Greeks themselves? Were they simply recording what they felt to be true; and is this another way of saying that such primitive and exotic societies provided the Greeks with a cherished image of the childhood, if that is the word, of their own society?

Be that as it may, Cook found it impossible to impose upon the native people of Tierra del Fuego and Tasmania a market economy and all that might have flowed from it. Those who cannot produce a surplus for themselves cannot produce it for others. In the fullness of time the Fuegians and the Tasmanians incapable of rising to the novel freedom of the European market were brought to the verge of extinction.

However, Polynesian societies rose to the challenge. In Tahiti, Tonga, Hawaii, New Zealand, Cook's pre-colonial trading proceeded at great pace. The introduction of iron tools not only changed the character of island craftsmanship, it changed also the balance of power among chieftains, who began to gain prestige by warfare rather than by geneaology. Both Tahiti and Hawaii became centralised under dynasties. In Hawaii the war god Kukalimoku achieved greater prestige than the more passive gods, such as the harvest god Lono, with whom Cook, in his last fatal days became identified. In both Hawaii and Tahiti iron increased internecine tribal warfare; it produced a time comparable to that first iron age described by Hesiod, when right was might and held in the power of the fist, and the gods abandoned their peoples.

The effects of European penetration upon the peoples of the Pacific has, naturally, been much studied and is well understood. Less attention has been given to the changes that Cook's trading and collecting stimulated in the European culture. On all three voyages trading in natural-history and cultural artefacts was much indulged in by all aboard. 'Today' (14 July 1774), wrote J.R. Forster,

218

a Saylor offered me 6 shells . . . all of which were not quite compleat & he asked half a Gallon brandy for them, which is now worth more than half a Guinea. This shews however what these people think to get for their Curiosities when they come home, & how difficult it must be for a Man like me, sent out on purpose by Government to collect Natural Curiosities, to get these things from the Natives . . . as every Sailor whatsoever buys vast Quantities of Shells, birds, Fish etc. so that the things are dearer & scarcer than one would believe, & often they go to such people, who have made vast collections, especially of shells. viz the Gunner & Carpenter, who have several 1000 shells.[18]

Such collections stimulated the British market for specimens of natural history and cultural exotics. The abundant supply of Pacific artefacts encouraged demand, taste and theory. The collector and dealer Thomas Martyn developed a new classification for shell collections and published on shells from the south seas in 1784.[19] Corals brought back from Cook's first voyage helped John Ellis to convince Linnaeus and Pallas that corals were animals not vegetables.[20] This was typical of the new empirical pressures that Pacific exotics began to place upon the taxonomy of natural science. If Cook was Adam Smith's first global agent, Joseph Banks was the first global agent of Linnaeus. The Linnaean system, based upon the description of the sexual organs of plants and animals, was binary in character. Species were named by genus and differentia. It was also essentialist and ultimately Aristotelian in character. For Linnaeus as for Aristotle, the world of nature was an ordered and immutable chain of being. When Cook first sailed into the Pacific, it was the influence of Greek thought (for it was ultimately Greek) that still prevailed in the systematics of classification. And in other fields also. Buffon, for example, in his *Histoire naturelle*, assured anatomists that if they wanted best to understand the proportions of the human body they could do no better than study the canons of the sculptors of antiquity.[21] And Pope reminded Englishmen that antiquity had provided the norms for the understanding of the natural world:

> The rules of old discovered not devised,
> Are nature still but nature methodised.

And a great deal that Cook's men saw in the Pacific supported the well-tested norms of classicism.

They had prepared themselves for it. Sydney Parkinson took copies of the *Iliad* and *Odyssey* with him, probably in Pope's translation.[22] So too, one suspects, did William Wales. 'I must confess', he wrote on one occasion while in Vanuatu,

> I have been often lead to think of the Feats which Homer represents his heros as performing with their Spears a little too much of the Marvelous to be admitted into an Heroic Poem, I mean when confined within the straight Stays of Aristotle; nay even so great an Advocate for him as Mr Pope acknowledges them to be *surprising*. But since I have seen what these People can do with their wooden ones; and them badly pointed and not of a very hard nature either, I have not the least exception to any one Passage in that Great Poet on this Account. But if I can see fewer exceptions I can find an infinite number more beauties in him as he has I think scarce an Action circumstance or discription of any kind whatsoever relating to a Spear, which I have not seen & recognised amongst these People as their whirling motion & whistling noise as they fly. Their quivering motion as they Stick in the Ground when they fall. Their

meditating their aim when they are going to throw & their shaking them in their Hand as they go along &c &c.[23]

In this connection we might note also J.R. Forster's comments on the armed fleet of canoes he saw assembled in Matavai preparing to attack neighbouring Morea:

Their warships seem to be of the same kind as the *mille carinae*, that went to fight the famous city of *Troy*, & perhaps the nature of their wars seems to have been very much the same, though the Greeks were better armed on account of the use of Iron & Brass . . . Some of their war-Canoes require 100 men to paddle & but a few have less than fifty & therefore the Number of people, who went to fight *Troy*, may have been very probably between 50 & 100,000. Their navigation from Isle to Isle in the Archipelago is pretty similar to the expeditions of these people among the isles of the South Sea, & they know so as the ancient Greeks well enough to navigate in the night time by the Stars, of whom they know a great many, & for them have peculiar names. Their petty Chiefs, like the Greek Heroes, go to war & get fame by their Exploits. In short I could continue the similitude by almost all the various stages of their wars if necessary.[24]

When they returned to England, J.R. Forster did indeed extend the similitude considerably in his son's published account of the voyage. At the end of the expanded comparison George Forster wrote, 'what I have said is sufficient to prove, that men in a similar state of civilisation resemble each other more than we are aware of, even in the most extremes of the world'.[25]

George, however, then added a significant qualification. 'I should be sorry', he concluded, 'to have made these slight remarks, if they should unfortunately lead some learned schemer on a wrong scent. The itch of tracing the pedigree of nations has lately made such havock in history, by endeavouring to combine the Egyptians and Chinese, that the learned must sincerely wish, it may never become a contagious distemper'.[26]

The 'learned schemer' George Forster and his father had in mind was probably Voltaire. But even though they were wary about sentimentalising over noble savages they did their best, as George pointed out in the preface to his voyage, to look upon all the tribes of mankind with an equal favour,[27] and this led them inevitably to comparative studies. It was Forster senior who, from an assessment of the linguistic evidence he had collected on the voyage, first enunciated the theory, now generally accepted, that the Polynesian societies had spread into the Pacific from earlier migrations from south-east Asia.

Yet even for the Forsters the Greek analogy continued to exercise a potent influence. It gave sanction to the long-standing belief that there were stages in the history of human society, and that some were more to be admired than others.[28] The work of the Forsters deeply influenced Herder. To the extent that Polynesia reminded men like Banks and the Forsters of ancient Greece, they admired it. For was not Greek society the source and fountain of European civilisation? Polynesians as *soi-disant* Greeks enabled Europeans, it was felt, better to understand their own civilisation. But the comforting analogy steadily collapsed under the weight of new knowledge. Archaeology, by increasingly historicising ancient Greek culture, destroyed it as an atemporal standard for Europeans of their own cultural values. The discovery of Herculaneum and Pompeii on the one

220

hand and of Paestum on the other stimulated the great neo-classical debate:[29] which architecture, which culture, served as the better model for modernity— Greece or Rome? In the end, neo-classicism opted for Greece: it was the earlier culture that was preferred; that which was first was best. In this respect the Greek Revival may be seen as the first of the modern primitivisms. Perhaps no one summed it up better than Marx in contemplating why it was that the moderns still admired Greek art although Greek technology had long been surpassed. 'The Greeks', he wrote, were 'normal children'.[30] The brilliance of their childhood provided a standard that an adult liberated humanity was yet to attain.

And, like archaeology in the Near East, the exploration of the Pacific as it continued put an enormous pressure upon the classic as standard. The analogy, the memory of Greece, could only be sustained if it continued to be identified with the vigour of the primitive. One image, one trope, at least, that of Tahiti as Arcadia, satisfied this requirement. 'One would think himself', the explorer Bougainville wrote, 'in the Elysian fields'.[31] 'The scene', Joseph Banks wrote a few months later, 'was the truest picture of an Arcadia of which we were going to be kings that the imagination can form'.[32] The history of that image through the nineteenth century, its effect upon the men of the *Bounty*, upon the artists Hodges and La Farge, the writers Loti, Melville and Stevenson, need not be told again here. But it was doomed to disintegrate. Once standards are embodied in concrete exemplars, the deficiencies of both the standards and the exemplars soon become apparent. There is, surely, a strange kinship of mood and feeling between Gauguin's best Tahitian paintings and much archaic Greek sculpture. Tahiti as Arcadia genuinely inspired his work in a way that it inspired no other European artist. Yet he was also the first self-consciously modernist painter of Europe, the first primitivist in his life as in his art. It was Gauguin who wrote to his friend Daniel de Montfried, 'keep the Persians, the Cambodians, and a bit of the Egyptians, always in mind . . . The great error is the Greek, however beautiful it may be . . . it is necessary to go back further, very much further than the horses of the Parthenon, as far as the dada of my childhood, the good rocking horse of my infancy.'[33]

However much Europeans attempted to embody the experiences of the Pacific within memories of the alleged childhood of their own culture, the vision faded. From the beginning, real knowledge of the Pacific worked steadily against the use of the classic as a standard. It was Hodges who launched in 1786 the first extended attack to be written in English on the supremacy of Greek architecture as a standard for European architecture, two years after he returned from India.[34] Two years before, John Douglas, the editor of the official account of Cook's third voyage, in his preface challenged the classical as the arbiter of the rule of taste:

> it is a favourite study with the scholar to trace the remains of Grecian and Roman workmanship; he turns over his Montfaucon with learned satisfaction and he gazes with rapture on the noble collection of Sir William Hamilton. The amusement is rational and instructive. But will not his curiosity be more awakened, will he not find even more real matter for important reflection, by passing an hour in surveying the numerous specimens of the ingenuity of our newly-discovered friends, brought from the utmost recesses of the globe, to enrich the British Museum, and the valuable repository of Sir Ashton Lever? If

221

194 (left). *A Man of the Sandwich Islands*, engraving by J.K. Sherwin after John Webber, in Cook and King, *A Voyage to the Pacific Ocean*, 1784, pl. 64.

195 (above right). Battle relief from the heroön at Gjölbashi-Trysa, *c*.420–410 BC, Kunsthistorisches Museum, Vienna.

196. Wicker helmet from Hawaii collected on Captain Cook's third voyage, height 31 cm., Australian Museum, Sydney.

the curiosities of Sir Ashton's Sandwich room alone were the only acquisitions gained by our visits to the Pacific Ocean, who that has taste to admire, or even eyes to behold, could hesitate to pronounce that Captain Cook had not sailed in vain? The expense of his three voyages did not, perhaps, far exceed that of digging out the buried contents of Herculaneum. And we may add, that the *novelties* of the Society or Sandwich islands, seem better calculated to engage the attention of the studious in our times, than the *antiquities*, which exhibit proofs of Roman magnificence [pl. 194].[35]

Roman, not Grecian, magnificence. For the archaeology of Greece and the ethnology of the Pacific were pulling in the one direction: towards the archaic, the cult of childhood, the childhood of the human race. To cite but one example: a striking, though no doubt superficial, parallel could be found in the helmets of Hawaiian warriors and those of the warriors of fifth-century Greece (pls 195, 196).

The history of modern primitivism remains to be written. Writers like Robert Goldwater,[36] who have addressed themselves mainly to those moments in the late nineteenth and early twentieth centuries, when artists such as Gauguin, Nolde, Picasso and others began to look appreciatively at ethnological collections of non-European art, have failed to begin at the substantive beginnings. Their perspective has been foreshortened and thereby distorted by the modernist presupposition that significant changes in art and taste are promoted by reciprocal exchanges within an autonomous aesthetic realm. But the cultural pressures that encouraged Picasso and his generation to fragment the human figure itself–the origin and fountain of classical naturalism–into a cuboid constellation of inter-faceted planes had been building up steadily since the late eighteenth century. For more than a century anthropologists and dealers in exotics had been creating a taste for other kinds of antiquity, a taste that eventually led to the dissolution of classical naturalism as the norm of European art, as it had been constructed by Greek artists of the sixth and fifth centuries BC.

And as in art and taste so in science. The power of Greek thought to provide enduring models failed to hold. Banks and his successors attempted for half a

222

century or more to classify the natural exotics of the Pacific according to Linnaeus's modern rationalisation of Aristotle.[37] In the end they failed. The fifty years prior to the publication of *The Origin of Species* is a testing time, when an increasing number of exotic anomalies, drawn mostly from the world of the Pacific, challenge Creation theory and the belief in the immutability of species. Nor was the Pacific merely the theatre from which most of the intractable, empirical material came, it was also the place where most of the pioneers of natural selection (the first scientifically convincing theory of evolution), trained as young men – Darwin, Hooker, Huxley, Wallace. It was only the geologist Lyell, among all the pioneers of natural selection, who did not engage in field work in the Pacific basin; and it was Darwin and Wallace who convinced Lyell.

Now, the intellectual and aesthetic pressure that the exploration and eventual colonisation of the Pacific by Europeans exerted upon classical conventions in nineteenth-century art and thought finds its first exemplar in the Hellenistic world. Here, too, it was new knowledge drawn from the ends of the known world that weakened the Greek classical canons. Such pressure exerts itself during the change from the *polis* to the metropolis, from the cultural to the multicultural, when the stranger is within the gates both at home and in the provinces, with his alien views and strange loyalties, and is reproducing his children at an alarming rate; a time when the old gods decline in power and the long-standing constraints in the conventions of religion, morality and art are weakened, a time when naturalism comes to prevail in art and thought.

Ernst Gombrich has propounded a theory concerning the emergence of naturalism in Greek art that has attracted wide attention. Greek sculptors and painters, Gombrich argues, broke from the long-established conventions of Egyptian art in the process of learning how to illustrate adequately the Greek epics. For Homer, Gombrich reminds us, tells his listeners not only what happened, but how it happened, and it was in the depiction of the how as well as the what of the epics (how Achilles behaved in his anger, for example), that Greek art was led along the long, new path of naturalism.[38] It is an intriguing theory and helps us to understand the character of classic Greek art during the fifth and fourth centuries BC, the period of classical naturalism, and it helps us to understand also the hypostatisation of classical naturalism as an academic norm that was to prevail in European art until the end of the nineteenth century. But it tells us only one part of the story of the emergence of naturalism. For there is a weakness in Gombrich's argument that he seems to be aware of himself, but does not take full account of.[39] For he would not deny that there are highly expressive moments in Babylonian, German and Indian epics, as in Greek. Why, then did not the artists of those societies also create a naturalistic art in illustration of their epics?

More recently John Onians has suggested that the increase in naturalism in Hellenistic art was due to the greater popularity of comedy with its emphasis upon particularities of contemporary life.[40] There are doubtless powerful interactions between epic and art during the period of classical Greek culture and comparable interactions between comedy and art during Hellenistic times. These are both special applications of Horace's comment that poetry is like painting. But do such interactions between the arts provide us with a sufficient explanation for the emergence of naturalism as a significant innovation in the arts of the ancient world? Horace's comment may be applied also, presumably, to the poetry and art of other contemporary societies, such as Egypt and Persia, the arts of which do not reveal comparable developments in naturalism. Gombrich and Onians, it seems to me, like Goldwater in his account of primitivism, assume too great an autonomy for the aesthetic realm in their account of naturalism.

Michael Baxandall's notion of a cognitive style is better designed to cope with such problems. 'A society', Baxandall observes, 'develops its distinctive skills and habits, which have a visual aspect.'[41] Distinctive skills are developed by the application of new knowledge to art practices. In the case of expanding societies such as Greece, a great deal of this new and fascinating knowledge takes the form of new information concerning other lands and peoples. If the rules, precepts and canons by which practice is governed are not so rigidly codified as to reject the new, then art itself becomes among other things a vehicle of information and repository of visual knowledge.

Such new visual knowledge worked against the limitations of classical naturalism and its narrow ideals of beauty and perfection. Hellenistic sculpture depicts the old as well as the young, the deformed and the beautiful, the impoverished and the heroic, not only the Hellene but the Italic, the Libyan, the Gaul. It moves away from an exclusively human-centred art into the intricacies of nature, into landscape and its atmospheric effects, and is fascinated by the peculiarities of marine flora and fauna. It is an empirical naturalism in which nature rather than man becomes the measure of things, and is signalled by the difference between Plato's conception of mimesis and its radical reworking by Aristotle. Even though we do not know whether Alexander, as legend has it, sent his teacher specimens of plants and animals collected on his extensive military expeditions, it is clear that Aristotle's organic conception of the beautiful owes everything to his lifelong interest in natural science. For Plato, any kind of imitation by the artist is something to be distrusted. For Aristotle, even the imitation of the ugly provides a source of pleasure.

In all this, Hellenistic culture is akin to that of nineteenth-century Europe. Naturalism fed by imperial expansion promotes cults of the exotic, the sublime and the archaic; promotes landscape art and Hellenistic kinds of impressionism. Ruskin, in so many ways, is the nineteenth-century counterpart of Aristotle and learnt immensely from him. In both times, too, though so widely separated, a loss of faith in the old gods gave rise to a philosophical naturalism. Lucretius anticipates Darwin. And it is perhaps in Lucretius that the cognitive style of the Hellenistic age is most optimistically expressed. Though the gods had failed, human skill, developed and transformed by experience and the rational intellect, could bring the arts to heights that they had not previously reached.

> Sailings, the tillage of ploughlands, and ramparts and edicts and arms and
> Roads, garb, all of the kind, all prizes, withal the delights of
> Life, whatsoever, as poems, and pictures, and statues of fine-wrought
> Polish—were all of them taught unto man, as by practice, by tireless
> Mind's experience little by little, as forward advanced he
> Step by step, Thus time draws each thing forward to men's midst
> Gradually, whilst to the borders of light 'tis uplifted by reason,
> Seeing that one thing after another by intellect saw they
> Grow clear, till in the arts now reach they the highest perfection.[42]

An optimism and hubris possible perhaps only at the apogee of Empires.

224

10 COOK'S POSTHUMOUS REPUTATION

> Lives of great men all remind us
> We can make our lives sublime,
> And, departing, leave behind us
> Footprints on the sands of time.
>
> 'The Reaper and the Flowers',
> Henry Wadsworth Longfellow (1807–82)

UNQUESTIONABLY, COOK'S REPUTATION prior to his death was considerable. At the age of thirty-four, six years before embarking on his first Pacific voyage, he was described by his superior officer Lord Colville as a man of 'genius and capacity'.[1] At the time of his death, his achievements were famed throughout Europe. In the Pacific, many thousands of the indigenous peoples had encountered him personally and knew good reasons why they should fear, cherish or in some cases, detest his memory. In Hawaii, he was revered as a god.

Cook's tragic death at Kealakekua Bay on 14 February 1799, however, propelled his memory far beyond the level of mere fame into those exalted realms of the human imagination where only gods, saints, heroes and martyrs dwell. This chapter will provide an outline account of some of the channels by which Cook's posthumous reputation was moulded and transmitted to later generations. As there is much material relevant to this subject still to be investigated, what I shall have to say here should be considered no more than a tentative foray into a fascinating field, an exercise in the ideology of reputation and, at least by implication, in the relation between the creation of reputation and the writing of history.

In embarking upon such an enquiry it is desirable to keep constantly in mind two distinguishable kinds of intention: the intention of those disposed to provide to the best of their ability an accurate account of what occurred at various times during Cook's remarkable life; and the intention of those who have concerned themselves with celebrating his life while using it, even if unwittingly, to support their own interests and concerns. These contrasting intentions are summarised for us in two of his portraits: in the realism of Hodges (pl. 197) and the idealism of Lucien Le Vieux (pl. 198). Admittedly, an absolute distinction is impossible, since even the most careful observer is not neutral. John Beaglehole, the finest and most meticulous of Cook scholars, did not flinch on several occasions from describing Cook as 'our Hero'; and if Beaglehole can be shown to possess an occasional blind spot, it will serve to remind us of our own. Indeed, the problem is built into the discipline. Clio is a schizophrenic muse who insistently enjoins historians to praise famous men while telling the truth, the whole truth, and nothing but the truth.

After his death, Cook's life and achievements provided the material from which a new kind of hero, one admirably adapted to the needs of the new industrial society of Europe, with its ambitions of global expansion, was fashioned. Cook

Capt. James Cook
of the Endeavour.

197. William Hodges,
Captain James Cook, oil on
canvas, 76 × 63.5 cm.,
c.1775, National Maritime
Museum, London.

198. Lucien Le Vieux,
James Cook, marble, 1790,
National Portrait Gallery,
London.

became the first and the most enduring hero of European expansion in the Pacific; or, to put it bluntly, the prototypical hero of European imperialism.

The first men to assess Cook's character and achievement knew him and worked with him at close quarters. They ranged from some of the most significant figures in contemporary European science, such as Banks and the Forsters, to common seamen. All of them, though aware of his weaknesses, revered and fostered his memory. They were disposed towards making sober assessments; as members of a scientific voyage, that is what they had been trained to do, and this was Cook's disposition also. 'The public will, I hope,' he wrote on one occasion, 'consider me as a plain man, zealously exerting himself in the service of his country.'[2] The tone is anti-heroic, in keeping with his temperament and calling. Yet we must be careful about accepting such modesty entirely at face value. By the time he made it, Cook's disclaimer was already something of a literary *topos*. More than once he had occasion to point out that he had been bred to the sea, and that the sea was no school for fine writers.[3] Bougainville, whose works were essential reading for Cook, had already pointed out that it 'was not in the forests of Canada nor on the breast of the sea, that one learns the art of writing'.[4] And others before Bougainville had made the same point. Cook is not so much admitting a literary deficiency as maintaining the ideals of a new kind of rhetoric, that art of plain speaking that Thomas Sprat in his *History of the Royal Society* (1667) had sought from the society's fellows (and remember Cook was one from 1776): 'a close, naked, natural way of speaking; positive expressions, clear sense; a native easiness, bringing all things as near the mathematical plainness as they can; and preferring the language of Artisans, Countrymen and Merchants before that of wits and scholars'.[5] What Diderot much later was to describe as 'le ton de la chose'[6]—a language, that is to say, suited to the needs of the new sciences, and one that was beginning, during Cook's lifetime, to affect the tone of literary discourse also. About twenty years after Cook's death, Wordsworth, in the Preface to the *Lyrical Ballads* (1798), recommended it as the language appropriate to poetry.[7]

226

It was not the new plain rhetoric, however, that provided the mould within which Cook's heroic posthumous reputation first came to be fashioned, although we must note in passing that the basic information from which the reputation was constructed in the journals of Cook, Banks, the Forsters, King, Samwell and others was composed in the plain style. Because it carried the authority of those who were there and knew Cook, it came to exercise a sobering and transforming constraint upon the heroising process. It is a case of the plain style of the medium helping to determine in the long run the tone and substance of the heroic message.

Shortly after his death, Cook's reputation was submitted quite consciously and deliberately to a heroising process, not by his fellow-voyagers but by academicians, poets and artists whose imaginations had been gripped by the magnitude of his achievement. Most of these people had already embraced with considerable warmth the attitudes and values of the Enlightenment. This is not surprising, for two reasons. Firstly, Cook himself adopted many, though by no means all, of the attitudes of the Enlightenment. Secondly, the initial phase in the construction of this heroic reputation was completed during the ten intellectually high-spirited years that elapsed between his death and the outbreak of the French Revolution. In saying that Cook's first hero-builders embraced the attitudes and values of the Enlightenment I mean, to quote Peter Gay's admirable description, that they adopted 'a programme of secularism, humanity, cosmopolitanism, and freedom, above all, freedom in its many forms—freedom from arbitrary power, freedom of speech, freedom of trade, freedom to realize one's talents, freedom of aesthetic response, freedom, in a word, of moral man to make his own way in the world'.[8]

The beginnings of the heroising process may be studied in the eulogies to Cook delivered and published by Continental academicians during the 1780s and early 1790s. The work of the eighteenth-century literary academies has not been fully studied, but it is already clear that they and not the universities were the institutions in which the ideas and values of the Enlightenment were discussed and tried out on the educated public.[9] The eulogy or funeral oration was one of the main literary genres employed for this purpose, and one in which the literary devices of classical rhetoric were given full play. It had reached its apogee in the great funeral orations of Bossuet a century before the death of Cook, but in the 1780s it was still very much alive, serving as a medium for the propagation of the values not of the Church but of the Enlightenment. Even so, its elaborate, forensic rhetoric was by the 1780s somewhat old-fashioned.

One of the earliest of the eulogies to Cook occurs as a section of the poem *Les Jardins* by Jacques Delille, published in Paris in 1782.[10] Delille had been admitted to the Académie Française in 1772, but his admission had been deferred because Louis XV suspected him of being an *encyclopédiste*. *Les Jardins*, which is modelled on Virgil's *Georgics*, is a dull poem, but it does provide some early pointers to the direction that the heroising of Cook was to take. Cook is praised because he brought the agricultural arts of his country, instead of the roar of the cannon, to the Pacific. In fact, of course, he brought both; but the heroising process required the selection of facts from a moral standpoint, and the setting of those facts as evidence of heroic behaviour against their antitheses, since heroes, in order to exist, require antagonists. War himself forgot his dire commands at the sight of Cook's ships: a reference to the French government's decision not to molest the *Resolution* and the *Adventure* following the outbreak of war with Spain in 1779. It is fitting, Delille observes, that such a universal hero should receive the laurel wreath from a foreign hand. He then proceeds to enquire, rather cheekily, by way of concluding his eulogy, why it is that the fierce sons of Britain cannot be truly great like their own hero, instead of always seeking despotic sway over their equals. Already we may glimpse here a rift appearing between Cook's potential role as universal hero and as patriotic hero.

Delille's piece is but a fragment. What appears to be the first of the complete eulogies to Cook, that of Michelangiolo Gianetti, was published by the Royal Academy of Florence in 1785.[11] For Gianetti, as for Delille, Cook's achievements were of the kind that greatly advanced the Enlightenment programme. Our hero, he informs us, has banished terror from the seas, where not a shoal has been neglected, not a depth untried, and not a danger unexplored. Cook has subdued human terror also, embracing his prisoners and winning their affections with gifts and kindnesses. Gianetti contrasts unfavourably the deeds of the old military heroes—Alexander, Scipio, Cortez, Pizarro—with those of this new man of peace whose excellences are not physical but mental, and who has revealed the whole earth to us under a new form that is safe for navigation and commerce.

Yet, Gianetti hastens to point out, Cook possessed the traditional virtues also: 'An Enlightened Monarch, an Enlightened Society and an admiring people had commanded him: "... go to the Island of Otahiete ... and there regulate the stars by your calculations; haste, examine, and make discoveries, bear the British name to New Zeland, rectify false opinion, improve Geography, discover new passages, and return with glory worthy of your Country, and yourself".'[12] And Cook, hearing the awful voice of his country which claims a hero for herself, took sorrowful leave, like Regulus, of his wife, and went. Gianetti's Cook is a blend of Enlightenment and patriotic hero. But he does select one aspect of Cook's life of special relevance to my theme. Cook is the self-made man. While hidden among the obscurity of the vulgar, he contemplated the stars and raised himself above his station in life by assiduous application to his studies. Now, the genesis of most of the technology that launched the industrial revolution was due mainly to the intense assiduity and resourcefulness of such self-made men, who possessed also a consuming interest in the application of science and mathematics to the practical problems of their trades and callings.

Gianetti's characterisation of Cook, though couched in the elaborate rhetoric of the late-baroque eulogy, is pretty much on mark. Cook, we suspect, might well have seen himself like that, though he would have put it more modestly. Nevertheless, it is a conventional tribute that does not enquire into the potential significance of his work for future generations. For this we must turn to the finest of the academic eulogies, Pierre Lémontey's *Eloge de Jacques Cook*, which won a prize for eloquence awarded by the Academy of Marseilles on 25 August 1789–a few weeks after the fall of the Bastille.[13]

Lémontey is worthy of more attention than he has received hitherto from Cook historians. Born at Lyons in 1762 of a merchant family, he studied law and practised as a barrister up to and during the early part of the Revolution. He was a powerful advocate for the civil rights of Protestants and played a leading part in organising the petition from the Lyonnaise to Louis XVI for the recall of Necker. Elected as a deputy from the Loire to the Legislative Assembly, later, in December 1791, he became its president. He aligned himself with the moderate minority and failed in his efforts to preserve the constitutional monarchy. After the insurrection of 10 August that captured the Tuileries and overthrew the

228

monarchy, Lémontey found it prudent to leave France for Switzerland, where he lived until 1795, when he returned to Lyons. In later life he wrote several plays and some historical works. His *Eloge de Jacques Cook*, written when he was twenty-seven, was the first of his literary productions. The fact that it was written in the year of the Revolution or shortly before and published in Paris in 1792 at the height of the struggle for power may help to explain the fervently optimistic, almost millenarianist tone that prevails throughout.

The reputation of Captain Cook, Lémontey assures us, will not be subjected to the twists and turns of the goddess Fortune, because the impact of his discoveries will increase from age to age, and mankind will confer upon him that kind of veneration that it reserves for those who bring universal benefits to mankind. Cook is the very personification of Europe. For him, movement was freedom. In movement he realised his innermost nature; to remain at home was, for him, to be a captive. Europe is like that: a geographical imperative impels it; it must be on the move or perish. Just consider the fanatical pilgrimages of the Crusades, the bloody brigands of Mexico and Peru, the tyrannous calculator of India (perhaps a reference to Warren Hastings, whose trial had just begun), and consider, too, the adventurers and philosophers of the South Seas. But Lémontey asks us, where can Europe possibly expand now? It cannot go on Crusade again; we shall only hurt ourselves or starve in India; and since the Americans have won their freedom, they are determined to bring European culture to the new continent themselves.

There is only one part of the world left: that made available by Cook, the harbours of the south (*les échelles du sud*). This is Lémontey's phrase for all the discoveries made, re-enlivened or promised by Cook, and it becomes the *leitmotif* of his eulogy. The merchant navies, he continues, are the prime movers of the European nations, they are changing the centres of gravity and the balance of power. Each nation strives for a larger mercantile marine, for the creation of which Europe is depopulating its forests. We shall have to reach out to the Isle of Pines and the forests of New Zealand to replenish our stores. And commerce grows with this growth of merchant navies; for commerce feeds on its own excess and impoverishes all that it does not swallow. But Cook has found new routes, new ports, new foods, and brought knowledge of them to existing ports in Indochina and the Philippines. The Sandwich Islands will become a new entrepôt for the colonies of Russia and England for the purchase of cloth, skins and furs, bows and arrows. All this is but further evidence of a continuing conspiracy among the inhabitants of the land against the inhabitants of the sea, of those periodic crusades when maritime peoples unite to make the sea a fertile field that nourishes the human race: for the sea itself is a school of vigour, skill and courage. The fishermen of England, France and Holland will unite and sail right up to the ice of the Southern Thule in search of those whales that long hunting is causing to desert the northern latitudes.

Furthermore, with the growth of the *échelles du sud*, population will increase and parochial prejudice dissolve in one great sphere of human activity. Although it is difficult, Lémontey concedes, to estimate the social effects of discoveries where chance and passion prevail, the promise of gold being mined abundantly and easily in New Caledonia may have the beneficial effect of the abandonment of those hellish caverns of America in which the Inca perished. How astonished, he adds with a flourish, the sun itself would be were the land to be returned to his own ancient admirers.

For Lémontey, the *échelles du sud* are of the first importance, for they hold out promise of a new kind of commerce which will not involve the misery of indigenous tribes or black Africans. Their wealth will be based upon work that is free. Already England has planted a new colony at Botany Bay consisting of a frightful mixture of convicted and depraved men, but, like Rome of old, they will develop into a strong nation. Human manure in the hands of good cultivators can produce golden harvests and spreading vines. New Holland will become a meeting place of the world. China will deposit her surplus population, which is the cause of her present feebleness, there. The Japanese, now so isolated, will mix themselves there with the great human family where Europeans, Malays, Americans and Asians will encounter one another with astonishment; and there, too, the plants and animals of the north and south will mingle and flourish to the advantage of all.

Lémontey, you will recall, came of a merchant family and successfully entered a prize piece to the Academy of a city that was, one might say, the great *échelle du sud* of France, with a proud mercantile history first as a Phoenician, then as a Greek and Roman colony which prospered commercially and culturally as it extended its sway over the barbarous tribes of its hinterland. What, Lémontey enquires of us, is the true grandeur of ancient nations? The ruins of Carthage, the ostentatious debris of Thebes and Palmyra? Of course not. It is rather the colonies that they spread in all regions: Gaul civilised, Lyons and Marseilles embellishing themselves from age to age. These are the true monuments of antiquity. Europe, therefore, Lémontey concludes, must throw herself without relaxing into the new hemisphere. May the nations long dispute the honour of carrying into this new world Europe's force of life, order and fecundity, which like a miracle produces dwellings, harvests and cities.

The last eulogy to which I wish to refer is that by Pierre-Louis Paris, published in 1790 and probably written, like Lémontey's, the year before.[14] Paris was a member of the Oratoire and several academies. Like Lémontey, he contrasts the earlier European voyages of exploration based upon rapine and slaughter with the peaceful, philosophic and, above all, useful voyages of Cook. Paris was a religious, and his text is clustered with christological *topoi*. While the nations compete with one another, each in its own domain studying science, a great event is prepared in the heavens, and Cook is charged with taking English scientists to the Pacific to watch the transit of Venus. The wise are jealous of this young man who was not educated in the right schools, but he confounds them and instructs them in the true geography. Paris, like Lémontey, presents Cook as the new hero of free and civilised trading. Whereas Columbus sought gold, Cook respected the rights of humanity. Indeed, if one possessed the genius of Cook, it might be possible to trace the ascent of man from the state of the lowest savages of Tierra del Fuego up to that of those Europeans who could give birth to a genius like Cook himself.

This brief outline of the substance of some of the eulogies will already have provided an impression of the literary techniques involved in the heroising process. For example, no mention is made of any of Cook's associates by name; if given a corporate mention, they function only in the capacity of assistants or disciples. On one occasion, when he found it necessary to mention Banks, Paris apologised in advance to his hero for mixing the praise of a stranger with his own. It was a strict convention of the eulogy to keep the spotlight of fame fixed on the hero. Again, as I mentioned briefly earlier, the treatment of facts and events differs greatly from their treatment in logs and journals. In the latter case, facts were collected and set down to provide new information for a growing number of new sciences; but in the eulogy, facts are selected to illustrate the virtues of the hero and to edify the audience. Further, the sequence of events may be altered for aesthetic reasons. For example, Paris had the *Endeavour* breach its hull on a coral shoal in the Tasman Sea between New Zealand and Australia, not in the Coral Sea, doubtless in order to provide a dramatic turn of events at a point in the story where it was felt to be needed.

The hero of the eulogies is a blend of the new and the old. By a continuous use of classical and biblical *topoi*, Cook's legitimate descent from the heroes of the past is traced. Although he discovers in Tahiti an Arcadia as alluring as Circe's grotto, he alone among his company resists the seductions of the sorceresses and, again like Ulysses, guides his little company through the Scylla and Charybdis of the coral shoals; and in the underworld of Antarctica faces the terrors of the deep: hideous marine monsters, frightening waterspouts, mountains of ice. Like Christ, he comes of humble human origins but confounds wise men and comes bringing a new message—free trading and civilised behaviour—to the gentiles of the south. Like Christ, too, he identifies with all humanity, treating all men as his brothers, rebuking, as Peter was rebuked, his crew from acts of violence against the native peoples. 'The life of one man', Paris asserts unequivocally 'was more precious in the eyes of Cook than the knowledge of a continent.'[15] In discovering new lands, he comes into his own kingdom; everything new reminds him of home, and he names the unknown rivers and seas, headlands and islands after his friends and benefactors, claiming them all in the name of his sovereign king. In my father's house there are many islands. And in the final episode of his life he is likened in Anna Seward's *Elegy on Captain Cook* (1780) to Orpheus, torn limb from limb by the very savages to whom he had carried the arts of civilisation.

Yet Cook is also a new kind of hero for a new time. His wisdom is based upon his command of the new technologies which he uses to practical advantage, such as the maintenance of the health of his crew. Unlike the old navigators, he publishes his voyages: freedom of trade is dependent upon freedom of knowledge. He upgrades a whole range of homely virtues that were neglected by previous military and naval heroes but that are essential for success in the coming industrial age: professionalism, competence, prudence, thoroughness, stubbornness, patience, a constrained pride in achievement. The old-style genius had been a man inspired by the gods and guarded by a tutelary benefactor. Cook did not depend much upon God: he kept his powder dry, mentioned Providence rarely and performed the Sunday naval service intermittently; but he was perfectly willing to play god himself, as he did at Hawaii, if the cultivation of peaceful cultural relations depended on it. Almost a century before Carlyle defined this new kind of self-dependent genius that the times had need of as 'the transcendent capacity for taking trouble',[16] Cook had already demonstrated the new type in the Pacific.

I propose now to turn to a brief consideration of the part played by the visual arts in the heroising process. Like the logs and journals kept by Cook and his companions, the visual records executed on the voyages had as their object a complete and accurate documentation of the peoples, places and things encountered. And even when such works were further developed as art works destined for the Royal Academy and other such prestigious places, they were still—despite their aesthetic modifications—directed towards the new visual

rhetoric of naturalism which sought to tell, within the limitations of painting, truths about geography and environment, light and weather. The application of painting to the heroising process, while also providing a truthful account of events, constituted a problem. For the process demands the selection of a series of crucial incidents linked in temporal succession: the humble birth, the illuminating call to the mission, the embarkation and fulfillment of the mission, and finally, the heroic death. But as Lessing, who was Cook's exact contemporary, pointed out, painting does not lend itself to heroising in the way that verbal narration does. The painter must respect the non-temporal character of his medium and choose a crucial moment in the hero's life, and by concentrating on the expressive potential of that one moment, reveal within it the events preceding and the events succeeding. In the case of Cook, as for most martyr-heroes, the crucial moment for the painter was obviously the moment of death or that immediately preceding death.

Let us examine some of the paintings of the death of Cook that appeared (like the eulogies) during the 1780s and early 1790s. In doing so, we may observe in the heroising process two modes paralleling those of the corresponding verbal rhetoric: a plain style that keeps close to the eyewitness accounts of Cook's death; a grand style that elevates and allegorises the events.

The first paintings of Cook's death were composed to illustrate faithfully the event as recorded in the official account of the third voyage by Captain James King. John Webber, the only artist who might possibly have witnessed Cook's death (though we have no evidence that he did) follows King's account closely: the two boats offshore, with the marines firing from the more distant, and a couple struggling in the water to gain the boats (pl. 199); Lieutenant Phillips, fallen to the ground, firing at his assailant; Cook about to be stabbed in the back

203. *Death of Cook*, lithograph, in *Narrative of Captain James Cook's Voyages around the World*, London, 1839, fp. 376.

by a huge native as he turns and gestures towards the launch. The gesture is key to the emotional tone of the painting, and is enigmatic. Is Cook waving to Williamson to stop firing and pull in so that he can escape, or is he commanding him to stop firing at the natives? The ambiguity is sufficiently strong to support a reading of Cook as martyr-hero willing to sacrifice his life rather than command the death of his native friends. John Cleveley's aquatint—which was based, it is alleged (obviously erroneously), on a drawing by his brother James, who was carpenter on the *Resolution*—also focuses the action upon a similar enigmatic gesture and makes use of a puff of musket fire to provide a halo for the hero (pl. 200). Significantly, these two paintings provided the basic material for those innumerable illustrations of Cook's death that appeared in books recounting his life and voyages. Those which chose moments in the death struggle less central to the tragedy were, predictably, used less. George Carter, for example, depicts Cook in a fit of desperation going for his assailant with the butt of his rifle (pl. 201). It may well have occurred;[1] but that is not at all the way a prospective hero should behave. D.P. Dodd also portrayed Cook in an unheroic position, at the moment when he had fallen face downwards and was being either pushed into or pulled out of the water by his attackers (pl. 202). It is significant that neither Carter's nor Dodd's paintings were much copied or adapted by later illustrators of Cook's death.

It is possible to trace the descent of the image of Cook as martyr-hero from the Webber and Cleveley paintings from their day to ours, as they came to be interpreted in the light of their own interests: by men imbued with the values of the Enlightenment, then by schoolteachers and evangelists; by philosophical beachcombers, colonial nationalists and novelists in search of a good adventure story for boys. Two examples will have to suffice. Firstly, an attractive primitive lithograph which appeared in a collection of Cook's *Voyages* published in 1839 (pl. 203). It depicts Cook completely disarmed, passively awaiting the *coup de grâce* from one native who looks like an English village blacksmith, and another like

204. Gordon Browne, *Death of Captain Cook*, in C.R. Lowe (ed.), *Captain Cook's three voyages round the world*, London, 1895, p. 470.

233

205. Frontispiece to *The British Nepos; or Mirror of Youth, Consisting of Selected Lives of Illustrious Britons*, by William Fordyce Mavor, London, 1798, engraving by W. Taylor after John Thurston.

Edmund Kean playing a villanous role at Drury Lane. Secondly, the illustration by Gordon Browne, which appeared in Lowe's collected edition of the *Voyages*, published in 1895 (pl. 204). A general feature of these illustrations of the late nineteenth and early twentieth centuries is the tendency to emphasise the bestiality of Cook's assailants: they are portrayed sometimes to look, as in an illustration by Will Robinson, remarkably like monkeys (pl. 55).

The life of Cook came to exercise a profound effect upon the younger sons of those large Victorian families in all parts of the United Kingdom who found it necessary to leave home in order to better themselves. One of the first writers to present Cook as a British worthy and model for schoolboys to emulate was William Fordyce Mavor, the schoolmaster of Woodstock, who included a life of Cook in his *British Nepos; or Mirror of Youth, Consisting of Selected Lives of Illustrious Britons* (1798). The frontispiece depicts the 'Genius of Biography directing British Youth to the Temple of Honour in the path of Industry & Perseverance' (pl. 205).

When a martyr dies, he is received into glory. Complementing the martyr-victim images of Cook, we have those that apotheosise him. The Greek practice of transforming heroes into gods was revived in the seventeenth century in the baroque ceiling paintings of Italy and central Europe, from whence it spread to book illustration. Despite the religious implications, the apotheosis became a popular visual trope by which the Enlightenment sought to venerate famous men. For though they questioned immortality, the Philosophes were great promoters (by way of compensation, perhaps) of secular fame.

Johann Ramberg, a German historical painter and illustrator who is said to have studied under Reynolds and Bartolozzi, depicted Cook being received into glory for the frontispiece of the Reverend Thomas Bankes's *New System of Geography* (1787) (pl. 206). Cook is depicted, looking uncomfortable, in an uncharacteristic pose midway between that of the *Apollo Belvedere* and the strut of a rococo dancing master. He stands on a rock that is changing into a cloud, though it is still solid enough for a sceptical astronomer to stand on. Fame trumpets his arrival, while a Genius crowns him with a wreath of oak. Neptune

206. Frontispiece to *New System of Geography*, by Rev. Thomas Bankes, London, 1787, engraving after Johann Ramberg.

207. *The Apotheosis of Captain James Cook*, engraved from a design by P.J. de Loutherbourg and John Webber, published 20 January 1794 by J. Thane, London.

introduces him to History (or it may be Clio's research assistant), who has started to take down from Cook's personal dictation the heavenly edition of the *Voyages*. Below, and this is central to my thesis, Britannia receives tribute from the Four Continents, personified in that most typical of baroque motifs, as four typically dressed young matrons of generous proportion. To the right, the *Resolution* and the *Adventure* sail into port with new treasure from the southern seas.

Phillip James de Loutherbourg's *Apotheosis of Captain James Cook*, published as an engraving in 1794, is more dramatic and less utilitarian than Ramberg's (pl. 207). Below, we see the tragic attack at Kealakekua Bay in progress; above, Cook is depicted ascending into the clouds clutching his sextant in one hand while he endeavours to fend off with the other the advancing buttocks of Universal Fame, only to fall into the welcoming lap of Britannia. The women of heaven, he seems to be thinking, are rather like those of Tahiti.

The neo-baroque style, like the rhetoric of the eulogies, was rather old-fashioned by the time these apotheoses were executed. It was left to Johan Zoffany, who might have joined the second voyage had Banks got his way, to paint a death of Cook in the more contemporary neo-classical manner (pl. 208). Here, as Charles Mitchell has indicated,[18] contemporary history is re-created on a timeless and ideal plane. Cook is presented to us as a hero-victim in the pose of the *Dying Gladiator*, while his huge antagonist is posed with equal dignity in the manner of the *Discobolos*; and Cook reveals no emotion upon his face, only that 'fixed expression of suffering' that characterises the antique tragic mask. The tragedy is thus elevated into a realm of timeless ideality.

The death of the hero was one of the central themes of neo-classical painting and sculpture. Cook's death was but one of the many deaths of contemporary famous men for which heroic parallels with antiquity were sought, the best-known and one of the first in the field being Benjamin West's *Death of Wolfe* (1771).[19] Although it is rightly famed beyond any painting associated with Cook and became enormously popular with the British public after its highly successful engraving by Woollett, it was Cook, it seems to me, the quiet man whose effective

208. Johan Zoffany, *The Death of Cook*, oil on canvas, 137.2 × 185.5 cm., *c.*1795, National Maritime Museum, London.

charting of the St Lawrence helped make Wolfe's victory possible, who was endowed with an heroic status more potent and durable than Wolfe's. For Wolfe was an old-fashioned military hero, not a man for a new time. And this might also be said of that other great hero of Empire, Horatio Nelson. Intrepidity, skill, courage: Nelson's virtues had all been demonstrated, and in many cases demonstrated better, by the heroes of antiquity. Dallying with Emma Hamilton on shore leave and kissing Hardy as he expired may well have been engaging and typical foibles in a British sailor-lad, but they were not–Trafalgar Square notwithstanding–the sort of qualities that make a modern hero durable. Cook, I would argue, grew in stature as an imperial hero because his life story was better fitted to the ideological belief–however distant from the true state of affairs–in a world-wide empire dedicated to the arts of peace (a *Pax Britannica*), not one based upon war. Perhaps it was the vision that haunted the men of the Enlightenment of a *Pax Universitas* that inspired the French sculptor Lucien Le Vieux, in 1790 at the height of the Revolution, to model a bust of Cook in the idealised image of the young Augustus Caesar, the creator of the *Pax Romana* (pl. 198).

This universal peace, however, was to be erected upon the principles of free trade, and Cook was to become the hero, as Napoleon once put it in a state of irritation, 'of a nation of shopkeepers'. For Cook, the realist, was well aware that the survival of his company depended upon his capacity to establish and maintain markets with the native people encountered at each of his major landfalls, as we have seen. Tools and toys (I use the latter word in its eighteenth-century sense) from Birmingham were exchanged, as Cook himself put it, for 'refreshments', that is to say, fresh food and the rights to fuel and water essential to the life and health of his company. In the process of establishing these markets, Cook developed a technique of culture contact with primitive peoples that proved to be highly successful. By means of friendliness and force, the conventions that were necessary for the maintenance of a free market (such as the European conception of private property) were impressed upon the native mind. Cook must have been the first European to *practise* successfully on a global scale the use of tolerance for the purpose of domination, an administrative technique that came to play a vital role in the European colonisation of the world during the nineteenth century.[20]

On such matters the parallel between Cook and Adam Smith, to which I have alluded earlier, is interesting. Smith was born five years before and died eleven years after Cook. In the lectures that Smith delivered in Edinbugh during 1748-9, he became an effective and influential champion of the new rhetoric which insisted upon a plain style, non-artistic arguments, and direct proofs;[21] a style that Cook adhered to firmly in writing up his daily transactions. This is not to say that Cook was influenced by Smith's ideas on rhetoric but that he belonged linguistically and temperamentally to the same intellectual movement. Smith's great work, *The Wealth of Nations*, appeared in March 1776, when Cook was taking on provisions prior to departing on his last voyage, the official account of which was placed, as noted earlier, in the hands of Strahan and Cadell, the publishers of *The Wealth of Nations*. As Smith's global agent, Cook developed markets and spread the notion of enlightened self-interest, bringing to prehistoric cultures the disguised checks and balances of a market economy regulated by what Smith described as a 'hidden hand'–though Cook had to reveal that hand from time to time, when natives made off with the boats or the chronometers, in order to instruct them in the rules of the new game.

Seen in this light, Cook emerges as a Promethean hero who brings metallurgy and its related forms of culture to primitve man. He achieved this great task by displaying a range of virtues—patience, tolerance, fortitude, perseverence, stubbornness, attention to detail, professionalism and so forth—about which Beaglehole and others have written eloquently. But this array of virtues, we may remind ourselves, is precisely that by which men seek to attain the efficiency of machines. Although Cook possessed in considerable measure what we might describe for the purposes of our discussion as the pre-industrial virtues—physical courage, loyalty, devotion, humility, faith, hope and charity—he was, admittedly, weak on some of them, and all of them were less relevant to the performance of his task. Yet there is little reason to doubt that Cook on any reading was a man of great virtue; my point is rather that we should recognise the sociality, the timeliness of his array of virtues, his inborn capacity to exercise an ethics of situation. To say this is not to accuse him of expedience but rather to stress that, when he was most himself, he was most in harmony with the new, secular, industrial order that was emerging as the new world order during his lifetime: his array of virtues made it possible for him to rediscover the Golden Age in the Pacific and to bring to it the values of the Iron Age so long in preparation in Europe.

To identify the spread of a British empire based upon industry and free trade with the universal progress of human culture was the theme with which the Royal Society of Arts and Manufactures chose to adorn the great hall of their new building by Robert Adam in the Adelphi. It was an appropriate theme, for the society was one of the earliest, and has continued to be one of the most effective, institutions dedicated to the progress of the agricultural and industrial arts. Painted by James Barry and entitled 'The Progress of Human Culture' (1777–83), it set out to depict the stages of man's development, beginning with *Orpheus Reclaiming Mankind from a Savage State* and culminating with *Navigation, or the Triumph of the Thames*, which depicted, to quote Joseph Burke's fitting description, 'the expansion and sharing of benefits under the new Olympians, the British' (pl. 209). Among the Tritons and Nereids swim Sebastian Cabot, Raleigh, Drake, 'the late Captain Cook of amiable memory', and Barry's friend the musical historian, Dr Charles Burney.[22] It puzzled many to find Burney there—though his son did travel with Cook twice. Barry, however, insisted that he wished to introduce 'the personification of music' into 'this scene of triumph and joy'.[23] Nevertheless, Burney's inclusion did create discussion. 'It irks one to see my good friend Dr Burney', an indignant dowager of the time remarked on seeing the painting, 'paddling in a horse pond with a bevy of naked wenches'.[24] But to describe that ample allegorical ocean as a horse pond was quite unfair to Barry, and to the enormous Pharos, supported by a giant whose hand alone, as Professor Burke has noted, is far larger than the ship below; all this is very much in the

209. James Barry, *Navigation, or the Triumph of the Thames*, oil on canvas, 335.5 × 462.5 cm., 1777–83, Royal Society of Arts, London.

spirit of that commercial utopia of the *échelles du sud* which Lémontey was to describe in his eulogy five years after Barry had completed his painting.

There are other paths along which Cook's heroic image was transmitted to later generations and maintained: for example, the editorial processes by which the original accounts of the voyages were transformed into books of edification and adventure for children, inspiring them to go out and do likewise as missionaries, explorers, colonial administrators or even as beachcombers–those pioneering drop-outs from industrial society of whom Cook would not have approved. There is the process by which the heroic image of Cook has developed, like a multi-facial Indian god, its own avatars: the posthumous history of Cook not only as a manifestation of the god Lono in Hawaii[25] but also as the manifestation of the hero transformed into a founding father, or historical Adam, for the new nations of the Pacific. As founding father he performs the primal historical act, that of taking possession in the name of the British sovereign.[26] This act has been commemorated continually in the striking of medals and the issue of postage stamps upon suitable occasions; in the execution of historical paintings and the preservation of Cook relics in the national libraries and museums of Australia, New Zealand and elsewhere; in the erection of obelisks, memorial tablets and statues at almost every beach in the Pacific Ocean where he is known to have stepped ashore; and in the re-enactment, in these sacro-secular groves at periodic intervals, determined by the movement of those stars that Cook studied with such scientific detachment, of appropriate rites to celebrate his memory.

Finally, we might consider that topic so close to the discipline of history which Arnold Toynbee once described as the 'inspiration of historians'. In this case it would be the relationship that subsists between the funding of celebrations commemorating Cook and the historical investigations supported by them. It might help to throw a little more light on Clio's mental problem: the role of history in the manufacture of fame, and history as critical enquiry.

A true hero invariably possesses a worthy antagonist who becomes the agent of the hero's death. That is the moral of Zoffany's painting. But the antagonist is only an agent; the hero dies because the charisma of the gods deserts him. Cook based his relations with native peoples largely upon his own personal courage and peaceful temperament, and a careful appraisal of the situation, going up to them alone with gifts in his hand and a welcome on his face. It was only as a last resort that he made use, as he once put it, of 'the smart of our fire' from the small line of marines held in support behind. At Hawaii, however, the device of looking them in the eye, the well-tried procedures of peaceful domination, failed; and Cook died, struck down from behind, his body hacked to pieces by daggers fashioned from iron spikes[27] which had quite probably been manufactured in Boulton's Birmingham factory. They had been brought out, as Cook had put it in his requisition order to the Admiralty, 'to be distributed to them in presents towards obtaining their friendship'.[28]

Like his celebrants, Cook's antagonists have continued to be active long after his death. I have not studied the activities of the anti-Cook party in detail, and I shall only suggest some pointers towards further research that should repay detailed examination.

The base for the criticism of Cook and his achievements originates in those apects of Enlightenment thought that placed greater emphasis upon the natural rights of men to decide their own moral destiny than upon the growth of free trade and the progress of civilisation. The criticism, in fact, appears prior to Cook in Diderot's *Supplément au voyage de Bougainville*, written in 1772 but not published until 1796, a book that was, in part, the result of Diderot's misreading of Rousseau on the nobility of savages. But it was George Forster, the only man to travel with Cook who embraced the whole critical programme of the Enlightenment, and probably the most intelligent and farsighted of them all, who first voiced concern at the likely outcome of Cook's voyages. In a much-quoted passage in his *Voyage*, he wrote: 'If the knowledge of a few individuals can only be acquired at such a price as the happiness of nations, it were better for the discoverers and the discovered, that the South Seas had still remained unknown to Europe and its restless inhabitants.'[29]

Forster's apprehensions and concerns were taken up, as we know, by the satirists and more seriously by moralists like Gerald Fitzgerald. In his poem *The Injured Islanders* (1779),[30] Fitzgerald expressed grave concern about the effects that the introduction of European commerce and European diseases would have upon the Polynesians: 'The imaginary value annexed to European toys and Manufactures and the Ravages of a particular disorder, have already injured their morals and their peace; even the instruments of iron, which must facilitate the ordinary Operations of Industry have been used as weapons of Destruction, or perverted to the purposes of Ambition and Revenge.'

Even the French academic eulogists of Cook had to take note of such criticism. At one point in his eulogy, Lémontey breaks off from his paean to Cook and puts in a word for the other side. 'An arm arrests me', he announced oratorically:

> Cease imprudent orator, usurper of the language of posterity, or be impartial as it is. Dare you judge without understanding the law? Are not the benefits of Cook rather mixed? When a victor marched to the Capitol, the curses of the Parthians and the Numidians mingled with the cheers of the Roman people. The hero of the Tiber was only a brigand on the banks of the Danube. Praise yourselves, civilised peoples, wise nations exalt those discoveries which flatter your pride, increase your wealth, perfect your knowledge; it is not you who pays for them with your happiness. But the ignorance of how many innocent tribes have you not violated by your barbarous curiosity and enflamed their passions by the fatal presence of your vices and your needs? The Eulogy of Cook is only a reckoning, a catalogue of egoism, and its laurels will perish on the theatre of its glory.[31]

Lémontey was aware of the anti-Cook case, but it was not his case. He introduced it only to destroy it. Introducing arguments drawn from Montesquieu and others based on geographical determinism and the role of Europe in civilising the world, he set out to demolish it.

I suspect that through most of the nineteenth century the anti-Cook case remained a kind of prehistoric and sub-literate resentment among the indigenous peoples of the Pacific that rarely surfaced. When it did take a written form, it came from Europeans who were disposed to discredit Cook in order to advance their own interests. John Stokes has shown that the strong anti-Cook sentiment that prevailed in Hawaii from the later 1830s up till quite recent times was largely the result of the work of the Reverend Sheldon Dibble, an American missionary and schoolteacher who encouraged his pupils to interview old Hawaiians to provide material for a local history. The memories of these old people conflated Cook's activities with that of subsequent early visitors. Then Dibble himself edited the interviews and wrote up the history to the discredit of Cook. Stokes argues convincingly that there was little anti-Cook sentiment in the island prior to Dibble's history, which was used as a text in schools.[32] This is an interesting example of the creation of an anti-Cook ideology. As a missionary, Dibble was antipathetic to Cook's secular pragmatism in accepting the impersonation of Lono that was largely thrust upon him, and as an American he was strongly influenced by the anti-British sentiment engendered by the war of 1812 and still present in Hawaii in the 1840s as a significant factor in island politics. Nevertheless, I do not think we can take Stokes's account of the growth of anti-Cook feeling entirely at its face value. It is doubtful whether Hawaiian opinion about Cook is best assessed from the written accounts of what Hawaiians were prepared to tell missionaries and visiting voyagers in the days before Dibble, even though they venerated Cook as a god prior to their conversion to Christianity. We should remind ourselves that on the first occasion, when they venerated him as a god, they also killed him. Furthermore, Dibble's spurious history found a receptive soil to flourish in through the nineteenth century. My point is this: though it may satisfy a European mind to distribute praise and blame among individuals in the precise way that Stokes does, the conflation of Cook's acts with those of his less high-minded successors exemplifies the process by which heroic legend is constructed and then countervailed. It will always be difficult for the native historians of the indigenous peoples of the Pacific as they come increasingly to write their histories to draw a fine line between Cook the individual and the culture their ancestors inherited in the wake of his vessels. Cook is not their culture hero, nor was he regarded as a culture hero by the republican circles that sprang up in the Australian colonies in the 1880s.[33]

Although the tone of this chapter in places may have given that impression, I want to emphasise that it has not been part of my intention to discredit the achievements of Cook. My intention has been to suggest that it is timely that they be placed in a new perspective. Amidst the collapse of the European colonial empires, amidst mounting criticism of the cultural consequences of high technology, it seems desirable that Cook and his achievements be interpreted in a less Eurocentric fashion than they have been in the past. We might have to admit, for example, that he discovered little in the way of new lands: that wherever he came there were usually people who had been settled for centuries. They provided, through trading, the provisions so crucial for the successful prosecution of his ventures. The discovery of the world is really a subject for prehistorians. Cook was not a discoverer of new lands in any fundamental sense of the word. He was the highly successful leader of three well-balanced, scientific research teams; a communications man, who was instrumental in bringing a mixed bag of goods— ironware and syphilis, written language and centralised government, and much more—to the Pacific. It could be said of Cook more than of any other person, that he helped to make the world one world; not a harmonious world, as the men of the Enlightenment had so ardently hoped, but an increasingly interdependent one. His ships began the process of making the world a global village.

NOTES

ABBREVIATIONS

Banks, *Endeavour Journal*   Sir Joseph Banks, *The Endeavour Journal of Sir Joseph Banks*, ed. J.C. Beaglehole, 2 vols, Sydney, 1962.

Cook, *Journals*   James Cook, *The Journals of Captain James Cook on his voyages of Discovery*, ed. J.C. Beaglehole, 3 vols, Cambridge, 1955–68.

Joppien and Smith   R. Joppien and B. Smith, *The Art of Captain Cook's Voyages*, 3 vols, Sydney, New Haven and London, 1985–7.

P.R.O.   Public Record Office, London.

Smith   B. Smith, *European Vision and the South Pacific* (2nd edn), New Haven and London, 1985.

PREFACE

1. Edmund Blunden, *in lit.* 5 Feb. 1957.
2. Kathleen Coburn, *in lit.* 1 Dec. 1959.
3. E.L. Griggs, *in lit.* 13 Sept. 1957.
4. A.D. Hope, *in lit.* 11 Nov. 1954.
5. Blunden, *in lit.* 5 Feb. 1957.
6. Edward W. Said, *Orientalism*, London, 1978.

1 ART IN THE SERVICE OF SCIENCE AND TRAVEL

1. W. Ivins, *Prints and Visual Communication*, London, 1953, p. 92.
2. *The Educational writings of John Locke*, ed. J.L. Axtell, London, 1968, p. 265.
3. The subject is discussed in detail in Kim Sloan, 'The Teaching of non-professional artists in Eighteenth-Century England', Ph.D. thesis, University of London, 1986. See also Martin Hardie, *Water-Colour Painting in England*, ed. D. Snelgrove, J. Mayne and B. Taylor, 1968, vol. 3, pp. 212–44.
4. Edmund Burke, *A Philosophical Enquiry into the Origin of our Ideas of the Sublime and Beautiful*, ed. J.T. Boulton, London, 1958, p. 77.
5. Otto Pächt, 'Early Italian Nature Studies and the Early Calendar Landscape', *Journal of the Warburg and Courtauld Institutes*, vol. 13, nos 1–2, 1950, p. 21; to which this whole section is much indebted.
6. See E.H. Gombrich, 'The Renaissance Theory of Art and the Rise of Landscape', in his *Norm and Form*, London, 1966.
7. It is possible that the invention of pictorial perspective itself may have been due to an early use of the camera obscura. See Shigeru Tsuji, 'Brunelleschi and the Camera Obscura', *Art History*, vol. 13, no. 3, Sept. 1990.
8. Edward W. Said, *Orientalism*, London, 1978.
9. William Eisler, 'Terra Australis. Art and Exploration 1500–1768', in *Terra Australis the Furthest Shore*, ed. W. Eisler and B. Smith, Art Gallery of New South Wales, Sydney, 1988.
10. Hugh Honour, *The European Vision of America*, Cleveland Museum of Art, 1975, item 6 (cat.).
11. On Le Moyne see P. Hulton *et al.*, *The Work of Jacques Le Moyne de Morgues*, 2 vols, London, 1977.
12. *Ibid.*, p. 119. Quoted from 'The Narrative of Jacques Le Moyne de Morgues'.
13. See the appraisal by W.C. Sturtevant in Hulton, *op. cit.*, pp. 69–71.
14. Quoted from Hulton, *op. cit.*, p. 141.
15. *Ibid.*, p. 163.
16. For eighteenth-century relationships between the exotic and erotic see G.S. Rousseau and R. Porter, eds, *Exoticism and the Enlightenment*, Manchester and New York, 1990; particularly the essays by R. Porter (pp. 117–44) and S.R. Pucci (pp. 145–74).
17. Quoted from P. Hulton, *The Complete Drawings of John White*, London, 1984, p. 8.
18. *Ibid.*
19. Mary F. Keeler, *Sir Francis Drake's West Indian Voyage, 1585–86*, London, 1981, p. 290; and Helen Wallis, 'The Cartography of Drake's Voyage', in *Sir Francis Drake and the Famous Voyage 1577–80*, ed. N.J. Thrower, Berkeley, Los Angeles and London, 1984, p. 123.
20. Quoted from D.B. Quinn and A.M. Quinn, *The English New England Voyages, 1602–1608*, London, 1983, p. 193.
21. Svetlana Alpers, *The Art of Describing. Dutch Art in the Seventeenth Century*, Chicago, 1983, p. 149.
22. R. Joppien, 'The Dutch Vision of Brazil of Johan Maurits and his artists', in *Johan Maurits van Nassau, 1601–1679, A Humanist Prince in Europe and Brazil*, ed. E. van den Boogart, The Hague, 1979.
23. On typical landscape see Smith, pp. 4–5, *et al.*
24. Joppien, *op. cit.*, p. 302.
25. See P.J.P. Whitehead and M. Boaseman, 'A Portrait of Dutch 17th Century Brazil. Animals, plants and people by the artists of Johan Maurits of Nassau*, Amsterdam, Oxford, New York, 1989.
26. Joppien, *op. cit.*, p. 347.
27. Alpers, *op. cit.*
28. Joppien, *op. cit*, p. 354.
29. Whitehead and Boaseman, *op. cit.*, pp. 123–6.
30. See Smith, pp. 205f.
31. Louis Renard, *Poissons, Ecrivisses et Crabes, de Diverses Couleurs et Figures Extraordinares, que l'on Trouve Autour des Isles Moluques, et sur les Côtes des Terres Australes* (2nd edn), Amsterdam, 1754.
32. J.P. de Tournefort, *A Voyage into the Levant*, 2 vols., London, 1718, vol. 1, pp. 2, 15.
33. Cited from E. Cassirer, *The Philosophy of the Enlightenment*, Princeton, 1951, pp. 79–80.
34. E. Sprat, *History of the Royal Society*, ed. J. Cape and H.W. Jones, Seattle, 1958, p. 111.
35. J. Ellis, *An Essay towards the Natural History of the Corallines*, London, 1755, pp. v–vi.
36. *Ibid.*, p. vii.
37. Quoted by E.H. Gombrich in 'Leonardo's Method for Working out Compositions', in his *Norm and Form*, pp. 58–9.
38. On the baroque imagination see A. Blunt, 'Gianlorenzo Bernini: illusion and mysticism', *Art History*, vol. 1, no. 1, 1978, pp. 67–8.
39. See N. Pevsner, *Academies of Art past and present*, London, 1940; A. Boime, *The Academy and French Painting*, London, 1971; and Q. Bell, *The Schools of Design*, London, 1963.
40. See Jessica Christian, 'Paul Sandby and the Military Survey of Scotland', in *Mapping the Landscape*, ed. N. Alfrey and S. Daniels, University Art Gallery, Castle Museum, Nottingham, 1990.
41. Nicholas Alfrey, 'Landscape and the Ordnance Survey, 1795–1820', in *Mapping the Landscape*, p. 24.
42. See Sloan, *op. cit.*
43. For a considered examination of the period of the 'take off' see A. Thompson, *The Dynamics of the Industrial Revolution*, London, 1973, pp. 19–23. Thompson argues that it is not until the 1780s that the Industrial Revolution got fully under way.
44. Francisco Algarotti, *An Essay on Painting*, London, 1764, pp. 72–3. Algarotti was more interested in contemporary science than was Reynolds. His interest in Newton's optics led him to prefer white to the conventional red grounds preferred by most of the painters of his time. For its likely influence on the lightening of Tiepolo's palette see F.J.B. Watson, 'Giovanni Battista Tiepolo', *Connoisseur*, vol. 136, 1955, pp. 212–15.
45. Reynolds, *Discourses*, ed. R.R. Wark, New Haven and London, 1975, p. 200.
46. G.E. Lessing, *Laocoon*, trans. J.M. Dent, London, 1930.
47. Its emergence may be traced in part from 'the new bourgeois taste for small works suitable for the informal rooms of the eighteenth century' (A. Blunt, *Art and Architecture in France, 1500 to 1700*, London, 1953, p. 282) and its

'descent' from history painting through the growing interest in France of scenes from the *commedia dell'arte*, Watteau's *fêtes galantes* and Philip Mercier's adaptation of them for English taste. It is an aspect of that wider process of the acculturation of the natural that Ann Bermingham has called 'the naturalisation of the sign' (A. Bermingham, *Landscape and Ideology*, London, 1986, p. 15).

48. Hardie, *op. cit.*, vol. 2, p. 247. For the emergence of photography from within the contexts of drawing, painting and the reproductive techniques of engraving and lithography, see A. Scharf, *Art and Photography*, London, 1968, pp. 1–18.

49. George Edwards, *History of Birds*, 7 vols, London, 1743–64, vol. 1, p. xiii.

50. *The Works of Jonathan Richardson*, London, 1792, p. 63.

51. Edwards, *op. cit.*, p. xv.

52. *Ibid.*, pp. xv–xvi.

53. See *Moses Griffith 1747–1819. Artist and Illustrator in the Service of Thomas Pennant*, Welsh Arts Council Touring Exhibition, Caernarfon, 1979.

54. T. Pennant, *British Zoology*, London, 1776, preface.

55. Burke, *op. cit.*, p. 13.

56. Pennant, *op. cit.*, preface.

57. *Ibid.*

2 THE INTELLECTUAL AND ARTISTIC FRAMEWORK

1. R.A. Skelton, 'Captain James Cook as a Hydrographer', *The Mariner's Mirror*, vol. 40, no. 2, Nov. 1954, p. 111.

2. On Cook's ships see A.P. McGowan, 'Captain Cook's Ships', *The Mariner's Mirror*, vol. 65, no. 2, May 1979, pp. 109–18.

3. Sir James Watt, 'Medical aspects and consequences of Captain Cook's Voyages', in R. Fisher and H. Johnston, eds, *Captain James Cook and His Times*, Vancouver, 1979, pp. 129–57.

4. In his provocative and occasionally illuminating book, *The Road to Botany Bay. An Essay in Spatial History* (London, 1987), Paul Carter makes the sharpest of distinctions between Cook as 'explorer' and Banks as 'discoverer'. For Carter, exploring is a form of knowledge valuable in itself; discovering, no more than classifying the unknown according to known taxonomies. But he nowhere demonstrates the need for such a distinction. I find his argument unconvincing. In his astronomy and cartography Cook worked as much within the concepts of trigonometry as Banks in his botanising worked within the concepts of the Linnaean classification. Perception itself implies conceptualisation, and both exploring and discovering, if we *must* distinguish between them, imply the perception of differences. That, at least, is an epistemological assumption upon which this book has been written. All that need be insisted upon here, however, is that Banks's botanising obviously depended upon the quality of Cook's navigating. Cook's mathematics made a space for Banks's botany.

5. As this bibliographical aspect of Cook's voyages is still not fully appreciated it will be useful to list the books Banks is known to have taken with him on *Endeavour*. They include:

William Piso and George Marcgrave, *Historia Naturalis Brasiliae* (1648).

Hans Sloane, *Catalogus plantarum, guae in insula Jamaica sponte proveniunt, vel vulgo coluntar* (1696).

Hans Sloane, *A voyage to the Islands Madera, Barbados, Nieves, S. Christophers and Jamaica, with the natural history of the last of those islands*, London, vol. 1 (1707), vol. 2 (1725).

C. Siron, *Curiositez de la nature et de l'art, aportées dans deux voyages, l'un aux Indes d'Occident en 1698 et 1699, et l'autre aux indes d'Orient en 1701 et 1702, avec une relation abregéede ces deux voyages* (1703).

Jobus Baster, *Opusculas subseciva, observationes miscellaneas de animalculis et plantis guibusdam marinis, eurumque ovariis et seminibus continentia* (1759–65).

George Edwards, *A natural history of uncommon Birds, and of some other rare and undescribed Animals*, 4 vols (1743–51).

Georges-Louis Leclerc, comte de Buffon et Louis Jean-Marie Daubenton, *Histoire naturelle générale et particulière, avec la description du cabinet du Roi* (1749–67; 15 vols of the then incomplete work).

George Everard Rumphius, *Herbarium Ambioinense* (1750).

Pehr Osbeck, *Dagbok ofwer en ostindisk Resa Aren 1750, 1751, 1752, med anmarkn. uti Naturken digheten . . .* (1757).

Patrick Browne, *The civil and natural history of Jamaica* (1756).

Carolus Linnaeus, *Systema naturae, sive regna tria naturae systematice proposita per classes, ordines, genera, et species* (1759).

Carolus Linnaeus, *Species plantarum* (1762–3).

Carolus Linnaeus, *Genera Plantarum* (1764).

Nicholas Joseph Freiherr von Jacquin, *Enumerato systematica plantarum* (1760).

Nicholas Joseph Freiherr von Jacquin, *Selectarum stirpium Americanarum historia* (1763).

Mathurin Jacques Brisson, *Regnum animale . . .* (1762).

Peter Simon Pallas, *Elenchus Zoophytorum* (1766).

Peter Simon Pallas, *Miscellanea zoologica* (1766).

Thomas Pennant, *British Zoology* (1766).

A. Cary Taylor drew attention to Banks's library on the *Endeavour* in his 'Charles de Brosses, the Man behind Cook', in *The Opening of the Pacific, Maritime Monographs and Reports*, no. 2, 1971, pp. 3–13. A more complete list was assembled from the works mentioned by Banks in his *Endeavour Journal* by Harold Carter, to whom I am indebted for the list published here. For his comments on Banks's library on the *Endeavour*, see his *Sir Joseph Banks 1743–1820*, London, 1988, pp. 72–3.

6. For the complete list of Parkinson's *Endeavour* library see Joppien and Smith, vol. 1, pp. 51–2.

7. The most complete account of Parkinson's contribution to the natural sciences on the *Endeavour* voyage will be found in D.J. Carr, ed., *Sydney Parkinson, Artist of Cook's Endeavour Voyage*, Canberra, 1983.

8. Morton's *Hints* are given in full in Cook, *Journals*, vol. 1, pp. 514–19.

9. This is despite the late Dr Averil Lysaght's research into Buchan's possible Scottish origin. See 'Banks's Artists and his *Endeavour* Collections', *The British Museum Yearbook*, vol. 3, 1979, pp. 16–22.

10. The definitive study on his life and work is by Michael E. Hoare, *The Tactless Philosopher: Johann Reinhold Forster 1729–98*, Melbourne, 1976.

11. See Lesli Bodi, 'George Forster: The Pacific Expert of Eighteenth Century Germany', *Historical Studies Australia and New Zealand*, vol. 8, May 1959, pp. 345–63.

12. These included:

Francois Pyrard, *Voyage . . . aux Indes orientales, Maldives, etc.* (1615).

William Piso and George Marcgrave, *Histoire naturalis Brasiliae* (1648).

Francois Laboullaye le Gouz, *Voyages et Observationes* (1653). (Laboullaye travelled widely in Europe, Persia, India and the Near East.)

J.F. Gamelli Carreri, *Giro del Mondo* (1699–1700). (Carreri travelled in Egypt, Persia, the Indes, China, the Philippines and Mexico.)

Jean de Thevenot, *Relation d'un voyage au Levant* (1664–84).

Engelbert Kaempfer, *Ameonitates exoticae* (1712). (Kaempfer travelled widely through Persia, the Caspian Sea area, Ceylon, Bengal and Batavia.)

Amédée, F. Frézier, *A voyage to the South-Seas, and along the coasts of Chili and Peru* (1717). (Forster used the English translation of Frézier.)

Peter Kolb, *Caput Bonae Spei Hodiernum.* (A work on the natural history of the Cape which Forster studied in either the German (1719) or Dutch (1727) editions.)

Hans Sloane, *Voyage to Jamaica* (1725).

William Dampier, *Voyage round the World* (1729).

François Valentjin, *Oud en Nieuw Oost-Indien* (1724–6).

Samuel Dale, *History and Antiquities of Harwich* (1730).

Eusebius Renaudot, *Ancient Accounts of India and China by two Mohammedan Travellers* (1733). (Forster appears to have used this English edition. The original French edition was published in Paris (1718).)

Johannes Burmann, *Thesaurus Zeylandicus* (1737).

Pierre Barrere, *Nouvelle relation de la France Equinoxiale* (1743).

George Edwards, *A natural history of uncommon birds* (1743–51).

Georges-Louis Leclerc, comte de Buffon, *Histoire naturelle*, 15 vols (1749–67).

R.A.C. de Renville, *Receuil des Voyages* (1754).

Patrick Browne, *The civil and natural history of Jamaica* (1756).

M.J. Brisson, *Ornithologie* (1760).

J.D. Michaelis, *Fragen an eine Gesellschaft gelehrter Manner* (1762). (Michaelis, philologist and theologian, was one of the leaders of the early German Enlightenment.)

Nicholas de la Caille, *Journal historique* (1763). (La Caille led a French expedition to the Cape and wrote on its natural history.)

Pehr Kalm, *Travels into North America* (1770–1). (A translation by Forster of the original text.)

Peter Simon Pallas, *Spicilegia zoologica* (1769).

A.J. Pernety, *Journal historique d'un voyage aux iles Malouines . . . et deux voyages au detroit de Magellan* (1769). (English translation (1771).)

This list has been compiled from the books cited by J.R. Forster in his journal kept on the voyage. See M.F. Hoare, ed., *The Resolution Journal of Johann Reinhold Forster 1772–1775*, 4 vols, London, 1982.

13. On Hodges, see I.C. Steube, *The Life and Work of William Hodges*, New York, 1979; Joppien and Smith, vol. 2.

14. On Omai, see E.H. McCormick, *Omai: Pacific Envoy*, Auckland and Oxford 1977; and R. Joppien, 'Philippe Jacques de Lutherbourg's Pantomime "Omai, or a Trip round the World" and the Artists of Captain Cook's Voyages', *British Museum Yearbook*, vol. 3, 1979, pp. 81–136.

15. The journals of Anderson and Samwell are published in Cook, *Journals*, vol. 3.

16. For a detailed account of the life and work of John Webber see R. Joppien in Joppien and Smith, vol. 3.

17. Their work is discussed in detail in B. Smith and A. Wheeler, eds, *The Art of the First Fleet and Other Early Australian Drawings*, Melbourne, 1988.

18. On Baudin's voyage see F. Horner, *The French Reconnaissance*, Melbourne, 1987; J. Bonnemains, E.C. Forsyth and B. Smith, eds, *Baudin in Australian Waters*, Melbourne, 1988; and N.J.B. Plomley, *The Baudin Expedition and the Tasmanian Aborigines 1802*, Melbourne, 1982.

19. In Hooker's *On the Flora of Australia*, London, 1859, p. cxiv.

20. E.g., Wilfred Blunt, *The Art of Botanical Illustration*, 1950, pp. 195–202.

21. For Flinders's life and voyages, see G.C. Ingleton, *Matthew Flinders: Navigator and Chartmaker*, Guildford, 1986.

22. On Bauer, see Blunt, *op. cit.*; Marlene J. Norst, *Ferdinand Bauer: The Australian Natural History Drawings*, Melbourne, 1989.

23. On Westall, see T.M. Perry and D.H. Simpson, eds., *Drawings by William Westall*, London, 1962.

24. Ingleton, *op. cit.*, p. 99.

3 ART AS INFORMATION

1. See the comments concerning the ending of the poem made by Robert Bridges, A Quiller-Couch, I.A. Richards and T.S. Eliot quoted in J.M. Murray, *Keats*, London 1930; see also Cleanth Brooks, *The Well Wrought Urn*, London, 1947; and W.H. Evert, *Aesthetic and Myth in the Poetry of Keats*, Princeton, 1965.

2. Although the naturalistic illustration of birds appeared even earlier in Emperor Frederick II's *De arte venandi cum avibus* (*c.*1250), a treatise on falconry. See Otto Pächt, 'Early Italian Nature Studies and the Early Calendar Landscape', *Journal of the Warburg and Courtauld Institutes*, vol. 13, 1950, pp. 13–47, and above, p. 4.

3. For example, Martin Hardie's authoritative *Water-colour Painting in Britain*, ed. Dudley Snelgrove with Jonathan Mayne and Basil Taylor, 2 vols, London, 1966–7, mentions neither Alexander Buchan nor Sydney Parkinson, and Hodges's art is noted mainly with reference to his later work in India. Yet Parkinson is for the Pacific what Paul Sandby was for Britain, and the work of Hodges in the Pacific foreshadows the naturalism of Constable and Turner.

4. For what is known see the admirable introduction to P. Hulton and D. Quinn, *The American Drawings of John White. 1577–1590*, Chapel Hill, 1964.

5. *Philosophical Transactions*, vol. 1, 1665–66, pp. 140–2.

6. George Anson, *A Voyage Round the World*, compiled by Richard Walter, London, 1748, introduction (n.p.).

7. See Banks, *Endeavour Journal*, with various references; and Cook, *Journals*, vol. 1, p. 58.

8. Anson, *op. cit.*, introduction, (n.p.).

9. See Harold B. Carter, *Sir Joseph Banks 1743–1820*, London, 1988, pp. 51, 53, *et al.*

10. Banks, *Endeavour Journal*, vol. 1, p. 227.

11. 'At the elementary level the pupil was required to copy engravings, called *models de dessin* . . . Although this form of instruction had been practised since the seventeenth century, at no time was it adopted in the Ecole des Beaux-Arts during the nineteenth century. It was employed only in the private ateliers, in the industrial schools and in the drawing programme of the State school system.' A. Boime, *The Academy and French Painting in the Nineteenth Century*, London 1971, p. 24. Although Boime is referring to Continental practice, a similar practice prevailed in England during the eighteenth century.

12. Banks, *Endeavour Journal*, vol. 1, pp. 217–18.

13. *Ibid.*, vol. 1, p. 214. It is possible that the copy of Shelvocke on board the *Endeavour* is that with the call number 981.d.3 in the British Library. It bears Banks's bookstamp and came to the Library with some 17,000 volumes from Banks's fine library.

14. 'An Indian Town of Terra del Fuego'. Ill. in Joppien and Smith, vol. 1, pl. 1.4.

15. Buchan, 'Inhabitants of the Island of Terra del Fuego in their Hut' and Parkinson, 'Natives of Terra del Fuego with their Hut'. Both ill. in Joppien and Smith, vol. 1, pls 1.6; 1.5.

16. See Smith, p. 40; and Joppien and Smith, vol. 1, pp. 16–19.

17. On a drawing of Bow Island (Hao). Ill. in A. David *et al.*, *The Charts and Coastal Views of Captain Cook's Voyages. The Voyage of the Endeavour 1768–1771*, pl. 1.93.

18. British Library, Add. MS. 9345, f. 13.

19. H. Wölfflin, *Principles of Art History*, trans. M.H. Hottinger, Dover edn (n.d.), p. 11.

20. British Library, Add. MS. 9345, f. 44 v. Ill. in Joppien and Smith, pl. 1.19.

21. A. Bermingham, *Landscape and Ideology. The English Rustic Tradition*, London, 1986.

22. C.P. Barbier, *William Gilpin*, Oxford, 1963, pp. 4–5.

23. Smith, pp. 153–4.

24. Their situation anticipates that of several influential painters of the nineteenth century who also travelled south towards the sun: Delacroix to Morocco; Van Gogh to Arles; Gauguin to Martinique and Tahiti. In Gauguin's case colour was freed from the controls of both chiaroscuro and naturalism for the 'freedoms' of pre-classical art. But by then the 'savage' was beginning to hit back.

25. See for example 'Maoris in a canoe'. Ill. in Joppien and Smith, vol. 1, pl. 2.33.

26. Cook, *Journals*, vol. 2, p. 410.

27. Smith, pp. 57–9.

28. E.g., his 'View in Tahiti', ill. in Jopien and Smith, vol. 2, pl. 2.51.

29. Hodges to William Hayley, London, 27 April 1793. Holograph letter, Alexander Turnbull Library, Wellington.

30. In the case of Tiepolo's paintings of the 1740s, however, it is possible that the lightening of his palette may have been due to discussions with Algarotti about Newton's optics: 'as a result of his [Algarotti's] Newtonian researches he seems to have affected technical practice by urging painters to use a lighter or white ground in contrast to the dark brown preparation which was generally adopted in Venice at that period' (F.J.B. Watson, 'Giovanni Battista Tiepolo', *Connoisseur*, vol. 136, 1955, pp. 212–15.

31. W. Hodges, *Travels in India*, London 1793, p. 155.

32. Hodges to Hayley, cited above, note 29.

33. J.G.A. Forster, *A Voyage round the World*. London, 1777, vol. 1, pp. 427–8.

34. Ill. in Smith, pl. 58.

35. See A.L. Kaeppler, 'Eighteenth Century Tonga', *Man*, vol. 6, June 1971, p. 209.

36. J. Cook and J. King, *A Voyage to the Pacific Ocean*, London, 1784, vol. 1, p. 5.

37. This, it would seem to me, is the crucial distinction between the two modes of history painting–ancient and modern–that Edgar Wind, in his important article 'The Revolution of History Painting', *Journal of the Warburg and Courtauld Institutes*, vol. 2, 1938, pp. 116–27, does not develop. For though Wind discusses the portrait sketches that Thornhill and Hogarth made of criminals, and also the on-the-spot sketches made by these two artists, he does not concern himself with the basic distinction, as evidence for an historic event, between drawings made on-the-spot at the time of the event, and a 'realism' such as West's and Copley's, assembled after the event, or even a 'realism' as aesthetically potent as David's Death of *Marat*, based on the artist's memory of the murdered Marat the day *before* his death.

38. Cook, *Journals*, vol. 3, p. ccxi.

39. R. Joppien, 'The Artistic Bequest of Captain Cook's Voyages', in R. Fisher and H. Johnston, eds, *Captain Cook and His Times*, Vancouver, 1979, pp. 187–210.

4 PORTRAYING PACIFIC PEOPLE

1. Banks, *Endeavour Journal*, vol. 1, p. 258.
2. Georges-Louis Leclerc, comte de Buffon, *Histoire Naturelle*, vol. 4, p. 546.
3. A. Sparrman, *A Voyage Round the World with Captain James Cook in H.M.S. Resolution*, ed. O. Rutter, London, 1944, p. 44.
4. Sydney Parkinson, *A Journal of a Voyage to the South Seas*, London, 1773, pp. 17–18.
5. In an earlier version of this chapter (*Art History*, Sept. 1934), I compared the engraving to the *Apollo Belvedere*, but David Solkin has shown in his 'Great Pictures of Great Men, Male Portraiture and the Power of Art', *Oxford Art Journal*, vol. 9, no. 2, 1986, that a closer parallel and likely source of the Ramsey and Reynolds portraits, already mentioned above, lies in Roman magisterial statuary of the *adlocutio* type. Chambers's engraving, doubtless, possesses a similar source.
6. Parkinson, *op. cit.*, pp. vii–viii.
7. *Philosophical Transactions*, 1746.
8. Parkinson, *op. cit.*, p. 93.
9. W. Hogarth, *Analysis of Beauty*, ed. J. Burke, London, 1955, p. 160.
10. Banks, *Endeavour Journal*, vol. 2, p. 134.
11. See Parkinson, *op. cit.*, with Stanfield's preface and John Fothergill's reply; also, Joppien and Smith, vol. 1, pp. 53–4.
12. W.T. Stearn, 'A Royal Society Appointment with Venus in 1769: The Voyage of Cook and Banks in the Endeavour in 1768–1771 and its Botanical Results', *Notes and Records of the Royal Society of London*, vol. 24, 1 June 1969, p. 85.
13. Parkinson, *op. cit.*, p. 135.
14. *Ibid.*, p. 134.
15. *Ibid.*
16. Banks, *Endeavour Journal*, vol. 2, p. 54.
17. *Ibid.*, vol. 2, p. 133.
18. *Ibid.*, vol. 2, p. 53.
19. *Ibid.*, vol. 2, p. 84.
20. J.R. Forster, *The Resolution Journal of Johann Reinhold Forster*, ed. M.E. Hoare, London, 1982, vol. 4, p. 660.
21. Parkinson, *op. cit.*, p. vii.
22. *Ibid.*, p. 15.
23. Cook, *Journals* vol. 1, p. 399.
24. Parkinson, *op. cit.*, p. 15.
25. *Ibid.*, pp. 146–7.
26. Banks, *Endeavour Journal*, p. 293.
27. Cook, *Journals*, vol. 1, p. 395.
28. Parkinson, *op. cit.*, p. 153.
29. In his drawing *Tongatabu or Amsterdam*, Australian National Library, Canberra. Ill. in Joppien and Smith, vol. 2, pl. 2.74.
30. On the work of the 'Artist of the Chief Mourner', see Joppien and Smith, vol. 1, pp. 60–3.
31. Banks, *Endeavour Journal*, vol. 2, p. 53.
32. J.G.A. Forster, *A Voyage round the World*, London, 1777, vol. 1, pp. 137–8.
33. Cook, *Journals*, vol. 2, p. clviii.
34. *Ibid.*, vol. 2, p. 175.
35. Forster, *op. cit.*, vol. 1, p. 368.
36. *Ibid.*, vol. 1, p. 213.
37. *Ibid.*, vol. 1, p. 484.
38. E. Burke, *A Philosophical Enquiry into the Origin of our Ideas of the Sublime and Beautiful*, ed. J.T. Bolton, London, 1958, p. 44.
39. W. Hodges, *Travels in India*, 1793, p. 155. Hodges here distinguishes between fancy and imagination, a distinction, of course, that will later concern Coleridge; see Chapter 6.
40. From the William Wales journal in Cook, *Journals*, vol. 2, p. 822.
41. Forster, *op. cit.*, vol. 1, pp. 289–92.
42. *Ibid.*, vol. 1, p. 327.
43. Cook, *Journals*, vol. 2, p. 410.
44. In a letter to John Douglas, editor of the official accounts of the second and third voyages, quoted in Cook, *Journals*, vol. 3, pp. 319–20.
45. *Voyage of Governor Phillip to Botany Bay*, London, 1789, pp. 293–4.
46. *Ibid.*, pp. 233–4.
47. What is known of its history is recounted by Beaglehole in Cook, *Journals*, vol. 3, p. cxi.
48. Robert Goldwater's pioneering *Primitivism in Modern Art*, New York, 1938, as the title implies, is concerned primarily with the more recent manifestations of primitivism. Since the first version of this chapter was written, an excellent series of relevant essays has appeared in *Primitivism in 20th Century Art*, ed. W. Rubin, 2 vols, Museum of Modern Art, New York, 1984.

5 WILLIAM HODGES AND ENGLISH *PLEIN-AIR* PAINTING

1. Note Banks's comment on the occasion of the death of Alexander Buchan, his figure artist on Cook's first voyage: 'his loss to me is irretrevable, my airy dreams of entertaining my friends with the scenes I am to see here are vanished. No account of the figures and dresses of men can be satisfactory unless illustrated with figures: had providence spard him a month longer what an advantage would it have been to my undertaking', Banks, *Endeavour Journal*, vol. 1, p. 259. On Zoffany, see Mary Webster, *Johan Zoffany 1733–1810*, National Portrait Gallery, London, 1976.
2. On Wilson, see W.G. Constable, *Richard Wilson*, London and Cambridge, Mass., 1953; David H. Solkin, *Richard Wilson: The Landscape of Reaction*, Tate Gallery, London, 1982.
3. On Vernet's likely influence on Wilson in the painting of *plein-air* oil sketches, see Philip Conisbee, 'Pre-Romantic plein air painting', *Art History*, vol. 2, no. 4, Dec. 1979, p. 425.
4. *Ibid.*, p. 415ff.
5. 'Memoirs of Thomas Jones', *Walpole Society*, vol. 32, 1946–8, p. 58.
6. Solkin, *op. cit.*, p. 49.
7. Lawrence Gowing, *The Originality of Thomas Jones*, London 1985; John Gere, 'Thomas Jones: An Eighteenth Century Conundrum', *Apollo*, vol. 91, no. 100, June 1970; Ralph Edwards, 'Thomas Jones 1742–1803, a Reappraisal of his Art', *Connoisseur*, vol. 168, no. 675, May 1968, pp. 8–14.
8. Gere, *loc. cit.*
9. Richard Wollheim, *Painting as an Art*, Washington, 1987, p. 345.
10. 'Memoirs of Thomas Jones', *loc. cit.*, p. 111.
11. Wollheim, *op. cit.*, p. 344.
12. Gere, *loc. cit.*, p. 469.
13. On Farington see Kenneth Garlick and Angus Macintyre, *The Diary of Joseph Farington*, New Haven and London, 1978, vol. 1, introduction.
14. *Gilpin to Ruskin: Drawing Masters and their Manuals, 1800–1860*, Fitzwilliam Museum, Cambridge, 1987, p. 9.
15. Quoted in Cook, *Journals*, vol. 2, p. clviii.
16. *Ibid.*, vol. 2, p. 21.
17. *Ibid.*, vol. 2, p. 687.
18. W.G. Constable, *Richard Wilson*, London, 1952, p. 139.
19. 'Memoirs of Thomas Jones', *loc. cit.*, pp. 42–3.
20. I have discussed the relationship between Hodges and Wales and the painting itself in more detail in Smith, pp. 57–9.
21. Cook, *Journals*, vol. 2, p. 119.
22. *Ibid.*, vol. 2, p. 118.
23. I.C. Steube, *The Life and Work of William Hodges*, New York, 1979, p. 142.
24. *Ibid.*
25. Conisbee, *loc. cit.*, p. 426.
26. J.R. Forster, *The Resolution Journal of Johann Reinhold Forster*, ed. M.E. Hoare, London, 1982, vol. 3, pp. 512–13; and J.G.A. Forster, *A Voyage round the World*, London 1777, vol. 2, pp. 104–7.
27. No. 1174, 25–8 April 1777, p. 1.
28. Cf. 'Truth is the base of every work of mine' (Hodges to Hayley, London, 27 April 1793. Holograph letter, Alexander Turnbull Library, Wellington).
29. Solkin, *op. cit.*, p. 50.
30. 'Memoirs of Thomas Jones', *loc. cit.*, p. 37.
31. *Ibid.*

6 COLERIDGE'S *ANCIENT MARINER*

1. 'European Vision and the South Pacific', *Journal of the Warburg and Courtauld Institutes*, vol. 13, 1950, pp. 65–100.
2. In *The Road to Xanadu*, Cambridge, Mass., 1927. Quotations in this chapter are from the second English edition, London, 1951.
3. Described in the Mitchell Library's *Bibliography of Captain James Cook (1928)* under *Second Voyage–Manuscript journals, etc.*, as follows: 'Wales, William–Journal on the Resolution, June 21st, 1772, to October 17th, 1774; with pen-and-ink charts. pp. 376 (original MS. journal kept in log form).' It was purchased from the Museum Book Store, London, in 1923.
4. *The English Cyclopaedia*, 1857.
5. Charles Hutton, *Philosophical and Mathematical Dictionary*, London, 1815. Article on William Wales.
6. 'Astronomical Observations made by Order of the Royal Society, at Prince Wales's Fort, on the North-West Coast of Hudson's Bay', by W.W. and Joseph Dymond, *Philosophical Transactions*, vol. 59, pp. 467–88; and 'Journal of a Voyage, made by Order of the Royal Society, to Churchill River, on the North-West Coast of Hudson's Bay; of Thirteen Months Residence in that Country; and of the Voyage back to England; in the Years 1768 and 1769', by W.W., *Philosophical Transactions*, vol. 60, 1770, pp. 100–36; and 'Observations on the State of the Air, Winds, Weather, etc. made at Prince of Wales's Fort, on the North-West Coast of Hudson's Bay, in the Years 1768 and 1769',

by Joseph Dymond and W.W., *Philosophical Transactions*, vol. 60, 1770, pp. 137–78.

7. These include: *Original Astronomical Observations made in a Voyage towards the South Pole*, by W.W. and W. Bayly, London, 1777; *Remarks on Mr. Forster's Account of Captain Cook's last Voyage round the World, in the years 1772, 1773, 1774, and 1775*, London, 1778; John Robertson's *Elements of Navigation*, rev. by W.W., London, 1780; 'A Defence of the Arguments advanced in the int. to Cook's last Voyage against the existence of Cape Circumcision', see James Cook and James King, *A Voyage to the Pacific Ocean*, London, 1784; *Astronomical Observations made in the Voyages . . . for making discoveries in the Southern Hemisphere . . . by Byron . . . Wallis . . . Carteret . . . and . . . Cook*, London, 1788; *The Method of Finding Longitude at Sea, by Timekeepers: to which are added tables of equations to equal altitudes*, London, 1794; dissertation on the rising of the Constellations, see Arrian, *The Voyage of the Nearchus from the Indus to the Euphrates*, London, 1797.

8. W. Trollope, *History of Christ's Hospital*, London, 1834, p. 94.

9. *Life and Works of Charles Lamb*, ed. A. Aiken, London, 1899, vol. 2, p. 28.

10. Ed. J.E. Morpurgo, London, 1949, p. 60.

11. See the plan of the old school in E.H. Pearce, *Annals of Christ's Hospital*, London, 1901, p. 300.

12. I.e., boys of the Upper Grammar School destined for the University.

13. Minutes of the Committee of Almoners of Christ's Hospital, 22 April 1795, quoted by Lawrence Hanson, *Life of S.T. Coleridge*, London, 1938, p. 439.

14. *Ibid.*, p. 50, *et passim*.

15. MS. journal, p. 315 (13 May 1774).

16. *Coleridge: Studies by Several Hands*, ed. E. Blunden and E.L. Griggs, London, 1934, p. 66.

17. Gordon Hake, *Memoirs of Eighty Years Ago*, London, 1892, p. 28.

18. Lamb, *op. cit.*, vol. 2, pp. 17–18.

19. *Letters of Samuel Taylor Coleridge*, ed. E.H. Coleridge, London, 1895, vol. 1, p. 20.

20. Trollope, *op. cit.*, pp. 187–8.

21. I.e., pupils of the Mathematical School.

22. Pearce, *op. cit.*, p. 107.

23. Trollope, *op. cit.*, p. 200. Edmund Blunden has since informed me that 'the Mathematical library was apparently in its place when I remember it; it was subsequently disturbed and some things were sold' (*in lit.*, 5 Feb. 1957).

24. Hanson, *op. cit.*, p. 18. J.E. Bullard, then Librarian of Christ's Hospital, has since informed me (*in. lit.*, 8 Feb. 1957) that a copy of George Forster's *A Voyage round the World* was in the school library during the nineteenth century, but that it had since disappeared.

25. It is just possible that Coleridge may have seen something of Wales's manuscript journal, since it would have most probably been among his teacher's personal papers at the school. But it is unlikely, and not important for the argument developed here. Verbal accounts of the voyage from Wales or garbled accounts from other boys are much

more likely, and more likely to have made a lasting impression. Nevertheless, that sailors' logs did hold a fascination for Coleridge, see the note to his poem 'To Captain Findley', in his *Complete Poetical Works*, ed. E.H. Coleridge, Oxford, 1912, vol. 2, p. 980.

26. *The Friend*, vol. 2, 1818, p. 72.

27. Written on the fly-leaf of his copy of William Law's edition of the works of Jacob Behmen (vol. 1), now in the British Library. I am indebted to Kathleen Coburn for drawing my attention to this inscription.

28. MS. journal, 29 April 1773. Also published in Cook, *Journals*, vol. 2, p. 782.

29. *Letters of Samuel Taylor Coleridge*, ed. cit., vol. 1, p. 21.

30. Hanson, *op. cit.*, p. 29. Mathematics at Cambridge seems to have been something of a let-down after the stimulation of Wales's classes; for in 'A Fragment Found in a Lecture-Room', Coleridge writes: 'Where all Boeotia clouds the misty brain,/The owl Mathesis pipes her loathsome strain.'

31. He also had the important duty of keeping the chronometers of Harrison and Arnold, which were being tested for their accuracy (see above, p. 45). Cf. Coleridge, 'A philosopher's ordinary language . . . are as his watch compared with his astronomical timepiece' (*Table Talk*, London, 1835).

32. *Philosophical Transactions*, vol. 60, 1770, p. 131.

33. *Ibid.*

34. *Ibid.*, p. 113. Cf. 'The stars were dim, and thick the night' (*The Ancient Mariner*).

35. Ibid., pp. 129–30.

36. MS. journal, 21 Sept. 1772. Cf. 'the thin but grey cloud is spread on high. It covers but not hides the sky' (*Christabel*). The frequently quoted entry is for 24 March 1798 from Dorothy Wordsworth's Alfoxden journal, and undoubtedly records the experience upon which the stanza in *Christabel* is based; but this does not preclude the possibility that *behind* the experience itself lay the influence of a teacher who had helped Coleridge to look at the heavens with a clearheaded and yet passionate enjoyment.

37. *Ibid.*

38. *Ibid.*

39. Hunt, *op. cit.*, p. 102.

40. *Prelude*, vi, pp. 266–70.

41. John Marra, *Journal of the Resolution's Voyage*, London, 1775, p. 113.

42. *Letters of Samuel Taylor Coleridge*, ed. cit., vol. 1, p. 2.

43. Benjamin Franklin, *Experiments on Electricity*, London, 1774. Cf. J.G.A. Forster, *A Voyage round the World*, London, 1777, vol. 1, p. 193, 'His [i.e., Franklin's] ingenious hypothesis that whirlwinds and waterspouts have a common origin has not been invalidated by our observations.'

44. *Op. cit.*, vol. 1, pp. 103–5 And Cook writes: 'it was very plain to us that these spouts were caused by whirlwinds'.

45. Forster, *op. cit.*, vol. 1, pp. 190–3.

46. 17 May 1773.

47. *Original Astronomical Observations*, p. 346.

48. *Ibid.*

49. Quoted from the Gutch notebook, British Library, ff. 25a–25b. Reproduced in K.

Coburn, *The Notebooks of Samuel Taylor Coleridge*, London, 1957, vol. 1, p. 174.

50. Edmund Blunden, *in lit.* 5 Feb. 1957, and in his essay 'The Head Master's Album', in *Modern English Literature: Essays presented to Professor Rintaro Fukuhara on his 60th Birthday*, Japan, 1956, p. 410.

51. Pp. 107–8, 111–12.

52. Pp. 105–7.

53. Another image of polar ice will be found in the first act of *The Fall of Robespierre*, wherein one of the characters, Legendre, asserts that 'love and friendship . . ./Shine like the powerless sun on polar ice', on the 'coward heart' of Robespierre. The act was written in September 1794 when Coleridge was lodging at the Angel, an inn close to Christ's Hospital, and visiting the school daily to see the Grecians (see above, p. 138).

54. Kathleen Coburn, *in lit.*, 1 Dec. 1959.

55. Southern Thule, which turned out to be an island, but neither Cook nor Coleridge was to know that.

56. *Op. cit.* vol. 1, p. 91.

57. *Ibid.* vol. 1, p. 92.

58. *Ibid.*, vol. 1, p. 93.

59. *A Voyage towards the South Pole*, vol. 1, p. 22.

60. This was not the only occasion on which Wales compared the height of floating ice to the height of the mast: cf. 'Passed within a cable's length of a very large island of ice . . . It was about as high out of the water as our maintop, and adorned on its top and sides with spires; and indented in the most romantic manner that can be imagined' (*Philosophical Transactions*, vol. 60, 1770, p. 104).

61. *Ibid.*, pp. 115–16.

62. *Op. cit.*, vol. 1, p. 101.

63. *Observations made during a Voyage round the World on Physical Geography, Natural History, and Ethnic Philosophy*, London, 1778, p. 72.

64. *Op. cit.*, vol. 2, p. 538.

65. *Op. cit.*, p. 74.

66. MS. journal, *loc. cit.*

67. Marra, *op. cit.*, p. 125.

68. *A Voyage towards the South Pole*, vol. 1, p. 38.

69. Coleridge, *Poems*, ed. A. Dyce, London, 1852, pp. 383–4.

70. MS. journal, *loc. cit.*

71. *Voyage towards the South Pole*, vol. 1, p. 13.

72. *Ibid.*, vol. 1, p. 38. The two Forsters were the most unpopular men on board the *Resolution*, for they were aloof, dogmatic and given to complaints. Much of the dislike was probably owing also to chauvinism. Wales developed an intense dislike of the Forsters because he felt that they were inclined to be critical of his hero, Cook. Whether the fact that they shot several albatrosses (partly in pursuit of their duty as the natural historians of the voyage) added to their unpopularity among the more superstitious must remain a matter of speculation.

73. A. Sparrman, *A Voyage Round the World with Captain James Cook in H.M.S. Resolution*, ed. O. Rutter, London, 1944, p. 60.

74. MS. journal. See also Cook, *Journals*, vol. 2, p. 787.

75. Sparrman, *op. cit.*, p. 49.

76. Concerning the friendly swallow see Arnd Bohm, 'George Forster's *A Voyage Round the*

World as a source for the Rime of the Ancient Mariner', *Journal of English Literary History*, vol. 50, 1983, pp. 363–77.

77. *Philip Quarll, The English Hermit*, London, 1924, p. 157. On Quarll, see also Lowes, *op. cit.*

78. J.G.A. Forster, *op. cit.*, vol. 1, p. 527.

79. Stephen M. Weissman, *His Brother's Keeper: A Pyschobiography of Samuel Taylor Coleridge*, Madison, Conn., 1989, p. 121.

80. See, for example, Vincent Buckley, 'Coleridge: Vision and Actuality', *Melbourne Critical Review*, vol. 4, 1961, pp. 3–17.

81. J.R. Forster, *op. cit.*, p. 117.

82. MS. journal, *loc. cit.*

83. Wales's *Original Astronomical Observations* contains an abbreviated version of the MS. journal, pp. 337–65. Some of the notes quoted for this chapter from the journal are published in this book, but as they are rather effectively hidden towards the end of a book which is mainly a mass of figures providing astronomical, meteorological and navigational data, it is rather unlikely that the published comments played much part in the genesis of *The Ancient Mariner*.

84. *Op. cit.*, pp. 66–7.

85. *Voyage towards the South Pole*, vol. 1, p. 15.

86. J.R. Forster, *op. cit.*, p. 61; J.G.A. Forster, *op. cit.*, vol. 1, p. 54.

87. MS. journal, *loc. cit.*

88. *Op. cit.*, p. 61.

89. *Op. cit.*, vol. 1, p. 54.

90. *Op. cit.*, p. 62.

91. Father Bourzes, 'Luminous Appearances in the wake of Ships in the Sea', *Philosophical Transactions*, vol. 5, p. 215.

92. *A Voyage to the Pacific Ocean*, vol. 2, p. 257. The context explains that the description has been taken from William Anderson's MS. journal of the voyage.

93. *Op. cit.*, p. 103.

94. *Philosophical Transactions*, vol. 26, 1794, pp. 429–34; vol. 27, pp. 435–40.

95. *A Voyage to the Pacific Ocean*, vol. 2, p. 114.

96. Wales and Bayly, *Original Astronomical Observations*, p. 42.

97. *Op. cit.*, p. 120.

98. MS. journal, 16 Feb. 1773.

99. *Ibid.*

100. *Ibid.*

101. *Ibid.*

102. E.g., 'To that superb work of scholarship [i.e., *The Road to Xanadu*] there is nothing to add. What we have to consider is not how "The Ancient Mariner" came into existence, but what it is and what it means' (C.M. Bowra, *The Romantic Imagination*, Oxford, 1949).

103. Lowes, *op. cit.*, p. 60.

104. For a criticism of Lowes in the light of Coleridge's own writing on the nature of the imagination, see I.A. Richards, *Coleridge on Imagination*, London, 1934, pp. 31–5, *et passim*; Humphrey House, *Lectures on Coleridge*, London, 1953; and A.D. Hope in the preface to this present book, pp. x–xi.

105. See Sir F.C. Bartlett, *Remembering*, Cambridge, 1932, pp. 197–214, *et passim*; and E.J. Furlong, *A Study in Memory*, London, 1951.

106. *The Friend*, vol. 3, 1818, pp. 223–5. Quoted

by Kathleen Coburn, *Inquiring Spirit*, London, 1951, p. 76.

107. *Ibid.*

108. *Biographia Epistolaris*, ed. A. Turnbull, London, 1911, vol. 2, p. 182. The metaphor most probably derives from Sir Humphrey Davy's lectures. Coleridge was a close friend and attended Davy's lectures because he said they were good to gain metaphors from.

109. *Biographia Literaria*, ed. J. Shawcross, Oxford, 1907, p. 79.

110. *The Friend, loc. cit.*

111. *Osorio*, Act IV, 224–6.

112. Weissman, *op. cit.*

113. Cf. Furlong, *op. cit.*: 'Our account brings out a feature of memory which deserves emphasis, namely, that when we remember a past situation we do not merely have a visual or other image which we refer to the past; rather we image, in a more or less spontaneous way, our whole state of mind on the past occasion ... we do not merely remember sense data: we also remember what we, active subjects, did about those sense-data–what we believed, felt and wished.'

114. *Op. cit.*, vol. 1, p. 178, quoted in Coburn, *op. cit.*

7 STYLE, INFORMATION AND IMAGE

1. Edward W. Said, *Orientalism*, London, 1978.

2. *Ibid.*, p. 58.

3. *Two Treatises on Government*, ed. P. Lovett, New York, 1965. See Ronald L. Meek, *Social Science and the Ignoble Savage*, Cambridge, 1976, pp. 37–67, *et. seq.*

4. The National Gallery of Victoria, Melbourne.

5. E.H. McCormick, *Omai: Pacific Envoy*, Auckland and Oxford, 1977, p. 174, fig. 40 and pl. III.

6. Joseph Burke, *English Art 1714–1800*, Oxford, 1976, p. 205.

7. Sir Joshua Reynolds, *Discourses on Art*, ed. R.R. Wark, New Haven and London, 1975, pp. 59–60.

8. See Joppien and Smith, vol. 1, catalogue 1.87C.

9. Sydney Parkinson, *A Journal of a Voyage to the South Seas*, London, 1773.

10. *Gentleman's Magazine*, Jan. 1785, p. 52.

11. See, for example, Joppien and Smith, vol. 2, pls 35, 36, 51.

12. *Ibid.*, catalogue, cf. 2.55 and 2.55A.

13. *Ibid.*, catalogue, cf. 2.54 and 2.54A.

14. *Ibid.*, catalogue 2.128A.

15. *Ibid.*, catalogue 2.73.

16. On Forster, see Lesli Bodi, 'The Pacific Expert of Eighteenth Century Germany', *Historical Studies Australia and New Zealand*, vol. 8, no. 32, May 1959, pp. 345–63.

17. British Library, Egerton MS 2180, f. 3. Quoted by Beaglehole in Cook, *Journals*, vol. 2, p. cxlvi.

18. William Wales, *Remarks on Mr. Forster's Account of Captain Cook's last Voyage round the World*, London, 1778, p. 79.

19. On Fuseli and Mannerism, see F. Antal, *Fuseli Studies*, London, 1956, pp. 28–54, 78–104.

20. On Vien, see F. Aubert, 'Joseph-Marie Vien',

Gazette des Beaux-Arts, vols 22–3, 1867, and M. Levey in W.G. Kalnein and M. Levey, *Art and Architecture of the Eighteenth Century in France*, Harmondsworth, 1972, pp. 122–3.

21. George Duplessis, ed., *Memoirs et Journal de J.G. Wille graveur du Roi publiés d'après les manuscrits autographs de la bibliothèque impériale*, Paris, 1857. See entries for 2 Mai 1761; 12 Avril 1763; 9 Janvier 1766.

22. Cook, *Journals*, vol. 3, p. 1174.

23. Joppien and Smith. vol. 3, pls 29, 30, 31, 152.

24. *Ibid.*, vol. 3, p. 156.

25. *Ibid.*, catalogue, 3.52A.

26. On Camper, see *The Works of the Late Professor Camper on the Connection between the Science of Anatomy and the Arts of Drawing, Painting, Statuary, etc. etc ...*, trans. from the Dutch by T. Coglan, M.D., London, 1794.

27. Quoted from Rhys Jones, 'Images of Natural Man', in *Baudin in Australian Waters*, ed. J. Bonnemains, E.C. Forsyth and B. Smith, Melbourne, 1988, p. 22.

28. Camper, *op. cit.*, p. 22.

29. Cook, *Journals*, vol. 3, p. 785.

8 CONSTRUCTING 'PACIFIC' PEOPLE

1. In this chapter I have drawn heavily upon the combined research of Dr Rüdiger Joppien and me from volume three of *The Art of Captain Cook's Voyages* (Oxford University Press, Melbourne, 1987) for many of the facts presented. I am particularly indebted to Dr Joppien for his recent research on the early life and training of John Webber. In other cases where I have drawn directly on Dr Joppien's personal research this is mentioned in the notes. Apart from that, the opinions expressed are my own.

2. For a detailed account of Webber's early life and training see R. Joppien, in Joppien and Smith, vol. 3.

3. Admiralty to Cook, 24 June 1777, quoted in Cook, *Journals*, vol. 3, p. 1507.

4. Joppien and Smith, vol. 3, p. 223.

5. For a more detailed discussion of this point see Joppien, in Joppien and Smith, vol. 3, pp. 189–96.

6. Cook, *Journals*, vol. 3, p. ccxxiii.

7. *Ibid.*

8. *Ibid.* Cf. Cook's instructions for the first voyage, *Journals*, vol. 1, p. cclxxx, and for the second, *Journals*, vol. 2, p. clxviii.

9. 'Car je soutiens que celui ne fait qu'exécuter des ordres ne fera jamais grandes figures dans les découvertes', quoted in Cook, *Journals*, vol. 2, p. 695.

10. See J.C. Beaglehole, *The Life of Captain James Cook*, London, 1974, pp. 439–40.

11. British Library, Egerton MS 2180, f. 3, quoted by Beaglehole in Cook, *Journals*, vol. 2, p. cxlvi.

12. Cook, *Journals*, vol. 3, p. 52.

13. *Ibid.*, vol. 3, p. 54.

14. See Joppien in Joppien and Smith, vol. 3, p. 193 *et al*. The remainder of this chapter develops the implications of this initial insight of Dr Joppien.

15. Sydney Parkinson, *A Journal of a Voyage to the South Seas*, London, 1773, pl. xxvii, f.p. 134.

16. J.G.A. Forster, *A Voyage round the World*, London, 1777, vol. 2, pp. 257–8.

17. William Wales, *Remarks on Mr. Forster's Account of Captain Cook's last Voyage round the World*, London, 1778, p. 71.
18. J.G.A. Forster, *Reply to Mr. Wales's Remarks*, London, 1778, p. 34.
19. On 12 July 1776.
20. On Omai in general, see E.H. McCormick, *Omai: Pacific Envoy*, Auckland, 1977.
21. See Joppien and Smith, vol. 3, catalogue 3.272, 3.273, 3.274.
22. Marshall McLuhan, *Understanding Media*, London, 1967, pp. 15–30.
23. *Captain Cook's Final Voyage: The Journal of Midshipman George Gilbert*, ed. Christine Holmes, London, 1982, pp. 33–34.
24. Cook, *Journals*, vol. 3, p. 995.
25. *Captain Cook's Final Voyage*, p. 20.
26. Edgar in Cook's *Journals*, vol. 3, p. 231, n. 5.
27. *Captain Cook's Final Voyage*, p. 47.
28. In *Captain James Cook and His Times*, ed. Robin Fisher and Hugh Johnston, Vancouver, 1979.
29. Quoted in Cook, *Journals*, vol. 1, p. 514.
30. *Ibid.*, vol. 1, p. 399.
31. *Ibid.*, vol. 2, pp. 174–5.
32. *Ibid.*, vol. 3, pp. 61–2.
33. See *The Periplus of the Erythraean Sea*, ed. G.W.B. Huntingford, London, 1980.
34. Cook, *Journals*, vol. 3, p. 1492.
35. 'He intends only his own gain, and he is in this, as in many other cases, led by an invisible hand to promote an end which was no part of his intention' (Adam Smith, *Wealth of Nations*, ed. R.H. Campbell, A.S. Skinner and W.B. Todd, Oxford, 1976, vol. 1, p. 456).
36. 'They received everything we gave them without the least appearance of satisfaction . . . they either retrieved it or threw it away without so much as tasting it' (Cook in Adventure Bay, *Journals*, vol. 3, p. 52).
37. *Ibid.*, vol. 3, p. 306.
38. The story is told by James Burney, first lieutenant on the *Discovery*, who had it from Anderson. It is recounted in Burney's *Chronological History of North-Eastern Voyages of Discovery*, London, 1819, pp. 233–4 and quoted in Beaglehole, *op. cit.*, pp. 568–9.
39. Clerke in Cook, *Journals*, vol. 3, pp. 1317–18.
40. See his manuscript 'Catalogue of Drawings and Paintings in Oyl by Mr Webber' under 'Portraits in Oyl Colour. New Zealand. Kahowre a Chief'. National Library of Australia, Canberra.
41. Cook, *Journals*, vol. 3, p. 69.
42. Joppien and Smith, vol. 3, pp. 19 and 285.
43. On these dark and profound matters of ethnohistory, see Marshal Sahlins, *Historical Metaphors and Mythical Reality*, Ann Arbor, 1980; and Greg Dening, 'Sharks that walk on the Land. The Death of Captain Cook', *Meanjin*, vol. 4, 1982, pp. 427–37.

9 GREECE AND THE COLONISATION OF THE PACIFIC

1. G.P.M. Dumont, *Suite de plans, coupes, profils, élévations géometrales et perspectives de trois temples antiques qu'ils existaient en 1750 dans la bourgade de Paesto qui est la ville de Paestum de Pline . . .*, Paris, 1764; J.J. Winckelmann, *Geschichte der Kunst des Altertums*, Dresden, 1764.
2. *Antiquités étrusques, grecques et romaines*, 4 vols, Naples, 1766–7.
3. D.L. Oliver, *Ancient Tahiti Scoiety*, Honolulu, 1974, vol. 1, p. 229.
4. Cook, *Journals*, vol. 3, pp. 1013–14.
5. *Ibid.*, vol. 2, p. 923.
6. J.R. Forster, *The Resolution Journal of Johann Reinhold Forster 1772–1775*, ed. M.E. Hoare, London, 1982, vol. 3, p. 496.
7. Adrienne L. Kaeppler, 'The Significance of Cook's Third Voyage for the Study of Hawaiian Art and Society', typescript of paper given at the conference, 'Captain James Cook and His Times', Simon Fraser University, B.C., April 1978, p. 22.
8. Cook, *Journal*, vol. 3, p. 306.
9. *Ibid.*, vol. 2, p. 477.
10. *The Periplus of the Erithraean Sea*, ed. G.W.B. Huntingford, London, 1980, pp. 30, 23.
11. P. Bourdieu, *Ce que parler veut dire: l'économie des échanges linguistiques*, Paris, Fayard, 1981.
12. Cook, *Journal*, vol. 3, pp. 52–5.
13. On soft primitivism, see A.O. Lovejoy and G. Boas, *Primitivism and Related Ideas in Antiquity*, Baltimore, 1935.
14. Cook, *Journal*, vol. 1, p. 399.
15. *Ibid.*, vol. 3, p. 774.
16. Quoted from *The Periplus of the Erythraean Sea*, *ed. cit.*, p. 182. For an extended account of fish-eaters, see also *Agatharchides of Cnidus on the Erythraean Sea*, trans. and ed. Stanley M. Burstein, London, 1989, pp. 78 ff.
17. *Iliad*, XIII, 3 f; *Odyssey*, IV, 561–8.
18. J.R. Forster, *op. cit.*, vol. 4, p. 555.
19. T. Martyn, *The Universal Conchologist*, London, 1784.
20. *The Natural History of many uncommon zoophytes collected by John Ellis, arranged and described by D.C. Solander*, London, 1786.
21. Georges-Louis Leclerc, comte de Buffon, *Histoire naturelle*, 15 vols, Paris, 1749–67, *Histoire naturelle de l'homme*, p. 546.
22. See Joppien and Smith, vol. 1, p. 52.
23. Cook, *Journals*, vol. 2, p. 862.
24. J.R. Forster, *op. cit.*, vol. 3, pp. 502–3.
25. J.G.A. Forster, *A Voyage round the World*, London, 1777, p. 106.
26. *Ibid.*, pp. 106–7.
27. *Ibid.*, preface.
28. On the four-stages theory of civilisation, see R.L. Meek, *Social Science and the Ignoble Savage*, Cambridge, 1976.
29. On this debate, see R. Wittkower, 'Piranesi's Parere sull'architettura', *Journal of the Warburg Institute*, vol. 2, 1938, pp. 147–8.
30. *A Contribution to the Critique of Political Economy*, introduction.
31. L. Antoine de Bougainville, *A Voyage Round the World*, trans. J.R. Forster, London, 1772, pp. 244–5.
32. Banks, *Endeavour Journal*, vol. 1, p. 252.
33. *Lettres de Gauguin à Daniel de Monfried*, ed. Mme Joly-Segalen, Paris, (n.d.), p. 113.
34. William Hodges, *Select Views in India*, 1786.
35. James Cook and James King, *A Voyage to the Pacific Ocean*, London, 1784, vol. 1, p. lxix.
36. R.J. Goldwater, *Primitivism in Modern Painting*, New York, 1938. But note the important publication *Primitivism in 20th Century Art*, ed. W. Rubin, New York, 1984.
37. On Linnaeus's indebtedness to Aristotle, see F. Stafleu, *Linneaus and the Linneans*, Utrecht, 1971.
38. E. Gombrich, *Art and Illusion: A Study in the Psychology of Pictorial Representation*, New York, 1960, pp. 116–45.
39. E.g., 'There can be no recital of events that does not include description of one kind or another, and nobody would claim that the Gilgamesh Epic or the Old Testament is devoid of vivid accounts', *Art and Illusion*, p. 129.
40. J. Onians, *Art and Thought in the Hellenistic Age*, London, 1979.
41. M. Baxandall, *Painting and Experience in Fifteenth Century Italy*, Oxford, 1972, p. 152.
42. Lucretius, *De Rerum Natura*, trans. L.L. Johnson, Fontwell, Sussex, 1963, Book v, 1449–57.

10 COOK'S POSTHUMOUS REPUTATION

1. Colville to Cleveland, 30 Dec. 1762, P.R.O. Adm. 1/482. Quoted in J.C. Beaglehole, *The Life of Captain James Cook*, London, 1974, p. 59.
2. Quoted in J.R. Muir, *The Life and Achievements of Captain James Cook*, London, 1939, p. 22.
3. See Beaglehole, *op. cit.*, p. 471.
4. 'Ce n'est ni dans les forêts du Canada ni sur le sein des des mers, que l'on se forme à l'art d'écrire' (*Voyage autour du monde*, quoted in Peter France, *Rhetoric and Truth in France*, Oxford, 1972, p. 79).
5. Thomas Sprat, *History of the Royal Society*, ed. J. Cape and H.W. Jones, Seattle, 1958, pp. 111 ff.
6. *Oeuvres complètes*, vol. 2, p. 208. Quoted by France, *op. cit.*, p. 79.
7. 'To chuse incidents and situations from common life, and to relate or describe them, throughout, as far as was possible in a selection of language really used by men' (*Lyrical Ballads*, 3rd edn, 1802, p. vii).
8. Peter Gay, *The Enlightenment: an interpretation*, London, 1973, p. 3.
9. See France, *op. cit.*, p. 73.
10. *Les Jardins, ou l'Art d'embellir les Paysages*, Paris, 1782, trans. in *Gentleman's Magazine*, vol. 53, Dec. 1783, pp. 1044–5.
11. *Elogio del Capitano Giacomo Cook letto da M Gianetti nella pubblica adunanza della Reale Accademia Fiorentina*, Florence, 1785 (with parallel texts in Italian and English).
12. *Elogio del Capitano Giacomo Cook*, p. 25.
13. Pierre Lémontey, *Eloge de Jacques Cook avec des notes: discours qui a remporté le prix d'éloquence au jugement de l'Académie de Marseille, le 25 Aout 1789*, Paris, 1792.
14. Pierre-Louis Paris, *Eloge de Cook*, Riom, 1790.
15. 'La vie d'un homme seroit à ses yeux plus précieuse que la connaissance d'un continent' (Paris, *op. cit.*, p. 62).
16. *Frederick the Great*, London, 1858–65, book 4, ch. 3.
17. Cook, *Journals*, vol. 3, p. 556.
18. Charles Mitchell, 'Zoffany's Death of Captain Cook', *Burlington Magazine*, vol. 84, 1944, pp. 56–61.
19. Benjamin West, *The Death of Wolfe*, oil, National Gallery of Canada, Ottawa.
20. For the *theory* of repressive tolerance (in relation to Auguste Comte), see Herbert Marcuse, *Reason and Revolution*, Boston, 1960,

pp. 353 ff.

21. See W.S. Howell, 'Adam Smith's Lectures on Rhetoric: an Historical Assessment', *Essays on Adam Smith*, ed. A.S. Skinner and T. Wilson, Oxford, 1975, pp. 11–43.

22. Joseph Burke, *English Art 1714–1800*, Oxford, 1976, p. 249.

23. Sir Henry T. Wood, *A History of the Royal Society of Arts*, London, 1913, p. 76.

24. Quoted by Burke, *op. cit.*, p. 249.

25. On the posthumous veneration of Cook on Hawaii as Lono, see J.F.G. Stokes, 'Origin of the Condemnation of Captain Cook in Hawaii', *Hawaiian Historical Society, Annual Report*, vol. 39, 1930, pp. 69–104; E.S.C. and E.G. Handy, 'Native Planters in Hawaii. Their Life, Lore and Environment', *Bishop Museum Bulletin*, vol. 233, 1972, p. 372. Cook's fascinating transfiguration after death into a manifestation of the Hawaiian god Lono is beyond the limits of this chapter.
See Marshal Sahlins 'The Apotheosis of Captain Cook' in *Between Belief and Transgression*, ed. M. Izard and P. Smith, trans. by L. Leavitt, Chicago, 1982; and G. Dening, 'Sharks that walk on the Land', *Meanjin*, vol. 4, 1982, pp. 427–37.

26. J. Williamson, 'I Now took Possession in Right of His Majesty King George III', frontispiece to J. Varrow, ed., *Cook's Voyages of Discovery*, London, 1904.

27. Cook, *Journals*, vol. 3, pp. 556–7.

28. *Ibid.*, p. 1492.

29. J.G.A. Forster, *A Voyage round the World*, vol. 1, p. 29.

30. Gerald Fitzgerald, *The Injured Islanders: or, the Influence of Art upon the Happiness of Nature*, Dublin, 1779.

31. Lémontey, *op. cit.*, p. 51 (author's trans.).

32. Stokes, *op. cit.*, pp. 68–104.

33. I am indebted to Professor Manning Clark for drawing my attention to this point.

I should like to acknowledge the valuable assistance of Jane De Teliga in collecting material related to this chapter.

SELECT BIBLIOGRAPHY

Alfrey, N., 'Landscape and the Ordnance Survey, 1795–1820', in *Mapping the Landscape*, ed. N. Alfrey and S. Daniels, University Art Gallery, Castle Museum, Nottingham, 1990, pp. 23–7.

Algarotti, F., *An Essay on Painting*, London, 1764.

Alpers, S., *The Art of Describing. Dutch Art in the Seventeenth Century*, Chicago, 1983.

Anson, G., *A Voyage Round the World*, comp. by R. Walter, London, 1748.

Antal, F., 'Reflections on Classicism and Romanticism, V', *Burlington Magazine*, vol. 78, 1941, pp. 14–22.

Antal, F., *Fuseli Studies*, London, 1956.

Banks, Sir Joseph, *The Endeavour Journal of Sir Joseph Banks*, ed. J.C. Beaglehole, 2 vols, Sydney, 1962.

Barbier, C.P., *William Gilpin*, Oxford, 1963.

Barrell, J., *The Dark Side of the Landscape*, Cambridge, 1980.

Barrell, J., 'The private comedy of Thomas Rowlandson', *Art History*, vol. 6, no. 4, Dec. 1983, pp. 423–41.

Barrell, J., *The Political Theory of Painting from Reynolds to Hazlitt*, New Haven and London, 1986.

Baxandall, M., *Painting and Experience in Fifteenth Century Italy*, Oxford, 1972.

Beaglehole, J.C., *The Life of Captain James Cook*, London, 1974.

Benisovitch, M., 'The history of the Tenture des Indes', *Burlington Magazine*, Sept. 1943, pp. 216–25.

Bermingham, A., *Landscape and Ideology. The English Rustic Tradition*, London, 1986.

Bicknell, P., and Munro, J., *Gilpin to Ruskin: Drawing Masters and their Manuals, 1800–1860*, Fitzwilliam Museum, Cambridge, 1987.

Blunt, W., *The Art of Botanical Illustration*, London, 1950.

Blunt, W., and Stearn, W.T., *Captain Cook's Florilegium*, London, 1968.

Bodi, L., 'The "Pacific Expert" of Eighteenth Century Germany', *Historical Studies Australia and New Zealand*, vol. 8, no. 32, May 1959, 32, pp. 345–63.

Bodi, L., 'Captain Cook in German Imaginative Literature', in W. Veit, *Captain James Cook Image and Impact*, Melbourne, 1972.

Bodkin, T., 'Les Nouvelles Tentures des Indes', *Burlington Magazine*, March 1944, pp. 65–6.

Bohm, A., 'George Forster's *A Voyage Round the World* as a source for the Rime of the Ancient Mariner', *Journal of English Literary History*, vol. 50, 1983.

Boime, A., *The Academy and French Painting in the Nineteenth Century*, London, 1971.

Bowra, C.M., *The Romantic Imagination*, Oxford, 1949.

Boxer, C.R., *The Dutch in Brazil, 1624–1654*, Oxford, 1957.

Buckley, V., 'Coleridge: Vision and Actuality', *Melbourne Critical Review*, vol. 4, 1961.

Buffon, George-Louis Leclerc, comte de, *Histoire Naturelle*, 15 vols, Paris, 1749–67.

Burke, E., *A Philosophical Enquiry into the Origin of our Ideas of the Sublime and Beautiful*, ed. J.T. Boulton, London, 1958.

Burke, J., *English Art 1714–1800*, Oxford, 1976.

Burney, J., *Chronological History of the North-Eastern Voyages of Discovery*, London, 1819.

Burstein, S.M., trans. and ed., *Agatharchides of Cnidus on the Erythraean Sea*, London, 1989.

Camper, P., *The Works of the Late Professor Camper*, trans. from the Dutch by T. Coglan, London, 1794.

Carr, D.J., ed., *Sydney Parkinson, Artist of Cook's Endeavour Voyage*, Canberra, 1983.

Carter, H.B., *Sir Joseph Banks 1743–1820*, London, 1988.

Carter, P., *The Road to Botany Bay. An Essay in Spatial History*, London, 1987.

Cassirer, E., *The Philosophy of the Enlightenment*, trans. Fritz C. Koeln and James P. Pettergrove, Princeton, 1951.

Chinard, G., *L'Amérique et le rêve exotique dans la littérature Française au XVIIe au XVIIIe Siècle*, Paris, 1934.

Christian, J., 'Paul Sandby and the Military Survey of Scotland', in *Mapping the Landscape*, ed. N. Alfrey and S. Daniels, University Art Gallery, Castle Museum, Nottingham, 1990. pp. 18–22.

Cole, D., and Tippett, M., 'Pleasing Diversity and Sublime Desolation. The 18th Century British Perception of the North-West Coast', *Pacific Northwest Quarterly*, vol. 65, Jan. 1974, pp. 1–7.

Coleridge, S.T., *Letters of Samuel Taylor Coleridge*, ed. E.H. Coleridge, London, 1895.

Coleridge, S.T., *Biographia Literaria*, ed. J. Shawcross, Oxford, 1907.

Coleridge, S.T., *Biographia Epistolaris*, ed. A. Turnbull, London, 1911.

Coleridge, S.T., *Biographia Literaria*, ed. J. Engell and W. Jackson Bate, Princeton, 1983.

Conisbee, P., 'Pre-Romantic Plein air painting', *Art History*, vol. 2, no. 4, Dec. 1979.

Cook, James, *A Voyage towards the South Pole and Round the World*, 2 vols, London, 1777.

Cook, James, *The Journals of Captain James Cook on his voyages of Discovery*, ed. J.C. Beaglehole, 3 vols, Cambridge, 1955–68.

Cook, James, and King, James, *A Voyage to the Pacific Ocean*, 3 vols and folio of plates, London, 1784.

Cordingly, D., ed., *Capt. James Cook Navigator*, Sydney and London, 1988.

David, A., Joppien, R., and Smith, B., eds, *The Charts and Coastal Views of Captain Cook's Voyages. The Voyage of the Endeavour 1768–1771*, London, 1988.

Degérando, M.J., *The Observation of savage Peoples*, trans. and intr. essay by F.C.T. Moore, London, 1969.

Delille, J., *Les Jardins, ou l'Art d'embellir les Paysages*, Paris, 1782.

Dening, G., 'Sharks that walk on the Land. The Death of Captain Cook', *Meanjin*, vol. 4, 1982, pp. 427–37

Duplessis, G., *Memoirs et Journal de J.G. Wille*, Paris, 1857.

Edwards, G., *History of Birds*, 7 vols, London, 1743–64.

Edwards, R., 'Thomas Jones 1742–1803, a Reappraisal of his Art', *Connoisseur*, vol. 168, no. 675, May 1968.

Eisler, W. 'Terra Australis. Art and Exploration 1500–1768', in *Terra Australis the Furthest Shore*, ed. W. Eisler and B. Smith, Art Gallery of New South Wales, Sydney 1988.

Fairchild, F.N., *The Noble Savage. A Study in Romantic Naturalism*, New York, 1928.

Farington, J., *The Diary of Joseph Farington*, ed. K. Garlick and A. Macintyre, New Haven and London, vol. 1, 1978.

Ferguson, A., *An Essay on the History of Civil Society*, Edinburgh, 1767.

Forster, J.G.A., *A Voyage round the World*, 2 vols, London, 1777.

Forster, J.R., *Observations made during a Voyage round the World*, London, 1778.

Forster, J.R., *The Resolution Journal of Johann Reinhold Forster 1772–1775*, ed. M.E.

Hoare, 4 vols, London, 1982.

Frantz, R.W., *The English Traveller and the Movement of Ideas: 1660–1732*, Lincoln, Nebraska, 1934.

Friedman, J., 'Cook, Culture and the World System', *Journal of Pacific History*, vol. 10, no. 4, Oct. 1985.

Frost, A., 'Captain James Cook and the Early Romantic Imagination', in *Captain James Cook: Image and Impact*, ed. W. Veit, vol. 1, Melbourne, 1972, pp. 90–106.

Frost, A., 'The Pacific Ocean–The Eighteenth Century's "New World"', in *Captain James Cook: Image and Impact*, ed. W. Veit, vol. 2, Melbourne, 1979, pp. 5–49.

Fruman, Norman, *Coleridge: The Damaged Archangel*, New York, 1971.

Gage, J., *A Decade of English Naturalism, 1810–1820*, Norwich Castle Museum, 1969.

Galassi, P., *Corot in Italy. Open-Air Painting and the Classical-Landscape Tradition*, New Haven and London, 1991.

Gardner, A.T.E., 'Scientific Sources of the Fulllength landscape', *Metropolitan Museum of Art Bulletin*, vol. 55, 1945, pp. 59–65.

Garfinkle, N., 'Science and Religion in England 1790–1800: the Critical Response to the Work of Erasmus Darwin', *Journal of the History of Ideas*, vol. 16, 1955, pp. 376–88.

Gauguin, P., *Lettres de Gauguin à Daniel de Monfried*, ed. Mme Joly-Segalen, Paris (n.d.).

Gay, P., *The Enlightenment: an Interpretation*, London, 1973.

Gere, J., 'Thomas Jones: An Eighteenth Century Conundrum', *Apollo*, vol. 91, no. 100, June 1970.

Gianetti, M., *Elogio del Capitano Giacomo Cook*, Florence, 1785 (with parallel texts in Italian and English).

Gilpin, W., *Observations made in 1772 . . . on Several Parts of England*, London, 1786.

Gilpin, W., *On the Principles on which the Author's Sketches are Composed*, London, 1804.

Gilpin, W., *Three Essays*, London, 1804.

Goldwater, R., *Primitivism in Modern Art*, New York, 1938.

Gombrich, E.H., *Meditations on a Hobby Horse*, New York, 1963.

Gombrich, E.H., *Norm and Form*, London, 1966.

Gombrich, E.H., *Art and Illusion: A Study in the Psychology of Pictorial Representation*, New York, 1960.

Gowing, L., *The Originality of Thomas Jones*, London, 1985.

Griffith, M., *Moses Griffith 1747–1819*, Welsh Arts Council, Caernarfon, 1979.

Hackforth-Jones, J., 'Imagining Australia and the South Pacific', in *Mapping the Landscape*, ed. N. Alfrey and S. Daniels,

University Art Gallery, Castle Museum, Nottingham, 1990, pp. 13–17.

Handy, E.S.C. and E.G., 'Native Planters in Hawaii', *Bishop Museum Bulletin*, vol. 233, 1972.

Hanson, L., *Life of S.T. Coleridge*, London, 1938.

Hardie, M., *Water-colour Painting in Britain*, ed. D. Snelgrove, J. Mayne and B. Taylor, 2 vols, London, 1966–7.

Hawkesworth, J., *An Account of the Voyages undertaken by the order of His Present Majesty for making Discoveries in the Southern Hemisphere*, 3 vols, London, 1773.

Herder, J.G., *Outlines of a Philosophy of the History of Man*, trans. T. Churchill, 2 vols, London, 1803.

Herrmann, L., *British Landscape Painting of the Eighteenth Century*, London, 1973.

Hill, J.S., *A Coleridge Companion*, London, 1983.

Hipple, W.J., *The Beautiful, The Sublime and the Picturesque in Eighteenth Century British Aesthetic Theory*, Carbondale, 1957.

Hoare, M.E., *The Tactless Philosopher: Johann Reinhold Forster 1729–98*, Melbourne, 1976.

Hodges, W., *Travels in India*, London, 1793.

Hogarth, W., *Analysis of Beauty*, ed. J. Burke, London, 1955.

Honour, H., *The European Vision of America*, Cleveland Museum of Art, 1975.

Honour, H., *The New Golden Land*, New York, 1975.

House, H., *Lectures on Coleridge*, London, 1953.

Howell, W.S., 'Adam Smith's Lectures on Rhetoric: an historical assessment', *Essays on Adam Smith*, ed. A.S. Skinner and T. Wilson, Oxford, 1975.

Hulton, P., *et al.*, *The Work of Jacques Le Moyne de Morgues*, 2 vols, London, 1977.

Hulton, P., *The Complete Drawings of John White*, London, 1984.

Hulton, P., and Quinn, D.B., *The American Drawings of John White. 1577–1590*, Chapel Hill, North Carolina, 1964.

Humboldt, Alexander von, *Aspects of Nature*, trans. Mrs Sabine, London, 1849.

Humboldt, Alexander von, *Cosmos*, trans. Mrs Sabine, 4 vols, London, 1846–58.

Hume, Robert D., 'Kant and Coleridge on Imagination', *Journal of Aesthetics and Art Criticism*, vol. 28, no. 4, Summer 1970, pp. 485–96.

Huntingford, G.W.B., ed., *The Periplus of the Erythraen Sea*, London, 1980.

Hyde, J.H., 'The Four Parts of the World as represented in old time pageants and ballets', *Apollo*, vol. 4, 1926, pp. 232-38, and 5, 1927, pp. 19–27.

Ivins, W., *Prints and Visual Communication*, London, 1953.

Ivor, James, *The Source of the Ancient Mariner*, 1977.

Jacquier, H., 'Le mirage et l'exotisme

tahitiens dans la littérature', *Bulletin de la Société des Etudes Ociennes*, Dec. 1944, June 1945, Sept. 1945.

Jarry, M., 'Les Indes. Série Triomphale de L'Exotisme', *Connaissance des Arts*, May 1959, pp. 62–9.

Jones, R., 'Images of Natural Man', in *Baudin in Australian Waters*, ed. J. Bonnemains, E.C. Forsyth and B. Smith, Melbourne, 1988.

Jones, T., 'Memoirs of Thomas Jones', *Walpole Society*, vol. 32, 1946–8, pp. 1–142.

Joppien, R., 'The Dutch Vision of Brazil of Johan Maurits and his artists', in *Johan Maurits van Nassau, 1604–1679. A Humanist Prince in Europe and Brazil*, ed. E. van den Boogart, The Hague, 1979.

Joppien, R., 'The Artistic Bequest of Captain Cook's Voyages', in *Captain James Cook and His Times*, ed. R. Fisher and H. Johnston, Vancouver, 1979, pp. 187–210.

Joppien, R., and Smith, B., *The Art of Captain Cook's Voyages*, 3 vols, Sydney, New Haven and London, 1985–7.

Kaeppler, Adrienne L., *'Artificial Curiosities' being an exposition of native manufactures collected on the three Pacific Voyages of Captain James Cook, R.N.*, Bernice P. Bishop Museum Special Publication 65, Honolulu, 1978.

Kames, H.H., *Sketches of the History of Man*, 3 vols, Edinburgh, 1813.

Keate, G., *An Account of the Pelew Islands*, London, 1788.

Knight, R. Payne, *The Progress of Civil Society*, London, 1796.

Knight, R. Payne, *An Analytical Enquiry into the Principles of Taste*, London, 1806.

Lafebre, M., *Samuel Taylor Coleridge: A Bondage of Opium*, New York, 1974.

Lémontey, P., *Eloge de Jacques Cook*, Paris, 1792.

Lessing, G.E., *Laocoon*, trans. J.M. Dent, London, 1930.

Locke, J., *Two Treatises on Government*, ed. P. Lovett, New York, 1965.

Locke, J., *The Educational Writings of John Locke*, ed. J.L. Axtell, London and New York, 1968.

Lovejoy, A.O., 'The Supposed Primitivism of Rousseau's Discourse in Inequality', *Modern Philology*, vol. 21, 1923, pp. 165–86.

Lovejoy, A.O., *The Great Chain of Being*, Cambridge, Mass., 1948.

Lovejoy, A.O., and G. Boas, *Primitivism and related Ideas in Antiquity*, Baltimore, 1935.

Lowes, J.L., *The Road to Xanadu*, London, 1951.

McCormick, E.H., *Omai: Pacific Envoy*, Auckland and Oxford, 1977.

McGowan, A.P., 'Captain Cook's Ships', *The Mariner's Mirror*, vol. 65, no. 2, May 1979, pp. 109–18.

Malthus, T., *Essay on the Principles of*

Population, (2nd edn), London, 1803.

Marshall, P.J., and Williams, G., *The Great Map of Mankind. British Perceptions of the World in the Age of the Enlightenment*, London, 1982.

Martyn, T., *The Universal Conchologist*, London, 1784.

Meek, R.L., *Social Science and the Ignoble Savage*, Cambridge, 1976.

Milton, M.L.T., *The Poetry of Samuel Taylor Coleridge. An Annotated Bibliography of Criticism, 1935–1970*, New York and London, 1981.

Mitchell, C., 'Zoffany's Death of Captain Cook', *Burlington Magazine*, vol. 84, 1944, pp. 56–61.

Monboddo, J.B., *On the Origins and Progress of Language* (2nd edn), Edinburgh, 6 vols, 1774–92.

Oliver, D., *Ancient Tahiti Society*, 3 vols, Honolulu, 1974.

Onions, J., *Art and Thought in the Hellenistic Age*, London, 1979.

Pächt, O., 'Early Italian Nature Studies and the Early Calendar Landscape,' *Journal of the Warburg and Courtauld Institutes*, vol. 13, 1950.

Park, Roy, 'Coleridge and Kant: Poetic Imagination and Practical Reason', *British Journal of Aesthetics*, vol. 8, no. 4, Oct. 1968, pp. 335–46.

Parkinson, S., *A Journal of a Voyage to the South Seas*, London, 1773.

Parris, L., and Shields, C., *Landscape in Britain c. 1750–1850*, Tate Gallery, London, 1973.

Pearce, E.H., *Annals of Christ's Hospital*, London, 1901.

Pennant, T., *Tour in Scotland* (2nd edn), London, 1774.

Pennant, T., *British Zoology*, London, 1776.

Pennant, T., *The Literary Life of Thomas Pennant*, London, 1793.

Pevsner, N., *Academies of Art past and present*, London, 1940.

Phillip, A., *The Voyage of Governor Phillip to Botany Bay*, London, 1789.

Philosophical Transactions (of the Royal Society), London.

Pickering, C., *The Races of Man, and their Geographical Distribution*, London, 1850.

Pinkerton, J., *Modern Geography*, 3 vols, London, 1807.

Price, U., *Essays on the Picturesque*, 3 vols, 1810.

Reynolds, Sir Joshua, *Discourses on Art*, ed. R.R. Wark, New Haven and London, 1975.

Richards, I.A., *Coleridge on Imagination*, London, 1934.

Robertson, J., *The Captain Cook Myth*, Sydney, 1981.

Rousseau, G.S., and Porter, R., eds, *Exoticism in the Enlightenment*, Manchester and New York, 1990.

Rousseau, J.J., *A Dissertation on the Origin and Foundation of Inequality among Mankind*, in *Works*, trans. from the French, London, 1773–4.

Rubin, W., ed., *Primitivism in Twentieth Century Art*, 2 vols, New York, 1984.

Sahlins, M., *Historical Metaphors and Mythical Reality*, Ann Arbor, 1980.

Sahlins, M., 'The Apotheosis of Captain Cook', in *Between Belief and Transgression*, ed. M. Izard and P. Smith, Chicago, 1982.

Said, E.W., *Orientalism*, London, 1978.

Scharf, A., *Art and Photography*, London, 1968.

Shelvocke, G., *A Voyage Round the World by way of the Great South Sea, performed in the years 1719–1722*, London, 1726.

Skelton, R.A., *Captain James Cook after two hundred years*, London, 1969.

Skelton, R.A., 'Captain James Cook as a Hydrographer', *The Mariner's Mirror*, vol. 40, no. 2, 1954, pp. 92–119.

Sloan, K., 'The Teaching of non-professional artists in Eighteenth-Century England', Ph. D. thesis, University of London, 1986.

Sloan, K., *Alexander and John Robert Cozens*, New Haven and London, 1986.

Smith, B., *European Vision and the South Pacific* (2nd edn), New Haven and London, 1985.

Smith, R.C., 'The Brazilian Landscapes of Frans Post', *Art Quarterly*, vol. 1, 1938, pp. 230–62.

Solkin, D.H., *Richard Wilson: The Landscape of Reaction*, Tate Gallery, London, 1982.

Solkin, D.H., 'Great Pictures of Great Men', *Oxford Art Journal*, vol. 9, no. 2, 1986.

Sousa-Leao, J. de, 'Frans Post in Brazil', *Burlington Magazine*, vol. 80, 1942, pp. 59–61.

Sparrman, A., *A Voyage to the Cape of Good Hope, towards the Antarctic Polar Circle, and Round the World*, trans. from the Swedish, 2 vols, London, 1785.

Sparrman, A., *A Voyage Round the World with Captain James Cook in H.M.S. Resolution*, ed. O. Rutter, London, 1944.

Spate, O.H.K., *Paradise Found and Lost. The Pacific since Magellan*, vol. 3, Canberra, 1988.

Stafford, B.M., 'Towards romantic perception: illustrated travels and the rise of "singularity" as an aesthetic Category', *Art Quarterly*, Autumn 1977.

Stafleu, F., *Linneaus and the Linneans*, Utrecht, 1971.

Stainton, L., *British Landscape Watercolours, 1600–1860*, London, 1985.

Stearn, W.T., 'A Royal Society Appointment with Venus in 1769: The Voyage of Cook and Banks in the Endeavour in 1768–1771 and its Botanical Results', *Notes and Records of the Royal*

Society of London, vol. 24, 1 June 1969.

Steube, I.C., *The Life and Work of William Hodges*, New York, 1979.

Stokes, J.F.B., 'Origin of the Condemnation of Captain Cook in Hawaii', *Hawaiian Historical Society, Annual Report*, vol. 39, 1930.

Tinker, C.B., *Nature's Simple Plan*, Princeton, 1922.

Tournefort, J.P. de, *A Voyage into the Levant*, 2 vols, London, 1718.

Trollope, W., *History of Christ's Hospital*, London, 1834.

Tsuji, S., 'Brunelleschi and the Camera Obscura', *Art History*, vol. 13, no. 3, Sept. 1990.

Veit, W., ed., *Captain James Cook: Image and Impact*, 2 vols, Melbourne, 1972, 1979.

Veit, W., 'Captain Cook and Comparative Literature', in *Captain James Cook: Image and Impact*, ed. W. Veit, vol. 1, Melbourne, 1972.

Wales, W., MS. journal, 21 June 1772–7 October 1774, Mitchell Library, Sydney.

Wales, W., *Remarks on Mr. Forster's Account of Captain Cook's last Voyage round the World*, London, 1778.

Wales, W., and Bayly, W., *The Original Astronomical Observations made in the course of a Voyage towards the South Pole*, London, 1777.

Watson, J.B., 'Giovanni Battista Tiepolo', *Connoisseur*, 1955, vol. 136, pp. 212–15.

Watt, J., 'Medical aspects and consequences of Captain Cook's Voyages', in R. Fisher and H. Johnston, eds, *Captain James Cook and his Times*, Vancouver 1979, pp. 129–57.

Webber, J., *Views in the South Seas*, London, 1808.

Webster, M., *Johan Zoffany 1733–1810*, National Portrait Gallery, London, 1976.

Weissman, S.M., *His Brother's Keeper: A Psychobiography of Samuel Taylor Coleridge*, Madison, Conn., 1989.

Whitehead, P.J.P., and Boaseman, M., *A Portrait of Dutch 17th Century Brazil. Animals, plants and people by the artists of Johan Maurits of Nassau*, Amsterdam, Oxford, New York, 1989.

Whitehurst, J., *Enquiry into the Original State and Formation of the Earth*, London, 1778.

Winckelmann, J., *The History of Ancient Art*, trans. G.H. Lodge, 2 vols, London, 1881.

Wind, E., 'The Revolution of History Painting', *Journal of the Warburg and Courtauld Institutes*, vol. 2, 1938, pp. 116–27.

Williams, G., 'Seamen and Philosophers in the South Seas in the Age of Captain Cook', *The Mariner's Mirror*, vol. 65, Feb. 1979, pp. 3–22.

Williams, G., and Frost, A., *Terra Australis to Australia*, Melbourne, 1988.

Williams, I.A., 'Thomas Pennant and

Moses Griffith', *Country Life*, 2 July 1938, pp. 8–9.

Williams, I.A., 'Moses Griffith', *Walker's Quarterly*, Aug.–Sept. 1938.

Wilton, A., *The Art of Alexander and John Robert Cozens*, New Haven and London, 1980.

Wittkower, R., 'Marvels of the East, A study in the History of Monsters', *Journal of the Warburg and Courtauld Institutes*, vol. 5, 1942, pp. 159–97.

Wittkower, R., 'Piranesi's *Parere sull'architettura*', *Journal of the Warburg and Courtauld Institutes*, vol. 2, 1938.

Wölfflin, H., *Principles of Art History*, trans. M.H. Hottinger, Dover edn (n.d.).

Wollheim, R., *Painting as an Art*, Washington, 1987.

Wood, G.A., 'Ancient and Medieval Conceptions of Terra Australis', *Journal of the Royal Australian Historical Society*, vol. 3, 1916, pp. 455–65.

Wood, Sir H., *A History of the Royal Society of Arts*, London, 1913.

ILLUSTRATIONS

Works illustrated in R. Joppien and B. Smith, *The Art of Captain Cook's Voyages*, 3 vols, Sydney, New Haven and London, 1985–7, are indicated by the abbreviation 'JS', followed by the volume and catalogue number.

1. A photograph taken in 1919 to confirm Einstein's hypothesis concerning the action of gravity upon light. *Philosophical Transactions* (of the Royal Society), vol. 220, 1920, series A, pl. 1, fp. 292.

2. Wenzel Hollar, *View of Engers with the Rhine*, pen and watercolour on paper, 11 × 27.1 cm., 1636, Devonshire Collection, Chatsworth. Reproduced by permission of the Chatsworth Settlement Trustees. Photograph courtesy of the Courtauld Institute of Art, London.

3. Bird studies from *The Art of Falconry* (*De arte venandi*) by Frederick II, folio 36 × 25 cm., mid-thirteenth century, Vatican, Rome (MS Pal. Lat. 1071, f. 22r).

4. A page from the Cocharelli Manuscript, showing animal borders, folio 26 × 18 cm., British Library, London (Add. MS 27695, f. 3v).

5. A page from the Cocharelli Manuscript, showing animal borders, folio 17 × 10.9 cm., British Library, London (Add. MS 28841, f. 3).

6. Pisanello, studies for an Epiphany, silverpoint, pen and bistre, 27.3 × 20.4 cm., early fifteenth century, Graphische Sammlung Albertina, Vienna.

7. Pisanello, studies of stags' heads, pen and ink, 27.3 × 20.4 cm., 1455, Graphische Sammlung Albertina, Vienna.

8. Giovannino de' Grassi, *Hoopoe*, watercolour, 25.5 × 20 cm., late fourteenth century, Biblioteca Civica, Bergamo.

9. Illustration of *Nigella* (Love-in-the-Mist) from the *Compendium Salernitanum*, folio 36 × 24.5 cm., early fourteenth century, British Library, London (Egerton MS 747, f. 68v).

10. Illustration of a violet from the *Carrara Herbal*, folio 35 × 24 cm., late fourteenth century, British Library, London (Egerton MS 2020, f. 94).

11. A page from the *Nuremburg Chronicle* (*Liber Chronicarum*), 1493, depicting and describing the fabulous race at the limits of the known world. Mitchell Library, Sydney. By permission of the Trustees of the State Library of New South Wales.

12. The world map from the *Nuremburg Chronicle* (*Liber Chronicarum*), 1493, showing Japheth (Japhet), Shem (Sem) and Ham (Cam) dispersing the peoples. Mitchell Library, Sydney. By permission of the Trustees of the State Library of New South Wales.

13. Jan Mostaert, *West Indian landscape*, oil on oak panel, 86.5 × 152.5 cm., c.1542, Frans Hals Museum, Haarlem.

14. Attributed to Vasco Fernandes, *The Adoration of the Magi*, oil on panel, 134 × 82 cm., c.1505, Museu de Grão Vasco, Viseu, Portugal.

15. Artist unknown, *Inferno*, oil on panel, 119 × 217.5 cm., c.1550, Museu Nacional de Art Antiga.

16. Hans Burgkmair the Elder (after), *People of Calicut*, woodcut, 41 × 58.5 cm., 1517–18. One of the series of woodcuts of the Triumph of Maximilian I. Department of Prints and Drawings, British Museum, London. By permission of the Trustees of the British Museum.

17. Jacques Le Moyne de Morgues, *Athore shows Laudonnière the marker column set up by Ribault*, watercolour and gouache with touches of gold vellum, 18 × 26 cm., after 1566, New York Public Library.

18. Jacques Le Moyne de Morgues, *A Young daughter of the Picts*, watercolour and gouache on vellum, 25.6 × 18.4 cm., c.1585–8, Yale Center for British Art, New Haven, Paul Mellon Collection.

19. *The Chief's chosen wife carried in procession on a litter*, engraving after Le Moyne, in De Bry, *America*, part two, 1591, pl. 37.

20. John White, *A Festive Dance*, watercolour over pencil touched with white, 27.4 × 35.8 cm., c.1585, British Museum, London. By permission of the Trustees of the British Museum.

21. Diego Prado de Tovar, *The Natives of the islands off the southern shores of New Guinea* (Torres Strait), watercolour, 28.7 × 42.8 cm., 1606, Archiveo General de Simancas, Mapas, Planos y Dibujos (Caja XVIII, f. 83).

22. Frans Post, *Sao Francisco river and Fort Maurits*, oil on canvas, 62 × 95 cm., 1639, Louvre, Paris.

23. Frans Post, *Landscape in Brazil*, oil on canvas, 282.5 × 210.5 cm., 1652, Rijksmuseum, Amsterdam.

24. Albert Eckhout, *Tapuya woman seated*, crayon, 33.2 × 21.6 cm., c.1637–44, Kupferstichkabinett, Staatliche Museen, Berlin.

25. Albert Eckhout, *Negro woman and child*, oil on canvas, 273 × 176 cm., Ethnography Collection, National Museum of Denmark, Copenhagen.

26. Albert Eckhout, *Tapuya dance*, oil on canvas, 168 × 294 cm., c.1645, Ethnography Collection, National Museum of Denmark, Copenhagen.

27. Albert Eckhout, *Le Cheval rayé*, from the *Tenture des Indes* Gobelins tapestries, 475 ×

375 cm., 1687–1730, Mobilier National, Paris.

28. *Monster representing a siren*, hand-coloured engraving, in Louis Renard, *Poissons, Ecrivisses et Crabes . . . que l'on Trouve Autour des Isles Moloques, et sur les Côtes des Terres Australes*, Amsterdam, 2nd edn, 1754.

29. *Groupes of different Corallines growing on shells, supposed to make this Appearance on the Retreat of the Sea at a very low Ebbtide*, engraving after Charles Brooking by A. Walker, in John Ellis, *An Essay towards the Natural History of the Corallines*, 1755, frontispiece.

30. Paul Sandby, *Surveying party by Kinloch Rannoch*, 17 × 24 cm., 1749, Map Library, British Library, London.

31. George Edwards, frontispiece to his *History of Birds*, 1743–64.

32. John Webber, *Captain James Cook*, oil on canvas, 114.3 × 91.4 cm., 1782, private collection.

33. Benjamin West, *Joseph Banks*, oil on canvas, 234 × 160 cm., 1771, Usher Gallery, Lincoln.

34. John Flaxman, *Daniel Carl Solander*, medallion bust designed for Josiah Wedgewood, 1775.

35. *Sydney Parkinson*, frontispiece to his *Journal of a Voyage to the South Seas*, 1773, engraved by James Newton.

36. Lord Morton. Detail from Jeremiah Davison, *James Douglas, 13th Earl of Morton, and his family*, oil on canvas, 241.3 × 284.7 cm., 1740, Scottish National Portrait Gallery, Edinburgh.

37. John Francis Rigaud, *Johann Reinhold Forster and George Forster in Tahiti*, engraving by D. Beyel, 1781.

38. *William Hodges*, engraving after a painting by Richard Westall, 1791.

39. William Parry, *Omai, Banks and Solander*, oil on canvas, c.1776, private collection.

40. Johann Daniel Mottet, *John Webber*, oil on canvas, 67.2 × 55.2 cm., 1812, after a contemporary miniature, Historisches Museum, Bern.

41. Paul Klee, *The Snake Goddess and her Enemy*, 1940. By permission of Benteli Verlag, Bern.

42. Sebastiano Ricci, *Achilles surrendering Hector's corpse to Priam*, pen and wash, 22.3 × 31 cm., Graphische Sammlung Albertina, Vienna.

43. Rembrandt, *A Beggar and his family*, chalk drawing, Graphische Sammlung Albertina, Vienna.

44. Animal drawings in the main chamber,

253

Lascaux, Service Photographique, Caisse Nationale des Monuments Historiques et des Sites, Paris. Arch. Phot. Paris. S.P.A.D.E.M.

45. Sydney Parkinson, *Medusa-pelagica*, pen and wash, 23.5 × 28.5 cm., 1768, Zoological Library, British Museum, Natural History (Parkinson's drawings, iii, 54). By permission of the Trustees of the British Museum.

46. Alexander Buchan, *Part of a panoramic view of Rio de Janeiro*, 26.7 × 50.8 cm., 1768, British Library (Add. MS 23920, f. 7). Ill. in Andrew David, *Charts and Coastal Views of Captain Cook's Voyages*, London, 1988, vol. 1, 1.39.

47. Alexander Buchan, *A View of the Endeavour's Watering-place in the Bay of Good Success*, gouache on vellum, 24.8 × 33.7 cm., 1769, British Library (Add. MS 23920, f. 11b). (JS 1.3)

48. Alexander Buchan, *A Man of the Island of Terra del Fuego*, gouache, 36.8 × 26.7 cm., 1769, British Library, London (Add. MS 23920, f. 16). (JS 1.8)

49. Alexander Buchan, *A Woman of the Island of Terra del Fuego*, gouache, 36.8 × 26.7 cm., 1769, British Library, London (Add. MS 23920, f. 17). (JS 1.12)

50. *Two Californian Women, the one in bird's skin, the other in that of a Deer*, engraving by John Pine, in George Shelvocke, *A Voyage Round the World*, London, 1726, fp. 404.

51. Alexander Buchan, two drawings of Tierra del Fuegans, pencil on one sheet, 27 × 10.1 cm., 1769, British Library, London (Add. MS 23920, f. 18a, b). (JS 1.7)

52. G.B. Cipriani, *A View of the Indians of Terra del Fuego in their Hut*, wash and watercolour, 20.8 × 28.5 cm., 1772, Dixson Library, Sydney (PXX 2, 43). By permission of the Trustees of the State Library of New South Wales. (JS 1.6A)

53. Sir Joshua Reynolds, *Lady Sarah Bunbury sacrificing to the Graces*, oil on canvas, 242 × 151.5 cm., 1765, Art Institute of Chicago. By permission of the Art Institute of Chicago.

54. *A View of the Indians of Terra del Fuego in their Hut*, detail from the engraving by F. Bartolozzi after Cipriani, 1779, in Hawkesworth's *Account of the Voyages*, vol. 2, pl. 1, fp. 55.

55. Will Robinson, *A few of the natives brandished spears*, from J. Lang, *Story of Captain Cook*, London, 1906.

56. Sydney Parkinson, *Red-tailed tropic bird (Phaethon rubricauda melanorhynchos*, Gm 1789), watercolour, 29 × 31.5 cm., 1769, Zoological drawings, British Museum, Natural History. By permission of the Trustees of the British Museum.

57. Herman Spöring, *Oberea's Canoe, Otaheite*, pencil, 18.7 × 32.5 cm., 1769, British Library, London (Add. MS 23921, f. 23a). (JS 1.56)

58. Sydney Parkinson, *Otaheite. View up the river among rocks*, wash drawing, 241 × 295 cm., 1769, British Library, London (Add. MS 23921, f. 7b). (JS 1.34)

59. Paul Sandby, *Romantic landscape with figures and a dog*, pen and wash, 47.2 × 58.2 cm., Yale Center for British Art, New Haven,

Paul Mellon Collection. By permission of the Yale Centre for British Art.

60. Sydney Parkinson, *Vessels of the Island of Otaha (Tahaa)*, pencil and wash, 29.8 × 47.7 cm., 1769, British Library, London (Add. MS 23921, f. 17). (JS 1.91)

61. William Hodges, *In Dusky Bay, New Zealand*, wash and watercolour, 38.2 × 54.3 cm., 1773, Mitchell Library, Sydney (PXD 11, 31). By permission of the Trustees of the State Library of New South Wales. (JS 2.14)

62. William Hodges, *Head of a Polynesian man*, oil on canvas, 10 × 6.4 cm., c.1774–5, Mitchell Library, Sydney (SSV, MAO, ib). By permission of the Trustees of the State Library of New South Wales. (JS 2.145b)

63. *Otoo [Tu] King of Otaheite*, engraving by J. Hall after William Hodges, in Cook, *Voyage towards the South Pole and Round the World*, 1777, vol. 1, pl. 38, fp. 254.

64. William Hodges, *Tu*, red chalk, 54 × 36.8 cm., 1773, National Library of Australia, Canberra. (JS 2.54)

65. William Hodges, *The Resolution and Adventure 4 Jan 1773 taking in Ice for Water. Lat. 61 s.*, wash and watercolour, 38 × 54.5 cm., 1773, Mitchell Library, Sydney (PXD 11, 26). By permission of the Trustees of the State Library of New South Wales. (JS 2.6)

66. William Hodges, *View from Point Venus, Island of Otaheite*, oil on panel, 24.1 × 47 cm., c.1775, National Maritime Museum, London, on loan from the Ministry of Defence, Navy. (JS 2.45)

67. William Hodges, *A View in the Island of New Caledonia*, oil on canvas, 135.2 × 193 cm., c.1777, National Maritime Museum, London, on loan from the Ministry of Defence, Navy. (JS 2.140)

68. William Constable, *Dedham Vale, Suffolk*, oil on canvas, 43.5 × 34.4 cm., 1802, Victoria and Albert Museum, London. By permission of the Trustees of the Victoria and Albert Museum.

69. *The Landing at Middleburgh (Eua)*, engraving by J.K. Sherwin after William Hodges, in Cook, *Voyage towards the South Pole and Round the World*, 1777, vol. 1, pl. 54, fp. 192.

70. John Webber, *An Interview between Captain Cook and the natives in Adventure Bay – Van Diemen's Land*, pencil, pen and wash, 66 × 97.2 cm., 1777, Naval Library, Ministry of Defence, London. (JS 3.12)

71. John Webber, *A Boxing match before Captain Cook*, pen, wash and watercolour, 56 × 98.7 cm., 1779, Bernice P. Bishop Museum, Honolulu. By permission of the Bishop Museum. (JS 3.300)

72. John Webber, *A Native prepared for hunting, Nootka Sound*, pen, ink and watercolour, 43.2 × 30.5 cm., 1778, Peabody Museum of Archaeology and Ethnology, Harvard University, Cambridge, Massachusetts. By permission of the Peabody Museum. (JS 3.215)

73. John Webber, *Dancers of Owhyhee*, pen and wash, 30.5 × 48 cm., 1779, Bernice P. Bishop Museum, Honolulu. By permission of the Bishop Museum. (JS 3.302)

74. Edouard Manet, *Concert in the Tuileries*, oil on canvas, 76.2 × 118 cm., 1862, National

Gallery, London. By permission of the Trustees of the National Gallery.

75. Illustration depicting the Linnaean system of classification, engraving after G.D. Ehret.

76. Sydney Parkinson, *A Brazilian vine (Serjania guarumina)* (Vell)C Martius, pencil and watercolour, 27.5 × 44 cm., 1768, British Museum, London, Natural History (Parkinson drawings). By permission of the Trustees of the British Museum.

77. *Tyche of Antioch*, Roman copy of a Greek work by Eutychides, Vatican, Rome. Photo: Alinari.

78. Antonio Zucchi, *America*, from 'The Four Continents' eating-room, Osterley Park, Middlesex, 101 × 139.7 cm., c.1780. By permission of the Trustees of the Victoria and Albert Museum, London.

79. John Webber, *A View in King George Sound*, pen, wash and watercolour, 57.2 × 36.8 cm., 1778, Department of Prints and Drawings, British Museum, London. By permission of the Trustees of the British Museum. (JS 3.212)

80. *Dying Gaul*, Roman copy after a bronze original, c.230–20 BC from Pergamon, Capitoline Museum, Rome. Photo: Alinari.

81. *America*, engraving by Cornelis Visscher (c.1650–60).

82. Sydney Parkinson, *Portrait of a New Zeland Man*, pen and wash, 39.4 × 29.8 cm., 1769, British Library, London (Add. MS 23920, f. 54a). (JS 1.126)

83. Sydney Parkinson, *Portrait of a New Zeland Man*, pen and wash, 38.7 × 29.5 cm., 1769, British Library, London (Add. MS 23920, f. 55). (JS 1.104)

84. Sydney Parkinson, *Sketch of a New Zeland Man*, pencil, 37.5 × 27 cm., 1769, British Library, London (Add. MS 23920, f. 56). (JS 1.103)

85. *A Native of Otaheite in the Dress of his Country*, engraving by R.B. Godfrey, from Parkinson, *A Journal of a Voyage to the South Seas*, 1773, pl. III, fp. 14.

86. *Heads of Divers Natives of the Islands of Otaheite, Huaheine and Oheiteroah*, engraving by T. Chambers, from Parkinson, *A Journal of a Voyage to the South Seas*, 1773, pl. VIII, fp. 26.

87. Sydney Parkinson, *A Tahitian, shewing distortions of the mouth used in dancing*, pencil, 18.8 × 16.2 cm., 1769, British Library, London (Add. MS 23921, f. 51b). (JS 1.86)

88. Sydney Parkinson, *Attitudes of defiance. New Zeland*, six pencil sketches, each approx. 20.3 × 16.8 cm., 1769, British Library, London (Add. MS 23920, f. 60). (JS 1.107)

89. Illustration of facial expressions, James Parson's Croonian Lectures, 1745, *Philosophical Transactions*, 1746.

90. Sydney Parkinson, *New Zealand War Canoe bidding defiance to the Ship*, pen and wash, 29.9 × 48.3 cm., 1770, British Library, London (Add. MS 23920, f. 50). (JS 1.139)

91. Herman Spöring, *New Zealand War Canoe, The Crew bidding defiance to the Ship's Company*, pencil, 26.7 × 41.6 cm., 1769, British Library, London (Add. MS 23920, f. 48). (JS 1.120)

92. Sydney Parkinson, *New Zealand War Canoe,*

254

The Crew Peaceable, pen, 27.9 × 42 cm., 1770, British Library, London (Add. MS 23920, f. 51). (JS 1.140)

93. Sydney Parkinson, *Two Australian Aborigines and other drawings*, pencil, 18.4 × 23.5 cm., 1770, British Library, London (Add. MS 9345, f. 14v). (JS 1.171)

94. Sydney Parkinson, sketches of various objects including a Javanese house, pencil, 18.4 × 23.5 cm., 1770, British Library, London (Add. MS 9345, f. 20v). (JS 1.177)

95. John Frederick Miller, *Five spears and a shield from New Zealand, Australia and New Guinea*, pen and wash, 20.6 × 16.5 cm., 1771, British Library, London (Add. MS 23920, f. 35). (JS 1.176)

96. *Two of the Natives of New Holland Advancing to Combat*, engraving by T. Chambers after Sydney Parkinson, from Parkinson, *Journal of a Voyage to the South Seas*, 1773, pl. xxvii, fp. 134.

97. Charles Praval, *An Australian Aborigine from the Endeavour River*, pen, 26.7 × 21.6 cm., c.1771 (copied from a lost drawing by Sydney Parkinson), British Library, London (Add. MS 15508, f. 13). (JS 1.174)

98. Sydney Parkinson, studies of Australian Aboriginal artefacts and other drawings, pen, 18.4 × 23.5 cm., 1770, British Library, London (Add. MS 9345, f. 20). (JS 1.175)

99. Artist of the Chief Mourner (possibly Joseph Banks), *Australian Aborigines in bark canoes*, pencil and watercolour, 26.3 × 36.2 cm., 1770, British Library, London (Add. MS 15508, f. 10a). (JS 1.172)

100. William Hodges, *A Maori holding a hatchet*, red chalk, 21.1 × 76 cm., 1773, Department of Prints and Drawings, British Museum, London (201. c.5 no. 282). By permission of the Trustees of the British Museum. (JS 2.19)

101. William Hodges, *A Maori woman carrying a child*, red chalk, 17 × 8.7 cm., 1773, Department of Prints and Drawings, British Museum, London (201 c.5 no. 283). By permission of the Trustees of the British Museum. (JS 2.20)

102. William Hodges, *Old Maori man with grey beard*, red chalk, 54 × 37.7 cm., 1773, National Library of Australia, Canberra (R749). By permission of the National Library of Australia, Canberra. (JS 2.31)

103. William Hodges, *Maori man with bushy hair*, red chalk, 54.3 × 37.5 cm., 1773, National Library of Australia, Canberra (R751). By permission of the National Library of Australia, Canberra. (JS 2.30)

104. William Hodges, *A Maori chieftain*, red chalk, 54.1 × 37.3 cm., 1773, National Library of Australia, Canberra (R747). By permission of the National Library of Australia, Canberra. (JS 2.90)

105. William Hodges, *Head of a man of Easter Island*, pen and pencil, 11 × 10 cm., 1774, Department of Prints and Drawings, British Museum, London (201 c.5 no. 275). By permission of the Trustees of the British Museum, London. (JS 2.95)

106. William Hodges, *Potatow*, red chalk, 53.9 × 37.1 cm., 1773, Mitchell Library, Sydney (PXD 11, N 17). By permission of the

Trustees of the State Library of New South Wales. (JS 2.55)

107. John Webber, *The Inside of a house in Nootka Sound*, pen, wash and watercolour, 22.5 × 37.5 cm., c.1781–3, Dixson Library, Sydney (PXX 2, 24). By permission of the Trustees of the State Library of New South Wales. (JS 3.202)

108. John Webber, *Tu*, oil on canvas, 36.2 × 27.9 cm., 1777, Alexander Turnbull Library, Wellington, New Zealand. (JS 3.113)

109. Richard Wilson, *Tivoli: the Cascatelli Grandi and the Villa of Maecenas*, oil on canvas, 50 × 66 cm., 1752, on National Gallery of Ireland, Dublin. Courtesy of the National Gallery of Ireland.

110. Richard Wilson, *Tivoli: the Temple of the Sybyl and the Campagna*, oil on canvas, 50 × 66 cm., 1752, National Gallery of Ireland, Dublin. Courtesy of the National Gallery of Ireland.

111. Thomas Jones, *View of Penkerrig*, oil on paper, 22.9 × 30.4 cm., 1772, City of Birmingham Art Gallery.

112. Thomas Jones, *Buildings in Naples with a view of the Castel Nuovo*, oil on paper, 22.2 × 28.6 cm., 1782, National Museum of Wales, Cardiff. By permission of the National Museum of Wales.

113. Thomas Jones, *Buildings in Naples*, oil on paper, 14 × 21.6 cm., 1782, National Museum of Wales, Cardiff. By permission of the National Museum of Wales.

114. Thomas Hearne, *Sir George Beaumont and Joseph Farington sketching a waterfall*, pen and brown and grey wash, 44.5 × 29.2 cm., c. 1777, The Wordsworth Trust, Dove Cottage, Grasmere, Cumbria.

115. Joseph Farington, *Richard Wilson painting from Nature in Moor Park*, pencil, 1765, Farington Sketchbook, Victoria and Albert Museum, London. By permission of the Trustees of the Victoria and Albert Museum.

116. William Hodges, *The Resolution in the Marquesas*, pen and wash, 28.9 × 23.1 cm., 1774, National Maritime Museum, London. (JS 2.104)

117. William Hodges, *Two coastal profiles of the Isle of Mayo, Cape Verde Islands*, watercolour on one sheet, 36.8 × 54 cm., 1775, Mitchell Library, Sydney (PXD 11, f. 2). By permission of the Trustees of the State Library of New South Wales.

118. John Elliott, *Savage Island* (Niue), wash, 37.7 × 55 cm., 1774, Dixson Library, Sydney. By permission of the Trustees of the State Library of New South Wales.

119. William Hodges, *The North Entrance to Dusky Bay, New Zealand*, wash, 22 × 33 cm., 1773, Mitchell Library, Sydney (PXD 11, 32a). By permission of the Trustees of the State Library of New South Wales. (JS 2.28)

120. William Hodges, *View of Funchal*, wash, 47 × 67.3 cm., 1772, private collection, Madeira. (JS 2.1)

121. William Hodges, *View of Funchal*, oil on canvas, 36.9 × 48.9 cm., 1772, private collection, England. (JS 2.2)

122. William Hodges, *View of the Cape of Good Hope, taken on the spot, from on board the Resolu-*

tion, oil on canvas, 96.5 × 125.7 cm., 1772, National Maritime Museum, London. (JS 2.4)

123. William Hodges, *Waterfall in Dusky Bay, New Zealand with a Maori canoe*, oil on panel, 27.2 × 35.5 cm., 1772 or c.1776, National Maritime Museum, London. (JS 2.23)

124. William Hodges, *Cascade Cove, Dusky Bay, New Zealand*, oil on canvas, 134.6 × 191.1 cm., 1775, National Maritime Museum, London. (JS 2.25)

125. William Hodges, *View in Pickersgill Harbour, Dusky Bay, New Zealand*, oil on canvas, 65.4 × 73.1 cm., 1773, National Maritime Museum, London. (JS 2.18)

126. William Hodges, *View of Point Venus and Matavai Bay, looking east*, oil on canvas, 34.3 × 51.4 cm., 1773, National Maritime Museum, London. (JS 2.44)

127. William Hodges, *View of Fare Harbour, Huahine*, oil on canvas, 34.3 × 51.5 cm., 1773, National Maritime Museum, London. (JS 2.62)

128. William Hodges, *View of the part of the Island of Ulietea* (Raiatea), oil on canvas, 33 × 48.9 cm., 1773, National Maritime Museum, London. (JS 2.66)

129. William Hodges, *View of the Islands of Otaha and Bola Bola* [Tahaa and Pora Pora] *with part of the Island of Ulietea* (Raiatea), oil on canvas, 33 × 48.9 cm., 1773, National Maritime Museum, London. (JS 2.67)

130. William Hodges, detail from *View from Point Venus, Island of Otaheite* (see pl. 66).

131. William Hodges, *The Resolution and Adventure in Matavai Bay*, oil on canvas, 137.1 × 193 cm., 1776, National Maritime Museum, London. (JS 2.49)

132. William Hodges, *View of Fare Harbour*, oil on canvas, 30.1 × 45.7 cm., c.1775, private collection, England. (JS 2.63)

133. William Hodges, *View of part of Fare Harbour*, oil on canvas, 45.7 × 61.5 cm., c.1775, National Maritime Museum, London. (JS 2.64)

134. William Hodges, *Province of Oparee* (Pare), oil on panel, 76.2 × 123.2 cm., c.1775, National Maritime Museum, London. (JS 2.53)

135. William Hodges, *Monuments of Easter Island*, oil on panel, 77.5 × 121.9 cm., c.1775, National Maritime Museum, London. (JS 2.94)

136. William Hodges, *View of Resolution Harbour, Vaitahu Bay, Marquesas*, oil on canvas, 47.6 × 62.9 cm., 1774, National Maritime Museum, London. (JS 2.101)

137. William Hodges, *The Otaheite fleet at Appany* [Pare] *Bay*, pen and wash, 37 × 54.5 cm., 1774, Mitchell Library, Sydney (PXD 11 N 14). By permission of the Trustees of the State Library of New South Wales. (JS 2.112)

138. William Hodges, *Review of the war galleys of Tahiti*, oil on panel, 24.1 × 47 cm., 1776, National Maritime Museum, London. (JS 2.114)

139. William Hodges, *War boats of the Island of Otaheite*, oil on canvas, 177.8 × 301 cm., 1777, National Maritime Museum, London. (JS 2.115)

140. William Hodges, *Tahiti Revisited*, oil on

255

canvas, 97.7 × 138.4 cm., 1776, National Maritime Museum, London. (JS 2.43)

141. John Russell, *William Wales*, pastel, oval 38 cm. wide, 1794, in the possession of H.O. Stafford Cooke, Esq.

142. *Waterspouts in Cook's Straits, in New Zealand*, engraving after William Hodges in Wales and Bayly, *Astronomical Observations, made in the course of a Voyage towards the South Pole*, 1777, pl. 4.

143. William Hodges, *A View of Cape Stephens in Cook's Strait with Waterspout*, oil on canvas, 137.2 × 193.1 cm., 1776, National Maritime Museum, London. (JS 2.29)

144. William Hodges, *The Resolution passing a large island of ice*, wash and watercolour, 32.4 × 47.2 cm., 1773–4, Mitchell Library, Sydney (PXD 11, N.27a). By permission of the Trustees of the State Library of New South Wales. (JS 2.8)

145. George Forster, *Ice islands with ice-blink*, gouache, 35 × 54.5 cm., *c*.1772–3, Mitchell Library, Sydney (PXD 11, N.30). By permission of the Trustees of the State Library of New South Wales. (JS 2.10)

146. William Hodges, *The Resolution and Adventure among icebergs*, wash and watercolour, 36.7 × 54.6 cm., *c*.1772–3, Mitchell Library, Sydney (PXD 11, N.28). By permission of the Trustees of the State Library of New South Wales. (JS 2.9)

147. George Forster, *Wandering Albatross Diomedea exulans*, Linn, watercolour, 33.2 × 48 cm., 1758, British Museum, London, Natural History, Zoological Library (Forster's paintings, f. 99). By permission of the Trustees of the British Museum.

148. William Hodges, *Ice islands*, wash and watercolour, 42.9 × 30.5 cm., *c*.1773–4, Mitchell Library, Sydney (PXD 11, N.27). By permission of the Trustees of the State Library of New South Wales. (JS 2.7)

149. William Hodges, *Ice islands*, wash and watercolour, 27 × 38 cm., *c*.1773–4, Mitchell Library, Sydney (PXD 11, N.29). By permission of the Trustees of the State Library of New South Wales. (JS 2.11)

150. G.B. Cipriani, *A Dance in Raiatea*, oil on oval canvas, 33 × 73.7 cm., *c*.1772, Goodwood House, West Sussex. (JS 1.87C)

151. *A Buddhist procession*, engraving from François Valentijn, *Oud en Nieuw Oost-Indien*, 1724–6.

152. *Captain Wallis, on his arrival at O'Taheite, in conversation with Oberea the Queen*, engraving from Hawkesworth's *Account of the Voyages*, 1773, vol. 1, pl. 22.

153. Sir Joshua Reynolds, *Omai*, oil on canvas, 604 × 370 cm., *c*.1775, Castle Howard, Yorkshire.

154. *Potatow*, engraving by John Hall after Hodges, in Cook, *A Voyage towards the South Pole and Round the World*, 1777, pl. LVI, fp. 159.

155. Sydney Parkinson, *Sketch of a Dancing Girl, Raiatea*, pencil, 28.7 × 22.9 cm., 1769, British Library, London (Add. MS 23921, f. 37c). (JS 1.83)

156. G.B. Cipriani, *A View of the inside of a house in the Island of Ulietea* [Raiatea], *with the representation of a dance to the music of the country*, pen and wash, 21.2 × 33.7 cm.,

c.1772, Dixson Library, Sydney (PXX 2, 14). By permission of the Trustees of the State Library of New South Wales. (JS 1.87A)

157. Raphael, *Christ's charge to Peter*, cartoon for tapestry, 343.5 × 532.8 cm., Victoria and Albert Museum, London. By permission of the Trustees of the Victoria and Albert Museum.

158. Sydney Parkinson, *Distortions of the Mouth used in Dancing*, pencil, 18.8 × 16.2 cm., 1769, British Library, London (Add. MS 23921, f. 51a). (JS 1.86)

159. Joseph-Marie Vien, *Greek girl at the bath*, oil on canvas, 90.2 × 67.3 cm., 1767, Museo de Arte, Ponce, Puerto Rico.

160. John Webber, *A Night Dance by Women*, pencil and pen, 48.9 × 66 cm., *c*.1777, British Library, London (Add. MS 15513, f. 10). (JS 3.48)

161. *Borghese Gladiator*, two engravings by Jan van der Gucht from Bernardino Genga, *Anatomia per uso et intellegenza del disegno*, Rome, 1691, pls XXX and XXXIV.

162. John Webber, *A Boxing match, Friendly Islands*, pen, pencil and wash, 31.1 × 45.1 cm., 1778, British Library, London (Add. MS 15513, f. 9). (JS 3.47)

163. John Webber, *A Hottentot woman*, pencil, pen and wash, 32.9 × 19 cm., 1780, British Library, London (Add. MS 17277, no. 49). (JS 3.421)

164. John Webber, *A Man of Hawaii dancing*, wash and watercolour, 24.1 × 17.8 cm., *c*.1781–3, Dixson Library, Sydney (PXX 2, 36). By permission of the Trustees of the State Library of New South Wales. (JS 3.301)

165. John Webber, *A Man of Kamchatka*, pencil, chalk and wash, 27.9 × 20.3 cm., 1779, Francis P. Farquhar Collection, Berkeley, California. (JS 3.343)

166. Illustrations from *The Works of the Late Professor Camper...*, trans. T. Cogan, London, 1794.

167. Nicolas Petit, *Head of an Aborigine of Van Diemen's Land*, pencil and wash, 11.5 × 14.5 cm., probably 1802, Museé d'Histoire Naturelle, Le Havre, France, Lesueur Collection (2008.2).

168. John Webber, *A Native of Van Diemen's Land*, pencil and wash, 35.5 × 29.2 cm., 1777, Allport Library and Museum of Fine Arts, State Library of Tasmania, Hobart. (JS 3.11)

169. John Webber, *A View in Vaitepiha Valley*, oil on canvas, 58.4 × 80.4 cm., 1787, Honolulu Academy of Arts, Honolulu. (JS 3.90)

170. John Webber, *A View in Annamooka, one of the Friendly Isles*, coloured etching, 28.7 × 42.4 cm., 1787, Department of Prints and Drawings, British Museum, London. By permission of the Trustees of the British Museum. (JS 3.44A)

171. Sydney Parkinson, *A Morai with an offering to the dead*, wash, 23.8 × 37 cm., 1769, British Library, London (Add. MS 23921, f. 28). (JS 1.72)

172. *A Toupapow with a corpse on it*, engraving by William Woollett after a drawing by William Hodges, in Cook, *A Voyage towards the South Pole and Round the World*, 1777, vol. 1, pl. XLIV, fp. 184.

173. *Monuments in Easter Island*, engraving by William Woollett after a drawing by William Hodges, in Cook, *A Voyage towards the South Pole and Round the World*, 1777, vol. 1, pl. XLIX, fp. 294.

174. John Webber, *A Human sacrifice at Otaheite*, pen, wash and watercolour, 42.2 × 62.5 cm., *c*.1777, British Library, London (Add. MS 15513, f. 16). (JS 3.99)

175. John Webber, *Poedua*, oil on canvas, 142.2 × 94 cm., 1777, National Maritime Museum, London. (JS 3.149)

176. John Webber, *Rural landscape with drover and flock*, pen and watercolour, 20.1 × 27.9 cm., 1773, Stadelsches Kunstinstitut, Frankfurt.

177. John Webber, *Abraham and the three angels*, oil on canvas, 90 × 115 cm., *c*.1755–6, Landesmuseum, Münster.

178. John Webber, *A Man of New Holland*, pencil and red crayon, 47.3 × 32.4 cm., 1777, British Library, London (Add. MS 15513, f. 4). (JS 3.10)

179. John Webber, *A Woman of New Holland*, pencil, 45.7 × 32.1 cm., 1777, British Library, London (Add. MS 15513, f. 5). (JS 3.13)

180. E. Rooker, *A Representation of the Attack of Captain Wallis in the Dolphin by the Natives of Otaheite*, engraving in Hawkesworth's *Account of the Voyages*, vol. 1, pl. 21.

181. *The Landing at Erramanga, one of the New Hebrides* (Vanuatu), engraving by J.K. Sherwin after William Hodges, in Cook, *A Voyage towards the South Pole and Round the World*, 1777, vol. 2, pl. 62.

182. *The Landing at Erramanga, one of the New Hebrides*, oil on panel, 24.1 × 47 cm., *c*.1776, National Maritime Museum, London. (JS 2.128)

183. John Webber, *Captain Cook in Ship Cove, Queen Charlotte Sound*, pen, wash and watercolour, 60.7 × 98.5 cm., 1777, National Maritime Museum, London. (JS 3.14)

184. John Webber, *The Reception of Captain Cook at Hapee* (Lifuka, Tonga), watercolour, 22.4 × 38.1 cm., 1777, British Library, London (Add. MS 15513, f. 8). (JS 3.46)

185. John Webber, *Summer huts of the Chukchi*, pencil, pen and wash, 25.4 × 48.9 cm., 1778, British Library, London (Add. MS 17277, no. 26). (JS 3.273)

186. John Webber, *Two Chukchi armed*, pencil, pen, wash and watercolour, 25.4 × 37.8 cm., 1778, British Library, London (Add. MS 17277, no. 27). (JS 3.272)

187. John Webber, *Captain Cook's meeting with the Chukchi at St Lawrence Bay*, pencil, pen, wash and watercolour, 64.8 × 99.1 cm., 1778, National Maritime Museum, London. (JS 3.269)

188. John Webber, *The Harbour of Annamooka*, pen, wash and watercolour, 44.8 × 100 cm., 1777, British Library, London (Add. MS 15513, f. 7). (JS 3.38)

189. John Webber, portrait sketch of a chief of Bora Bora, pencil and wash, 37.8 × 25.4 cm., 1777, British Library, London (Add. MS 17277, no. 10). (JS 3.161)

190. John Webber, *A Chief of Oparapora* (Bora Bora), pencil and wash, 31.4 × 48.6 cm., 1777, British Library, London (Add. MS 15513, f. 24). (JS 3.160)

191. John Webber, *The Chief Kahura*, pen and wash, 43.8 × 31.3 cm., 1777, Dixson Library, Sydney. By permission of the Trustees of the State Library of New South Wales. (JS 3.22)

192. William Hodges, *The Landing at Tanna* [Tana] *one of the New Hebrides*, oil on panel, 24.1 × 45.7 cm., c.1775–6, National Maritime Museum, London. (JS 2.134)

193. John Webber, *A View of Christmas Harbour*, watercolour, 22.2 × 37.8 cm., c.1781–3, Dixson Library, Sydney (PXX 2, 1). By permission of the Trustees of the State Library of New South Wales. (JS 3.4)

194. *A Man of the Sandwich Islands*, engraving by J.K. Sherwin after John Webber, in Cook and King, *A Voyage to the Pacific Ocean*, 1784, pl. 64.

195. Battle relief from the heroön at Gjölbashi-Trysa, c.420–410 BC, Kunsthistorisches Museum, Vienna.

196. Wicker helmet from Hawaii collected on Captain Cook's third voyage, height 31 cm., Australian Museum, Sydney.

197. William Hodges, *Captain James Cook*, oil on canvas, 76 × 63.5 cm., c.1775, National Maritime Museum, London.

198. Lucien Le Vieux, *James Cook*, marble, 1790, National Portrait Gallery, London.

199. John Webber, *The Death of Cook*, engraving; figures by F. Bartolozzi, landscape by W. Byrne.

200. *View of Owhyhee, one of the Sandwich Islands*, aquatint by Francis Jukes after John Cleveley, published 5 July 1788 by Thomas Martyn.

201. *Death of Captain Cook*, oil, after George Carter.

202. *The Death of Captain James Cook, F.R.S. at Owhyhee in MDCCLXXIX*, engraving by T. Cook after D.P. Dodd, in Cook and King, *A Voyage to the Pacific Ocean*, London, 1784, fp. 199.

203. *Death of Cook*, lithograph, in *Narrative of Captain James Cook's Voyages around the World*, London, 1839, fp. 376.

204. Gordon Browne, *Death of Captain Cook*, in C.R. Lowe (ed.), *Captain Cook's three voyages round the world*, London, 1895, p. 470.

205. Frontispiece to *The British Nepos; or Mirror of Youth, Consisting of Selected Lives of Illustrious Britons*, by William Fordyce Mavor, London, 1798, engraving by W. Taylor after John Thurston.

206. Frontispiece to *New System of Geography*, by Rev. Thomas Bankes, London, 1787, engraving after Johann Ramberg.

207. *The Apotheosis of Captain James Cook*, engraved from a design by P.J. de Loutherbourg and John Webber, published 20 January 1794 by J. Thane, London.

208. Johan Zoffany, *The Death of Cook*, oil on canvas, 137.2 × 185.5 cm., c.1795, National Maritime Museum, London.

209. James Barry, *Navigation, or the Triumph of the Thames*, oil on canvas, 335.5 × 462.5 cm., 1777–83, Royal Society of Arts, London.

257

INDEX